DATE DUE

12/28/11			

Demco

WOMEN'S ROLES
IN THE RENAISSANCE

WOMEN'S ROLES
IN THE RENAISSANCE

**Meg Lota Brown and
Kari Boyd McBride**

Women's Roles through History

GREENWOOD PRESS
Westport, Connecticut • London

Library of Congress Cataloging-in-Publication Data

Brown, Meg Lota.
  Women's roles in the Renaissance / Meg Lota Brown and Kari
Boyd McBride.
      p. cm. — (women's roles through history, ISSN 1553-5088)
  Includes bibliographical references and index.
  ISBN 0-313-32210-4 (alk. paper)
  1. Women—History—Renaissance, 1450-1600. 2. Sex role—
Europe—History. 3. Social role—Europe—History. 4. Social
change—Europe—History. 5. Europe—Social conditions. I. McBride,
Kari Boyd. II. Title.
  HQ1149.E85 B76 2005
  305.4'094'0903—dc22   2005005217

British Library Cataloguing in Publication Data is available.

Library of Congress Catalog Card Number: 2005005217
ISBN: 0-313-32210-4
ISSN: 1553-5088

First published in 2005

Greenwood Press, 88 Post Road West, Westport, CT 06881
An imprint of Greenwood Publishing Group, Inc.
www.greenwood.com

Printed in the United States of America

The paper used in this book complies with the
Permanent Paper Standard issued by the National
Information Standards Organization (Z39.48-1984).

10 9 8 7 6 5 4 3 2 1

Dame Gertrude More, "Magnes Amoris Amor," in Dorothy L. Latz,
"*Glow-Worm Light*": *Writings of 17th Century English Recusant
Women from Original Manuscripts* (Salzburg: Institut für Anglistik
und Amerikanistik Universität Salzburg, 1989). © by Dorothy L. Latz.
Reprinted with permission.

for the children:
Aaron, Caitlyn, Jacob, Mallory, Jamie,
Madison, Riley, Cole, Carlos, Christiana, and Holden

Contents

List of Illustrations

Series Foreword

Women's history is still being reclaimed. The geographical and chronological scope of the **Women's Roles through History** series contributes to our understanding of the many facets of women's lives. Indeed, with this series, a content-rich survey of women's lives through history and around the world is available for the first-time for high school students to the general public.

The impetus for the series came from the success of Greenwood's 1999 reference *Women's Roles in Ancient Civilizations,* edited by Bella Vivante. Librarians noted the need for new treatments of women's history, and women's roles are an important part of the history curriculum in every era. Thus, this series intensely covers women's roles in Europe and America, with volumes by the century or by era, and one volume each is devoted to the major populated areas of the globe—Africa, the Middle East, Asia, and Latin America and the Caribbean.

Each volume provides essay chapters on major topics such as

- Family Life
- Marriage and Childbearing
- Religion
- Public Life
- Lives of Ordinary Women

- Women and the Economy
- Political Status
- Legal Status
- Arts

Country and regional differences are discussed as necessary.

Other elements include

- Introduction, providing historical context
- chronology
- glossary
- bibliography
- period illustrations

The volumes, written by historians, offer sound scholarship in an accessible manner. A wealth of disparate material is conveniently synthesized in one source. As well, the insight provided into daily life, which readers find intriguing, further helps to bring knowledge of women's struggles, duties, contributions, pleasures, and more to a wide audience.

Acknowledgments

Our first and greatest thanks go to our families, especially the children, who inspired this work and put up with its long residency in their lives. What kept us excited about the project was the prospect of creating a resource that young scholars might one day use and learn from. We wish to acknowledge the many books on early modern women that paved the way for ours, in particular the groundbreaking work of Bonnie S. Anderson and Judith P. Zinsser, Roland H. Bainton, Alice Clark, Natalie Zemon Davis, Susan Karant-Nunn, Ruth Kelso, Linda Nochlin, Joan Thirsk, Merry E. Wiesner-Hanks, and the mother of all feminist history, Virginia Woolf. More near at hand, we would like to thank Gordon K. McBride, who read our manuscript and saved us from many historical infelicities; David L. Graizbord, who read portions of the manuscript and offered suggestions for sources and for revision and elaboration of the text; and Christina Kenworthy-Brown, CJ, who provided invaluable information on Mary Ward and her Companions. Any errors that remain are, of course, ours. We are grateful to David Orvis, who searched the world helping us to identify and locate illustrations for the book, to Ruth Dickstein, who pointed us to sources when we were stumped, and to Audrey Tinkham, whose elegant work on the index was indispensable. Thanks to Mary Wildner-Bassett and Albrecht Classen for help with the early modern German. We particularly appreciate the support of Wendi Schnaufer, our editor at Greenwood Press, for her astute guidance, her enthusiasm for our work, and her patience. Writing this book was entirely collaborative; our names are placed in alphabetical order.

Added to our collective thanks is our individual appreciation. Kari Boyd McBride: I would like to acknowledge the importance to this project of my time at St. Catharine's College, Cambridge, where I was Visiting Scholar in the autumn of 2003. I am grateful to the Master, David S. Ingram, and Fellows of the College for that precious time to read, think, and write and for the gift of a friendly and learned scholarly community. I especially wish to thank Paul Hartle, Senior Tutor at St. Catharine's, who brought together a lively group of early modern scholars and fellows that term, and my fellow Visitor, Graham Parry, Professor Emeritus of York University. Their erudition is a polestar whose reach exceeds the grasp of most mere mortals. I am grateful to Ed Donnerstein, Dean of the University of Arizona College of Social and Behavioral Sciences, and to Elizabeth Lapovsky Kennedy, former Head of the University of Arizona Women's Studies Department, who fostered the sabbatical that allowed me that glorious time in Cambridge. I also acknowledge the support of the faculty of Women's Studies—especially Julia Balen, Miranda Joseph, Judy Temple, and Sarah Deutsch, Interim Head—whose encouragement of their colleagues' scholarship goes beyond any reasonable expectation. They carried a massively increased teaching and service load in fall 2003, giving the rest of us the greatest gift of all: time. I am blessed in having Meg Lota Brown as my friend and coauthor, a splendid and learned collaborator whose enthusiasm, generosity, wisdom, and megawatts of pure brilliance touch and inspire everyone who has had the good fortune to work with her as a student or colleague. For her patience, good humor, and generosity and for carrying on during my long absence, I am grateful to Gretchen. I acknowledge my immense good fortune and discernment in my choice of Gordon, a generous friend, companion in the intellectual life, and partner in love. He has been the sounding board for most of the arguments here, and whatever is good is so in part because of his thoughtful listening. To the children, who bless my life and who inspired this work, I dedicate this book.

Meg Lota Brown: I would like to thank Larry Evers, Head of the University of Arizona Department of English, and Chuck Tatum,

Dean of the University of Arizona College of Humanities, for the time to write and for their invaluable professional support. For their generosity and the example they set in every aspect of their lives, I thank Rosie Mills, Mary Webster, Alexandra Jankovic, Ann Brigham, Angela Balla, Helen Wilcox, Claude Summers, and Paul Parrish. I cannot imagine a better collaborator than Kari Boyd McBride; her sagacity, humor, extraordinary knowledge, typing prowess, and friendship have made writing this book—and the prospect of more—a pleasure. For their wisdom and a lifetime of love, I thank Nancy Simpkins, Rick Teagarden, and Heather Wilson. To the ineffable Mallory, Aaron, and Rick Brown, I give my love, appreciation, and this book.

Timeline

1294   *La Vita Nuova* [The New Life] published by Dante Alighieri (1265–1321), in which he tells of his love for the beautiful, pure, unattainable young woman, Beatrice. She became the model for the female beloved in male poets' writings, especially the sonnet as it developed throughout Europe in the Renaissance. In Dante's most famous work, *The Divine Comedy*, Beatrice is the poet/dreamer's guide to paradise.

1336   *Canzoniere* [Book of Songs] published by Francesco Petrarch (1304–1374), in which, following Dante, Petrarch celebrates his love for Laura, both a beautiful, pure, unattainable young woman and a symbol of the poet's laurel wreath of fame.

          In this same period, Italian humanists, led by Petrarch, began to recover and disseminate throughout Europe the writings of ancient Rome and Greece. Such works, especially those of Quintillian, became the basis for education in the early modern world.

1347   Birth of Catherine of Siena (d. 1380); a tertiary (an uncloistered associate of the Dominicans), she had mystical visions throughout her life and attracted a large following. She, like Francis of Assisi, manifested the stigmata, the marks of Christ's wounds. Feeling called to the public life, she corresponded with people of all social rank and led the movement for a crusade against the so-called Infidels, the Turks who practiced Islam and held territory that included Jerusalem and the Holy Land.

In creating this timeline, we consulted decades.com, <http://www.decades.com>.

1379 Birth of Elizabeth of Nassau Saarbrücken (d. 1456), German translator of chivalric romances.

1383 Birth of Baptista di Montefeltro (d. 1450), noted Italian scholar and orator to whom Leonardo Bruni (1369–1444), Italian humanist and the Apostolic Secretary to three popes, addressed his treatise on women's education.

1394 Charles VI of France issued a decree for the expulsion of Jews from France.

ca. 1400 Birth of Helene Kottanner (d. aft. 1458); as chambermaid of Queen Elizabeth of Hungary, she kept a record of the historic events of her life at court.

ca. 1407 Birth of Alessandra Macinghi Strozzi (d. 1471), wealthy Florentine whose collection of 72 letters, addressed to her banished sons, is a model of classical and Renaissance epistolary (letter-writing) conventions and of didactic advice.

1415 Henry the Navigator, Prince of Portugal, attracted cartographers and shipbuilders and inspired a series of expeditions to Africa, inaugurating the European exploration and exploitation of colonies and plantations in Africa, the Orient, and the Americas.

Bohemian religious reformer Jan Hus charged the Church with corruption and was burned at the stake as a heretic.

1418 Birth of Isotta Nogarola (d. ca. 1466), Italian humanist; she never married, but lived as a scholar and maintained, in contrast to many male humanists, that women were innately virtuous and good.

1421 Viennese synagogue burned with its Jewish occupants.

1429 Birth of Margaret of Anjou (d. 1482), skilled French negotiator of political and martial support for her husband, King Henry VI of England.

1430 Jews expelled from Bohemia.

1433 Birth of Elenore of Austria (d. 1480), translator of German courtly romances.

1440 Creation of the Vinland Map, the first known map of America.

1444 African slaves first brought to Europe by Portuguese adventurers.

1449 Birth of Osanna Andreasi of Mantua (d. 1505), Italian Dominican tertiary.

1450 Jews expelled from Lower Bavaria.

1451 Birth of Isabella of Castile (d. 1504), Spanish queen who consolidated power in her country against Muslims and Jews and a leading figure in the emergence of Spain as a European superpower.

1452 Johannes Gutenberg published the first book, a Bible, printed with movable metal type.

1453 Constantinople fell to the Muslim Turks under Muhammad II, ending the Byzantine Empire. Byzantine scholars poured into Italy, bringing with them the treasures of Greek philosophy and literature and fueling the humanist revolution.

Forty-one Jewish martyrs burned at the stake in Poland.

1463 Birth of Italian Neoplatonist and humanist Pico della Mirandola (d. 1494). He offered to debate any scholar on all possible topics (a list of nine hundred theses drawn from various Greek, Latin, Hebrew, and Arabic authors). He wrote *On the Dignity of Man,* in which he argues that "man" is the center of the universe.

1465 Birth of Italian scholar Cassandra Fedele (d. 1558).

1467 Birth of Colomba of Rieti (d. 1501), Italian founder of a convent of Dominican tertiaries, including young women and widows.

Birth of Caritas Pirckheimer (d. 1532), German scholar who defended women's right to be educated and to write.

1469 Birth of Laura Cereta of Brescia (d. 1499); proficient in Latin language and literature, she lived as a scholar and argued for women's right to education.

1470 Princess Juana of Portugal (1439–1475) first popularized the farthingale, the cone-shaped skirt stiffened by wooden canes or whale bone that was popular in England in the sixteenth century, perhaps introduced there via Spain by Catherine of Aragon, Queen of England.

1471 Birth of Chiara (Clara) Bugni (d. 1514), Franciscan tertiary and visionary from Venice who became Prioress of the Ospedale del Santo Sepolcro.

1473 Birth of astronomer Copernicus in Poland (d. 1543); he theorized that the earth and other planets revolve around the sun.

1474 Birth of Beatriz Galindo (d. 1534), Spanish intellectual and Latin tutor to Queen Isabella of Spain.

1476 In England, the printer William Caxton published Chaucer's *Canterbury Tales*.

1480 Queen Isabella and King Ferdinand of Spain established the Inquisition to seek out Moorish and especially Jewish converts to Christianity who were suspected of practicing their old religion in secret. The Inquisition later hunted suspected Christian heretics and apostates as well as witches.

Birth of Lucretia Borgia, Duchess of Ferrara (d. 1519), daughter of Pope Alexander VI and patron of the arts; though she has been romanticized as an incestuous lover and murderer, she was probably neither.

Birth of Margaret of Austria (d. 1530), Regent of the Netherlands for more than twenty years, skilled political negotiator, patroness of the arts, and guardian to four wards who were to become some of the most powerful monarchs of Europe.

1483 Anne de Beaujeu (1460–1522) made Regent of France on the death of her brother.

1484 Pope Innocent VIII issued a bull censuring the spread of witchcraft and heresy in Germany. He ordered that all cats belonging to convicted witches also be burned.

1485 Henry Tudor (Henry VII; 1457–1509) defeated Richard III (1452–1485) at the Battle of Bosworth Field, inaugurating the Tudor dynasty in England; a minor noble of Lancastrian lineage, Henry married Elizabeth of York (1466–1503), uniting the warring factions of the Wars of the Roses and ending that hundred-year conflict.

Birth of Catherine of Aragon (d. 1536), Spanish princess, first wife of Henry VIII, and mother of Mary Tudor (later Mary I of England).

Birth of Veronica Gambara, Italian Petrarchan poet (d. 1550).

1486 Dominican friars Heinrich Kraemer and Johann Sprenger published *Malleus maleficarum* [The Witches' Hammer], the definitive work on witchcraft in Europe.

Birth of Caterina Mattei of Racconigi (d. 1547), Italian Dominican nun and visionary who manifested the stigmata (wounds resembling those of Christ).

1490 Birth of Properzia de' Rossi (d. 1530), the only Italian woman of the era to sculpt in marble.

1491 Birth of Ignatius Loyola (d. 1556), Spanish soldier and founder of the Society of Jesus (the Jesuits); the Jesuits' mission was to defend Catholicism against Protestant heresy, and their "mixed life" (following a rule but active in the world) provided the model for two early modern women's orders, the Ursulines and the Institute of the Blessed Virgin Mary (IBVM).

1492 Birth of Vittoria Colonna, Marchesa di Pescara (d. 1547), Italian erudite and socially prominent poet. Her *Litere* [Letters] (1544) was among the most celebrated collections of letters ever published and provided a model for many educated women of the sixteenth century.

Isabella and Ferdinand ruled a united, Christian Spain after driving the Moors from most of Granada, their last stronghold, and expelling the Jews from Spain—all except those of both faiths who would "choose" to convert to Christianity; the joint monarchs funded the Genoan adventurer Cristobal Colon (Christopher Columbus) in his voyage to the Indies under their patronage.

One hundred thousand Jews expelled from Sicily.

Birth of French aristocrat Marguerite of Navarre (d. 1549); author of the celebrated and influential *Heptameron* [Seven Days], a collection of 73 stories (published posthumously), Marguerite advocated women's education as well as religious reform.

1493   Birth of Anna Bijns (d. 1575); poet, schoolteacher and zealous defender of Catholicism, she is thought to have been the most important and widely read Renaissance woman writer in Dutch.

1494   Columbus began using Indians of the Americas as slaves.

1495   Birth of Marie Dentière (d. 1561), French author who insisted on women's right to preach in church and other assemblies.

1496   Alhambra near Granada, the last Moorish outpost in Western Europe, surrendered to the forces of the Spanish Christian troops of Ferdinand and Isabella.

    Treatyse of Fyshynge wyth an Angle, written by Dame Juliana Berner in the early fourteenth century, first published.

1497   Jews given the so-called choice of forced conversion or expulsion from Portugal.

1499   Birth of Katharina von Bora (d. 1522), a German nun at the time of Martin Luther's reformation of the German church. When her convent was dispersed, she proposed to Luther; he married her, he said, "to spite the devil."

1500   World population about 400 million, with 100 million in Europe and Russia.

    Practice of medicine first restricted to qualified male doctors, barring many women from earning their living through the practice of healing.

    Birth of Anne Boleyn (d. 1536), second wife of King Henry VIII of England and mother of Elizabeth Tudor (later Elizabeth I of England). A fervent and learned Protestant, Anne was executed by Henry VIII on trumped-up charges of adultery when she failed to produce a male heir.

    Birth of Dianne de Poitiers (d. 1566), influential mistress of King Henry II of France, skilled politician, diplomat, and patron of the arts and sciences.

1505   Birth of Margaret More Roper (d. 1544); daughter of Thomas More (1478–1535), she benefited from an extensive humanistic education and translated works from Greek to Latin and Latin to English, including *The Treatise on the Lord's Prayer,* by Desiderius Erasmus (1466–1536).

1510   Birth of Beatrice Benveniste de Luna in Portugal (d. 1569) to a wealthy Jewish family. Forced to flee after the expulsion of the Jews, she and her family lived for a time as Christians in Venice, though they continued to practice their Judaism in secret; later, she and her sister moved to Ferrara and then to the Ottoman Empire, where they were able to practice their religion openly (and where she took the Jewish name Gracia Nasi) and helped to resettle other Jews.

Lea Ráskai, the first woman to write in Hungarian, wrote the *Legend of Blessed Margaret.*

ca. 1510   Birth of Levina Teerline (d. 1576), Flemish painter to the court of three English monarchs, Edward VI, Mary I, and Elizabeth I.

1512   Birth of Katherine Parr (d. 1548); an ardent Protestant, she was Henry VIII's last wife. As an adult, she taught herself Latin and Greek to further her religious studies and also published two books, *Prayers or Medytacions … Collected out of Certayne Holy Workes* (1545) and *The Lamentacion of a Synner* (1547).

1515   Spanish explorer and colonist and later Dominican priest Bartolome de Las Casas (1484–1566) returned to Spain from Hispaniola (present-day Haiti and the Dominican Republic) to report on the barbaric treatment of the indigenous peoples and to petition King Ferdinand for a change in Spanish policy toward them. He was initially successful, but the brutal policy was later restored under pressure from the colonists and plantation owners.

Birth of Teresa of Avila, Spanish nun and spiritual leader (d. 1582); she entered a Carmelite convent at age 20, where she developed the spiritual practice described in *The Interior Castle,* a metaphor for the soul's journey, room by room, toward union with God. Teresa ultimately founded a number of Carmelite convents in Spain that followed a spiritual practice based on her writings, and her method influenced houses of friars (male religious) as well. She also published her autobiography, *Life Written By Herself.*

1516   Birth of Mary Tudor, later Mary I of England (d. 1558); a staunch Catholic, she returned the English Church to Catholic practice and governance following the reigns of her father, Henry VIII (who broke with Rome in order to divorce Mary's mother, Catherine of Aragon), and her zealously Protestant elder brother, Edward VI.

1517 Archduke Charles of Austria (1500–1588) gave Florentine merchants a monopoly in the African slave trade.

Martin Luther (1483–1546) nailed his Ninety-Five Theses to the door of the Wittenberg castle church, inaugurating the Protestant Reformation in Europe.

1518 Swiss cleric Ulrich Zwingli (1484–1531) supported Martin Luther's reformist proposals. In 1519, he launched the Swiss Reformation with his preaching in Zurich.

1520 Anabaptist movement grew in northern Europe; Anabaptists held that all members of the sect—women and men, children and adults—were entirely equal. Women held worship services, presided over sacraments, and taught. Anabaptists were persecuted throughout Europe, and many women were martyred alongside men.

Birth of Marie Bessemers (d. 1600), Dutch artist as well as grandmother and first teacher of the painter Jan Breughel (1568–1625).

Birth of Madeleine Neveu (d. 1587), French intellectual renowned for her scholarship.

ca. Birth of Pernette Du Guillet (d. 1545), popular French poet whose
1520 collection of verse, *Rymes,* was published in 1545.

Birth of Louise Labé (d. 1566), French poet whose published work includes one of the first sonnet cycles in France.

1521 Pope Leo X excommunicated Martin Luther from the Roman Catholic Church. The same year, the pope granted King Henry VIII of England the title Defender of the Faith for his defense of the seven Catholic sacraments in response to Martin Luther's Protestant reform movement.

1522 Birth of Caterina de' Ricci (d. 1590); an Italian Dominican nun known for her ecstatic visions, she manifested the stigmata, wounds resembling those of Christ.

Birth of Portuguese scholar Luisa Sigea (d. 1560).

1523 Publication of *De Institutione Feminae Christianae,* by Juan Luís Vives (1492–1540), which promoted women's education; the work was translated into English by Richard Hyrde as *The Instruction of a Christen Woman,* and published in 1527. Vives's book was dedicated to the English Queen Catherine of Aragon.

1524 Birth of Gaspara Stampa (d. 1554), Italian love poet who adapted the Petrarchan tradition by portraying women as agents of love and not just passive objects.

1525   English biblical scholar and reformer William Tyndale (ca. 1484–1536) published his translation of the New Testament in Worms, Germany.

Martin Luther wrote his tract "Against the Murderous and Thieving Hordes of Peasants" in an attempt to stop the widening religious and political protest in Germany, calling on all Germans "to smite, slay, and stab, secretly or openly," the protestors. The peasant protest was savagely put down and thousands of peasants, both women and men, were killed.

1526   Jews expelled from Hungary by order of Maria of Hapsburg.

1527   Henry VIII appealed to Pope Clement VII for permission to divorce his wife of nearly twenty years, Catherine of Aragon (1485–1536), mother of Mary (Tudor) I of England.

Birth of Elizabeth Talbot, Countess of Shrewsbury (d. 1608); known as Bess of Hardwick, she amassed a fortune by surviving four husbands, each wealthier than the last, and oversaw the design and building of the palatial Hardwick Hall.

ca.   Birth of Caterina van Hemessen (d. 1566), court painter for Mary
1527   of Hungary.

1528   On Henry VIII's orders, Cardinal Thomas Wolsey (1475–1529) dissolved 22 English religious houses, including nunneries, and used the money to found several men's colleges, including Cardinal College, Oxford.

1529   Civil war began between Catholic and Reformed cantons in Switzerland.

Agrippa von Nettesheim (1486–1535), author of many tracts on the occult and esoterica, published *De nobilitate et praecellentia foeminae sexus* (On the Nobility and Excellence of Women), which provided the source for many of the later arguments about "women's worth."

1531   Henry VIII broke with the Church in Rome and took the title Supreme Head of the Church of England.

1533   Birth of Marguerite de Valois, queen of France and Navarre (d. 1615), daughter of Catherine de' Medicis and King Henry II of France; her marriage in 1572 (as a Catholic) to Henry, the Protestant king of Navarre, was meant to settle the religious wars, but the bloodshed continued unabated.

Birth of Soeur Anne de Marquets, Dominican nun born of a noble family in Normandy (d. 1588); she wrote a book in support of the French Catholic Church against the Huguenots, the French Calvinist Protestants, as well as a collection of religious poetry, *Spiritual Sonnets* (1605).

The Archbishop of Canterbury annulled Henry VIII's marriage to Catherine of Aragon and declared his secret marriage to Anne Boleyn (ca. 1500–1536) to be valid.

Birth of Elizabeth I (d. 1603) to Anne Boleyn and Henry VIII; following the deaths of her brother, Edward VI, and sister, Mary I, Elizabeth was crowned in 1558. She oversaw the development, implementation, and enforcement of the Elizabethan settlement, a moderate Protestantism that maintained many of the ritual aspects of Catholicism.

ca. 1535
Birth of Sofonisba Anguissola (d. 1625), innovative and internationally celebrated Italian portraitist who served at the Spanish court of Philip II for 10 years.

1536
French theologian and law scholar John Calvin (1509–1564) published *The Institutes of the Christian Religion,* a document that criticized Catholicism and proposed a Protestant church and state. Calvin led the creation of a Protestant state in Geneva. French followers of Calvin called themselves Huguenots (confederates or companions).

Publication of Marie Dentière's history of the early Reformation in Geneva, *The War for and Deliverance of the City of Geneva, Faithfully Prepared and Written Down by a Merchant Living in That City;* a former abbess, the French Dentière (1490–1560) became an outspoken Reformed preacher, polemicist, author, and defender of women's spiritual authority.

King Henry VIII of England married his third wife, Jane Seymour (ca. 1509–1537). She gave birth to Henry's only son to survive adulthood, the future King Edward VI (1537–1553), but she died within two weeks of his birth.

1537
Birth of Lady Jane Grey (d. 1554); a highly educated and erudite woman, she was the great-granddaughter of Henry VII. On the death of King Edward VI, Protestant factions proclaimed Grey queen to prevent the Catholic Mary Tudor from ascending the throne. However, Mary, Edward's sister and the rightful heir, had strong support, and Grey was imprisoned and executed.

1538
Publication of *Les Angoysses douloureuses qui procedent d'amours* [The Torments of Love], by Hélisenne de Crenne (pen name for Marguerite Briet, ca. 1515–1550).

1540
Ruffs, elaborate pleated collars, brought to Europe from India and popularized by Marguerite de Valois, Queen of France and Navarre.

King Henry VIII of England married his fourth wife, Anne of Cleves. The marriage was annulled six months later, and she lived on in her own house as a royal "sister."

ca. 1540 Birth of Maddalena Casulana (d. ca. 1590), Italian lutenist, singer, and composer who published several volumes of her music.

1541 Henry VIII married Catherine Howard (b. 1521); within four months, she was imprisoned in the Tower of London and was executed for adultery the next year.

1542 Birth of Mary, Queen of Scotland (d. 1587); mother of King James VI of Scotland (later James I of England) and a Catholic, she was executed by Elizabeth I for plotting against the crown.

Birth of Catherine Neveu (d. 1587), French scholar celebrated for her erudition.

1543 English King Henry VIII married Katherine Parr (1512–1548), his sixth and last wife; he died in 1547.

1545 The Catholic Church Council of Trent began meeting, launching the Counter-Reformation.

1546 Anne Askew (b. 1521), a member of the Reformed religion of England, imprisoned, tortured, tried, and executed under King Henry VIII for holding and voicing Protestant beliefs; she left a record of her trial and torture in her *Examinations*.

Birth of Veronica Franco (d. 1591), Venetian prostitute and published poet.

1547 Birth of Diana Scultori Ghisi, also known as Diana Mantuana (d. 1612), Italian engraver and printmaker.

ca. 1548 Birth of Isabella Whitney (d. after 1573), English middle-class poet who published several collections of popular verse.

1552 Birth of Lavinia Fontana of Bologna (d. 1614); the most prolific female artist in Renaissance Europe, she amassed great wealth for her paintings and royal commissions and was elected to the Roman Academy.

Publication of *Lettere a Gloria del sesso femminile* [Letters in Praise of Women] by the Italian Lucrezia Gonzaga (1536–1538).

1553 King Edward VI of England died of tuberculosis. In order to prevent the coronation of the Catholic Mary Tudor (1516–1558), next in line for the throne, Protestant leaders attempted to place Lady Jane Grey on the throne, but Mary had wide support and was proclaimed the rightful heir and queen of England.

1557 Thomas Tusser (1524–1580) published *A Hundreth Good Pointes of Husbandrie*, detailing the duties of all members of a well-ordered household, especially those of the housewife.

Birth of Anne Howard, Countess of Arundel, British recusant (convert to Catholicism) (d. 1630); Howard hid the Catholic Robert Southwell (1561–1595) in her home for a time and later founded the novitiate of the Jesuits at Ghent. Her husband, Philip, 1st Earl of Arundel (1557–1595), was tortured and executed for his faith.

1558 Mary Tudor died; Elizabeth I (1533–1603) crowned queen of England.

Publication of *The First Blast of the Trumpet Against the Monstrous Regiment of Women,* by John Knox (1505–1572); a misogynist diatribe against female rule directed at Mary Tudor; Mary, Queen of Scots; and Mary of Guise, its publication coincided with Elizabeth I's coronation, incurring her wrath.

1560 Birth of Marietta Tintoretto (d. 1590), Italian artist whose paintings were often attributed to her famous father, Jacopo Robusti Tintoretto (1518–1594).

1561 Birth of Mary Sidney, later Mary Herbert, Countess of Pembroke (d. 1621), author, translator, and patron of the arts and sciences. Following the death of her brother, Sir Philip Sidney, she completed his translation of the Psalms (undertaking herself the translation of more than half of the 150 Psalms) and saw their publication; his prose romance *Arcadia* is dedicated to her.

1563 Birth of Louise Bourgeois, French midwife to Marie de Médicis (d. 1636); she wrote *Diverse Observations on Sterility, Miscarriages, Fertility, Childbirth, and Illnesses of Women and Newborn Children,* the definitive work on midwifery.

Jews expelled from France by order of Charles VI.

Publication of *Lettere amorose* [Love letters], by the Italian Celia Romana (ca. 1524–1557).

ca. 1563 Birth of Elizabeth Grymeston (d. 1603), English author of the very popular mother's advice book *Miscelanea, Meditations, Memoratives* (1604).

1569 Birth of Aemilia (Bassano) Lanyer (d. 1645), author of *Salve Deus Rex Judaeorum* [Hail, God, King of the Jews] and perhaps the first country-house poem in English, "The Description of Cooke-ham."

1570 Queen Elizabeth I of England excommunicated by Pope Pius V for heresy and for contributing to the growth of "the ungodly" as the "pretended queen" of England and head of the English (Protestant) church.

1571 Birth of Lady Margaret Hoby (d. 1633); she kept a diary from 1599–1605, detailing her daily activities, including her prayer life.

1572 St. Bartholomew's Day Massacre resulted in the deaths of more than seventy thousand people, mostly Protestants, in France.

After the failed attempt by Queen of France Catherine de' Medicis (1519–1589) to have the Huguenot (Protestant) leader Comte de Coligny (1590–1572) assassinated, the Catholic nobility who had gathered in Paris for the wedding of her daughter, Marguerite de Valois, took up the cause and began a murderous rampage beginning with the killing of Coligny. The violence spread throughout Paris and then France, even after a royal decree ordered the Catholic loyalists to cease. News of the massacre quickly spread throughout Europe and heightened divisions between Catholics and Protestants. Many Huguenots fled France for Protestant countries, especially England.

Isabel Warwike licensed to practice medicine in York, England.

1575 Birth of Lady Arbella Stuart (d. 1615), claimant to the English throne who tried to resist the efforts of Queen Elizabeth I and King James I to control nearly every aspect of her life—social, political, amatory, and reproductive—to prevent her from encroaching on their sovereignty.

1578 Birth of Fede Galizia (d. 1630), Italian leader in the early production of still-life paintings.

1580 Publication of *Lettere familiari* [Letters to Friends] by the Italian Veronica Franco (1546–1591).

Birth of Dorothy Lawson (d. 1632), English Catholic and recusant who illegally harbored Catholic priests in her home.

1581 Birth of Elizabeth Grey, Countess of Kent (d. 1651); English herbalist and specialist in medical practices and medicines, she collected her medicines and cures in *A Choice Manuall, or Rare and Select Secrets in Physick* (first published in 1653 and much reprinted).

1584 Publication of Reginald Scot's *Discovery of Witchcraft,* which was banned by King James I of England because it disputed the existence of witches.

Birth of Anna Owena Hoyers (d. 1655), a learned German poet.

1585 Birth of Mary Ward, founder of the IBVM, in Yorkshire (d. 1645); the order was dedicated to the education of girls and modeled on the Society of Jesus, following the "mixed life" rather than cloistering its members.

Birth of Winifred Wigmore, one of Mary Ward's Companions (d. 1657); Wigmore was mistress of the IBVM school in Naples.

Birth of Elizabeth Tanfield (Cary, Lady Falkland) (d. 1639), convert to Catholicism and author of the first English play known to be written by a woman, *The Tragedie of Mariam, the Faire Queene of Jewry* (1613); she also translated religious works, wrote poetry, and wrote stories of the saints' lives and the life of Edward II.

1586   Englishwoman Margaret Clitherow (b. ca. 1556) put to death by *peine forte et dure* (crushing to death with heavy stones) for harboring Catholic priests and for having mass celebrated at her house, both against the law in Protestant England.

1587   Mary, Queen of Scots (b. 1542) executed for treason by order of Elizabeth I.

Birth of Lady Mary Wroth (d. 1651), English poet and prose romance writer, branded a hermaphrodite for publishing her work.

Birth of Francesca Caccini (d. aft. 1640), Italian vocalist and published composer who became the highest-paid performer in the Florentine court of the Medicis.

1588   Birth of Catherine de Vivonne, the Marquise de Rambouillet (d. 1665); an accomplished and erudite woman, she established the earliest literary salons, which were attended by the literati of France.

1590   Birth of Anne Clifford, Countess of Pembroke, Dorset and Montgomery (d. 1676); her father attempted to leave his estates to a distant male heir, though, as his only child, she was the legitimate heir. She maintained her claim to the family property throughout her life and finally inherited it when she had outlived the other claimants.

Birth of Lady Eleanor Davies (d. 1652), a devoutly Protestant author and religious polemicist who published more than sixty tracts in England and who was imprisoned for many years because of her outspokenness.

Birth of Italian artist and church decorator Caterina Ginnasio (d. 1660).

ca.   Birth of María de Zayas y Sotomayor (d. ca. 1661), Spanish author
1590   of numerous published novelas and defender of women.

1593   Birth of Artemisia Gentileschi (d. 1652); believed by many to be the most important female artist in Renaissance Europe, she was distinguished as a member of the Florentine Academy of Design. Many of her paintings were long attributed to her father, Orazio Gentileschi (ca. 1563–1639).

1594   Birth of Clara Peeters in Antwerp (d. ca. 1657), one of the originators of a new form of still-life painting, the "banquet piece."

Birth of Maria Tesselschade (d. 1649), Dutch poet and member of a learned cultural coterie.

1595   Publication of the *Lettere* of the Italian Chiara Matraini (1515–1604).

Birth of Elizabeth Joscelin (d. 1622), English author of the post-humously published mother's advice book, *The Mothers Legacie to her Unborne Childe.*

1597   Publication of *Demonology,* a treatise on witchcraft, by James VI of Scotland (later James I of England).

Birth of Rachel Speght, English protofeminist polemicist (d. aft. 1621); in addition to *A Mouzell for Melastomus* (1617), her response to Joseph Swetnam's 1615 misogynist pamphlet, Speght wrote *Mortalities Memorandum* (1621), a religious reflection on death.

1598   Robert Cleaver published the popular and much-reprinted Protestant marriage tract *A Godlie Forme of Householde Government.*

1599   Birth of Camilla Faà Gonzaga (d. 1662); she was secretly married in 1616 to Duke Ferdinando Gonzaga of Mantua, but he later divorced her, kept her from seeing their son, and forced her into a convent, where she wrote the story of her troubles, the first prose biography by an Italian woman, published in 1622.

Birth of Madeleine de Souvre, Marquise de Sablé (d. 1678), French author of a collection of maxims and leader of a celebrated and influential Parisian salon.

ca.   Birth of Ana Caro Mallén de Soto (d. ca. 1650), popular Spanish
1600   playwright.

Birth of Mariana de Carvajal (d. ca. 1663), Spanish author of novellas collected and published in 1663 as *Navidades de Madrid, y noches entretenidas, en ocho novelas* (Christmas in Madrid, or Entertaining Nights, in eight tales).

1601   Birth of Helen More (d. 1633); an English Catholic who joined the convent at Cambrai and took the name Gertrude, she wrote spiritual treatises and religious poetry.

ca.   Birth of Martine de Bertereau, Baroness de Beausoleil (d. 1640),
1602   French geologist who discovered over 150 ore deposits of iron, gold, and silver before she was imprisoned for using "black arts" to make the discoveries.

1603   English Queen Elizabeth I died and was succeeded by her cousin James VI of Scotland and James I of England.

1606   Sisters of Ursula (Ursulines) founded in France as a "mixed order"; like the Mary Ward sisters, the Ursulines combined contemplative withdrawal with worldly engagement.

Birth of Winifred Bedingfeld (d. 1666), one of Mary Ward's Companions and founding member of the IBVM school for girls in Munich.

1607 Birth of Madeleine de Scudery (d. 1701), one of the most celebrated and influential leaders of Parisian salons.

Birth of Anna Maria van Schurman (d. 1678); Dutch polyglot, Latin scholar, and advocate of women's education, she was internationally reputed to be the most learned female scholar of her time.

1609 Birth of Judith Leyster (d. 1660); a self-supporting Dutch painter and head of her own workshop of pupils, she was the only female member of the Haarlem painters' guild.

1610 Birth of Louise Moillon (d. 1696), popular French still-life painter.

ca. Birth of Maria Cunitz (d. 1664), Silesian (German) expert in astron-
1610 omy whose published scientific treatise, *Urania propitia* [She who is closest to Urania, the goddess of astronomy], was dedicated to Emperor Frederick III.

ca. Birth of Bathsua Makin (d. ca. 1673); scholar and governess to the
1612 English royal family, she founded a school for girls and published *An Essay to Revive the Antient Education of Gentlewomen* (1673) advocating women's education.

1614 Birth of Margaret Askew Fell (Fox) (d. 1702), itinerant Quaker preacher in England who wrote *Women's Speaking Justified* (1666) and who was persecuted for her religious beliefs.

1616 Posthumous publication in England of Dorothy Leigh's *The Mother's Blessing*, a mother's advice book.

Birth of Plautilla Bricci (d. 1690), Italian architect and one of the few female architects in Renaissance Europe.

1617 Publication in England of *Esther hath hanged Haman; or, An Answer to a lewd Pamphlet entitled The Arraignment of Women, With the arraignment of lewd, idle, froward, and unconstant men and Husbands,* by Esther Sowernam, a response to Joseph Swetnam's misogynist pamphlet *The Arraignment of Lewd, idle, froward, and unconstant women ...* (1615), which provoked a number of prowoman responses, most of them (like Sowernam's) published under a pseudonym.

Publication in England of *The Worming of a mad Dog; or, A Sop for Cerberus, the Jailor of Hell ...* (also a counterattack on Swetnam), by Constantia Munda [Pure Constancy].

1618 Birth of Madeleine Béjart (d. 1672), French actor (from a family of 11 children, many of whom were actors, including her sister

Armande) who led her own traveling troupe before joining the acting company of the playwright Molière (1622–1673), where she had numerous starring roles in his plays and others' and virtually managed the company.

Birth of Princess Elizabeth of Bohemia, Princess Palatine (d. 1680); an influential player in European and international politics, she gave asylum to William Penn (1644–1718) and other Quakers as well as the Dutch scholar and champion of women's rights, Anna Maria van Schurman (1607–1678).

The start of the Thirty Years' War; actually a series of wars that raged throughout the Holy Roman Empire between 1618 and 1648 over inextricably interconnected issues of religion and dynastic struggles.

1619 Birth of Barbara Strozzi (d. 1677); renowned vocalist, composer, and head of a music salon in Venice, she performed on many instruments and published eight volumes of cantatas and arias.

1620 Birth of Ninon de Lenclos (d. 1705), French courtesan of the nobility and friend of powerful politicians and literati.

1621 Birth of Sibylle Schwarz (d. 1638), German poet, prose writer, translator, and dramatist who insisted on women's right to write.

Birth of Leonora Christina of Denmark (d. 1698), scholar and princess whose memoir, *Memory of Sorrow,* was written in part during the nearly twenty-two years she was in prison.

1623 Birth of Margaret Lucas Cavendish, Duchess of Newcastle (d. 1673), English scientist, philosopher, translator, poet, biographer, playwright, autobiographer, and science-fiction writer.

1625 Birth of Geertruyd Roghman, Dutch painter and engraver (d. bef. 1657); she depicted domestic tasks featuring primarily women.

1626 Birth of Marie de Rabutin-Chantal, Marquise de Sévigné (d. 1696), erudite French aristocrat, celebrated for her wit and prolific letter writing.

Birth of Queen Christina of Sweden (d. 1689); she converted to Catholicism and abdicated the throne, leaving her strongly Protestant country for Rome and Vatican politics.

1627 Birth of Dorothy Osborne (d. 1695), Englishwoman whose clandestine correspondence with her fiancé is distinguished by self-analysis, wit, and learning.

1629 Birth of Mary Harvey, Lady Dering (d. 1704), first Englishwoman to publish music in her own name.

"Captain" Alice Clark led a grain riot in Essex, England.

1630   Birth of Maria van Oosterwyck (d. 1693), Dutch still-life painter commissioned by royalty throughout northern Europe.

1631   Publication in London of Richard Brathwaite's *The English Gentlewoman,* a popular conduct manual for women.

Birth of Anne Finch, Viscountess Conway (d. 1679), English philosopher and author of the posthumously published *Principles of the Most Ancient and Modern Philosophy,* which includes evaluation of the philosophy of Descartes, Hobbes, and Spinoza.

Birth of Katherine Philips (d. 1664), English poet, translator, and center of a literary coterie composed primarily of female friends.

1632   Birth of Mary Beale (d. 1697), prolific English portraitist who supported her family and trained artists in her own workshop.

Martha Moulsworth wrote "The Memorandum of Martha Moulsworth/Widow," one of the first autobiographical poems in English; the poem calls for an all-female English university to complement Oxford and Cambridge.

1633   Birth of Catharina von Greiffenberg (d. 1694); Austrian translator and author of Protestant lyrics, an anti-Islamic epic poem, and popular published devotionals, her work was widely acclaimed by contemporaries.

1634   Birth of Marie-Madeleine Pioche de la Vergne, Madame de LaFayette (d. 1693), celebrated French novelist, best known for *La Princesses de Clèves* (1678).

1637   Women of Edinburgh led a popular resistance movement to the Book of Common Prayer, which had been imposed on the Calvinist Scots by King Charles I and the Church of England.

1638   Birth of Elisabetta Sirani (d. 1665), successful Italian engraver and painter; internationally acclaimed, she received royal commissions, supported her entire family, and taught art to more than a dozen female students.

1640   Birth of Ludamilia Elisabeth, Countess of Schwarzburg-Rudolstadt (d. 1672), popular German religious poet.

ca. 1640   Birth of Aphra Behn (d. 1689), prolific playwright, novelist, and poet and the first British woman to support herself by selling her writings.

Birth of Marie Catherine Desjardins, Madame de Villedieu (d. 1683); popular French author whose publications include collections of poetry and letters, 3 plays, and 13 fictional narratives, she was one of the first European women to achieve financial independence through publication.

1641   Birth of Barbara Villiers, Countess of Castelmain (d. 1709), mistress of King Charles II of England.

1642   Birth of Antoinette Hérault (d. 1695), French miniaturist who trained her five daughters, all of whom became painters and married other artists.

Birth of Marie Champmeslé (d. 1698); one of the most successful actors in seventeenth-century France, she specialized in the role of tragic heroine.

1643   Queen Anne, the widow of Louis XIII of France, was granted sole and absolute power as regent by the Paris parliament, overriding the late king's will.

1645   French working women, led by la Branlaïre, waged a tax revolt in Montpellier. La Branlaïre is reported to have called for the death of tax collectors who were taking bread from children's mouths.

Birth of Armande Grésinde Claire Elizabeth Béjart (d. 1700), sister of Madeleine Béjart and leading comic actor at the Comédie Française theater celebrated at the French and English courts for her performances.

1646   Birth of Glückel of Hameln (d. 1724); a Jewish merchant who prospered in business both while married and as a widow, her diary spans 30 years of family life, trade, and spiritual reflection.

1647   Birth of Maria Sibylla Merian (d. 1717); German botanist, entomologist, engraver, watercolor artist, and author of *Wonderful Metamorphosis and Special Nourishment of Caterpillars* (1679), she revolutionized the fields of zoology and botany.

1648   Birth of Elizabeth Chéron (d. 1711), French artist whose earnings supported her extended family.

1649   Birth of Louise de Keroualle, Duchess of Portsmouth (d. 1734), *maitresse en titre,* or "official mistress," of King Charles II of England.

Ten thousand women signed a petition to Parliament calling for religious and political reform and asserting "an equal interest with men of this Nation." Anon. *To the supream authority of England ... The humble petition of diverse wel-affected weomen of the cities of London ... and places adjacent ...* (London, 1649).

1650   Birth of Nell Gwyn (d. 1687), English actress and mistress of King Charles II.

ca. **1650**	Birth of Madame d'Aulnoy (d. 1705), French author of numerous historical novels, memoirs, and fairy tales.
1652	Birth of Susan Penelope Rosse (d. 1700), English miniaturist, one of the most popular in history, whose paintings were commissioned by Charles II's court.
1654	Anna Trapnell, English mystical poet, imprisoned for singing verses against Cromwell (Oliver).
1656	Publication of Dorothy Waugh's *The Lamb's Defense Against Lies,* a justification of her public preaching for which she was sentenced to wear a scold's bridle.
	Birth of Luisa Ignacia Roldán (d. 1704), the first known female sculptor in Spain.
	Birth of Catharina Schrader (d. 1746), Dutch midwife who published a manual of cases drawn from her extremely successful career of participating in more than three thousand births.
	Birth of Mary Lee, Lady Chudleigh (d. 1710), published poet and polemicist whose *The Ladies Defence: or, the Bride-Woman's Counsellor answer'd* asserts females' intellectual powers and their right to education and humane treatment.
1658	Publication of Sarah Jinner's *Almanac,* the only extant English almanac written by a woman in the Renaissance.
	Birth of Elizabeth Barry (d. 1713), extremely popular English actor and successful businesswoman.
1660	First Shakespearian actress, either Margaret Hughes or Ann Marshall of the Killegrew company, appeared on an English stage as Desdemona in *Othello*.
	Birth of Isabella del Pozzo (d. 1700), court painter to Adelheid, wife of the Elector of Bavaria.
1662	Birth of Kata Szidónia Petrči (d. 1708); from Upper Hungary (now the Czech Republic), she was a poet and translator of German pietistic writings into Hungarian and zealously worked to prevent Reformed believers from converting to Catholicism.
1663	Katherine Philips's dramatic rendition of *Pompey* is the first play by a woman to be produced in London.
1664	Birth of Rachel Ruysch (d. 1750), court painter to the Elector of Palatine in Dusseldorf.
ca. **1664**	Birth of Elizabeth-Claude Jacquet de la Guerre (d. 1727), French composer who wrote instrumental works and opera.
1666	Birth of Mary Astell (d. 1731), English advocate of women's right to an education and critic of women's subordination.

ca.   Birth of Sarah Fyge Field Egerton (d. 1723), English poet and femi-
1670   nist polemicist whose *Female Advocate* defends women against
            misogynous attacks.

1671   Publication in England of Jane Sharp's influential and popular
            The Midwife's Book on the Whole Art of Midwifery.

1689   Birth of Lady Mary Wortley Montagu (d. 1762); English author and
            defender of Islam, she introduced inoculation for smallpox to
            England from Turkey, where she had learned the procedure.

Introduction

———✀———

Women and the Renaissance

Women's Roles in the Renaissance examines the lives of women and girls from a wide range of classes, religions, and nations in Europe from the fourteenth through the late seventeenth centuries (ca. 1300–1699). Throughout, this narrative is concerned with the perceptions that were both shared and disputed about women across cultures and across economic boundaries as well as with the distinctions that differentiated some women's experiences from those of others. The focus is both on the ideas that circulated about women and on the difference between representations of them and their experiences of everyday life. Attention is also paid to the significant influence women exerted on the economy, social structures, and culture of the Renaissance, despite the constraints on women's exercise of power. Women's limited opportunities, enforced dependence, and exclusion from politics ensured that they did not create history or influence events in the same ways men did. Women were generally denied participation in government, universities, warfare, science, law, medicine, philosophy, banking, and navigation or exploration. To locate most women in the period, one must look not only in the public record but also in private or domestic artifacts such as wills, letters, advice books, and diaries. In many cases, however, the historical evidence of women's existence is recorded only in terms of their relationship to males; in parish registers and other documents, they are denoted simply as their husband's wife or widow or their father's daughter, so one must often listen for the silences as well as the testimony of the period to locate women. What one hears in those voids and voices is that women were not only contributors to the cultural achievements of the Renaissance, but they were crucial laborers, though often unpaid and always valued less than their male counterparts in the economies of the period. Thus, the purpose of this book is to examine not only the attitudes and practices that shaped the roles of women in the Renaissance, but also the important ways that women shaped the world in which they lived.

Before proceeding with that examination, however, it is imperative to think through the very terms of the discussion. For scholars of the period, the use of the term *Renaissance* is intensely debated, especially among feminist scholars. In addition, an unexamined use of the term *woman* is problematic, because ideas about women and men and their roles and relationships have a history; that is, they are not constant through time. There is no one single, iconic woman. Rather, gender is inflected by other social categories like class, race, nationhood, and sexuality; by geography (whether women lived in urban or rural areas); and, in this period in particular, by religion. In many of their experiences and expectations of day-to-day life, elite women had more in common with elite men than they did with peasant women living within the same region. So discussions of women's roles must be qualified by carefully attending to the other markers of social identity that determine privileges, responsibilities, and privations. An elite, white, Protestant woman's identity was defined as much by her difference from peasant women, from "native" women, from Catholic women, and from Jewish women as it was by her difference from men. At the same time, the governing discourses about gender—ideals of womanhood and women's particular virtues and weaknesses—tended to generalize about women's household and maternal responsibilities and to demand women's submission to men in all spheres. These discourses did not exist only in the realm of debate and literature; they had real consequences for all women, however various their economic and social status. And, in the days before reliable birth control, all women were subject to at least the possibility of pregnancy and its sometimes devastating consequences, whether as a result of sex as sanctioned within marriage, or extramarital sex enjoyed with some level of consent, or rape. At the same time, women's *experience* of pregnancy depended almost entirely on their social and economic status. Elite women had the financial means to feed their children, whatever the circumstances of conception, and they traveled in social circles where extramarital births were sometimes tolerated or even celebrated. But then, as now, impoverished women struggled to feed children born to them within or outside marriage. Widows with children tended to be the poorest households in any area, and what was seen as sexual misconduct by poor women was excoriated; both they and their children were subject to punishment. On the other hand, aristocratic women might experience greater rates of maternal and infant mortality than some rural women of much lower, though sufficient, income, because elite women tended to live at least part of the time in urban areas, where disease was rampant. Moreover, elite women rarely breast-fed their children and tended to become pregnant more frequently than women who breast-fed, sometimes to the detriment of maternal and infant health. It is always important, then, to distinguish between discourses about women and gender and the ways in which those ideals of womanhood played out very differently for women of differing status.

The term *Renaissance* refers to a period of western European history that extended approximately from the fourteenth century in Italy to the late seventeenth century in Great Britain. (The term was not used by those who lived in this period but was first applied in this way in the nineteenth century.) The setting for the Renaissance spanned the European continent, from Italy to Scandinavia and from what is now Portugal to Russia. Traditionally, scholars have described the Renaissance as a time of intellectual expansion and opportunity. The term literally means "rebirth," and it refers to the rebirth of ancient or classical learning as well as the liberation of science, the arts, and the individual from what contemporary thinkers saw as the stranglehold of scholasticism and the medieval church. But if the Renaissance is understood solely in terms of arts and letters, it is obvious that only the elite among those living during this period, and men, in particular, will be included under this rubric. For the most part, it was elite men who spent their lives reading, writing, and discussing the works of literature and ways of thinking that had been recovered from the classical Greek and Roman past. Unlike this privileged group, the bulk of the population was illiterate, and few of those who could read knew classical languages. So the question arises, Was there a rebirth, a Renaissance, for most people, and, specifically, did women have a Renaissance?[1] Most scholars today think not, and they characterize this period instead as *early modern,* a name that emphasizes the ways in which social, economic, and cultural features of modern life were beginning to emerge in this era; unlike *Renaissance,* the term *early modern* allows for the fact that these changing features affected everyone, not only the elite. The recovery of ancient texts and philosophies was a piece of the changes that mark the period, but rebirth is not understood to be even a central feature of the early modern era. However, because the term *Renaissance* has a currency and familiarity to those even outside academia, in this book it is used interchangeably with *early modern* to refer to the lives, experiences, and histories of all peoples living in Europe at that time.

Given its focus on the rebirth of classical learning, the story of the Renaissance has characteristically been told as the story of elite male perspectives and experiences. Conventional accounts of the period define it as a time of intense curiosity, of dignifying the self and its capacity, and of believing that man was the measure of all things. Such an account, however, is not true for at least half of the European population. Women's curiosity, for example, was muzzled by illiteracy. Female self-assertion was considered disruptive and even monstrous; the ideal woman was chaste, silent, and obedient. She was taught to cultivate the virtues of passivity and modesty, not the skills to govern, teach, or conduct business. Her place was in the home, as wife, mother, or daughter. The German theologian Martin Luther (1483–1546) observed,

> The rule remains with the husband, and the wife is compelled to obey him by God's command. He rules the home and the state, wages war, defends his possessions, tills the soil, builds, plants, etc. The woman on the other hand is like a nail driven into the wall.... [That is why] the wife should stay at home and look after the affairs of the household.[2]

One scholar has noted that "[t]he favorite [early modern] metaphor for the virtuous wife was either the snail or the tortoise, both animals that never leave their 'houses' and are totally silent."[3] In the Renaissance, then, *man* was indeed the measure of all things, a measure against which even women were assessed. To contrast the substantial differences in women's experiences in the Renaissance to those of men is not to argue, however, that males and females had no common circumstances, misfortunes,

Woman spinning and man hunting. *Source: Roxburghe Ballads,* courtesy AMS Press.

or achievements. Inevitably, their lives were shared to a considerable extent. Wars, plague, famine, urbanization, religious reform, the pleasures of festivals, and the solace of spirituality shaped the world of both women and men.

The Renaissance was a time of tremendous change and instability—social, economic, religious, political, scientific, and cultural instability. In England, for example, official versions of the Truth, of God's immutable judgment regarding right and wrong, good and bad, shifted as often as a new monarch ascended to the throne. The terms and conditions of religion and law were repeatedly reconfigured, so that today's law-abiding, pious citizen was tomorrow's blasphemous felon. Queen Mary Tudor (1516–1558) would have subjects killed for believing the version of God's truth that her father and brother, Kings Henry VIII (1491–1547) and Edward VI (1537–1553), had legislated only a few years earlier. And her successor, Elizabeth I (1533–1603), silenced, exiled, and executed those who maintained their support for Mary and the Catholic Church. Parliament imprisoned subjects for supporting King

Charles I (1600–1649), and the pope damned Catholics to hell for pledging allegiance to Queen Elizabeth. On one hand, King James I (1566–1625) would fine anyone who missed Sunday church, while on the other hand he would order that priests who celebrated the Catholic Mass must be hung, drawn, and quartered.

Not just legal and religious truths were unstable. Traditional structures and institutions such as class hierarchy and marriage were destabilized as an emerging middle class began to acquire more social status through greater wealth and by marrying into the aristocracy. As merchants could afford more lavish lifestyles, it became increasingly difficult to distinguish a mere common-born person from an aristocrat, one whose privilege, wealth, and status were inherited and, thus, defined by blood. In other words, a person's outside—clothes, ornaments, home, and retinue—was no longer necessarily commensurate with or indicative of the supposedly inherent nobility on the inside. The plumage of privilege obscured rather than verified one's place in the traditional political hierarchy.

In addition, during the Renaissance there was a florescence of discoveries and technological inventions in astronomy, medicine, physics, and navigation, so that received modes of generating and ordering knowledge were also dislocated. All of these changes, and many more, caused tremendous anxiety amid cultures that were constantly having the rug of truth and familiarity pulled out from underneath them. The disruptions and anxieties of the period had significant effects on representations of certain social groups, as fear of the unknown was often displaced onto the body of marginalized peoples, including Conversos, those Jews who had converted to Christianity, and women. Their bodies came to signify the disturbing disparity between what was thought to be hidden inside and what merely appeared to be true on the outside. The sinful soul in a woman's beguiling body became an emblem of all the deceiving confusion of the period; she was often perceived, therefore, as a threat that must be controlled, contained, silenced, or destroyed.

At the same time, not all change was perceived as frightening. Indeed, the exploration, artistic developments, advances in science, and production of extraordinary literary works gave many an elevated sense of the possibilities of human achievement. This sense was especially evident as the Renaissance evolved from the era that preceded it, the Middle Ages. The shift in modes of life and thought that distinguished the Renaissance from the medieval world began in Italy a century earlier than it occurred elsewhere on the continent. The remnants of older land-based economic structures, the lack of urbanization in some areas, and a kind of cultural insularity slowed the advent of the Renaissance in northern countries. But in Italy (which had ongoing contact with other peoples and cultures from its vantage in the Mediterranean), commerce, industry, wealth, ideas, and art flourished, each sustaining and augmenting the other. The Italian Renaissance was primarily an urban phenomenon. An extraordinary migration from the country to the city in thirteenth-century Italy saw an increase of commercial opportunities and an emerging class of merchants and professionals. The city became the economic, political, and cultural center of civilization, and it contrasted significantly with the rural institutions and social structures of northern Europe at the time. Moreover, Italy was positioned on vital trade routes between the continent and nations to the east and south, and these routes enabled the exchange of commodities and ideas. With enhanced prosperity came tremendous support for the arts from patrons who paid to have their names and images preserved and celebrated.

Also central to the changes that mark off the Renaissance from earlier times and allow generalizations about it as a discrete historical period are both the explorations and the incursions that brought Europeans in contact with peoples of different geographies, histories, and cultures. The incursions came mostly from the Ottoman Turks, who encroached steadily upon eastern Europe and the Levant, occupying territory adjacent to—and, in some cases, once held by—city-states in Italy and various countries within the Holy Roman Empire. The Turks were both feared and respected for their military strength. Their successful imperial expansion westward toward the borders of Austria and what is now Italy occupied the monarchs of Europe for most of this period. The explorations that defined the era were mounted by European nation-states, most notably the Dutch, Portuguese, Spanish, English, and French. They sought wealth, land, and raw materials first in China and India—the so-called Orient or the East in contrast to which Europeans defined themselves as Western—and later in the Americas and Africa. In all these areas of exploration, to varying degrees and with mixed success, Europeans attempted to impose their rule and culture on indigenous peoples and their societies.

In fact, it is at this time that Europeans increasingly thought of themselves as belonging to a distinctive culture and a thing called "Europe," that is, to a particular entity with unique cultural, political, and social features. The notion of a universal Christendom uniting peoples of many ethnicities and histories under one faith had emerged in the Middle Ages but without many of the political and economic features that defined early modern alliances, relationships, and ideologies within Europe. For instance, in the Middle Ages, there was nothing like the modern nation-state, which ultimately came to form the building block of Europe. But in the Renaissance, these nations began to emerge as strong and distinctive political units, and people came to see themselves as having a nationality, be it English, French, or Dutch. Such changes happened gradually, and elite people living in urban areas identified with their nation sooner and more fully than people in remote rural regions; the latter were likely throughout this time to see themselves as inhabitants of a particular village or geographic area or simply as servants to a particular landlord. The sense of national identity developed at a different pace in different countries. Italy and Germany were slow to fold city-states or small dukedoms and princedoms into larger, national political units where power was invested in a monarch who had effective sovereignty over local leaders. In general, the countries that preserved small, localized political units were the very countries that did not engage in widespread exploration and colonization during the Renaissance. While one might argue that it was their very lack of centralized political organization that prevented them from mounting sustained exploration, plantation, and colonization, it is clear at the same time that exploration had the effect of catalyzing and solidifying national identity and driving the desire for even greater imperial expansion.

As a result of these many complex economic and political processes, Europe emerged over time as a cultural entity that included some people and excluded others. The majority, even those in rural areas who lived in nearly absolute cultural isolation, identified themselves in contradistinction to some negative "other"—they were not Muslim Turks, nor were they Jews; they were not pagan, not native, not brown or black. Out of this negative space emerged a people with some shared identity and self-image. They were white, a term that had no social meaning before widespread exploration and colonization; they followed what was for them the only true religion, Christianity, to which other peoples must be converted, by force, if necessary; and they were civilized, while all others were barbaric, beastly, or childish, and, therefore, in need of political and economic governance by Europeans. And though Jews, for instance, lived within all countries of Europe in varying numbers during this period, they did not enjoy the same political rights as their neighbors, and they were always in danger of attack or banishment. In some profound sense, they were seen as alien to the world in which they lived, despite the fact that they had never in recent memory lived anywhere else and were among the creators of Western culture as it has been inherited. At the same time, Ashkenazic Jews in particular "cultivated a punctillious sense of spiritual separateness from their 'idolatrous' [Christian] neighbors to compensate for the fact that Jews' survival depended on interaction with Christians."[4] They saw themselves as perennial exiles and foreigners in an alien land. But the Jews might paradoxically be credited with a significant role in creating national identities and the idea of Europe, as even in countries like England where there were very few Jews during this period, they served as a demonic "other" against which notions of "Englishness" were defined. It was only in later centuries that their positive contributions to Western culture were widely recognized, and the horrific wars of the twentieth century demonstrated the continuing widespread power of anti-Semitism and the degree to which Jews could still be imagined as essentially alien to Europe.

The notion that the Jews were outsiders is particularly ironic because of the contributions they made to the distinctive economic structures of the Renaissance. This period marks the emergence of capitalism, an economic system based in trade and empires rather than in the land and its produce and rents. (And even the land in many areas came to be farmed and managed in new ways under emerging agrarian capitalism.) The land—in particular, the great estates owned by aristocratic landlords—had been the basis of most medieval wealth. It had certainly determined the social and economic philosophy of that era, which defined individuals and classes by their relationship to the land: the nobility were those who owned the land and benefited from its wealth, while the peasantry were those who worked the land. But the value of land as a source of wealth declined in some countries during the Renaissance. This was partly because inflation drove up prices, while rents—what aristocrats received from their tenants who farmed the land—were fixed. Landowners were impelled to seek new sources of wealth, especially through mercantile activity. But those activities were open not only to aristocrats who had money to invest in exploration and merchant adventures, but also to enterprising urban merchants who might never have owned a great estate or had a title. By the end of the early modern era, the middle class, a group that had been nearly invisible to political theorists of the Middle Ages, had emerged all over Europe and had come to dominate the political life of some countries. And though Christian women, like the Jews, did not share in the full political rights accorded to Christian men in early modern states, their lives were nonetheless affected by the shifting of the economic center from the landed estate to the towns and cities where manufacturing provided women as well as men and people of all cultures and ethnicity with new opportunities for work and livelihood.

Capitalism emerged differently and at varying rates in the countries and economies of Europe in this period. In Britain and the Netherlands, though both maintained monarchies and systems of noble titles, the monarchs shared power with a governing assembly made up of middle-class men whose wealth came at least in part from mercantile activity. In France, on the other hand, though manufacturing and small-scale industry developed in towns and produced a prosperous middle class, land continued to support the economic and political dominance of the French monarchy and aristocracy up to the eve of the revolution in 1789. This difference is partly one of geography and climate; French land is far more agriculturally productive than Britain's, and its climate is more conducive to growing a wide variety of food for export, including grapes and grain. France had historically been a major exporter of food, especially luxury goods like wine, and that meant that the French aristocracy were never driven to undertake the same kind of improvements associated with agricultural capitalism that drove English practices. In addition, the French were not pushed into colonial mercantile activity to maintain their dominance. In a sense, French aristocrats had always been merchants, exporting and marketing the produce of their land. In another sense, their wealth and status remained tied to the land in ways that seemed very traditional and that did not provoke the

Geertruydt Roghman, *Woman Reading* (ca. 1640). *Source:* Museum of Fine Arts, Boston. Harvey D. Parker Collection. Photograph © 2004 Museum of Fine Arts, Boston.

same kind of political change that accompanied the emergence of mercantilism in other parts of Europe during this period.

It is also in the Renaissance that the precursor to mass media emerged, another feature that makes the period early modern. The printing press with movable type was invented in the middle of the fifteenth century and ultimately made possible the widespread distribution of printed materials. When printed books first became available, there was still a very small reading public, and initially the books were nearly as rare and valuable as manuscripts (handwritten books). But the very existence of printing created a readership, and, by the mid-sixteenth century, rates of literacy were rising quickly. This was especially true among the aristocracy, where nearly all women and men could read, and among the urban bourgeoisie, particularly in the Protestant north. The availability of printed materials made it possible for a growing public to buy printed books that broadcast new information and challenged traditional notions of authority, hierarchy, and truth.

The expansion of a reading public was also driven by Reformation theologies that held individual believers responsible for their own salvation; to assume that responsibility, women as well as men needed to be able to read the Bible in their own language. Paradoxically, the influence of these ideas was first spread through printed materials, creating a cycle of causation where theology drove printing, and printing drove theology. In fact, the Protestant Reformation could not have happened without the existence of mass printing. The religious ideas of the sixteenth-century reformers, those who wanted to reform the theology and structure of the Church, were not new; these ideas had circulated throughout Europe among elites since the fourteenth century. But when in 1517, as the story goes, Martin Luther nailed to the doors of the castle church in Wittenburg a list of challenges to and complaints about what he saw as the repressive practices and abuses of the Church, his ideas were broadcast throughout Europe by printed pamphlets and were soon being widely discussed. Very quickly, many countries became embroiled in responses to the Reformation insistence that only reason, conscience, and scripture—not institutions or authority figures—could guide Christians to truth. In response, in 1545 the Catholic Church convened the Council of Trent, which enacted wide-ranging reforms (leading to the Counter-Reformation or Catholic Reformation) as well as stricter censorship, surveillance, and active recruitment in Protestant regions. Of course, Protestant thinkers also advocated the censorship and surveillance of people, and they actively recruited Catholics.

While Protestant ideas prompted discussion and debate everywhere, a country's faithfulness to Catholicism or its conversion to Protestantism was not simply a result of theological dispute but also a matter of political expediency. The very nation-states that were coming into being in the Renaissance were in some sense the cause of the Reformation as much as the ideas of Luther or other reformers. Monarchs could not rule effectively if they had to share power in political and legal matters with the pope and if they did not control significantly more financial assets than any other rival to their power. For many rulers, a church headed by the pope, who was essentially seen as a foreign ruler, represented an unacceptable bar to the royal consolidation of power. As a result, many rulers moved to establish their sovereignty over church polity and to seize the assets of religious establishments. In some countries, such as England, that meant that the monarch declared himself head of the Church in place of the pope and took control of monastic wealth. Elsewhere, as in the Holy Roman Empire, the pope was generally a political ally of the emperor and, under a powerful leader like Charles V (1500–1558), was even subject to the emperor. In that case, there was no need to disrupt a system that actually served to increase the power of the emperor vis-à-vis other monarchs and his own subjects. Monarchs all over Europe made religious decisions for their countries for pragmatic reasons, though those reasons were usually cloaked in religious language.

At the same time, the ideas propounded by Reformation thinkers ultimately had a profound effect on political systems, in part because of the emphasis the Reformation placed on individual responsibility and, it ultimately came to be thought, on individual rights. The very notion of the individual, which has been inherited from the Renaissance and which has made the West the most thoroughgoing individualistic society ever, emerged in this period. It affected, for instance, the way contemporaries thought about artistic and literary production. Present culture has inherited ideas about the genius of the individual that influence and even, some might say, corrupt the way artists and their works are understood. That kind of thinking militated against the emergence of women artists, who were not thought to possess the individual spark of genius that would allow them to achieve greatness. And it has affected the ways in which art history and literary history are taught and theorized. These disciplines have overwhelmingly preserved the works of great men who, until recently, have been studied in a cultural vacuum, as if they were not products of their times. Renaissance ideas of the individual also ultimately contributed to the rise of radical and revolutionary political theories that claimed that all peoples—not just property-owning Christian men, but poor men, women, Jews, and people of color—have inalienable rights that no monarch or government has the right to abrogate. These ideas did not reach fruition until the nineteenth century, and people are still struggling, with varying success, to implement them, but they stand as ideals for a humane and moral political life, and they have their origin in the religious and political debates of the early modern era.

In spite of the fact that different peoples in different countries experienced the Renaissance differently, and that the history of the Renaissance varies significantly according to region and social status, there are, nonetheless, some generalizations that can be made about all women's lives within this wide geographic area over nearly four hundred years. None of the developments that characterize the Renaissance were entirely good news for women. Though her experiences were shaped by class, faith, nationality, or the work that she did, a woman's gender defined her and shaped her circumstances profoundly. For example, whether she was an English aristocrat, an Italian peasant, or a Jewish merchant, her legal identity depended on her relationship to men. That is, she was defined by whom she belonged to as a daughter, sister, or wife, because women were legally designated as the property of husbands, brothers, fathers, or other male relatives or guardians. Parents still arranged marriages for their daughters and minor sons, though it was generally thought cruel to force children to marry someone they found repugnant. Women in many parts of Europe did not inherit an equal share of property with their brothers on the death of their fathers, and the wealth they brought to their marriages became the property of their husbands, with the exception of an allowance that might be set aside for the women's particular use. (In Venice, by contrast, both married and single women controlled their own property.) Generally in this period, children legally belonged to the father rather than the mother, so that, for women, separation or divorce meant losing their children. Elite women might have more restrictions on their marriage or their freedom to go where they pleased than women of lower status because noblewomen were held to be the conduits for noble blood and lineage, the guarantors of rightful inheritance. Some nuns, noblewomen, and widows had more social autonomy than most women, and the emerging urban economies gave many women of the "middling" classes a hitherto unknown freedom to move and to earn a living, but the vast majority of women had fewer legal rights than men and more limited independence. Rather than liberation, expansion, and prosperity, women in the Renaissance experienced attempts to limit their education, repress their sexuality, and confine them primarily to a domestic sphere and to domestic labor.

However, moralists' very complaints about women's social, economic, geographic, and sexual mobility suggest that women's roles and expectations were changing; urban, middle-class women in particular had more earning opportunities and mobility in this era. Nonetheless, the proscriptions of women's liberty shaped women's sense of self and the horizons of their vision. Because domesticity was seen as the norm for all women, and because of constraints on their education and economic activities, it was extremely difficult for them to participate in or benefit from the cultural expansion of the Renaissance. Even when women were able to overcome illiteracy, they were frequently condemned as unnatural or transgressive for aspiring to intellectual or artistic achievement. The Italian Isotta Nogarola (1418–ca. 1466), for example, was renowned for her knowledge of languages and her intelligence. She wrote elegant Latin and Greek and attempted to discuss philosophy and theology with educated men of her time. But in 1438 she was attacked in an anonymous pamphlet that argued that her unnatural learning had led her to commit incest with her brother. The only proof the pamphlet offered was her erudition, since "an eloquent woman is never chaste."[5]

Indeed, concern about women's speech, writing, and unsupervised movement was almost always expressed in terms of their sexuality. A wife who "went gadding" outside the confines of her household was perceived as calling into question her chastity and disgracing her husband. Many women who wrote or painted, such as the Italian Artemisia Gentileschi (1593–1652), the English Aphra Behn (ca. 1640–1689), and the Spanish María de Zayas y Sotomayor (ca. 1590–ca. 1661) were condemned as whores. Lady Mary Wroth (1587–ca. 1651) was called both a whore and a hermaphrodite for publishing her work, the latter term implying that she was a monstrous combination of male (that is, artistic and creative) and female parts. The equating of women's speech or writing with their sexuality was perhaps the most common justification for silencing them throughout the Renaissance. Female writing and speech were perceived as a threat to the traditionally male domains of learning and professional services. Humanist changes in education were mostly directed toward preparing young men for public service—for wage earning and social advancement—a sphere that was emphatically closed to women. Female silence was necessary to prevent competition and to disable encroachment on male authority. Thus, many moralists held that women's education should be limited to basic literacy and that their learning to write was both unnecessary and inappropriate. Writing was seen as a kind of agency that could dismantle images of the helpless, passive, and intellectually inferior female.

Hostility toward women's independence and anxiety about their sexuality were partly grounded in economic considerations. Land, money, and other property had to be transferred from the father to his "legitimate" children, preferably sons. In some countries, such as England, a system of primogeniture and entail was made increasingly binding during this era. In this system, the eldest child, usually the eldest son, inherited the bulk of the estate, which was entailed on him; that is, it was legally required that the estate pass intact to the eldest, while any other children received much smaller inheritances. In other countries, including France, it remained the custom to divide estates equally among one's heirs. In either case, it was necessary that paternity be clearly established. Otherwise, the consolidated wealth of a family could pass out of the bloodlines to an outside male's lineage. So women's sexuality was strictly controlled in order to regulate the inheritance of property. Indeed, an unmarried girl's virginity was itself her father's property, and a husband owned his wife's chastity. Women's sexuality was a valuable commodity in the marriage market, one that might be bought and sold in arranged marriages so as to perpetuate family names, form political alliances, and consolidate or augment wealth. Even in nonaristocratic families, a father could sue a man for having intercourse with his unmarried daughter because the criminal had damaged the father's property. Similarly, the law supported a husband's right to charge his wife's lover with trespassing, and rape was a crime of property, not sexual violence. Social and economic power, ownership, and authority were at stake in men's regulation of female sexuality.

Early modern people also drew on ideas inherited from classical and biblical traditions in theorizing about men's and women's roles and relationships. Aristotle (384–322 B.C.E.) was the most influential of the classical philosophers, and he understood women to be by nature inferior to men in every way. Though Aristotle argued that only barbarians (i.e., those who were not Greek) thought women and slaves to be of the same nature and capabil-

Pious husband instructing his family, Thomas Sternhold, *Tenor of the Whole Psalmes in Foure Partes* (London, 1563), frontispiece, STC 2431, BL K.1.e.2. *Source:* Reproduced by permission of The British Library.

ities, he nonetheless saw both women and slaves through their relationship to male citizens. Aristotle theorized that both males and females started out as identical creatures in the womb, but that the natural "heat" of the male forced the genitals to the outside of the body and perfected other characteristics natural to men. A woman was less finished and less complete than a man, sharing the same characteristics but in a less perfect form. Aristotle posited that men were thus more suited to command than women, just as adults are superior to the young, and that this inequality was permanent and part of human nature. As an example, he noted that both men and women could possess courage, but their expression of this virtue was entirely different in each. He argued that a man's courage is shown in commanding, while a woman's is shown in obeying. Even in the case of procreation, Aristotle understood women to be merely suppliers of raw material, while men supplied the form of the child. The womb, then, was rather like garden soil into which the man planted his seed, the sperm, which contained the essence of the child to be born. At the same time that people of the Renaissance accepted this argument, there circulated an opposite theory holding that men and women were entirely different species, unalike in any way. But even in this model, women were thought to be inferior.

In addition to the works of Aristotle and other ancient writers, the Bible, both the Hebrew Bible (Old Testament) and the Christian Scriptures (New Testament), greatly influenced thinking about women in the Renaissance. That said, it is important to note that the books of the Bible, whether Old or New Testament, do not have only one thing to say about women. Rather, they are polyvocal texts written over a period of more than one thousand years, representing a variety of experiences and understandings about women and every other topic of interest to those ancient people. In the work of some Hebrew writers, women are seen as the occasion of sin, as sexual temptations, as images of unfaithfulness, and as inferior to men in every way. For most theorists, a reading of Genesis suggested that Eve's having been created from Adam's rib and her sin in eating the forbidden fruit meant that woman was subordinate to man. But others argued that the fact that woman was created last by God meant that she was the most perfect creature, while Adam/man was God's first attempt, as inferior to Eve/woman as the animals and plants were to humankind. Some books of the Hebrew Bible portray women as the saviors of the Jews (e.g., Deborah, Jael, and Judith) or as possessing particular virtue (such as Susanna). Those heroines of Jewish history were important to early modern writers who wished to exalt women's status. The stories of Judith and Susanna in particular were popular subjects of both art and poetry during this period. Likewise, women are portrayed in differing ways in the Christian writings of the first and second centuries. Those Renaissance writers who wished to limit and subordinate women seized on the most misogynist passages, while defenders of women's virtue and liberty focused on other biblical texts that offered an alternative vision.

The most oft-quoted passages regarding women come from the New Testament letters of Paul or those attributed to him. Yet even in these writings there is no single understanding of women and gender. For example, in 1 Corinthians, Paul ordains a strict hierarchy in which women are both inferior and subjected to men. Referring to the story of Adam's creation from earth and Eve's from his rib, the passage argues that

The head of every woman is the man…. A man indeed ought not to cover his head, forasmuch as he is the image and glory of God but the woman is the glory of the man. For the man is not of the woman; but the woman of the man. Neither was the man created for the woman; but the woman for the man. (11:3–13)

And the passage most frequently cited during the early modern period to silence women comes from this same epistle:

Let your women keep silence in the churches: for it is not permitted unto them to speak; but they are commanded to be under obedience, as also saith the law. And if they will learn anything, let them ask their husbands at home: for it is a shame for women to speak in the church. (14:34–35)

Ephesians (a pseudo-Pauline text) reiterates male dominion over the female: "Wives, submit yourselves unto your own husbands, as unto the Lord. For the husband is the head of the wife…. Therefore as the church is subject unto Christ, so let wives be to their own husbands in everything" (5:22–24). Yet Paul wrote in Galatians that, among Christians, "there is no longer Jew or Greek, there is no longer slave or free, there is no longer male and female, for all of you are one in Christ Jesus" (Gal. 3:28), a remarkably egalitarian statement for a man of the first century. And it is from Paul's letters that the names of a few women leaders of the Early Christian Missionary movement are known, including Prisca, who seems to have been more noted in that movement than Paul, and Junia. Women are also important in some of the gospel accounts, especially Luke (and its companion volume, Acts). In the Renaissance, these prowoman materials were used to defend women against their attackers.

At the same time, those who wished to condemn women and show them to be inferior to men repeatedly seized on the Pastoral Epistles, 1 and 2 Timothy (works that were known from the earliest Christian centuries not to have been written by Paul, though they nonetheless carried scriptural authority within the Church). 1 Timothy admonishes females to

adorn themselves in modest apparel, with shamefacedness and sobriety; not with braided hair, or gold, or pearls, or costly array. But (which becometh women professing godliness) with good works. Let the woman learn in silence with all subjection. But I suffer not a woman to teach, nor to usurp authority over the man, but to be in silence. For Adam was first formed, then Eve. And Adam was not deceived, but the woman being deceived was in the transgression. Notwithstanding she shall be saved in childbearing, if they continue in faith and charity and holiness with sobriety. (2:9–15)[6]

Prowoman writers also made use of these same biblical passages to defend women. Henricus Cornelius Agrippa von Nettesheim (1486–1535), known as Agrippa, wrote in his 1529 *De nobilitate et praecellentia foeminei sexus* [On the nobility and excellency of the female sex] that

Phyllis riding Aristotle, [Anon.], *The Deceyte of Women to the Instruction and Ensample of All Men Yonge and Olde, Newly Corrected* (London, 1557), titlepage, STC 6451. *Source:* Reproduced by permission of The British Library.

> by *Tradition* the Woman received this Commandment [not to eat of the tree of knowledge] from the Man, not by immediate *delivery* from God; which is so, we thence conclude, That by reason thereof the Woman might chance more easily to break this Law, than the Man; since the *All-glorious Majesty* of God that *commanded,* should take deeper impression in Man, than the *equality* of person that *related,* could in the Woman; the roaring of a *Lion* being more trembled at, than the braying of an *Ass*; the Commands of a *King* more powerful, than the words of one's *Companion.* At most, when Woman sinned, she did it, poor soul, unwittingly, being deluded by the insinuating Serpent: so that it appears the Man sinned against perfect knowledge, and the positive Command of his Maker; the Woman out of ignorance, seduced by the crafty wiles of the *Tempter,* with whom for a considerable time she *disputed* the matter.[7]

That is, Agrippa argues that Eve's having been deluded or deceived (in the words of the author of 1 Timothy) made her *less* culpable than Adam. This twist on the defense was taken up by many prowoman writers of the Renaissance, most of whom were influenced by Agrippa's interpretation of the biblical passage.

However, Renaissance writers used the biblical passages cited above to enforce the subjection of women in every sphere, not simply the marital or the domestic. The Bible was the ultimate authority, and interpretations of its teaching were often more oppressive than the text itself. Martin Luther argued that the prior creation of man demonstrated his precedence or superiority over woman, not only spiritually and intellectually but also physically. He infers from the anatomical difference of males and females a moral significance:

> God has created man with a broad chest, not broad hips, so that in that part of him he can be wise; but that part out of which filth comes is small. In a woman, this is reversed. That is why she had much filth and little wisdom.[8]

French theologian and reformer John Calvin (1509–1564) was a particularly severe commentator on women. His discussions of the fall in Genesis emphasize Eve's guilt and the blame and iniquity that all women have inherited from her originary wickedness. As a result of the first female's crime, all women must suffer greater subjection than men. If a wife does not submit to her husband, Calvin insists, she is blaspheming against God:

When they contend with their husbands, it is all one as if they would reject God…. Women must needs stoop [bow or submit] and understand that the ruin and confusion of all mankind came in from their side, and that through them we be all forlorn and accursed and banished from the kingdom of heaven: when women (say I) do understand that all this came of Eve and of the womankind (as Paul telleth us in another place), there is none other way but for them to stoop and to bear patiently the subjection that God hath laid upon them, which is nothing else but a warning to them to keep themselves lowly and mild.[9]

In spite of the fact that some arguments relied on protofeminist readings of these same biblical passages, interpretations like Luther's and Calvin's tended to predominate.

Order and hierarchy were important concepts in the Renaissance, and most theorists and moralists of the period worked out their philosophy in a schema of rank and subordination. Early modern people shared a literary, philosophical, and religious heritage that mostly argued for women's inferiority to men as well as peasants' inferiority to the nobility and aristocrats' inferiority to the sovereign. In addition, people of one religious confession usually held that people of other religions were misguided and mistaken. However, the Renaissance was a period of new thinking regarding religion, politics, and social roles and structures; all of the received wisdom of the ancient world as well as time-honored interpretations of the Bible were being challenged during this period. So, while most early modern people continued to hold rather traditional notions of hierarchy, there were challenges to almost every idea they had inherited. The Querelle des Femmes, or "Woman Controversy," a heated discussion about the nature of women, provided a forum for the most radical thinking about women and gender; the Reformation and the Counter-Reformation produced revolutionary ideas not only about the Bible but about religious authority and social structures, and some religious free-thinkers—like the Quakers, Levellers, and Anabaptists— argued for an entirely egalitarian society without rank or even marriage. Such thinking did not, of course, win the day in any Renaissance state, but the fact that such ideas were expressed opened up a world of possibilities for those whose daily lives were played out within political and social structures of rank and difference. The notable women of the period who did challenge conservative thinking about gender, whether through their artistic endeavors or their overtly political engagement in the debates of the day, no doubt drew inspiration, courage, and a certain authorization from the possibilities offered by the new thinking that emerged in the Renaissance.

The following chapters are organized according to topics that provide a frame of reference for analyzing and illustrating many aspects of women's roles in the Renaissance. Inevitably, these topics overlap. Daily experiences and roles in the Renaissance were interwoven and interdependent, as were ideological assumptions and practices. When one discussion in the book overlaps with another, the material is presented from several perspectives, so that topics can be understood as richly related. Viewing women's roles through a variety of lenses demonstrates ways in which gender, class, race, religion, work, and nationality are mutually shaped and shaping. The chapters and topics are cross-referenced throughout, so that nonspecialist readers can more fully develop their research interests. Chapter 1 examines women's education and conduct, including dress, speech, prescribed virtues, and proscribed vices. Chapter 2, entitled "Women and the Law," surveys regulations concerning family, marriage, dowries, and inheritance. It also discusses the legal ramifications of parenting, stepparenting, and fostering as well as attitudes and legislation regarding rape and witchcraft. Chapter 3, "Women and Work," investigates the economic roles and circumstances of women's lives, including labor conditions and employment options such as housekeeping, service, midwifery and healing, child care, membership in guilds and professions, and prostitution. Discussion of poverty is inevitably a part of the study of women and work. The fourth chapter, "Women and Politics," examines patronage, public life, female rulers and courtiers, and women's experiences of social protest and war. Considerations of socioeconomic status necessarily inform each of these subjects. "Women and Religion," chapter 5, discusses the positive and negative impact on women of the Reformation and Counter-Reformation as well as the pervasive effects of religion on the daily lives of all Renaissance peoples, whether they were Christian, Jewish, or Muslim. Chapters 6 and 7 examine women and literature, and women and the arts. The chapter "Women and Literature" explores the relationship between class and female authorship, print, and literacy as well as the ways in which literary genres were gendered and highly politicized in the period. "Women and the Arts" includes accounts of female painters, sculptors, musicians, and artisans as well as a discussion of the conditions and attitudes that affected women's ability and opportunities to create. The final chapter discusses women's pleasures: sport, dancing, festivals and fairs, drinking, eating, and loving.

NOTES

1.   This question was famously asked by Joan Kelly Gadol: "Did Women Have a Renaissance?" in *Feminism and Renaissance Studies,* ed. Lorna Hutson (New York: Oxford University Press, 1999) 21–47. Gadol's essay has significantly influenced subsequent feminist histories of the period.

2.   Qtd. in Jaroslav Pelikan, ed., *Luther's Works* (St. Louis, MO: Concordia, 1958), 1.202–03.

3.   Merry E. Wiesner, *Women and Gender in Early Modern Europe,* 2nd ed. (New York: Cambridge University Press, 2000), 25.

4.   David Graizbord, e-mail message. Thanks to Prof. Graizbord for his many helpful suggestions regarding Jews in the early modern period.

5.   Anonymous letter, qtd. in Margaret L. King and Albert Rabil, Jr., eds. and trans., *Her Immaculate Hand: Selected Works by and about Women Humanists of Qualtrocento Italy* (Asheville, NC: Pegasus Press, 2000), 17.

6.   This extremely conservative and hierarchical epistle also counsels slaves to "regard their masters as worthy of all honor," particularly if the masters are Christian, since, in that case, "those who benefit by their service are believers and beloved."

7.   *Female Pre-eminence: Or the Dignity and Excellency of that Sex, above the Male. An Ingenious Discourse: Written Originally in Latine, by Henry Cornelius Agrippa, Knight, Doctor of Physick, Doctor of both Laws, and Privy-Counselor to the Emperor Charles the Fifth. Done into English, with Additional Advantages By H[enry] C[are]* (London: Henry Million, 1670), 31. Care's translation of Agrippa is also available through EEBO, <http://eebo.chadwyck.com>

8.   Qtd. in Susan C. Karant-Nunn and Merry E. Wiesner-Hanks, eds. and trans., *Luther on Women: A Sourcebook* (New York: Cambridge University Press, 2003), 29.

9.   Qtd. in Kate Aughterson, ed., *Renaissance Woman: A Sourcebook* (New York: Routledge, 1995), 16–17.

SUGGESTED READING

Benson, Pamela J. *The Invention of the Renaissance Woman: The Challenge of Female Independence in the Literature and Thought of*

Italy and England. University Park: Pennsylvania State University Press, 1992.

Chojnacka, Monica. *Working Women of Early Modern Venice.* Baltimore: Johns Hopkins University Press, 2001.

Clarke, Danielle. *The Politics of Early Modern Women's Writing.* New York: Longman/Pearson Education, 2001.

Ferguson, Margaret W., Maureen Quilligan, and Nancy J. Vickers, eds. *Rewriting the Renaissance: The Discourses of Sexual Difference in Early Modern Europe.* Chicago: University of Chicago Press, 1987.

Henderson, Katherine Usher, and Barbara F. McManus. *Half Humankind: Contexts and Texts of the Controversy about Women in England, 1540–1640.* Urbana: University of Illinois Press, 1985.

Hufton, Olwen. *The Prospect before Her: A History of Women in Western Europe, 1500–1800.* New York: Alfred A. Knopf, 1996.

Karant-Nunn, Susan C., and Merry E. Wiesner-Hanks, eds. and trans. *Luther on Women: A Sourcebook.* New York: Cambridge University Press, 2003.

Kelso, Ruth. *Doctrine for the Lady of the Renaissance.* 1956. Urbana: University of Illinois Press, 1978.

King, Margaret L. *Women of the Renaissance.* Chicago: University of Chicago Press, 1991.

Labalme, Patricia H. *Beyond Their Sex: Learned Women of the European Past.* New York: New York University Press, 1980.

Lerner, Gerda. *The Creation of Feminist Consciousness, From the Middle Ages to 1870.* New York: Oxford University Press, 1994.

Maclean, Ian. *The Renaissance Notion of Woman: A Study in the Fortunes of Scholasticism and Medical Science in European Intellectual Life.* New York: Cambridge University Press, 1980.

Orgel, Stephen. *Impersonations: The Performance of Gender in Shakespeare's England.* New York: Cambridge University Press, 1996.

Wiesner, Merry E. *Women and Gender in Early Modern Europe.* 2nd ed. New York: Cambridge University Press, 2000.

1

—∞∞—

Women and Education

Though few people of the early modern era were literate, that is, few could read and write, all were educated to assume their proper place in society; often that education was quite programmed and intentional, despite the fact that very few children, girls or boys, went to school.[1] Parents were responsible for training their children (or sending them to others to be trained) to assume roles appropriate to their status, whether as agricultural laborers, household servants, skilled artificers, merchants, clergy, courtiers, or monarchs. And every girl, regardless of her social situation, was educated in domestic skills—something that set girls apart from boys. Any person of the era who wrote about education stressed that girls were to be instructed very differently from boys. All women learned sewing and needlework, which were often lauded as the mark of feminine virtue (something for which there was no equivalent for boys, whose training tended to depend very much on their class). Even when girls' education was not elaborately theorized (as, for instance, in the case of girls of low social status), they were still taught a very different set of skills from boys, though neither girls nor boys, men nor women among the peasantry were likely to be able to read or write at this time.[2] More than anything else, education was meant to fit a child for a particular social role, which is perhaps why some moralists thought that too much education was a danger for women and for all people of lower social status.

In addition, girls' education was always designed to protect and preserve their chastity and virtue, so some educators recom-

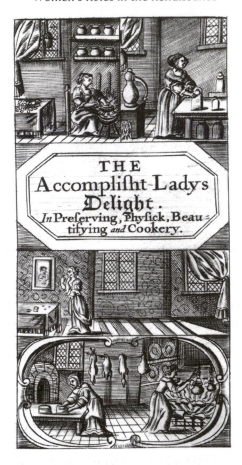

Housewifery, Hannah Woolley, *The Accomplisht Ladies Delight in Preserving, Physick, Beautifying and Cookery* (London, 1675), STC 19976. *Source:* © Bodleian Library, University of Oxford, Douce P42, Title Page.

mended limiting even elite girls to reading the Bible and religious works and discouraged their learning of Latin and Greek, which might expose them to obscene or frivolous literature. (Few educators encouraged boys to read such works, either, but it was assumed that elite boys needed to have Latin to read philosophy and other ancient literature.) Similarly, girls from most Jewish families were not encouraged to learn Hebrew, which was, like Latin and Greek, the language of scholarship and—even more importantly for both Christianity and Judaism—the language of Holy Scripture. Both Christian and Jewish scholars typically argued that girls who studied holy works in the ancient languages would become sexually promiscuous. The Mishnah (the collection of Jewish law and commentary) quoted the revered Rabbi Eliezer as saying, "Everyone who teaches his daughter Torah, it is as if he taught her lechery."[3] Too much learning was also thought to make girls masculine; one rabbi writing about learned women used masculine pronouns and suffixes to describe them. And Leon Modena (1571–1648), an Italian rabbi of Venice, though he taught both girls and boys as part of his official duties, did not educate his own daughters, who could neither read nor write. Indeed, even after their marriages, they could maintain contact with their father, renowned as "one of the greatest masters of Hebrew letter writing in Italy, if not all of Jewish history," only by having their husbands write letters for them.[4] For some Christian as well as Jewish moralists, too much learning or the wrong kind of learning would, at the very least, distract women from their duties as wives and mothers. At the worst, it would corrupt their chastity and virtue and perhaps turn them into mannish, lascivious monsters. Nonetheless, sources show that some "Jewish women in Italy taught children the Hebrew letters and the correct reading of scripture in Hebrew, though translation and commentary were reserved for male teachers."[5]

Indeed girls' education in general became more common in the Renaissance. Despite the widespread objections from many religious writers and cultural commentators, it is nonetheless a fact that many middle-class and aristocratic girls *were* educated, some of them as extensively as boys. In this case, as in many others, too much credence cannot be given to the writings of conservative moralists, whose diatribes against certain activities are often the best proof that those activities were common.

Works on pedagogy, that is, theories of education, were written by the hundreds during this period, and almost everyone who wrote on education felt obliged to include some mention of women's proper education. Authors would often append to the tract a list of learned women throughout the ages as a justification for their own educational theories. While many moralists were leery of overeducating women, a fair number of authors, both male and female, wrote enthusiastically in support of women's education and published elaborate programs of study for girls. Most elite children continued to be schooled at home by private tutors at this time. Such a practice had always guaranteed that many—perhaps most—girls from aristocratic families would have access to education up to a point (though they could not, of course, go to a university, which elite boys typically attended from about the age of 14). Indeed, one recent scholar has suggested that education was quite widely available to girls: "[i]t is modern scholarship, rather than early modern, which has caused the woman scholars of the sixteenth and seventeenth centuries to vanish."[6] Even middle-class girls began to enjoy greater and greater education during the Renaissance as schools proliferated in many parts of Europe. Children in these schools learned reading, writing, and mathematics; some were introduced to other languages, even Latin, which remained the mark of a true education throughout the era. Girls' schools of this sort were also noted for teaching dance and music, as these skills were thought to be particularly appropriate to women.

In some cases, girls' musical education might be quite advanced, as their teachers were among the finest musicians of the age. For instance, Antonio Vivaldi (1678–1741), one of the most admired musicians of the Baroque era, was for many years the *maestro di violino* (string instrument master or teacher) and later the *maestro de' concerti* (orchestra master) at the Ospedale della Pietà, a girls' orphanage in Venice. He wrote some of his finest compositions, including instrumental works and sacred vocal works, for the all-girl orchestra and chorus there. Similarly, when the Civil War in England (1639–1649) broke up the royal and aristocratic courts, musicians who were formerly employed writing court music and producing concerts and masques had to make a living outside those circles. Henry Lawes (1596–1662) had been Gentleman of the Chapel Royal and a member of the King's Musick, but after the breakup of the royal court, he took a job teaching at Mrs. Salmon's School in Hackney (near London). There he taught, among other young women, Mary Harvey, Lady Dering (1629–1704), the first Englishwoman to publish music under her own name. Elaborate musical and dramatic productions were quite common in both girls' and boys' schools. The composer Henry Purcell's (1659–1695) opera *Dido and Aeneas,* for instance, was first performed in 1689 by the "Young Gentlewomen" of "Mr. Josias Priest's Boarding School at Chesley" near London, according to the title page of the libretto published that same year. Convent girls' schools in northern Europe regularly staged plays, both ancient and modern; by the eighteenth century, girls in those schools were learning and performing the works of the French neoclassical dramatist Jean Racine (1639–1699) and others.[7] And many Continental convent schools were known for the high quality of their music and music instruction. The celebration for Margaret Clement's 50-year Jubilee (the 50th anniversary of her profession as a nun) at Louvain (Belgium) was marked by an entire week of musical performance, with choirs and viol consorts from all the local convents. The High Mass culminating the week of festivities featured her own nuns singing a piece specially composed for the event with viols accompanying the entire service. Even the musicians from the court of Archduke Albert of Austria (1559–1621) joined in the celebration.[8]

Literacy in one's own language—one's "mother tongue"—was generally on the rise in this period. Indeed, Protestants insisted on literacy, as they held that salvation was predicated *sola scriptura,* that is, on scripture alone, rather than on sacraments or penitential acts or good works. This belief led to the translation of the Bible into vernacular languages (the common languages of the people, like English, French, and German) not only by Protestants but also by Catholics, who wished to counter the overtly Protestant perspective of some translations with their own version. There developed, then, a literate population who believed that salvation was based on their ability to "read, mark, learn, and inwardly digest" the "holy Word" of God, as one collect (prayer) of the Church of England put it.[9] In addition, the fact that the Catholic Church continued to hold the Latin Bible (the Vulgate) in particular esteem during this period and continued to celebrate liturgies in Latin meant that Catholic children who were educated at all tended to learn at least some basic Latin, and sometimes they became quite fluent in the language. Despite the misgivings of conservative rabbis, many elite Jewish girls were also educated, sometimes learning Hebrew as well as Greek (for the study of philosophy) and Latin (for the study of poetry and rhetoric); as in the case of Christian girls, however, they were often kept from reading anything remotely corrupting or salacious, including the works of poets like Dante (1265–1321) and Petrarch (1304–1374), both of whom wrote in Italian.[10] The sixteenth-century woman Fioretta of Modena, Italy, was "very learned in Torah, Mishnah, Talmud, Midrash, Jewish law, especially Maimonides, and Kabbalistic literature." She raised her grandson, who became the scholar and author Rabbi

Forsake not the law of thy Mother. Prou:1:8

Mother teaching her daughter to read, BL Harleian 5974/121. *Source:* Reproduced by permission of The British Library.

Aaron Berechiah of Modena (d. 1639), and supervised his education. He in turn credited her with his scholarly gifts. Jewish women like Fioretta who were notably learned might be known by the title *rabit* or *rabanit,* a woman who participates in rabinnic discussions.[11] So the Renaissance was for some women a time of expanded opportunities in terms of what is usually thought of as education, that is, learning based on reading and writing. Furthermore, the Renaissance revival of learning—the recovery of ancient Greek and Roman philosophy, literature, and rhetoric—meant that the body of knowledge that one might study was exponentially expanded in this period. And the flowering of humanism—a philosophy that emphasized the accomplishments of human endeavor and arts rather than seeing human beings only in terms of life after death and the judgment of God— meant that academic and artistic accomplishment came to be seen as compatible with piety and as something to be desired rather than feared.

Some proponents of humanism, both Jewish and Christian, departed from the long tradition of resistance to girls' education and argued that elite girls as well as boys should be given a liberal education. Such learning included training in the *trivium* (grammar, rhetoric, and logic) and the *quadrivium* (arithmetic, geometry, music, and astronomy). Even girls who did not enjoy an extensive education benefited nonetheless from the humanist outlook and from the growing demands of urban culture and economy, which required a labor force of women and men with literacy and numeracy skills. Glückel of Hameln (1646–1724) is a good example of a woman who was fully competent in both writing and keeping accounts. She was able to take over her husband's business at his death in 1690; Glückel was merely one of thousands of Renaissance widows who managed businesses. (See also chapter 5: "Women and Religion.") Italian humanists saw it as the mother's particular duty to teach her children the alphabet and basic reading skills; children often learned first to read a vernacular Psalter (the 150 Psalms of the Bible), and many of them would memorize all the Psalms in this manner. Boys would then be sent away to schools where they would receive extensive training in literature as well as instruction in Latin, which was essential for anyone pursuing a public or academic career. In Italy as elsewhere, girls' education was concentrated on sewing, reading, and learning the virtues (*le virtú*). With some notable exceptions, girls were less likely than boys to be sent out to school; rather, they would continue their training at home in domestic arts and, among families of means who could afford special tutors, in music, dancing, and art. But, contrary to this norm, post-Reformation English Catholic families often sent their children to convent schools on the Continent for an education so as to avoid the explicit Protestantism of English schools.

There were also day schools for local girls in Italy early in this period, usually at a convent where they were taught by nuns; such establishments often became boarding schools by the late fifteenth century, where girls lived and learned until they reached marriageable age or made their vows as nuns.[12] For instance, Laura Cereta (1469–1499) of Brescia was sent to a convent school at seven years of age to learn reading, writing, needlework, and basic Latin. (By this time, Brescia had 10 monasteries for women housing eight hundred nuns, many of whom were involved in the work of educating young girls.) Though Cereta was back and forth between convent and home for the next few years, she was sent at the age of nine to the same "erudite woman" to be instructed in the Latin canon of literature. She was married at 15, but her husband died less than two years later; she spent the rest of her short life as a scholar, meeting regularly with other intellectuals of the region, giving public readings of her essays, and keeping up close friendships with many of the scholar-nuns of the area. Indeed, the scholarly life was thought inappropriate for a married woman, who would be distracted by her studies from her duties to her children and to overseeing the management of her household. Consequently, Italian women scholars of the fifteenth century tended to be either widows like Cereta or unmarried women or nuns, and all lived cloistered, whether at home or in a monastery or a convent. (Men, of course, could both marry and pursue the scholarly life, as they would have a wife to see to all the "distractions" of family life and personal care.) Cereta was particularly interested in women's education and argued that "[a]ll human beings, women included, are born with the right to an education":

> For some women are concerned with parting their hair correctly, adorning themselves with lovely dresses, or decorating their fingers with pearls and other gems. Others delight in mouthing carefully composed phrases, indulging in dancing, or managing spoiled puppies. Still others wish to gaze at lavish banquet tables, to rest in sleep, or, standing at mirrors, to smear their lovely faces. But those in whom a deeper integrity yearns for virtue, restrain from the start their youthful souls, reflect on higher things, harden the body with sobriety and trials, and curb their tongues, open their ears, compose their thoughts in wakeful hours, their minds in contemplation, to letters bonded to righteousness. For knowledge is not given as a gift, but [is gained] with diligence. The free mind, not shirking effort, always soars zealously toward the good, and the desire to know grows ever more wide and deep.[13]

Note that Cereta was careful to align her learning with chastity and virtue, a theme that occupied all writers on education, even women themselves.

Even before Cereta's time, there were Italian women well known as humanists, perhaps the most famous of whom was Isotta Nogarola (1418–ca. 1466). Although she was very well educated by her parents and lived out her entire life in their home engaging in continuing study, she was unable to enter the ranks of learned men, most of whom had no interest in a woman scholar. Nogarola engaged in a lengthy and spirited correspondence with the Venetian humanist Ludovico Foscarini wherein they argued about the guilt of Adam and Eve and, by implication, the relative virtue and wisdom of women and men. Nogarola argued that Eve was less to be blamed for sin than Adam because she was less capable and weaker—not the defense one would make today, but a skillful and creative handling of the scriptural materials and arguments that were available to her.[14]

Nogarola had been preceded in Italy by Baptista di Montefeltro (1383–1450), a learned woman who corresponded at some length with the Lord of Pesaro, a noted humanist. Upon marrying his son, she found herself in a miserable marriage to a man who was despised by all and who was ultimately exiled. She returned to her family's home and lived there until taking vows in the Franciscan Order of Santa Chiara. When Holy Roman Emperor Sigismund of Luxembourg (1387–1437) visited Urbino in 1433, he was greeted by a Latin oration that Montefeltro had composed. Leonardo Bruni (1369–1444), a celebrated Italian humanist and the Apostolic Secretary to three popes, addressed his treatise on women's education to her. He wrote, "I am led to address this Tractate to you, Illustrious Lady, by the high repute which attaches to your name in the field of learning; and I offer it, partly as an expression of my homage to distinction already attained, partly as an encouragement to further effort." Like all humanists, he was devoted to the study of correct Latin, and he recommended this even for women:

This leads me to press home this truth—though in your case it is unnecessary—that the foundations of all true learning must be laid in the sound and thorough knowledge of Latin: which implies study marked by a broad spirit, accurate scholarship, and careful attention to details. Unless this solid basis be secured, it is useless to attempt to rear an enduring edifice. Without it the great monuments of literature are unintelligible and the art of composition impossible. To attain this essential knowledge we must never relax our careful attention to the grammar of the language but perpetually confirm and extend our acquaintance with it until it is thoroughly our own.

He recommended the reading of Christian writers, of course, but also the ancient Greek philosophers Plato (427–347 B.C.E.) and Aristotle (384–322 B.C.E.), as well as the Latin authors Virgil (70–19 B.C.E.), Cicero (106–43 B.C.E.), Sallust (86–34 B.C.E.), Livy (ca. 60 B.C.E.–17 C.E.), Seneca (3 B.C.E.–65 C.E.), and Statius (45–96 C.E.).

However, Bruni argued that some studies are not appropriate to women:

> Thus there are certain subjects in which, whilst a modest proficiency is on all accounts to be desired, a minute knowledge and excessive devotion seem to be a vain display. For instance, subtleties of Arithmetic and Geometry are not worthy to absorb a cultivated mind, and the same must be said of Astrology. You will be surprised to find me suggesting (though with much more hesitation) that the great and complex art of Rhetoric should be placed in the same category. My chief reason is the obvious one, that I have in view the cultivation most fitting to a woman. To her neither the intricacies of debate nor the oratorical artifices of action and delivery are of the least practical use, if indeed they are not positively unbecoming. Rhetoric in all its forms—public discussion, forensic argument, logical fence, and the like—lies absolutely outside the province of woman.

The prospect of a woman trained in argumentation seemed to horrify even the most progressive pedagogue. Bruni does argue that women should study history and poetry, "a subject with which every educated lady must shew her self thoroughly familiar, for we cannot point to any great mind of the past for whom the Poets had not a powerful attraction." And she must study the Virtues. Though Bruni's pedagogical program for women is constrained compared with what men were to learn, it nonetheless represents for its time a remarkably liberal view of women's abilities and potential.[15]

Montefeltro was a particularly apt recipient for Bruni's educational tract, as she was known for her poetry as well as her Latin prose works. She in turn educated her granddaughter, Costanza Varano (1428–1447), a woman who "had a visible public role as a learned woman from as early as her teens" and who left "an extensive oeuvre": "four Latin orations, nine Latin letters, and eight poems, of which one oration, three letters, and one poem are addressed to other women." Costanza died in childbirth, leaving the deathbed poem "Constantia Sforza ad circumstantes demum ad virum in extremo vitae" [Costanza Sforza to the bystanders and to her husband, from her deathbed]. Her husband had their daughter, Battista Sforza, educated as extensively as her mother had been, and the girl gave her "first (miniature) public oration in Latin at the almost unprecedentedly tender age of four." Even after her marriage, she "continued studying Greek"; "[b]y the time she was fifteen, she was mandated full powers by her husband to rule his vicariates during his frequent absences…. Thus, her education was not an elegant accomplishment, but an aspect of her fitness for rule."[16] One can thus track four generations of learned women in one noble family, and this kind of inher-

Typus Arithmeticae, Gregor Reisch, *Margarita Philosophica* (Strassburg, 1504). *Source:* Reproduced by permission of the University of Arizona Library Special Collections, AE3 R36.

itance of learning was fairly common. It suggests that the education of but a single woman within a family might have an ongoing and growing influence on girls' learning, as women tended to pass along that tradition of education to their daughters and granddaughters.

Fra Sabba Castiglione (1480–1554), founder of a school in Faenza for poor children, also wrote about the ideal education for elite girls. Contrary to those who suggested that education made women unfit to be wives and mothers, he argued that the young woman who could not read the great Italian writers and poets—Dante, Petrarch, and Boccacio—would be seen as a "rustic" and as having been "poorly brought up." He counseled against too much reading of frivolous literature or focusing all girls' education on singing, music, and dancing. Rather, the bulk of young women's education should be based on their reading the Bible, saints' lives, and other religious and spiritual works. Similarly, Silvio Antoniano (1540–1603) advocated teaching elite girls arithmetic (so as to enable them to keep accounts and run a household), reading, and writing; he even argued that poor girls and those of lower social status should be able to read their prayers. But he thought learning languages, especially Latin and Greek, as well as the study of poetry and rhetoric to be a waste of girls' time—much better that they concentrate on sewing and cooking.[17]

Among the most influential early modern works on pedagogy was *The Education of a Christian Prince* (1516), written by Desiderius Erasmus (1466–1536); chief among the early modern humanist thinkers and writers of northern Europe. Erasmus is also known for his praise of one of the most accomplished and well-educated women of the early sixteenth century, Margaret More Roper (1505–1544). The daughter of Sir Thomas More (1478–1535), she was one of the first girls to benefit from the expansion of girls' education in England. Indeed, More and Erasmus seem to have used Margaret as the exemplar for a "humanist political project" that they hoped would revolutionize the courts of Europe. They wished to foster virtue and scholarship among the rulers of Europe in place of the hunting, dancing, fancy dressing, and other mindless pursuits, which they saw as frivolous and unworthy. More and Erasmus reasoned that if elite girls were well educated, they would attract and foster the development of virtuous noblemen rather than the greedy and self-serving fops that populated the courts of Europe.[18] Though this particular humanist plan did not bring about the kind of complete social revolution More and Erasmus had hoped for, Margaret's accomplishments exceeded all their ambitions: she was known for her learning among the literati of Europe. She was absolutely fluent in both Greek and Latin (as well as all modern European languages), so much so that she was able to translate a treatise by the Church Father Eusebius (ca. 260–ca. 341) from Greek into Latin and to translate Erasmus's own Latin treatise on the Lord's Prayer into English.

The German church reformer Martin Luther (1483–1546) also advocated that lower class girls as well as boys to be better educated, particularly in religion. The Protestant reformers John Calvin (1509–1564) and John Knox (1505–1572), on the other hand, were not particularly interested in girls' education; Knox did not even discuss the question, and Calvin advocated elementary education for girls, though always separate from boys, a common theme of the day. But Luther wrote that "Above all, in schools of all kinds the chief and most common lesson should be the Scriptures…. And would to God each town also had a girls' school, in which girls might be taught the Gospel for an hour daily, either in German or in Latin." He argued that "even a girl has enough time that she can go to school for an hour a day and still perform her household tasks." Though this statement seems dismissive of girls' academic potential, he called for the same amount of study for boys, who would spend the rest of their days working as apprentices to learn a trade. For children of higher social rank, he called for the study of languages, history, music, and "the whole course of mathematics."[19]

Though many educational reformers argued that girls should be taught by women, there were not nearly enough educated women for this purpose (a problem that, for obvious reasons, tended to replicate itself). Furthermore, many teachers of the day were itinerant or lived independently, something that was deemed unacceptable for women. Partly in response to this ongoing problem, the German educator Wolfgang Ratke (1571–1635) called for the establishment of a normal school to train teachers, one that would prepare an equal number of women and men for teaching. Ratke's ideas, as propounded in *The New Method* (1617), included the insistence that children not be taught by rote learning (the primary pedagogical method of the time) but rather that they understand the principles behind any study. He also thought that learning should proceed from experience. Ratke's theories inspired the great Czech-born educational theorist Johann (or Jan) Amos Comenius (1592–1670), a Moravian minister who published his theories in the *Great Didactic* (1632). He argued that all children should be educated, "boys and girls, both noble and ignoble, rich and poor, in all cities and towns, villages and hamlets."[20] He argued that since all human beings are rational creatures, and there is no way to know God's plan for them, girls as well as boys should learn in both the vernacular and Latin. Comenius carried his ideas to all parts of Europe, including Poland, Sweden, Germany, Hungary, and England, but most considered his theories too radical, and he saw little of his program implemented in his lifetime.

One of the most famous Renaissance educational programs for women was laid out in *De Institutione Feminae Christianae* or *The Instruction (or Education) of a Christian Woman* (1523) by Juan Luís Vives (1492–1540). Vives was a humanist and, like many scholars of the day, he was at home in a number of countries and cities, including his native Valencia as well as Paris, Bruges, and London. He was a friend and correspondent of Erasmus's and of other literati all over Europe. Vives dedicated his treatise to Catherine of Aragon (1485–1536), wife of Henry VIII (1491–1547) and Queen of England—something that made Vives persona non grata at the English court when Henry divorced Catherine in 1533 to marry Anne Boleyn (1500–1536). But Vives's educational program had a significant impact on elite English women, including Henry's daughters, Elizabeth I (1533–1603) and Mary I (or Mary Tudor, 1516–1558), both of whom were educated according to its principles and were remarkably learned and eloquent in many languages. Both women translated works from Latin into English when they were still quite young. Mary was a patron and promoter of learning during her short reign (1553–1558), and Elizabeth was able to lecture her Parliament in fluent Latin throughout her life. Though Vives was as concerned as any writer of the day with preserving young women's chastity and virtue, he stood apart from most cultural arbiters in his recommendation that elite girls be taught Latin (though this idea may have originated with Catherine of Aragon herself, who wished to see her children educated according to the most progressive humanist scholarship). Vives's educational program begins in infancy; like many writers of the era, he recommended that girls be suckled by their own mothers rather than a wet nurse so as to avoid ingesting anything evil or vile:

Humanist Education, Gregor Reisch, *Margarita Philosophica* (Strassburg, 1504). *Source:* Reproduced by permission of the University of Arizona Library Special Collections, AE3 R36.

The maid [girl child], whom we would have especially good, requireth all intendance [attention] both of Father and Mother, lest any spot of vice or uncleanliness should stick on her. Let her take no such [evil] things, neither by her bodily senses and wits, nor by her nourishing and bringing up. She shall first hear her Nurse, first see her, and whatsoever she learneth in rude and ignorant age, that will she ever labor to counterfeit and follow....

After that she is once weaned and beginneth to speak and go, let all her play and pastime be with maids of her own age, and within the presence either of her mother or her nurse or some other honest woman of sad [solemn, sober] age, that may rule and measure the plays and pastimes of her mind, and set them to honesty and virtue. Avoid all mankind away from her; nor let her not learn to delight among men.[21]

When the girl is ready to learn—some time between four and seven, depending on the child—Vives would have her learn to read, but, to keep her from idleness, she should learn at the same time to spin (something that would never have been recommended for boys): "Therefore let her both learn her book, and beside that to handle wool and flax, which are 2 crafts yet left of that old innocent world, both profitable and keepers of temperance, which thing specially Women ought to have in price [to prize]." She is also to learn cooking so as to be able to please her parents, husband, and children with delicacies. Vives defended his claim that girls should be taught, offering many examples of learned women who were chaste and who modeled their lives on the ideal woman "who clearly despised all pleasure of the body, and lived perpetually a maid."[22]

Like most moralists of the period, Vives seemed to contradict himself when it came to discussion of who should teach young girls, for the dominant opinion was that women should rarely speak and should not teach. So, like Bruni, Vives wrote that girls need not be taught eloquence, "As for eloquence, I have no great care, nor a woman needeth it not, but she needeth goodness and wisdome," which Vives suggested she can get only through study. So he compromised, naming a few women of the ancient world who were eloquent, and allowed that "If there may be found any holy and well learned woman, I had leaver [rather] have her to teach [girls]. If there be none, let us choose some man well aged, or else very good and virtuous, which hath a wife, and that right safe enough, whom he loveth well, and so shall he not desire other."[23] Note here how it is not the potentially adulterous man's responsibility to be virtuous, but all depends on the desirability of his wife and the adequate protection of the young pupil. Given this thinking about men's lack of responsibility for their actions, it is not surprising that parents and educators were concerned with protecting girls' chastity.

Vives provided an extensive list of those works a young woman should *not* read, and then recommended that she read Holy Scripture and religious works by the Church Fathers Ambrose (333–397); Jerome (ca. 342–420), who is today infamous among feminist scholars for his misogyny; Augustine of Hippo (354–430); and Gregory the Great (590–604); as well as the ancient authors Plato, Cicero, and Seneca.[24] Vives also laid out the appropriate diet for a young woman: no hot meat and no wine, but rather mild, cool foods that will keep her chaste. Likewise, she should have no "hot" exercise (especially dancing) or things that "fire the mind with filthy and lecherous heat."[25] And he argued at great length about her dress; she should wear only the most modest clothing and jewels.

Anna Maria van Schurman (1617–1678), a remarkably well educated Dutch woman who read Hebrew, Chaldean, Syriac, and Arabic as well as Latin and all the vernacular languages of Europe, also proposed a curriculum for girls. She wrote a treatise on education that

William Marshall, *Bathsua Makin*, NPG D13657. *Source:* Reproduced by permission of the National Portrait Gallery, London.

was first published in Latin in 1638 and later translated into French and then English as *The Learned Maid or whether a Maid may be called a Scholar* (1659).[26] The book is in the form of letters to a man who had lent the author some books but who objected to women's learning. Schurman argued that women's confinement to learning needlework was merely the result of custom and that "it is impossible that generous souls, which are capable of everything, should be contained with the strict limits which common error has prescribed for them."[27] Van Schurman's book inspired Bathsua Reginald Makin (ca. 1612–ca.1673), a learned woman and governess to the English royal family, to write *Essay to Revive the Antient Education of Gentlewomen in Religion, Manners, Arts and Tongues* (London, 1673). To support her argument, Makin provided an extensive list of learned and virtuous women of the past as well as those of her own time, including the daughters of Lord Burghley (Elizabeth I's chief minister); Queen Christina of Sweden; the Cooke sisters; King James VI and I's daughter, Princess Elizabeth; Lady Grace Sherrington Mildmay; Lady Arbella Stuart; and Margaret, Duchess of Newcastle. She also included the poets Mary, Countess of Pembroke; Katharine Philips; and Anna Maria van Schurman herself, among others. Such a list suggests that the learned women of Europe were aware of each other and of their "membership" in a community of female scholars. Makin corresponded with van Schurman, and she may well have done so with others she named. In her book, she argues that God must surely approve of women's education: "Had God intended Women onely as a finer sort of Cattle, he would not have made them reasonable. Bruits, a few degrees higher than Drils [Baboons] or Monkies, (which the Indians use to do many Offices) might have better fitted some men's Lust, Pride, and Pleasure; especially those that desire to keep [women] ignorant to be tyrannized over."[28] She laid out a detailed program for teaching grammar and language to children and advertised her own school "for gentlewomen" where, beginning at age eight or nine, girls could be educated in needlework, dancing, music, singing, writing, keeping household accounts, English grammar, Latin, and French. Those girls who wished to expand their knowledge might also have taken up Greek, Hebrew, Italian, and Spanish. Makin had already published a book entitled *Musa Virginea Greco-Latino-Gallica, Bathsvae R. (filiae Henrici Reginaldi Gymnasiarchae et Philogotti apud Londonenses) Anno Aetatis Suae Decimo Sexto edita* (The Virgin Muse in Greek-Latin-French, by Bathsua R. [daughter of Henry Reginald, schoolmaster and linguist of London], published in her sixteenth year). The small book consisted of poems to members of the royal family in Greek, Latin, and French. However, when Makin was later introduced to King James as a prodigy, scholar, linguist, and the author of the book, he asked, "Yes, but can she spin?"[29]

Most significant for the development of learned women in France was the tradition of the salon, literary gatherings in the houses of aristocratic women where the erudite exchanged ideas and read from their works and others'. (See also chapter 6: "Women and Literature.") The earliest salon was hosted by Catherine de Vivonne, the Marquise de Rambouillet (1588–1665), beginning after her retirement from court life in 1608 and running continually until mid-century. Moreover, Rambouillet's salon was imitated by many other women. The literati of France attended regularly, among them Marie de Rabutin-Chantal, the Marquise de Sévigné (1626–1696). The Marquise de Sévigné was a remarkably learned woman who had been raised by her grandfather and then, on his death, sent to be educated under the direction of her uncles. She was widowed young and never remarried, occupying herself instead with the education of her daughter and later her granddaughter. At her death, she left a collection of fifteen hundred letters addressed principally to her daughter (to whom she wrote daily), which were so highly esteemed for their wit and erudition that they were copied and circulated among the learned aristocracy of France. They were eventually collected into eight volumes and published in 1727. In the letters, she discusses an education program designed for her granddaughter that would focus on history, geography, and literature.

One of the most ambitious educational projects of the period was the mission of the women religious of the Institute of the Blessed Virgin Mary, founded by the English Catholic Mary Ward (1585–1645). Ward saw herself as called to lead a "mixed life," that is, to take vows and to live celibate under a religious rule but not to be cloistered. She believed her mission was to found an order dedicated to the education of young women. She inspired many followers, whom she called her Companions (as Ignatius of Loyola [1491–1556] had termed his seminarian colleagues), to work toward the same ends. Ward and her Companions founded many schools for girls, especially on the Continent, where girls were given an extensive education. Ward thought that training in Latin in particular was essential for girls' preparation for the spiritual life and

Mary Ward and her Companions. "In London in 1609, Mary has attracted through her virtuous life and diligent discourse several highly noble virgins for the divine bridegroom. They travel under her direction to St. Omar to escape the traps of the world. They want to serve God in holy orders, and Mary leads them through her example." *The Painted Life,* number 22. *Source:* Reproduced by permission of Tanner Werbung.

second only to prayer in their formation. She wrote in 1627 to Winifred Bedingfeld (1606–1666), Ward's Companion and founding member of the house in Munich, regarding two of Bedingfeld's pupils who were learning Latin,

> *Pax Christi!* These [greetings] are indeed chiefly to congratulate the unexpected progress of your Latin schools. You cannot easily believe the content I took in the themes of those two towardly [apt to learn] girls. You will work much to your own happiness by advancing them apace in that learning, and God will concur with you because his honour and service so require. All such as are capable invite them to it, and for such as desire to be one of us, no talent is so much to be regarded in them as the Latin tongue.[30]

Ward reiterated these sentiments in a letter to her close Companion Winifred Wigmore (1585–1657), then the novice mistress at the house in Naples, regarding the education of girls in her care. In this letter, Ward also responded to those who thought education would make girls less virtuous:

> I would have Cecilia and Catherina begin out of hand to learn the rudiments of Latin; fear not their loss of virtue by that means, for this must and will be so common to all as there will be no cause for complacency. I would not have their other work be hindered, but what time can otherwise be found besides their prayer, let it be bestowed upon their Latin.[31]

In addition to Latin, Ward thought girls should learn

> a sense of duty, Christian doctrine, good morals, how to serve God, reading the common and Latin languages, writing, household management, liberal arts [grammar, rhetoric, logic, music, arithmetic, geometry, and astronomy], singing, painting, sewing, spinning, curtain-making, in a word, all those liberal exercises which are more suitable for every state of life.[32]

Ward's curriculum represents a perhaps unique melding of girls' traditional education in domesticity and piety along with all the subjects that marked boys' education in the period. Ward's Institute was a remarkable success even in her lifetime. She had gathered 60 sisters before she died, many of whom headed the schools in operation for girls; there were more than a hundred in Germany alone by the next century. But the political situation in England—the hostility to Catholics and the prohibition against teaching Catholic doctrine—meant that Ward's educational program was not able to prosper there until after her death. The two schools that did open, one in Hammersmith near London in 1669 and another at the Bar Convent in York in 1686, operated in secret in the sixteenth and seventeenth centuries.[33]

Even children of lower social status who did not benefit from humanist learning and educational programs like Ward's were educated in the skills they would need as adults. For girls, this meant that they would learn domestic skills, whether domestic work itself or, in the case of middle-class and aristocratic women, how to manage a household. Either way, the work demanded a range of skills that girls learned first from their mothers and any older sisters and then, beginning around seven years of age, from other women, often in another household. In England in particular the practice of fostering—sending one's children to live with others and taking others' children into one's household—was nearly universal. Boys who were sent out in this manner to learn a trade were often formally apprenticed to a master, but girls were more likely to work as domestic servants or as ladies-in-waiting, depending on their social status. Some elite girls might even get a formal education in literature, languages, music, and art in this way, but it was considered most important for them to learn social skills and manners and to mix in society.

In addition to interest in pedagogy and women's education in this period, moralists were concerned with the behavior of women in all aspects of life, and there was a florescence of conduct manuals and books. These works laid out the appropriate behavior, dress, and activities for women as well as for men of the middle and upper classes. Such treatises served as a kind of ongoing education for people throughout their adulthood. Probably the most famous was Baldassare Castiglione's (1478–1529) *Il Libro del Cortegiano* (1528), translated into many languages, including Latin, Spanish, German, and English, notably by Sir Thomas Hoby as *The Book of the Courtier* (1561). At the heart of Castiglione's program is the idea of *sprezzatura,* the ability to display one's accomplishments artlessly and easily. While Castiglione claimed that "Everything that men can understand can also be understood by women," the bulk of his advice is for elite men. And, indeed, women play a very limited role in the dialog about courtiership that he invented in *The Courtier:* two of the women named do not contribute at all to the conversation. Above all for Castiglione, women were to cultivate virtue, particularly chastity, and "[t]o have a sweetenesse in language and a good uttrance to entertein all kinde of men with communication woorth the hearing, honest, applyed to time and place and to the degree and disposition of the person whiche is her principall profession."[34]

Among the most popular conduct books in England during the seventeenth century were Richard Brathwaite's (ca. 1588–1673) *The English Gentleman* (London, 1630) and *The English Gentlewoman* (London, 1631). What sets Brathwaite's work on women apart from his discussion of men is a focus on women's appearance: though women were frequently excoriated for their reputed obsession with clothes and makeup and counseled to care more about their inner virtues, here it is Brathwaite who seems obsessed with women's exterior and what it communicates about their virtue.

Even his subtitle demonstrates this focus: *The English Gentlewoman Drawn Out to the Full Body: Expressing What Habilliments [Clothes] Do Best Attire Her, What Ornaments Do Best Adorne Her, What Complements Do Best Accomplish Her.* (Compare his companion title: *The English Gentleman: Containing Sundry Rules, or Exquisite Observations, Tending to Direction of Every Gentleman, of Selecter Ranke and Quality; How to Demeane or Accommodate Himselfe in the Manage of Publick or Private Affaires.*)[35] Every chapter of Brathwaite's book for gentlewomen comments on their dress and appearance. In addition to conduct manuals, the treatises of the Woman Controversy, the early seventeenth-century English pamphlet debate on the nature of womanhood, always included a discussion of women's proper behavior and particular virtues and vices. Even literature on religious and romantic topics often had a didactic side; it functioned as a tool of continuing education for women and served to police their behavior and activity.

Education for early modern women was a disputed and contentious topic, but the very fact that it was being widely discussed implies that their education had come to seem less radical than in earlier centuries. The Renaissance is the first time in history that so many girls were educated, and some of them to the full extent of learning available. Many moralists continued to resist educating girls and, even more, having women teach, often referring to the biblical passage in 1 Timothy 2:11–14:

> Let the woman learn in silence with all subjection: But I suffer not a woman to teach, nor to usurp authority over the man, but to be in silence. For Adam was first formed, then Eve: And Adam was not deceived, but the woman being deceived was in the transgression.

But, as many women of the time pointed out, even in this very restrictive and misogynist passage, there seems to be an assumption that women will indeed learn, if only in silence. Defenders of women's access to learning used this loophole to frame their arguments, making the best of the conservative material that was at hand and continuing to struggle to make women's education the norm rather than a dangerous exception.

NOTES

1. It is very difficult to establish any reliable or meaningful figures about literacy rates in early modern Europe. Literacy was inflected by nationality, geography (i.e., urban or rural, village or discrete farms), reli-

gion, class, and gender. Urban, elite men were more likely to be able to read than women of similar social standing, but those women were far more likely to be able to read than, for instance, rural male peasants. Even if the data existed to compute an average figure, that average would be, for all practical purposes, useless for understanding a particular country or even city. The most literate group would have been urban men working in trades that demanded literacy or working as secretaries; perhaps 50–75 percent of them could read. Only 10–15 percent of urban day laborers would have been able to read, and even fewer rural agricultural laborers; probably less than 2 percent of rural women of the servant class were literate. H. G. Koenigsberger, George L. Mosse, and G. Q. Bowler, *Europe in the Sixteenth Century,* 2nd ed. (London: Longman, 1968), 80.

2.   In the Renaissance, reading and writing were taught as separate skills, and though all of the professional scribes and secretaries of the era were male, some girls did take instruction from writing masters.

3.   Qtd. in Howard Adelman, "The Literacy of Jewish Women in Early Modern Italy," in *Women's Education in Early Modern Europe,* ed. Barbara J. Whitehead (New York: Garland, 1999), 133.

4.   Adelman, "The Literacy of Jewish Women," 135, 137.

5.   Merry E. Wiesner, *Women and Gender in Early Modern Europe,* 2nd ed. (New York: Cambridge University Press, 2000), 146.

6.   Jane Stevenson, "Women and Classical Education in the Early Modern Period," in *Pedagogy and Power: Rhetorics of Classical Learning,* ed. Yun Lee Too and Niall Livingstone (New York: Cambridge University Press, 1998), 94.

7.   Margaret J. Mason, "Nuns and Vocations of the Unpublished Jerningham Letters: Charlotte Bedingfield, Augustinian Canoness (1802–1876), Louisa Jerningham, Franciscan Abbess (1808–1893), and Clementina Jerningham, Marquise de Ripert-Monclar (1810–1864)," *Recusant History* 21 (1993): 503–55.

8.   Caroline Bowden, "'For the Glory of God': A Study of the Education of English Catholic Women in Convents in Flanders and France in the First Half of the Seventeenth Century," *Paedagogica Historica,* Supplementary Series 5 (1999): 86.

9.   The collect for the Second Sunday of Advent, *The Book of Common Prayer.*

10.   Adelman, "The Literacy of Jewish Women," 137.

11.   Adelman, "The Literacy of Jewish Women," 141–42.

12.   Sharon T. Strocchia, "Learning the Virtues: Convent Schools and Female Culture in Renaissance Florence," in *Women's Education in Early Modern Europe: A History, 1500–1800,* ed. Barbara J. Whitehead (New York: Garland, 1999), 3–46.

13.   Qtd. in Margaret L. King and Albert Rabil, Jr., trans. and eds., *Her Immaculate Hand: Selected Works by and about the Women Humanists of Quattrocento Italy* (Asheville, NC: Pegasus Press, 2000), 83.

14. King and Rabil, Jr., trans. and eds., *Her Immaculate Hand,* 59.

15. W. H. Woodward, ed., *Vittorino da Feltre and Other Humanist Educators* (Cambridge: Cambridge University Press, 1921), 119–33.

16. Peter Davidson, "The *Theatrum* for the Entry of Claudia de' Medici and Federigo Ubaldo della Rovere into Urbino, 1621," in *Court Festivals of the European Renaissance: Art, Politics, and Performance,* ed. J. R. Mulryne and Elizabeth Goldring (Aldershot, UK: Ashgate, 2002), 331–34.

17. Paul F. Grendler, *Schooling in Renaissance Italy: Literacy and Learning, 1300–1600* (Baltimore: Johns Hopkins University Press, 1989), 88–89.

18. Mary Ellen Lamb, "Margaret Roper, the Humanist Political Project, and the Problem of Agency," in *Opening the Borders: Inclusivity in Early Modern Studies: Essays in Honor of James V. Mirollo,* ed. Peter C. Herman (Newark: University of Delaware Press, 2001), 83–108.

19. Qtd. in Phyllis Stock, *Better Than Rubies: A History of Women's Education* (New York: Putnam, 1978), 62.

20. Qtd. in Stock, *Better Than Rubies,* 66.

21. Juan Luís Vives, chapter 2, *A very frutful and pleasant boke called the Instruction of a christen woman, made fyrst in latyne, by the right famous clerke mayster Lewes Viues, and tourned out of latyne into Englishe by Rycharde Hyrde* (London, 1585), 4, 5. Hyrde's translation of Vives is available through EEBO, <http://eebo.chadwyck.com>, and in Foster Watson, ed., *Vives and the Renascence Education of Women* (New York: Longmans, Green, 1912).

22. Vives, 21.

23. Vives, 27, 28.

24. Vives, 31–41.

25. Vives, 64.

26. Wiesner, *Women and Gender in Early Modern Europe,* 160.

27. Qtd. in Stock, *Better Than Rubies,* 83–84.

28. Makin's work is widely available on the Internet through EEBO, <http://eebo.chadwyck.com>, through the Web site *Sunshine for Women,* <http://www.pinn.net/~sunshine/book-sum/makin1.html>, and in two modern editions, including most recently that edited by Frances N. Teague, *Bathsua Makin, Woman of Learning* (Lewisburg, PA: Bucknell University Press, 1998).

29. Qtd. in Teague, *Bathsua Makin,* 43.

30. Mary Ward, letter to Winifred Bedingfeld, 16 July 1627, in James Walsh, S. J., introduction to *Till God Will: Mary Ward through Her Writings,* ed. M. Emmanuel Orchard, IBVM (London: Darton, Longman and Todd, 1985), 96.

31. Mary Ward, letter to Winifred Wigmore, 10 October 1667, in Walsh, introduction, 97. Walsh also demonstrates Ward's extensive training in the forms of classical rhetoric and the way in which her prose follows the rhythms of the Vulgate (Latin Bible) and incorporates many Latin phrases.

32.   Qtd. in Orchard, *Till God Will,* 37.

33.   Material on Ward's life not otherwise cited comes from M. Immolate Wetter, IBMV, *Mary Ward: In Her Own Words* (Rome: Istituto Beata Vergine Maria, 1999); Henriette Peters, *Mary Ward: A World in Contemplation* (Leominster, UK: Gracewing, 1994); and Christina Kenworthy-Browne, CJ, e-mail message.

34.   Baldassare Castiglione, "Of the Chief Conditions and Qualities in a Waiting Gentlewoman," in *The Book of the Courtier,* trans. Thomas Hoby (London, 1561), z.r iii. Hoby's translation is available through EEBO, <http://eebo.chadwyck.com>.

35.   Brathwaite's *English Gentleman* and his *English Gentlewoman* were published together in one volume in 1641. All three books are available through EEBO, <http://eebo.chadwyck.com>.

SUGGESTED READING

Bowden, Caroline. "'For the Glory of God': A Study of the Education of English Catholic Women in Convents in Flanders and France in the First Half of the Seventeenth Century." *Paedagogica Historica.* Supplementary Series 5 (1999): 78–95.

Brink, Jean R., ed. *Female Scholars: A Tradition of Learned Women before 1800.* Montreal: Eden Press Women's Publications, 1980.

Grendler, Paul F. *Schooling in Renaissance Italy: Literacy and Learning, 1300–1600.* Baltimore: Johns Hopkins University Press, 1989.

Hunt, Margaret. *The Middling Sort: Commerce, Gender, and the Family in England, 1680–1780.* Berkeley: University of California Press, 1996.

King, Margaret L., and Albert Rabil, Jr., trans. and eds. *Her Immaculate Hand: Selected Works by and about the Women Humanists of Quattrocento Italy.* Binghamton, NY: Medieval and Renaissance Texts & Studies, 1992.

Labalme, Patricia H., ed. *Beyond Their Sex: Learned Women of the European Past.* New York: New York University Press, 1984.

Stevenson, Jane. "Women and Classical Education in the Early Modern Period." *Pedagogy and Power: Rhetorics of Classical Learning.* Ed. Yun Lee Too and Niall Livingstone. New York: Cambridge University Press, 1998. 83–109.

Stock, Phyllis. *Better Than Rubies: A History of Women's Education.* New York: Putnam, 1978.

Whitehead, Barbara J., ed. *Women's Education in Early Modern Europe: A History, 1500–1800.* New York: Garland, 1999.

2

——⊗⊗⊗——

Women and the Law

Early modern Europeans were governed by a complex and often confusing mixture of legal codes, including local customs, canon (church) law, Roman law (the principles derived from the commentaries of the sixth-century Roman emperor Justinian), statute law, and equity law. In addition, there were a variety of legal principles and regulations that had historic jurisdiction in particular areas or for particular peoples. These included English Common Law, the unwritten code that had its origins in Germanic cultures; Salic Law in France, infamous for its exclusion of women from inheritance even when there was no direct male heir; and Jewish law, which regulated daily life. The various codes would often contradict each other, thus becoming the battleground for political contention. The conflicts between Christian rulers and church officials were particularly turbulent, as it was during this period that nation-states emerged as powerful political units, often at the expense of ecclesiastical authority as well as local custom. In the daily lives of European Christians, matrimonial disputes (including divorce), sexual misconduct, and wills were under the purview of the church courts and canon law, while crimes of rape and other serious offenses were under the jurisdiction of secular courts. Even local guilds might enforce their laws and customs to regulate the lives of their members; in mid-sixteenth-century Augsburg, Germany, a guild member was not allowed to marry until he had attained the status of master craftsmen.[1] To add to this confusion and complexity, the laws of the various local and regional codes and their courts were in the process of changing, as many political and ecclesiastical groups attempted to make their particular legal systems more uniform and coherent.

Early modern women had a paradoxical relationship to the law. On the one hand, they had fewer legal rights than did men. Even elite women in some countries (with the few exceptions of queens in their own right such as Elizabeth I of England and Queen Christina of Sweden) could not overtly participate in politics or serve on juries. In some countries and towns, they were not allowed to make contracts or to initiate a lawsuit, though women could generally serve as witnesses in court. As the legal scholar Sir William Blackstone (1723–1780) put it in his *Commentaries on the Laws of England,* a summary of the legal theory that had developed by the end of the early modern period, "If the wife be injured in her person or her property, she can bring no action for redress without her husband's concurrence, and in his name, as well as her own: neither can she be sued, without making the husband a defendant." Indeed, the Common Law of England understood married women to be *civiliter mortuus* (civilly dead) and "covered" by the legal personhood of their husbands (hence the terms *coverture* and *femme couverte*). Blackstone explained,

> By marriage, the husband and wife are one person in law: that is, the very being or legal existence of the woman is suspended during the marriage, or at least is incorporated and consolidated into that of the husband: under whose wing, protection, and cover, she performs every thing; and is therefore called in our law-french [the language of law derived from French] a feme-covert; is said to be covert-baron, or under the protection and influence of her husband, her baron, or lord; and her condition during her marriage is called her coverture. Upon this principle, of an union of person in husband and wife, depend almost all the legal rights, duties, and disabilities, that either of them acquire by the marriage…. For this reason, a man cannot grant any thing to his wife, or enter into covenant with her: for the grant would be to suppose her separate existence; and to covenant with her, would be only to covenant with himself.

In other words, under the logic of coverture, a woman had no legal existence.

In a sense, an Englishwoman never became an adult under the law but remained a child in relationship to her husband as she had once been to her father. And just as a father or mother was legally entitled to "correct" a child, so might a husband discipline his wife:

The husband also (by the old law) might give his wife moderate correction. For, as he is to answer for her misbehavior, the law thought it reasonable to intrust him with this power of restraining her, by domestic chastisement, in the same moderation that a man is allowed to correct his servants or children; for whom the master or parent is also liable in some cases to answer.

Thomas Cecill, "A New Yeares Guift for Shrews": Who marieth a Wife uppon a Moneday. If She will not be good uppon a Tewesday. Lett him go to the wood uppon a Wensday. And cutt him a cudgell uppon the Thursday. And pay her soundly uppon a Fryday. And she mend not, the divil take her a Saterday. Then may he eate his meate in peace on the Sonday. *Source:* Thomas Cecill, © Copyright The Trustees of The British Museum.

And while Blackstone argued that "this power of correction was confined within reasonable bounds; and the husband was prohibited to use any violence to his wife," other legal scholars held that there was no legal limit to a husband's use of violence against a wife.[2] Indeed, wife beating as a form of "correction" was widely authorized. The following sixteenth-century adage epitomizes conventional attitudes about domination of women: "A good horse and a bad horse need the spur. A good woman and a bad woman need the stick."[3]

At the same time, many moralists and theologians decried men's use of violence against women. The English Homily on Matrimony of the late sixteenth century (one of more than twenty sermons produced by the authorities of the Church of England that clergy were required to preach) condemned husbands' violence:

> I meane not that a man should beat his wife, GOD forbid that, for that is the greatest shame that can be, not so much to her that is beaten, as to him that doth the deed. But if by such fortune thou chancest upon such an husband, take it not too heavily, but suppose thou, that thereby is laid up no small reward hereafter, & in this life time no small commendation to thee, if thou canst be quiet. But yet to you that be men, thus I speake, Let there bee none so grieuous fault to compell you to beat your wives. But what say I, your wives? no, it is not to be borne with, that an honest man should lay hands on his maide servant to beat her. Wherefore if it be a great shame for a man to beat his bondseruant, much more rebuke it is, to lay violent hands upon his free-woman.[4]

While advising wives that being beaten "is not to be borne with," the authors of the homily seem reluctant to counsel that abused women leave their husbands. Rather, they are to remember the "reward" in the "hereafter" that will be theirs as a result of their forebearance. Similarly, the German theologian and reformer Martin Luther argued that "Men should govern their wives not with great cudgels, flails, or drawn knives, but rather with friendly words and gestures and with all gentleness so that they do not become shy … and take fright such that they afterward do not know what to do. Thus, men should rule their wives with reason and not unreason, and honor the feminine sex as the weakest vessel."[5] Both Luther and the Church of England assumed, however, that men deserved wifely obedience as a result of Eve's punishment and had the right to correct their wives as they saw fit. Men might be dissuaded from violence, but they could not be prohibited from beating their wives, either by the law of God or the law of nations.

As women throughout Europe were understood by the elite scholars of the age to have the same legal status as children, imbeciles, and peasants, they were in some cases not held responsible for their actions. Nonetheless, in every European country, female adulterers were punished far more severely than were their male lovers or unfaithful husbands. Often, women who were raped had scant legal recourse, especially if the criminal were of a higher social status. Rape victims were commonly accused of promiscuity or prostitution. In seventeenth-century England, if an assaulted female became pregnant, she was assumed to have consented to intercourse because of the prevailing belief that conception could occur only with orgasm. When the sixteenth-century artist Artemisia Gentileschi accused her teacher of rape, the court tortured her with thumbscrews to test the veracity of her claims (the standard method at the time for securing truthful testimony). The rapist, who was found guilty, underwent no torture.

The degree of women's legal disenfranchisement varied from one country to another, but the principles of female subordination and incompetence were the norm throughout Europe. In some parts of Europe, single women, regardless of their age, were required to have a male guardian. Marriage as a transmission of property ownership from one male to another became symbolized in a woman's name change from that of her father to that of her husband; French brides altered their identity in this way from the fourteenth century, and the practice was common in England by the seventeenth century. In Eastern Europe, laws constraining women were less stringent than in the west, but the actual customs that were observed in marriage were even more disabling. For example, a Russian wife could be sold into slavery to pay off her husband's debts; if a Russian man were exiled, his spouse was required to accompany him, but if she were exiled, his disowning her was socially sanctioned. Throughout Europe, laws governing adultery were similarly skewed. The legally imposed double standard for infidelity allowed sixteenth-century French men to kill their adulterous wives while affording little opportunity for women to divorce or even file grievances against abusive or unfaithful spouses.

As is clear from these early modern religious and legal arguments, though a woman had no existence under the law, she was very much subject to the law, and her life choices were shaped by the law, particularly laws governing marriage. Furthermore, because it was assumed that unmarried women would someday marry, restrictions on married women's liberties were often understood to include all women, regardless of their marital status at any moment. Such limitations affected all young women before marriage as well as those 10 to 15 percent of early modern women who never wed. In the words of the popular English author Thomas Edgar in *The Law's Resolutions of Women's Rights; Or, the Law's Provision for Women,* "Women have no voice in Parliament, they make no laws, they consent to none, they abrogate none. All of them are understood either married or to be married and their desires are subject to their husband."[6] Though the concept of coverture as Blackstone articulated it was unique to England, the moralists and the leaders of other countries shared many of the basic understandings spelled out in the doctrine of coverture. Luther echoed Blackstone's assessment in religious terms when he said that "Women are not created for any other purpose than to serve man and to be his assistant in producing children." Elsewhere he said that as a result of Eve's sin, "woman is not able to be without the man. Wherever the man dwells the woman has to dwell too; the wife follows her husband wherever he may go. And beyond this, she is obligated to submit to the man; authority pertains to the husband in all matters of this life."[7]

Not all women meekly accepted their subordination within marriage, and, just as Luther had, some drew on the Bible to make their case for women's equal or even superior status. The English Lady Anne Southwell (1571–1636) used the Genesis story of Eve being made from Adam's rib to make an argument against a husband's dominance:

> All married men desire to have good wives,
> But few give good example by their lives.
> They are our head and would have us their heels;
> This makes the good wife kick—the good man reels.
> When God brought Eve to Adam for a bride,
> The text says she was tak'n from out man's side,
> A symbol of that side, whose sacred blood
> Flowed for his spouse, the Church's saving good.
> This is a mystery, perhaps too deep
> For blockish Adam that was fallen asleep.[8]

The "sacred blood" of Southwell's poem is the blood and water that flowed from the side of the crucified Jesus when he was speared; in Christian tradition, that came to be understood as the water and wine of the Mass. Southwell rereads the story of Adam and Eve by identifying women with the sacred blood and that "saving good" and not with Adam's rib. Rather than being Adam's inferior, Eve in this exegesis becomes a precursor of Christ and, by implication, Adam's superior. Southwell thwarts the expected response from men who might disagree with her reading by declaring it a sacred mystery, one that blockish or blockhead men will not be able to understand. Southwell's poem is but one of many rereadings of the creation narratives of Genesis that sought to counter the dominant, androcentric interpretations that were used to justify women's subordination. Clearly, not everyone in Renaissance society agreed on the nature of women's and men's social relationships and roles.

Nonetheless, a combination of religion, tradition, and law reinforced women's subservience in marriage. In Italy, though there was no legal provision for coverture, women at marriage tended to be much younger than their husbands and usually married as early as 14 or 15; this difference in age and experience effectively made the young wife her husband's childlike dependent. Because of the way that women throughout Europe at this time were infantilized through marriage, some cities and towns made provision for a married woman who engaged in business alongside her husband to declare herself to be a *feme sole,* that is, a single woman, a legal fiction that allowed her to make contracts and manage money and generally engage in commerce.

Among the middle and upper classes, marriage was not seen as primarily a symbol of romantic attachment but was understood as a means of establishing political alliances and securing property. Among the elite, who had vast tracts of land and other wealth that passed from generation to generation, marriages were more like the corporate mergers of today's world than a celebration of love, and the dowry or "marriage portion" that a woman brought to the relationship might itself amount to a small fortune. It was the woman's body, both materially and metaphorically, that represented and cemented these alliances, for her body both stood for the relationship between kinship groups and gave birth to the legal heir who would inherit the property that passed from family to family in marriage. As a reflection of the magnitude of these alliances, marriage contracts for the elite were sometimes massive parchment documents that listed in detail the disposition of all family property involved in the marriage alliance. Such marriage documents could be as large as five feet long and five feet wide, written in large, elegant script and flamboyantly sealed in red wax. The very size of the document spoke to the weight of the legal burdens that marriage imposed on the parties involved, particularly the women.

Within the middle classes, where there might be little real property to settle in a marriage document, there would not be a convocation of lawyers behind most marriage settlements, though the economic terms of the marriage would certainly be spelled out in some less extensive and ostentatious form. A woman usually brought a dowry to her marriage, even if it was no more than some household items like cooking pots and bed linens, and the dowry would be specified as part of the negotiations between the parents if the prospective marriage partners were still under their parents' dominion. In some parts of France, where there was plentiful work in the towns and villages, a girl might leave home in her early teens to work in the towns and then return to the country as an adult, having earned her own dowry and, thus, being free to choose her marriage partner. However the dowry was procured, there would usually be some items, known as paraphernalia, that were specified to remain in the woman's personal and absolute control, things such as clothing or jewelry and even, in some cases, furniture and household goods. In more elaborate settlements, there might also be an allowance settled on a woman for her personal expenses (in England, sometimes called her pin money) and provision made for her should she be widowed.

Customs of inheritance varied greatly from place to place. In France, where Salic Law prevented daughters from inheriting estates or farms, even if there was no son, daughters would be married to bring a son (in-law) into the family and, thus, to allow the property to continue in the family rather than being inherited by a distant male relative. In some areas, including Czech communities, the son or son-in-law would take over the running of the farm before the death of the father, inheriting the property with the provision that he would care for his wife's parents until their death. Similarly, in some parts of England, an estate holder might pass property to his son on his marriage, with the provision that the father would have "meat, drink, firing, and all his domestic needs for his lifetime" and that his new daughter-in-law would be "serviceable" to him.[9] In places like France where primogeniture was not the norm—that is, where the eldest son did not inherit the great bulk of the estate to the impoverishment of his younger siblings—sons, daughters, and their spouses all lived together on the land, though usually in separate houses, to prevent the fragmentation of the estate into economically unprofitable units. In England, primogeniture increasingly became the norm during this period. Consequently, estates tended to be passed mostly intact from father to son or father to daughter, as the bulk of the property was "entailed," that is, legally required to be kept whole and passed from generation to generation. In this case, younger sons and daughters would receive a relatively small inheritance—a little money, a house, or some land, depending on the wealth of the family. In such families, younger sons would either acquire their own estates through marriage to an heiress or pursue a career in the army, in politics, or in the Church; daughters would either marry and join another family and live on that estate or live at the mercy of their wealthy brothers, sisters, or cousins.[10] In French-speaking Flanders, on the other hand, the family house was typically passed to the youngest child, male or female, with the assumption that he or she was most likely to live the longest and, thus, most likely to ensure that the property would be kept in the family. Other property would be divided among all children, even bastards, for such children were thought to have inherited sovereign birthrights through the mother.[11]

Children of all classes were expected to obey their parents' wishes as to marriage partners, at least while they were minors, but it was thought wrong for parents to force their children to marry if they were absolutely repulsed by the proposed spouse. Indeed, Luther preached (and published) a sermon entitled "That Parents Should Neither Compel nor Hinder the Marriage of their Children and That Children Should not Become Engaged Without Their Parents' Consent" (1524). Nonetheless, such marriages were not unheard of—hence the need for such a sermon—especially when there was a great deal of property involved in the match. Blackstone summarized the law as holding that "whosoever marries any woman child under the age of sixteen years, without consent of parents or guardians, shall be subject to fine, or five years imprisonment: and her estate during the husband's life shall go to and be enjoyed by the next heir." The civil law indeed required the consent of the parent or tutor at all ages, unless the children were emancipated, or out of the parents' power. "If such consent from the father was wanting, the marriage was null, and the children illegitimate; but the consent of the mother or guardians, if unreasonably withheld, might be redressed and supplied by the judge, or the president of the province." That is, the mother's consent was not necessary to the arrangement; she could be overruled by legal or political officials. Blackstone further noted that "in France the sons cannot marry without consent of parents till thirty years of age, nor the daughters till twenty five; and in Holland, the sons are at their own disposal at twenty five, and the daughters at twenty."[12] Even in England, however, the situation described by Blackstone did not always obtain. For instance, when the English poet John Donne (1572–1631) eloped with Anne More, her influential father, George More, was unable to secure an annulment of their marriage, despite the fact that he had not consented to the match.

Indeed, recent research has shown that clandestine marriage (elopement and marriage in secret) was widespread in the early modern world. In such cases, the bride and groom bypassed the social and economic forms of parental guidance and consent as well as the dowry system and church authorities. The couple, in effect, declared themselves married and sealed the bargain through intercourse. In some parts of Europe, especially Portugal and Spain, clandestine marriage and the resulting domestic partnerships were rife. There, property was often equally owned by husband and wife, and clandestine marriage was common.[13] In Italy, however, the dowry system was entrenched, and such marriages were less common; in addition, the tradition that Italian girls marry in their early teens made it less likely they would have occasion to meet potential partners and be able to formulate and execute a plan to elope. Church and secular courts struggled to come to grips with these marriages that circumvented the elaborate religious, social, and economic mechanisms that had developed over time to buttress and control marriage and, hence, births. Church courts generally—though not always—accepted clandestine marriage as a fait accompli and blessed it after the fact, sometimes cajoling parental consent and requiring that a dowry be given to mark the marriage as legitimate.

It is not clear, however, that a woman would be better off in a relationship that began with elopement than in a marriage concluded through socially accepted modes. Marriage was an institution that fostered relationships of hierarchy and obedience rather than love and sentiment. Peasant couples in France addressed each other using the formal *vous* rather than the familiar *tu* from the day of their marriage, and the wife's subordination to the husband was repeatedly demonstrated by her standing while her husband sat to eat his meals. Many women would have shared the widely held view that marriage was a contract best made with the head rather than with the heart, as a woman's entire life depended on the partner she chose—his ability to provide for a family, his honesty, morality, kindness, and religious inclinations. A partner with solid economic resources and a pacific character would clearly provide her with a happier existence than the most seductive and handsome man of meager means and improvident habits. Furthermore, most women saw marriage as bringing them a kind of independence through the running of their own households that they could never have so long as they remained dependents in their parents' home.

Given the economic and social implications of a marriage contract, it is not surprising that many marriages were not consummated for love alone; if there was affection, it might grow over time, an ornament to marriage rather than its occasion. At the same time, the prudent marriage did not preclude strong bonds of affection and the expression of sexual desire. Especially in Protestant countries and among the middle classes during this period, the notion emerged that marriage existed to foster companionship, affection, and even a kind of honorable sexuality. Christian clergy as well as the laity in the Middle Ages had mostly understood sex to be sinful and corrupting, even when practiced within marriage. The Church Father Augustine of Hippo (354–430) had said that marital intercourse for the purpose of underlying lust or desire, rather than for procreation only, is a venial sin, and that attitude predominated among medieval theologians and moralists.[14] And, of course, it was a sin and crime to have sex outside the bonds of marriage, whether between men and women or in same-sex couples. Medieval ecclesiastics valued celibacy and understood the life of a monk or nun to be more excellent, perfect, and holy than the life of a married person. Sex was associated with sin, a presumption that was underscored by the culture's reading of the story of Adam and Eve, where the knowledge of good and evil that comes with eating the forbidden fruit was specifically understood to be a knowledge of sexuality. So it was that even married couples were not to have intercourse during seasons of penitence like Lent and Advent, on fast days (Wednesdays and Fridays), when the woman was menstruating, and on special days of national or local prayer and penitence. Jews did not share all Christian attitudes toward sex. Like Christians, they restricted sex during a woman's period: menstruating women were quarantined and declared unclean, as were men who had ejaculated.[15] And Jews placed great emphasis on the importance of procreation, restricting sex to heterosexual relationships. At the same time, Jews always valued the pleasure and companionship of sex between men and women. And both Christians and Jews could invoke the conjugal or marital debt, the obligation to have sex with one's partner if she or he demanded it.

But the notion that even within marriage sex was inherently sinful remained popular in the Renaissance among many Christians, both Catholic and Protestant. *The Roman Catechism,* the Catholic teachings that emerged from the Council of Trent, followed Augustine in counseling that

> marriage is not to be used for purposes of lust or sensuality.... It should be remembered that the Apostle admonishes: They that have wives, let them be as though they had them not, and that St. Jerome says: The love which a wise man cherishes towards his wife is the result of judgment, not the impulse of passion; he governs the impetuosity of desire, and is not hurried into indulgence. There is nothing more shameful than that a husband should love his wife as an adulteress.

Furthermore, couples should forbear "the marriage debt"—that is, sex—at particular times:

> [T]he faithful are also to be taught sometimes to abstain from the marriage debt, in order to devote themselves to prayer ... for at least three days before Communion, and oftener during the solemn fast of Lent.[16]

And some Protestant theologians, though they did not advocate a celibate clergy, nonetheless saw sex as defiling. Calvin argued that a man should "abstain from marriage only so long as he is fit to observe celibacy," and he counseled marriage only when a man's "power to tame lust fails him."[17]

Nonetheless, in rejecting celibacy, Protestants also affirmed the goodness and even holiness of marriage and made possible a different understanding of sex; some Protestants, including Luther, came to see sexual relations not only as a debt owed to one's spouse but even as a particular pleasure and comfort of marriage that married couples could enjoy and not be ashamed of. (See also chapter 8: "Women and Pleasures.") Later political and religious reformers went much further than Luther in their reassessment of marriage practices. The Anabaptists or Mennonites, who flourished briefly in Germany, Switzerland, Holland, and England in the sixteenth century, believed in polygamy. Anabaptist leaders briefly instituted that form of marriage in Münster in 1533–1534, where it was required of all women that they accept any marriage proposal made to them. Soon, however, the sect was violently dispersed by the religious and political authorities of the region (in part because of Luther's vocal opposition to them). In seventeenth-century England, radical political groups like the Levellers, Diggers, and Ranters called for the end to private property and the freedom to choose one's marriage partner. (See also chapter 5: "Women and Religion.")

Luther's celebration of the naturalness of desire was part of his widespread attack on the Catholic Church's insistence on celibacy, a virtue that Luther thought to be extremely rare and, in a fallen world, unnatural. In addition, his repeated insistence that women are divinely ordained to be in marital relationships with men was an attack on those women who preferred the single life, whether in the convent or in the world. The fact that he repeatedly censured the single life in his sermons and writings suggests that it was a life choice among even Protestant women and men. Many Catholics in early modern Europe continued to value celibacy and to follow a monastic life with its sex-segregated norms. For women who did not wish to marry, the Catholic Church in this period still offered a respected alternative to marriage in the religious life. Though nuns and other women religious were under vows of obedience that made them answerable to authority, they were not required to answer immediately to a man, and, of course, they were free from the duty of sexual service to a husband, a liberty that has been a crucial part of many women's decision to take religious vows in any age. Catholic women in Protestant England during this period left their families and homeland to join monastic orders on the Continent. But convents and monasteries were havens for only the elite; women needed a substantial dowry to enter a convent. For women of middling and lower classes and for Protestant women, there was no sanctioned escape from the pressure to marry—a pressure that was not only social but economic, as women have always had a limited range of work available to them, and always at a lower rate of pay than men's. For a lower middle class Protestant woman, the single life would have been a costly choice, economically and socially. Nonetheless, single women made up 10 to 25 percent of the population at any time, a testimony to such women's preference for the single life as well as the vagaries of the marriage market and the frailty of human life.

Among the elite, the great aristocrats and royal families, women could not avoid marriage, and marriages at this social level were often made in spite of individual preferences and affections. Male infidelity was tolerated and even expected; a monarch's duty was to father legitimate heirs, preferably males, and, once he had seen to that, his duty by his wife and his subjects was done. Charles II of England (1630–1685), for instance, had very public relationships with a series of mistresses whom he kept in great estate and with whom he consorted openly, notably Nell Gwyn (1650–1687), Barbara Villiers, Countess of Castlemaine (1641–1709), and Louise de Keroualle, Duchess of Portsmouth (1649–1734), who bore the title *maîtresse en titre* (official mistress). Indeed, some poets of the time, in particular John Wilmot, 2nd Earl of Rochester (1647–1680), wrote lewd poems about the king's sexual propensities, implying that he was ruled by his passions when he should be ruling the kingdom. As Rochester put it,

> His scepter and his prick are of a length;
> And she may sway the one who plays with th' other.[18]

Even the suspicion of such behavior in a queen would have been intolerable, of course, and might have even cost her her life, as it had two of Henry VIII's wives who were accused of unfaithfulness. Though their "crimes" were actually more political than sexual, infidelity was the most damning charge that could be made against a queen and could, in this and other cases, be made to stand for any woman's crime. Nonetheless, many elite women of noble status had a number of quite public affairs, and such arrangements were tolerated to a greater or lesser extent depending on the religious and cultural climate of the time and place. The children of these irregular alliances, the boys in particular, might attain significant social status; the bastard sons of kings, for instance, were often given titles, and many of the noble families of Europe had their beginnings in this manner. Other families also provided for children born out of wedlock to varying degrees. Anne Clifford, Countess of Pembroke, Dorset and Montgomery (1590–1676), one of the wealthiest women in seventeenth-century England, raised and provided for two daughters born of her first husband's infidelities.[19] And the Venetian composer and singer Barbara Strozzi (1619–1677) was born Barbara Valle, the "natural" daughter of a woman employed in the household of Giulio Strozzi, academician, librettist, and patron of music. No documents survive that explicitly name him as her father, but he gave her his name (she was known as "La Strozzi") and raised her as a daughter, providing her with a superb musical education and with a forum for displaying her musical talents. (See also chapter 7: "Women and the Arts.")

Less socially and economically powerful women who engaged in extramarital affairs might be subject to prosecution in church courts or to a variety of traditional shaming rituals that made their transgressions public. Women of "light carriage" could be publicly whipped and dragged through the streets on wooden carts or skimmingtons. The humiliating spectacle of the punishment was considered important as a deterrent of repeat offenses and as a cautionary lesson to others. Indeed, public disgrace was a central component of many penalties imposed on disobedient or uncooperative females. One transgression in particular was punished with ridicule and debasement: the crime of nagging or scolding. Particular instruments of discipline were designed to restrain such aggressive speaking. The branks, or scold's bridle, was a heavy iron cage that covered the head; a sharp spike projected into the woman's mouth, preventing her from speaking and sometimes mutilating her tongue. Locked into the mask, she was led through the streets on a chain held by a magistrate and then staked in the town square. Throughout her so-called penance, she was beaten, taunted, and pelted with rotten vegetables and excrement. More than fifty varieties of branks are on display in modern European museums and town halls, testimony to the grim requirements of female passivity in the Renaissance.

This cautionary image draws a connection between the open sewage of a typical Renaissance village and the moral filth of improper women. The woman dumping excrement from a chamber pot has befouled not only the street but also her husband, who stands in the doorway wearing cuckold's horns. Three other villagers pass by the rooting pig with a skimmington ride, a public humiliation for adulterous wives and cuckolds. *Source:* Skimmington, *Roxburghe Ballads,* courtesy AMS Press.

One of the few published accounts of wearing a scold's bridle is Dorothy Waugh's description of her "cruel usage by the Mayor of Carlisle." Waugh's testimony was included in *The Lambs defence against lyes,* an anonymous 1656 account of the persecution of Quakers. There Waugh stated,

> I was moved of the Lord to go into the market of Carlisle, to speak against all deceit and ungodly practices, and the mayor's officer came and violently haled me off the cross and put me in prison.... [The mayor] called to one of his followers to bring the bridle, as he called it, to put it upon me, and was to be on three hours. And that which they called so was like a steel cap, and my hat being violently plucked off, which was pinned to my head, whereby they tore my clothes to put on their bridle, as they called it, which was a stone weight of iron ... and three bars of iron to come over my face, and a piece of it was put in my mouth, which was so unreasonable big a thing for that place, as cannot be well related, which was locked to my head, and so I stood their time with my hands bound behind me

with the stone weight of iron upon my head, and the bit in my mouth to keep me from speaking.... And the man that kept the prison door demanded two-pence of everyone that came to see me while the bridle remained upon me. Afterwards it was taken off and they kept me in prison for a little season, and after a while the mayor came up again and caused it to be put on again and sent me out into the city with it on, and gave me very vile and unsavoury words, which were not fit to proceed out of any man's mouth, and charged the officer to whip me out of the town.[20]

In England, another standard punishment for women's transgressive speech was the ducking stool. As Blackstone explained in

Scold's bridle or branks, Ralph Gardiner, *England's Grievance Discovered* (London, 1655), 110. *Source:* © Bodleian Library, University of Oxford, 4° S21Jur.

his *Commentaries,* "a common scold, communis rixatrix, (for our law-latin confines it to the feminine gender) is a public nuisance to her neighborhood. For which offense she may be indicted; and, if convicted, shall be sentenced to be placed in a certain engine of correction called the trebucket, castigatory, or cucking stool, which in the Saxon language signifies the scolding stool; though now it is frequently corrupted into ducking stool."[21] This apparatus was a chair suspended over a lake or a river. The accused was strapped in the chair and repeatedly plunged into the water, to the accompaniment of jeering crowds. Though it was usually associated with women, the ducking stool was used as punishment for both men and women. Men who beat their wives could be ducked, and squabbling couples were sometimes tied back to back and ducked together. Some of the ducking stools were carved with offensive mottos or with images of devils seizing scolds.

Then as now, women were more likely to be punished for prostitution than men were. Men were rarely prosecuted either for being prostitutes or for paying for the sexual services of a prostitute. Prostitution was common in towns and cities throughout Europe at this time, and it was tolerated to a greater or lesser degree from place to place. The economic arrangements might take any number of forms: some women were pimped by others, either men or family members (including mothers) who sold the girls' services; in some places, prostitutes would live together, sharing the cost of housing and caring for each other's children and aged relatives. Providing sexual services was not the only means of earning money for such women, and they might combine sex work with various trades such as selling small wares or working as an artist's model part of the time. (See also chapter 3: "Women and Work.") Prostitutes were always among the followers of armies, and, then as now, army officials encouraged their being available to service military men and often supervised their behavior. In some urban areas, prostitutes were less liable to harassment and arrest so long as they kept to a designated area of the city, wore distinctive clothing or badges, were regularly examined by a doctor, and paid taxes or bribes to city officials. In some towns, the local officials were essentially in the sex business, managing and housing prostitutes, setting their fees, and taking a percentage of their income as a kind of tax. In some times and places, accomplished courtesans were an accepted part of society. Less powerful women who earned their living with their bodies ended up in jail from time to time and were subject to abuse and misuse, while royal mistresses and courtesans might move in the most elevated social circles and acquire significant wealth, property, and fame.

In most parts of Europe, a woman's children, whatever her status, were the legal property of her husband, and, in the case of divorce, she might lose all contact with them, a provision that surely kept many women in miserable alliances. This was especially true at a time when divorce, particularly for ordinary folk, was so rare as to be essentially unknown. The fact that marriage was seen as a sacrament in the Catholic tradition and as the will of God for all humankind in both the Protestant and the Jewish traditions made it very difficult to argue that marriages could be dissolved. Luther thought marriage "the business of the world," something that "it is not proper for us clergymen or servants of the church to arrange or govern," but he certainly understood the vows taken by husband and wife to be binding under civil authority. Even if a girl is "forced into marriage," that is, raped and abducted, that marriage is valid, he argued, "for although she was forced into it, she still consented to this coercion by her action, accepted it, and followed it, so that her husband has publicly acquired conjugal rights over her, which no one can now take from him."[22] Robert Cleaver, in his popular and much-reprinted Protestant marriage tract *A Godlie Forme of Householde Government* (1598), which borrowed heavily from an earlier tract by Heinrich Bullinger (1504–1575) (translated into English as *The Christen State of Matrimonye;* [1541]), argued that "the institution of Matrimonie is an indissoluble bond and knot, whereby the husband and wife are fastened together by the ordinance of God."[23]

But Christian monarchs and aristocrats, by virtue of their great political power, did frequently manage to receive ecclesiastical consent to divorce or to annul a marriage. When that was not forthcoming, powerful men might simply take the question of divorce under their own governance, as did Henry VIII in putting aside Catherine of Aragon. Some Protestants (notably John Milton) argued for the possibility of divorce, basing their arguments on Jewish "notions of marriage as a contract that can be completely dissolved—and remade with another party if so desired."[24] But such arguments were seen as radical, outlandish, and damaging to the very fabric of society, particularly as the relationship between husband and wife was held as a model and metaphor for the relationship between monarch and people. To understand marriage as consensual and transitory struck at the very foundations of governance and rule. Yet Mary Astell (1666–1731), in her protofeminist critique of marriage, drew on this same metaphor to attack marriage, comparing married women to the poor and oppressed:

> Man can't deny that [a woman] has by much the harder Bargain [in marriage]: because she puts herself entirely into her Husband's Power, and if the Matrimonial Yoke be grievous, neither Law nor Custom afford her that Redress which a Man obtains. He who has Sovereign Power does not value the Provocations of a Rebellious Subject; he knows how to subdue him with Ease, and will make himself obeyed: But Patience and Submission are the only comforts that are left to a poor People, who groan under Tyranny, unless they are Strong enough to break the Yoke, to Depose and Abdicate, which, I [am sure], would not be allowed of her. For whatever may be said against Passive-Obedience in another case, I suppose there's no Man but likes it very well in this; how much soever Arbitrary Power may be disliked on a Throne, not *Milton* himself would cry up Liberty to poor *Female Slaves,* or plead for the Lawfulness of Resisting a Private Tyranny.[25]

Works like Astell's illustrate the wide range of thinking on gender and legal issues during this period as well as the fact that what one might call feminist objections to women's subordination is not a modern phenomenon but rather has a long history.

Renaissance families were rarely limited to two parents and their natural children. Because of high maternal mortality rates and the relatively shorter life spans of all early modern peoples, many children were raised by at least one stepparent; between one-third and one-half of all children would have lost at least one parent by the time they themselves married. When children were heirs to significant wealth, they might also be subject to court-appointed guardians. As popular fairy tales and moralizing tracts attest, both stepparents and guardians were seen to be prone to abusing their power over the children in their care, forcing them into marriages they did not want or preventing them from marrying so as to have access to the children's wealth. In Britain, the monarch or a royal official was the de facto guardian of the estates of all elite children who had lost a father; the surviving mother in such a case had to purchase the guardianship of her children for them to marry or come into the property they had been left in their father's will. But the guardianship of the children might instead be sold to a higher bidder, perhaps a complete stranger, who would then have authority over the disposition of the child's education, upbringing, and marriage as well as access to the child's money and property. Even the most respectable among such officials commonly received bribes or gifts in exchange for their granting permission for the ward to marry.

English heiresses who brought extensive wealth to their marriages did not as married women administer or control that wealth; at the moment of marriage, a woman's property became her husband's to dispose of as he wished unless provision had been made for an allowance or land that remained in the wife's control. As the 1632 *Law's Resolutions of Women's Rights* put it,

> Whatsoever the husband had before coverture either in goods or lands, it is absolutely his own; the wife hath therein no seisin [entitlement] at all. If any thing when he is married be given him, he taketh it by himself distinctly to himself. If a man have right and title to enter into lands, and the tenant enfeoffe [entitle] the baron and feme [man and woman], the wife taketh nothing. The very goods which a man giveth to his wife are still his own; her chain, her bracelets, her apparel, are all the good-man's goods.... A wife how gallant soever she be, glistereth but in the riches of her husband, as the moon hath no light but is the sun's.[26]

Elsewhere the author added,

> For thus it is, if before marriage the woman were possessed of horses, neat [cattle], sheep, corn, wool, money, plate, and jewels, all manner of moveable substance is presently by conjunction the husband's, to sell, keep, or bequeath if he die. And though he bequeath them not, yet are they the husband's executor's and not the wife's which brought to her husband.[27]

In other parts of Europe, a husband and wife held property jointly. Such was the case in Holland, a country unique in its egalitarian inheritance laws. Whereas the inheritance laws of countries like England and France grew out of a system of aristocratic landholding and its particular concerns with property, Holland was thoroughly bourgeois in its social and economic systems, and its laws reflected a concern with the robust continuation of business and the health of the marketplace rather than the transmission of landed estates within a male-dominated aristocracy. As a result, not only did Dutch sons and daughters share equally in the transmission of property and movable goods, but widows in Leiden were legally granted independent status and the right to half of their deceased spouse's property. Because widows in Holland were recognized as independent heads of household, they were not constrained to return to the home of their parents or move in with their children, as did the legally disenfranchised widows in other parts of Europe.[28] And even among countries dominated by a land-based aristocracy, there was usually provision for widows' maintenance after the death of their husbands in the "dower," usually one-third of the husband's estate. In very wealthy families, the widow might have her own "dower house," her separate domestic establishment on the family estate; in middle-class families, she might be given a room within the family house. The dower, whether land, property, or money, was not hers to dispose of as she wished, however: it returned to the estate of her husband's heir on her death.

Despite their legal and economic disenfranchisement, widows and single women in most countries could make wills disposing of their property, while in some cases a married woman could make a will with her husband's approval (though those represented a tiny percentage of all those who made wills). Still, in many areas, women's wills represented no more than 10 percent of all the wills that survived, and almost all of those were written by widows. One particularly interesting will left by an Englishwoman in the early eighteenth century shows her to be attempting to use the legal authority of her will to subvert the doctrine of coverture. The will of Sarah Gooch begins typically by bequeathing her body to the earth and her soul to God, names her sister as executor of the will, and then makes distributions to various family members before making this declaration regarding her son-in-law's authority over her daughter's inheritance:

> I do hereby devise & will that the said sum of £100 & several sums of £600 so as aforesaid devised unto the said Leonard Buxton, Sarah Buxton, & Ann Buxton, & also the several shares of the rest & residue of my personal Estate belonging to the several children of the said John Buxton & Ann his Wife, which shall be living at the time of my Decease, shall from time to time be paid to, employed & disposed of, into the proper hands, & by the order & direction of Ann my Loving Daughter, the aforesaid Wife of John Buxton *without*

his Intermeddling therewith, and that the Interest & Produce of the said sum of £100, & several sums of £600 & of the several shares & proportions of the aforesaid younger children shall be also from time & as the same shall be made & raised, paid into the proper hands of the said Ann Buxton my Daughter *without the said John Buxton her Husband intermeddling therewith*—& that Her receipts under her separate hand for such sums of money & produce thereof shall also be a good & sufficient discharge for the same *notwithstanding her present Coverture or any other future Coverture.*[29]

Women could also witness others' wills and could serve as executors. In fact, when a woman survived her husband, she was usually his executor. Wills also tell us something about women's economic lives, especially when the widow of an artisan or a tradesman inherited the tools of her husband's trade. Clearly, these women were active in the family business and were expected to carry on after the death of the husband. In general, however, men were left land and tools, while women inherited linens and other domestic goods.

Women who committed crimes were subject to arraignment, trial, and punishment under a legal system that seems to us harsh and cruel, though courts tended to be more lenient with women than men, with several exceptions. As discussed earlier in this chapter, a female's "unbridled" speech—gossiping, nagging, scolding—was far more strictly punished than was a male's. And because a wife's subordination to her husband was seen as the bedrock of society, women who murdered, especially those who killed or tried to kill their husbands, were seen as monsters and were subject to the full penalty of the law. Women were also seen as liable to kill the infants who were the result of extramarital sex, and midwives were particularly charged with seeing to the survival of these babies. Such crimes, especially instances of murdering a husband, were the hot topic of gossip. They were frequently reported in the early modern equivalents of the tabloid, pamphlets, and in street ballads with titles like *Murther, Murther. Or, A Bloody Relation how Anne Hamton dweling in Westminster nigh London, by Pouson [Poison] Murthered her Dear Husband* (London, 1641) and *A Cabinet of Grief: Or, the French Midwife's Miserable Moan for the Barbarous Murther Committed upon the Body of her Husband* (London, 1688). Reports of wives murdering their husbands significantly outnumbered reports of wives being murdered, though it is likely that actual crime statistics ran the other

Moll Cut-purse, notorious thief who cross-dressed in man's clothing and was frequently arrested for cross-dressing, brawling, and other crimes. *Source:* © Museum of London.

direction, given that the law gave men the right to "correct" their wives, while women had no such rights with their husbands. In a kind of grim irony, though women ordinarily had little or no legal status, they were required to testify in court on their own behalf when they committed capital crimes.

Women were also subject to the law if they were suspected of heresy or witchcraft, both of which were seen as crimes against God, though in quite different ways. Given the many shifts in national Christian religious confession during this period, it is not surprising that both men and women might find themselves accused of illegal and blasphemous religious practices. In every European country during this time, a significant number of people were actively opposed to the country's official religion and practiced a different and often illegal version of Christianity. In England, under the pre-Reformation reign of Henry VIII (1491–1547) and during the reign of his daughter Mary Tudor (1516–1558), Protestants like Anne Askew (1521–1546) were persecuted, tortured, and even executed. Under the English Protestant monarchs, Catholics were liable to arrest, torture, imprisonment, and death. After Elizabeth I (1533–1603) was excommunicated by Pope Pius V (1504–1572) in 1570, some Catholics sought actively to undermine her authority and even to assassinate her; in that political climate, it became treasonous to practice Catholicism, to own the trappings of Catholic ritual such as "monstrances" that displayed holy relics, or to harbor (support and hide) Catholic priests.

English women were particularly important to clandestine Catholicism in England, providing safe haven for priests in their homes during long stretches when their husbands were imprisoned or exiled to the Continent because of their beliefs. Catholic homes often had a "priest's hole," a secret hiding place where a person might escape arrest should the house be searched by the Protestant authorities. Margaret Clitherow (ca. 1556–1586) harbored a series of priests until she was finally arrested, tortured, and, despite her Protestant husband's pleas on her behalf, executed by *peine forte et dure,* "crushed under heavy stones." Anne Howard, Countess of Arundel (1557–1630), was arrested for her Catholicism along with her husband, Philip; in fact, she gave birth to a daughter while in prison. Her cousin, Anne Vaux, gave protection to Henry Garnet (1555–1606), superior of the English Jesuits, for nearly twenty years and oversaw a network of safe houses where Jesuit clergy could find protection. She also served as a courier for the Jesuits and, with Anne Howard, provided significant financial support to the Catholic cause. Howard herself founded the novitiate of the Jesuits at Ghent at a time when there were no opportunities for Catholic priests to be trained within England itself and all such education happened on the Continent. As was so often the case, it was in times of social and cultural disruption that women were able to come to the fore and assume leadership roles unavailable to them in more peaceful times.

It is rather more difficult to summarize quickly the historical record of the early modern prosecution of witches, as women's role in that history continues to be much debated. The fact that women witches had been little studied before the twentieth century became a cause célèbre for many historians working to recover evidence of the lives of women; the scandal of witches' invisibility in the work of historians came to be seen as a symbol for the neglect of women in all scholarly disciplines. As historians of the 1970s and 1980s attempted to rectify this fault, many of them came to see accusations of witchcraft as an instance of genocide fueled by vitriolic misogyny and fostered by woman-hating Christian authorities who sought especially to silence *femes soles* (single women), midwives, social outsiders, elderly women, the poor, and other women who did not fit the passive, domestic, and subordinate role. Some scholars claimed that the Christian Church had caused the torture and death of up to 9 million women in Europe over the period of a few hundred years.

But more recent scholarship has complicated this picture, estimating that between one hundred thousand and two hundred thousand people were accused of witchcraft, and that between fifty thousand and one hundred thousand people were executed for that crime. Perhaps because of the nearly universal belief in women's tendency to wickedness, women were the majority of those accused in early modern towns and cities (80 to 85% of the whole), but men were persecuted as well. Indeed, in a few areas of Europe, men formed the majority of those accused, and in all places, women were as likely to be accusers as men. Furthermore, the women accused of witchcraft tended not to be outsiders, the poor and marginalized, but rather married members of the community, and the accusers tended to be of the same social status as the accused. Revisionist histories of the early modern witch craze suggest that it was not a top-down conspiracy against women, undertaken by an alliance of ecclesiastical and state authorities, but rather the evidence of widely held ideas about gender and the supernatural. Indeed, some scholars have suggested that belief in witches and sorcery was more a feature of the peasants' world-view, while the educated and the elite tended to dismiss claims and accusations of magic as the mark of ignorant superstition.

Yet many early modern church and state leaders were at the forefront of the witch hunts. Both Protestant and Catholic authorities hunted and executed witches, but the witch craze is a phenomenon of northern European Protestantism, and there were very few executions in the strongholds of Catholicism in southern Europe like Spain and Italy. At the same time, the most famous early modern treatise on witchcraft was the *Malleus maleficarum* [Hammer of Witches], written in 1486 by two German Dominican monks active in the Inquisition, an institution of the Catholic Church charged with rooting out and punishing heresy and defending the faith from false practices and false doctrines.[30] King James VI of Scotland (later James I of England) wrote the treatise *Demonology* in 1597, and he enjoyed being present when those accused of witchcraft were tortured to extract confessions. James initiated harsh statutes to seek out and prosecute witches, and he banned Reginald Scot's book *A Discovery of Witchcraft* (1584) because it disputed the existence of witches. So, though thinkers like Scot dismissed the phenomenon of witchcraft, some among the elite and the well-educated believed fervently in witches and the supernatural.

Women and men had been accused of being witches and brought to trial throughout the Middle Ages, but there was undoubtedly a great increase in the number of accusations and prosecutions of witches in the early modern period beginning in the fourteenth century and reaching what can aptly be called a witch craze between 1550 and 1650. Again, scholars disagree about what caused this increase (and what led to the disappearance of witch hunts in the eighteenth century), but most agree that there was no single cause for the phenomenon. It's safe to say that the persecution of women for witchcraft arose from a network of social attitudes that held the ideal woman to be silent and submissive yet, at the same time, more prone to demonic seduction and possession. As the writers of the *Malleus maleficarum* put it, women are "more credulous [than men], and since the chief aim of the devil is to corrupt faith, therefore he rather attacks them." Women "are more naturally impressionable," they "have slippery tongues, and are unable to conceal from their fellow-women those things which by evil arts they know." Moreover, a woman is "more carnal than a man, as is clear from her many carnal abominations." And how do the authors know such things to be true of women? Their argument, like that of most moralists of the time when it came to questions of gender, was a circular one: they know woman is more impressionable and carnal (that is, less spiritual) by the story of Adam and Eve.

Testing for a witch; a "real" witch would not sink, while an innocent woman would drown. [Anon.], *Witches Apprehended, Examined and Executed* (London, 1613), title page, STC 25872. *Source:* © Bodleian Library, University of Oxford, 4° E17Art(11).

And it should be noted that there was a defect in the formation of the first woman, since she was formed from a bent rib, that is, a rib of the breast, which is bent as it were in a contrary direction to a man. And since through this defect she is an imperfect animal, she always deceives.

The authors of the *Malleus* also catalog the qualities of good women who "have brought beatitude to men, and have saved nations, lands, and cities; as is clear in the case of Judith, Debbora, and Esther" and a host of postbiblical women leaders. But these women are clearly exceptions (indeed, hardly women at all, as their virtues deviate so greatly from the ideal of woman, who was to be chaste, silent, and obedient, not a leader of men). Most ordinary women are instead seen as more likely to stray from obedience into wickedness, since, as the authors say, quoting an ancient proverb, "When a woman thinks alone, she thinks evil."[31] Any threat of women's deviation from feminine ideals, through public speaking or through claims of supernatural power, was seen as a sign of profound social and religious disruption and danger. In fact, one scholar has suggested that it was these women's perceived deviation from their prescribed maternal role that marked them as evildoers, pointing to the many accusations against women that they had stolen milk or ruined crops through conjuring bad weather. Where the idealized woman nurtured, these women brought death and destruction.[32]

The economic and class changes and often violent disruptions that marked European society in the early modern period also contributed to the breakdown of the kinds of social "glue" that held together communities of peoples whose families had known each other from as far back as anyone could remember, making it easier to suspect one's neighbor of practicing witchcraft. And no doubt the events of the Reformation also influenced thinking about witches and the need to prosecute heretics. Both Catholic and Protestant theologians were increasingly interested in defining their own doctrinal adherence to the truth, and this focus inevitably resulted in the identification of new versions of heresy and blasphemy and the discovery of more heretics. The majority of prosecutions and executions of women and men for witchcraft happened in areas where the social and political frameworks were already profoundly disrupted because of the Thirty Years' War; these areas included parts of present-day Germany, northern France, and Switzerland, where violence, torture, and public executions had become a grisly part of daily life. In other parts of Europe, which were less violently affected by the Reformation, very few witches, male or female, were actually executed, though thousands were charged and tried. Such was the case even in the states and provinces of Italy most firmly under the control of the Vatican and in Spain, the home of the particularly brutal Inquisition. Likewise, in England, with a couple of notable exceptions, few witches were executed and never by burning at the stake.

Perhaps the most extreme example of early modern women transgressing gender norms is represented by those who took on male identities and cross-dressed; such behavior often resulted in their prosecution and punishment under the law. While wearing "mannish" clothing was stylish among the elite in the period, it was generally middle- or lower-class women who actually adopted male identity, dressing in men's clothing, doing work typically done by men, and even, in some cases, entering into sexual relationships and marriage with women. Women cross-dressed for a number of reasons. Some adopted male clothing to avoid marriage and men's sexual advances. A woman might cross-dress as a cover for a same-sex relationship, while another woman might have merely been seeking a single life. A woman whose profession or whose husband's profession involved travel might cross-dress to ensure her own safety, as women were more liable to be attacked, especially raped, than men. Cross-dressing could allow a woman to enter traditionally male occupations. For instance, a woman might cross-dress to travel with the army or navy, either because her husband was a soldier or sailor and she wanted to be with him, or in order to fight as a soldier or sailor herself. Those who cross-dressed to accompany their husbands used men's clothing to facilitate heterosexual relationships. But for other women, the adoption of what we would now call a transgendered identity allowed them to be in sexual relationships with women and to assume male identity in all their social interactions.[33]

One notorious English cross-dresser was Mary Frith (ca. 1584–1659), better known as Moll Cutpurse, a notorious outlaw in early modern London. ("Moll" is a woman's name but can also signify a pickpocket, prostitute, or thief's girlfriend; "cutpurse" was the early modern term for a thief.) She was memorialized in Thomas Middleton and Thomas Dekker's play *The Roaring Girl* (1611); in the anonymous pamphlet entitled *The Life and Death of Moll Cutpurse* (1662); and in the 1769 entry in *The Newgate Calendar, Or Malefactors Bloody Register* (1760), entitled "Mary Frith Otherwise Moll Cutpurse: A famous Master-Thief and an Ugly, who dressed like a Man, and died in 1663." Moll was noted for her "masculine spirit," her "manly" activities (smoking, fighting, disliking children), and her refusal of men's sexual advances.[34] Though Moll spent time in jail and was even convicted of murder, she avoided execution and lived a long life as a thief, fence, and dispenser of rough justice. The *Newgate Calendar* entry states that "Moll was always accounted by her neighbours to be an hermaphrodite," that is, she was thought to be of ambivalent gender. However, a postmortem physical examination showed her to have typical female genitalia.[35]

Others who cross-dressed were not treated with the same tolerance as was Moll. Despite Moll's adoption of masculine dress and activities, she did not claim to be a man; but those who misled the authorities and who were seen to transgress upon male privilege were subject to the harshest penalties of the law. The severest sentences were passed on those who used "material instruments" (dildos) to "counterfeit the office of a husband," or, in other words of another case, who used "illicit inventions ... to supplement the shortcomings of [their] sex."[36] In early eighteenth-century Germany, Catherine Margaretha Linck adopted male identity, dressing as a man, serving in the army, and marrying a woman. When Linck's wife complained to her mother about Linck's physical and sexual oddities, the mother took Linck to court in 1721. At the trial, it was noted that Linck used "a penis of stuffed leather with two stuffed testicles made from pig's bladder attached to it." The judge ruled that "a woman who commits sodomy with another woman with such an instrument" must be sentenced to death. Linck was executed, and Linck's wife was sentenced to three years in prison and then banished.[37] As a recent scholar notes, "sexual activities between women primarily came to the notice of medieval ecclesiastics when the women implicated seemed to be appropriating recognized male sexual roles. In those cases, the response could be, literally, deadly."[38]

Thus the law, in its many manifestations, defined the lives of women of all classes and in all places. One might even contend that the law increasingly defined what it meant to be female, as those characteristics that were thought to delineate women in opposition to men influenced legal writings and legal practice and were brought into sharper focus through legal codes that governed property, heresy, public speech, and both public and private behavior. As Leonardo Bruni (1369–1444), the Italian historian, politician, and papal secretary, said of the ideal woman, "Hers is not the task of learning to speak for and against witnesses, for and against torture, for and against reputation; she will not practice the commonplaces, the syllogisms, the sly anticipation of an opponent's arguments. She will, in a word, leave the rough-and-tumble of the forum entirely to men."[39] At its worst, the law saw women as profoundly flawed beings who were more prone to demonic and lustful actions than men and who, therefore, needed to be controlled, silenced, and domesticated. At its best, the law provided some protection for women, though often in a paternalistic fashion whereby they were protected into a kind of childlike helplessness. But some women—particularly elite women—were able to use the law and their rights under the law to their advantage. Moll Cutpurse was a survivor who lived on her own terms, mostly managing to flout social and legal strictures regarding gender. At the other end of the social scale was Anne Clifford (1590–1676), one of the richest women in England. As her parents' only child, she was entitled to inherit her father's estate (which was entailed on the eldest child regardless of gender), but her father wrote a will disinheriting her in favor of his brother's sons. After his death, Anne steadfastly refused to accept the terms of his will, arguing her right to inheritance by law. Neither the attempts of King James VI and I to sway her nor her first husband's willingness to forfeit the claim in exchange for a lesser inheritance dissuaded her. Although the estate passed for a time to her male cousin, in spite of the property's being entailed, Clifford finally inherited it on his death. Furthermore, thousands of unnamed widows and younger daughters were able to survive and remain economically independent because they were guaranteed a dower or an inheritance by law. While women were not welcome in court by the legal codes or the popular prejudices of the time, they nonetheless used the courts to claim and even enlarge their legal rights.

NOTES

1.   Lyndal Roper, "Going to Church and Street: Weddings in Reformation Augsburg," *Past and Present* 106 (1985): 85. On the other hand, guilds might provide dowries for the orphaned daughters of former craftsmen and so make it possible for them to marry.

2.   Sir William Blackstone, *Commentaries on the Laws of England* (1765–1769), 1.15.430–33. Blackstone's *Commentaries* are available online through the Avalon Project at Yale Law School, <http://www.yale.edu/lawweb/avalon/blackstone/blacksto.htm>, as well as in many modern editions.

3.   J. L. Flandrin, *Families in Former Times: Kinship, Household, and Sexuality,* trans. Richard Southern (New York: Cambridge University Press, 1979), 122.

4.   Church of England, Homily 18, "Of the State of Matrimony," in *The Elizabethan Homilies,* vol. 2 (1563–1571), 295–306. The Homilies are available online through UTEL (University of Toronto English Library), <http://www.library.utoronto.ca/utel/ret/homilies/elizhom.html>,   and

EEBO, <http://eebo.chadwyck.com>, as well as in the facsimile reprint *Certain Sermons or Homilies Appointed to Be Read in Churches* (Gainesville, FL: Scholars' Facsimiles & Reprints, 1968).

5.   Qtd. in Susan C. Karant-Nunn and Merry E. Wiesner-Hanks, eds. and trans., *Luther on Women: A Sourcebook* (New York: Cambridge University Press, 2003), 95.

6.   Thomas Edgar, section iii, "The Punishment of Adam's Sin," *The Law's Resolutions of Women's Rights: Or, the Law's Provision for Women* (London, 1632). Edgar's pamphlet is excerpted in M. H. Abrams, ed., *The Norton Anthology of English Literature,* vol. 1, *Early Seventeenth Century Topic: Gender, Family Household* (New York: Norton, 1993) in Early Seventeenth Century Topics: Gender, Family, Household, and is available online, <http://www.wwnorton.com/nael/17century/topic_1/laws.htm>.

7.   Qtd. in Karant-Nunn and Wiesner-Hanks, *Luther on Women,* 93.

8.   See Jane Stevenson and Peter Davidson, eds., *Early Modern Women Poets (1520–1700): An Anthology* (New York: Oxford University Press, 2001), 120. The spelling and punctuation have been modernized here.

9.   Margaret Spufford, "Peasant Inheritance Customs and Distribution in Cambridgeshire from the Sixteenth to the Eighteenth Centuries," in *Family and Inheritance: Rural Society in Western Europe, 1200–1800,* ed. Jack Goody, Joan Thirsk, and E. P. Thompson (New York: Cambridge University Press, 1976), 175.

10.   Primogeniture became increasingly prevalent during this period, not only in England but among the German states, in Spain, and in some parts of France, though it was never as widespread as in England. The fact that it never predominated in France is in part the consequence of French agricultural richness; French land had always generated more produce per acre than the less fertile land of England, and, thus, more English acres were needed to support a family. The English turn to primogeniture was, in this sense, a practical solution to an economic and geographic problem. At the same time, English primogeniture was an expression of the power of the landed classes vis-à-vis the monarch, an attempt to amass aristocrat wealth to counter the wealth and power of the monarchy.

11.   Emmanuel Le Roy Ladurie, "Family Structures and Inheritance Customs in Sixteenth-Century France," in Goody, Thirsk, and Thompson, *Family and Inheritance,* 67.

12.   Blackstone, *Commentaries,* 1.15.425.

13.   Jutta Sperling, "Marriage at the Time of the Council of Trent (1560–70): Clandestine Marriages, Kinship Prohibitions, and Dowry Exchange in European Comparison," *Journal of Early Modern History* 8 (2004): 67–108.

14.   Augustine of Hippo, *"De bono conjugali"* [On the Good of Marriage] 6.6, in *Saint Augustine: Treatises on Marriage and Other Subjects,*

ed. and trans. Charles T. Wilcox (Washington, DC: Catholic University Press of America, 1969). Augustine cautioned that sex for procreation should be engaged in sparingly, as it uses time that could otherwise be devoted to prayer.

15.   See Leviticus 15 for prohibitions concerning unclean "issues" of blood or other body fluids.

16.   "The Sacrament of Matrimony: The Use of Marriage," in *The Roman Catechism*. Also known as the Catechism of Trent, it is available online through the Catholic Information Network, <http://www.cin.org/users/james/ebooks/master/trent/tindex.htm>.

17.   John Calvin, *Institutes of the Christian Religion* 2.8.43. Widely available online and in print.

18.   "A Satyre on Charles II," lines 11–13.

19.   Richard T. Spence, *Lady Anne Clifford: Countess of Pembroke, Dorset and Montgomery (1590–1676)* (Stroud, UK: Sutton, 1997), 86.

20.   [Anon.], *The Lambs defence against lyes. And a true testimony given concerning the sufferings and death of James Parnell…. By such hands as were eye-witnesses, and have subscribed their names thereto….* (London, 1656), 29–30. This account is available through EEBO, <http://eebo.chadwyck.com>. On Waugh's account, see Kate Chedgzoy, "Impudent Women: Carnival and Gender in Early Modern Culture," *The Glasgow Review,* issue 1, <http://www.arts.gla.ac.uk/SESLL/STELLA/COMET/glasgrev/ issue1/contents.htm>, and David E. Underdown, "The Taming of the Scold: The Enforcement of Patriarchal Authority in Early Modern England," in *Order and Disorder in Early Modern England,* ed. Anthony Fletcher and John Stevenson (New York: Cambridge University Press, 1985), 116–36.

21.   Blackstone, *Commentaries,* 4.13.169.

22.   Qtd. in Karant-Nunn and Wiesner-Hanks, *Luther on Women,* 115, 114.

23.   John Deacon and Robert Cleaver, *A Godlie Forme of Householde Government: For the Ordering of Private Families, according to the direction of God's Word….* (London: Thomas Man, 1598), sig. G2. This tract is available through EEBO, <http://eebo.chadwyck.com>. For more on this tract and other similar works, see Sid Ray, "'Those Whom God Hath Joined Together': Bondage Metaphors and Marital Advice in Early Modern England," in *Domestic Arrangements in Early Modern England,* ed. Kari Boyd McBride (Pittsburgh, PA: Duquesne University Press, 2002), 15–47.

24.   M. Lindsay Kaplan, "Subjection and Subjectivity: Jewish Law and Female Autonomy in Reformation English Marriage," in *Feminist Readings of Early Modern Culture: Emerging Subjects,* ed. Valerie Traub, M. Lindsay Kaplan, and Dympna Callaghan (New York: Cambridge University Press, 1996), 230–31.

25.   Mary Astell, *Some Reflections Concerning Marriage,* 3rd ed. (London: R. Wilkin, 1706), 27.

26. Thomas Edgar, section viii, "That which a husband hath is his own," in *The Law's Resolutions of Women's Rights*. T. E.'s pamphlet is excerpted in M. H. Abrams, ed., *The Norton Anthology of English Literature,* vol. 1, *Early Seventeenth Century Topics: Gender, Family, Household* (New York: Norton, 1993), and is available online at <http://www.wwnorton. com/nael/17century/topic_1/laws.htm>.

27. Thomas Edgar, section ix, "That which the wife hath is the husband's," in *The Law's Resolutions of Women's Rights.* Edgar's pamphlet is excerpted in M. H. Abrams, et al., eds. *The Norton Anthology of English Literature,* vol. 1, *Early Seventeenth Century Topics: Gender, Family, Household* (New York: Norton, 1993), and is available online at <http://www. wwnorton.com/nael/17century/topic_1/laws.htm>.

28. Ariadne Schmidt, *Overleven na de dood. Weduwen in Leiden in de Gouden Eeuw* [Outliving the Dead: Widows in Leiden in the Golden Age] (Amsterdam: Prometheus, Bert Bakker, 2001).

29. Our emphasis; Sarah Gooch, will dated 1725, Buxton Papers 122.28, Cambridge University Library.

30. The Inquisition became notorious in fifteenth-century Spain under the joint monarchs Ferdinand and Isabella as it was used to seek out, torture, and execute (by burning at the stake) Jews and Muslims thought to be masquerading as Christians.

31. *Malleus maleficarum* [Hammer of Witches], part 1, question 6 (1486). The treatise is available in translation online through the Hanover Historical Texts Project, <http://history.hanover.edu/project.html>, and many other sites as well as in many printed versions, including that translated by Montague Summers (London: Rodker, 1928).

32. Nancy Hayes, "Negativizing Nurture and Demonizing Domesticity: The Witch Construct in Early Modern Germany," in *Maternal Measures: Figuring Caregiving in the Early Modern Period,* ed. Naomi J. Miller and Naomi Yavneh (Aldershot, UK: Ashgate, 2000), 179–200.

33. For a delineation of the various reasons women cross-dressed and a review of recent work on the topic, see Shasta Turner, "Disordered Subjects: Female Cross-Dressing and Sumptuary Regulation in Early Modern England," essay originally presented in the 1998 Huntington Library Graduate Seminars in Early Modern British History, updated 2004, <http:// www.majorweather.com/projects/000040.html>.

34. [Anon.], *The Life and Death of Moll Cutpurse,* in Janet Todd and Elizabeth Spearing, eds., *Counterfeit Ladies: The Life and Death of Moll Cutpurse and the Case of Mary Carleton* (London: William Pickering, 1994), 9. Thomas Decker and Thomas Middleton, *The Roaring Girl* (London, 1611), is available online through EEBO, <http://eebo.chadwyck.com>.

35. "Mary Frith," *Newgate Calendar,* 174.

36. Qtd. in Lillian Faderman, *Surpassing the Love of Men* (New York: William Morrow, 1981), 51, 52.

37.   Qtd. in E. Ann Matter, "My Sister, My Spouse: Woman-Identified Women in Medieval Christianity," *Journal of Feminist Studies in Religion* 2 (1986), 91; rpt. in Carol P. Christ and Judity Plaskow, eds., *Weaving the Visions: New Patterns in Feminist Spirituality* (San Francisco: Harper and Row, 1989). See also Brigitte Eriksson, "A Lesbian Execution in Germany, 1721: The Trial Records," *Journal of Homosexuality* 6 (1980/81): 27–40.

38.   Matter, "My Sister, My Spouse," 92.

39.   Qtd. in George Puttenham, *The Art of English Poesie* (London: Richard Field, 1589), 244.

SUGGESTED READING

Anderson, Michael. *Approaches to the History of the Western Family, 1500–1914.* Cambridge: Cambridge University Press, 2000.

Arkell, Tom, Nesta Evans, and Nigel Goose. *When Death Do Us Part: Understanding and Interpreting the Probate Records of Early Modern England.* Oxford: Leopard's Head Press, 2000.

Bever, Edward. "Witchcraft, Female Aggression, and Power in the Early Modern Community." *Journal of Social History* 35 (2002): 955–88.

Cressy, David. *Birth, Marriage, and Death: Ritual, Religion, and the Life-Cycle in Tudor and Stuart England.* New York: Oxford University Press, 1997.

Faderman, Lillian. *Surpassing the Love of Men: Romantic Friendship and Love between Women from the Sixteenth Century to the Present.* New York: Morrow, 1981.

Goody, Jack, Joan Thirsk, and E. P. Thompson, eds. *Family and Inheritance: Rural Society in Western Europe, 1200–1800.* New York: Cambridge University Press, 1976.

Karant-Nunn, Susan C., and Merry E. Wiesner-Hanks, eds. and trans. *Luther on Women: A Sourcebook.* New York: Cambridge University Press, 2003.

McBride, Kari Boyd, ed. *Domestic Arrangements in Early Modern England.* Pittsburgh, PA: Duquesne University Press, 2002.

Miller, Naomi J., and Naomi Yavneh, eds. *Maternal Measures: Figuring Caregiving in the Early Modern Period.* Aldershot, UK: Ashgate, 2000.

Purkiss, Diane. *The Witch in History: Early Modern and Twentieth-Century Representations.* New York: Routledge, 1996.

Slack, Paul. *The English Poor Law, 1531–1782.* Cambridge: Cambridge University Press, 1990.

Thomas, Kirsti S. "Medieval and Renaissance Marriage: Theory and Customs." *Medieval and Renaissance Wedding Page.* <http://www.drizzle.com/~celyn/mrwp/mrwed.html>.

Wiesner, Merry E. *Women and Gender in Early Modern Europe.* 2nd ed. New York: Cambridge University Press, 2000.

3

Women and Work

The concept of work and its social meaning were quite different in the Renaissance from how they are understood today. That era had inherited a socioeconomic perspective from the late Middle Ages that equated labor with the peasantry or servant class, while gentle status was defined by one's ownership of land and real estate that provided work for others. That is, gentlemen and gentlewomen did not work but rather lived on the income generated by the labor of others. This kind of thinking began to change somewhat in the late fifteenth century for several reasons. Land had ceased to be a reliable source of wealth for the nobility in some parts of Europe, and merchant activities, fueled by exploration and colonialism, increasingly became the basis of wealth. Indeed, the seventeenth century saw the emergence of what is now called the Protestant work ethic, a bourgeois (middle-class) outlook that values work not only for the wealth it produces but as a good in and of itself. At the same time, many who aspired to gentle status took pains to distance themselves from the actual mercantile labor that produced their wealth, and they often purchased traditional landed estates as a sign of their gentility. The emerging dominance of mercantilism also meant the emergence and ultimate political, social, and economic dominance of the middle class, those whose livelihoods were not primarily connected to the land but who tended to live in towns and cities rather than in the country and who developed other ways to advertise their wealth and status. For some groups of Renaissance people, most notably the Jews, mercantile activity was always the source of their work and wealth, as they were in most places pro-hibited from owning land.

While it is essential to distinguish between the kind of work done by people of different classes living in different parts of any coun-try, it is nonetheless accurate to say that all Renaissance women worked. The culture at large tended to see their work primarily in domestic and familial terms, however much they may have been involved in other kinds of labor, and any discussion of Renaissance women and work must deal with their experience of motherhood and domestic work. Then as now, most women would *not* have spent most of their lives engaged solely in tending to the needs of their own families, even when they lived in their own households. Though there was great regional variation in terms of family com-position, age of marriage, and women's domestic situation, the masses of people in all parts of Europe—female and male, wealthy and poor—would have spent at least part of their lives working in someone else's household. They would have served either as apprentices learning trades, as domestic servants, or as children "fostered" with other families to be trained, educated, and intro-duced to social and political duties. Most women would have worked as servants in other's households some or all of the time, either living there or returning home daily to their own families. Rural women whose families were tenants on a great estate would have spent part of their time working in the fields and tending live-stock. Elite women supervised the running of large households and their staffs and were responsible themselves for certain kinds of domestic work. And urban middle-class women, an emerging group in this period, would always have been active in family busi-nesses in addition to being responsible for domestic work and child-care. A small number of women were in charge of money-making activities, including widows of great landowners who con-trolled their own land and assets and women who ran businesses; among the latter, some were widows of urban merchants, and some went into business independently.

All that said, the essential work of raising children and all that it entailed, not to mention the work of giving birth to them and assisting in childbirth, fell almost entirely to women. However, it should not be assumed that men never lent women a hand in car-ing for children. Glückel of Hameln noted in her diary that "Abra-ham Kantor of Hildesheim was our first servant; he looked after our children."[1] And the German theologian Martin Luther coun-

This hurtlesse beast with meeke moode yelds his woll
And skin. to cloth our naked clotte of claye
He giues his flesh to feede our bellies full
Nought for him selfe he bringe but for our staye

June
Cancer

mayd milke cleane

Sheepshearing and milking, Thomas Fella, *Divers Devises and Sortes of Pictures. Source:* Reproduced by permission of the Folger Shakespeare Library, 51v, V.a.311.

seled men that "when a father goes ahead and washes diapers or performs some other mean task for his child, and someone ridicules him as an effeminate fool…, which of the two is most keenly ridiculing the other? God, with all His angels and creatures, is smiling—not because that father is washing diapers, but because he is doing so in Christian faith."[2] Luther's comments suggest that while men's tending to babies was open to ridicule, it was not uncommon. Nonetheless, in Luther's commendation of child care, there is an underlying assumption that the work is first and foremost women's work. Even nuns, who of course had no children of their own, would often provide schooling for privileged girls and so would be part of the network of caretaking women who guaranteed the survival and success of each household and community from one generation to the next. Many women worked in the nurseries of wealthy houses, feeding, bathing, teaching, playing with, and sleeping with babies and children. Elite women, both those who lived in great luxury and those of more modest means, did not necessarily breast-feed or care for their children's basic needs, but that work was always done by women nonetheless.

Bathing a child, Gregor Reisch, *Margarita Philosophica* (Strassburg, 1504). *Source:* Reproduced by permission of the University of Arizona Library Special Collections, AE3.R36.

Indeed, moralists of the era encouraged women to breast-feed their babies, arguing that the virtue and even the class status of the mother passed through her milk to the baby; the noble child breast-fed by a servant woman, they warned, would inevitably be tainted by her milk. As Jacques Guillemeau declared in a 1612 treatise on childbirth and infancy, "We may be assured, that the Milke (wherewith the child is nourish'd two years together) hath as much power to make the children like the Nurses, both in bodie and mind, as the seed of the Parents hath to make the children like them."[3] This logic fueled concerns of Catholic parents whose children were ingesting "Protestant milk," and vice versa. Moralists also equated true motherhood and, by inference, true womanhood with breast-feeding. Nonetheless, the practice of hiring wet nurses to feed babies gained in popularity among women during this period. Wet-nursing might free a new mother to do wage work in a job that did not allow her to bring her child along. At the same time, the practice provided the wet nurse with essential income, as she breast-fed both her own baby and the child of her employer. (In late fourteenth-century Italy, wet nurses for merchant families typically earned about twelve florin a year, which was equivalent to the salary earned by most female servants.) Sometimes (though not always) there would not be enough milk for both babies, and both the servant's child and her mistress's child would be undernourished, with the wet nurse's own child paying the larger price in terms of health, growth, and, in the worst cases, life itself. In other cases, the wet nurse would have ample milk, either because her own baby had died or had been weaned or because she was a healthy woman with plenty of milk for two babies.

Women were the primary educators of early modern children, whether their own or, in the case of convent schools in Catholic countries, of the daughters of elite families. A number of women's religious orders, including the Ursulines and the Institute of the Blessed Virgin Mary, were founded in the seventeenth century with the goal of educating girls; some convents housed highly skilled nuns who could teach music, art, and literature. Women in Protestant countries might also run small schools for middle-class children where they could learn their letters and numbers. Girls of all social classes were expected to be able to spin and sew. Daughters of aristocratic households, however, would learn elegant needlework rather than cloth making or lace making, which were for the most part urban industries in this period. Literate mothers taught their sons and daughters to read, and while sons in wealthy families would be sent to boarding schools at a very early age, the education of daughters was generally confined to the home. (See also chapter 1: "Women and Education.")

The nature of women's work was dependent on the kind of family or household in which a woman lived, and the composition of early modern families varied greatly from region to region. The nuclear family (parents and their children with perhaps a servant or two) was probably the norm within the lower and middle classes in parts of Europe at the time. This was particularly true in England, where only the greatest, most wealthy families lived in households that included multiple generations, the children of near and distant relatives, and servants of all sorts (including tutors and music teachers). The great households might even have a family priest and a number of artists, architects, and writers working on various projects, all of whom would be understood to be "in service" to the lord and lady of the estate or villa and to be part of the family household. In other areas, including parts of France, Germany, Italy, and Spain, the extended family household was far more common, even the norm. In such extended families, three or four generations of a variety of siblings, cousins, parents, aunts, uncles, and grandparents lived in the same household. But the pattern varied greatly from town to town, even within the same region, and it is very difficult to generalize for this period. In all areas, however, because of high rates of maternal mortality and generally short life spans, many households would have included stepchildren and orphaned children being raised by family members or godparents.

The number of children a woman had varied greatly according to class and place. While a childless marriage was seen as a drawback both in terms of familial affection and economic security, it could be a liability to have too many children, especially in times of economic hardship. Families with 7 to 14 live births were not uncommon among the wealthy during this period, but peasants generally had fewer children. Infants and mothers were always at tremendous risk of dying from infections and complications during birth. Malnutrition and a higher incidence of breast-feeding (including wet-nursing) resulted in a somewhat lower birthrate among the poor. Most couples controlled family size through contraception, abortion, the fostering of "surplus" children into domestic service or apprenticeship, or infanticide. Although the Church decreed as early as the ninth century that any form of contraception other than abstinence was an act of murder, many women of all classes tried to regulate the size of their family by preventing pregnancy.

> Peasant women had their own ways of avoiding conception and, once pregnant, of aborting the fetus. They believed in douches and purges, spermicides like salt, honey, oil, tar, lead, mint juice, cabbage seed; some abortificants like lead and ergot were effective but dangerous. With enough lead ingested, a woman became permanently sterile. Other substances might purge her system but would not directly affect the pregnancy, such as douches or teas of rosemary, myrtle, coriander, willow leaves, balsam, myrrh, clover seeds, parsley, and animal urine. More effective would be the cervical caps and vaginal blocks mentioned in German and Hungarian sources, like beeswax or a linen rag. Peasant women believed actions prevented conception: drinking cold liquids, remaining passive during intercourse, holding one's breath, jumping up and down afterward.[4]

When efforts to avoid conception failed, abortion was a hazardous option. Some mothers, especially unmarried women and particularly those among the poorest classes, practiced infanticide.[5] Records show that girls were more likely to be killed at birth than were boys; analysis of parish records throughout Europe suggests that female newborns died in far greater numbers than did males. In other cases, unwanted children might be abandoned, given to a foundling house (orphanage), a religious order, or a house of prostitution (blasphemously called a "nunnery" in early modern England) to be raised by the women there and trained in the trade. Despite such practices, however, most couples held that one of the primary duties of marriage was reproduction.

During the Renaissance, when the average life span was around forty for those who survived into adulthood (up to one-third of children died before age 5, and just under 50% survived to the age of 15), most people living in northern Europe married relatively late in their lives; the average age was around twenty-five for women and twenty-seven for men. In southern and eastern Europe, the typical marriage was between teenagers; they would live for a number of years in the household of his or her parents before establishing their own household or until the parents died and the younger couple became the householders. Another common marriage arrangement in these areas was between a man in his thirties and a much younger woman, often still in her teens. In northern Europe, on the other hand, couples were expected to be economically independent at their marriage, and this is one reason why smaller households and the nuclear family tended to predominate there. Between 10 and 25 percent of women in any area or time period never married at all. In southern Europe, where women married young, or in communities where marriages were still arranged by parents while the bride and groom were still very young (such as was the case in Jewish communities), women were less likely to remain unmarried.[6] Glückel of Hameln was betrothed at 12 and wrote of her marriage, "After my wedding my parents returned home and left me, a child not yet fourteen, in a strange town, among strangers."[7] Elite girls and women living in Catholic countries were likely to enter a convent or other religious order if they did not marry. Unmarried women in largely Protestant northern Europe were more likely to migrate to towns and cities where there were more opportunities for single women in emerging manufacturing and in mercantile work, though many of them would have ended up in domestic service.

Since the ideals of the period understood women's work in terms of the domestic sphere and motherhood, single women's mobility seemed particularly improper to their contemporaries; some laws sought to regulate women's mobility as well as that of the working poor, who might move from town to town looking for work and end up as beggars. England passed a series of "poor laws" to regulate the movements and opportunities for impoverished vagrants and to attempt to provide stopgap relief, but it was unclear whether and how society at large was responsible to provide relief to the poor. It had once been the responsibility of churches to care for the poor within their parish boundaries, but the Reformation broke down a system that had already been weakened by the Black Death. With the geographic mobility of laborers, the parish was no longer a functional economic unit. Nonetheless, authorities attempted to resettle vagrants, especially women, whose labor was seen as superfluous or as undermining men's employment opportunities, and to send them back to their previous dwelling or to the parish of their birth, however ridiculous that policy might be for someone who had left home ten or twenty years ago. The results were horrific, as the records of vagrant trials and their "passports" show. Passports were author-izations that allowed vagrants to travel through the countryside from the place where they had been arrested and to beg on their way to where they had been sent. The record of passports here (from the late sixteenth and early seventeenth centuries in Wilt-shire, England) lists the charges against the holders, their punish-ment (often whipping), and the amount of time they were allowed to travel on their way back to their place of residence. The docu-ments are of great interest because they provide a glimpse into the struggles of poor women and men to find work and to feed themselves and their families.

- Grace Martyn, wandering and begging, was punished. Passport to Lawnsowe, Cornw., where she says she was born; 1 month allowed. By order of the Lord Chief Justice she has taken her 3 children, William, Agnes, and Jane Martyn, being under the age of 7 years, with her.

- Rebecca Wilkes alias Seymor alias Anne Wilkes, a vagrant accompa-nied by four other idle persons, who confesses that she travels from fair to fair, was punished. Passport to Twyfford, Hants, where she says she was born; 2 days assigned.

- Olive Hallame, a wandering person using the trade of a petty chap-man [trader], selling small wares contrary to the statute, was pun-ished. Passport to St. James's parish, Bristoll, where she says her dwelling is; 5 days assigned.

- Anne Hamersley, wandering and a vagrant, confesses that she was in Fisherton gaol [jail] and was discharged out of the prison at the last assizes at Marleboroughe, and so came wandering to this city. She was punished. Assigned 8 days to go to St. John's Street, London, where she says she last dwelt.

- Thomas Pistoe and Joan his wife were taken idle, wandering, and using the trade of a tinker [mender of tin pots and other metal items]. He was punished and she was spared because she was great with child. Assigned 6 days to go to Wynscombe, Som., where their dwelling is.

- One naming herself Elizabeth Sherwood, wife of George Sherwood of St. Philip's parish, Bristoll, was found wandering and because she is with child her punishment was spared. Assigned 5 days to go to Bristoll. She stole venison from Mr. Sidenham's house.

- Margaret Farr, daughter of Thomas Farr, deceased, of Horton, Dors., whose last dwelling was with Jane Norris, widow, at Whit Waltham, Berks., where she was begotten with child by Wilding Norris, son of Jane, and who was delivered of the child at Wotton Bassett about three weeks ago, came to this city last Saturday to Elizabeth Wheler, a poorwoman, her mother-in-law, and brought with her the bastard child named Jeremy. Margaret affirmed that Wilding Norris is her husband. Because she was not dwelling here and her mother [in-law] is unable to relieve her, she has a passport to Waltham to her pretended husband.

- Alice Barley, widow, wandering, was spared her punishment because of her weakness and feebleness. Assigned 3 days to go to Upper Walloppe, Hants, where she says she was born.

- Agnes Symons, daughter of William Symons late of Lyttleton, Som., wandering and begging, was punished. She confessed that she had wandered for the last two years. Assigned 10 days to go to Lyttleton where she says she was born.

- Grace and Abraham Tuke, wandering with two small children, not giving any cause of their wandering, were punished. Passport to Froome Selwood, Som., where they say their dwelling is. Suspected of stealing a piece of cloth from Mr. Coward; they had a new pair of shoes and confess they had no money.

- Nathaniel Leache, a poor child about 9 or 10 years of age, likely to perish and die in the streets with cold, was taken begging and crying. Passport to Lyndhurste, Hants, where he says he was born.[8]

It is clear from these and other records that women who were widowed or orphaned, women who were impregnated by men who did not provide for them, or women who had left their husbands for reasons that can now only be guessed were particularly at risk. They and their children often had little recourse but to beg. In addition, they were always at the mercy of public prejudice and a legal system that stood ready to blame them for their poverty and to punish them for their misfortunes.

Throughout Europe, a disproportionate number of the adult poor were women. In a 1561 census for Segovia, Spain, women accounted for 60 percent of the urban poor. And less than a decade later in Norwich, England, female indigents outnumbered males by almost two to one. Increasingly, the poor were regarded with suspicion, contempt, and fear. Venetian poor laws in 1527, 1529, and 1545 required that all beggars must be licensed, and many other cities followed this practice. The laws were more punitive than protective; they specified that poor men and women would be required to work for their alms, whatever their physical debility.[9] During the Renaissance, city officials sometimes attempted to establish education and training programs for orphans and unem-

Woman begging with her children, [Anon.], *Cryes of the City of London*. *Source:* Reproduced by permission of the Folger Shakespeare Library, DA 688L2Cage.

ployed youth. In France and Italy in the early sixteenth century, such programs were instituted to teach orphans to read and write, and the boys were apprenticed to various artisans to learn trades. Girls were excluded from those apprenticeships for the most part (though some were taught to unwind silk for thread) and tended rather to be taught religion, good manners, and spinning in order to make them fit for domestic service. Girls and young women who had been prostitutes were invited to leave sex work and join the convent of Filles Repentiés (repentant girls) where they might earn a living doing needlework or other crafts. In France, repeated famines and the dislocation of workers led officials to abandon these programs, and a series of poor laws were passed to deal with the problem of "sturdy beggars" and vagabonds (the able-bodied poor), those who wandered from town to town looking for work and food. The latter were treated more harshly; either they were sent back to where they came from, as they were later in the century in England, or they were shackled and forced to do hard labor, the Renaissance version of the chain gang. Both women and men suffered this punishment; they were known as the *pauvres enchaînés* (the poor in chains). Others deemed deserving of help might receive assistance from the city coffers and from the guilds, but those from the "respectable" ranks of artisans were more likely to receive aid than those who had no such connections. Such a prejudice favored men over women (who were less likely to have learned such skills) and the middle class over peasants and servants. Children and women, particularly widows, suffered the most. While some widows were able to inherit property and a livelihood on their husband's death, many were thrown on the mercy of family members, if they had any. Many became day laborers, washerwomen, or prostitutes, never sure from day to day whether they would eat or be able to feed their children. Households headed by widows were always the poorest category in any region during this period. Children were especially vulnerable to poverty; without adult protection and support, only the strong and the lucky avoided an early death due to disease and malnutrition.

As the Wiltshire passport documents and other contemporary evidence reveal, sex and childbirth outside marriage were fairly common in some areas. The practice of confirming fertility through premarital sex and conception seems to have been more common in France than in other parts of Europe, and more common among the working poor than the upper classes. Premarital conception may have been especially widespread among farming families, where the labor of children was essential to economic survival and an infertile wife would be a great liability. (Women were more likely than men to be blamed for infertility.) Extramarital sex was directly linked to economic security for prostitutes, of course, and the recourse of married men to these sex workers was also a tactic to limit fertility within the family. Sex workers, then as today, included impoverished women who sold their services for a few pennies, independent women of essentially middle-class status who supported themselves by their sexual labor, and elite mistresses of kings and wealthy, powerful noblemen. Prostitution was often a state- or city-regulated activity, and in some areas, prostitutes had to wear distinctive clothing or armbands to mark them from other women. The popular English song "Greensleeves" may refer to a prostitute, as green was associated with loss of sexual innocence; one got a "green gown" by rolling in the grass with a sexual partner. Some cities, especially in Italy, were tolerant of prostitution, in part because they saw the use of prostitutes as a means for protecting the virginity of "good" women and in part because they saw it as an important economic activity that enriched the town coffers through taxes paid by the brothels. The same motives prompted the city government in Lisbon, Portugal, to build and operate a brothel that brought in significant tax revenue. Local councils in Nuremberg, Germany, and Toulouse, France, strictly regulated the profits of brothels and the activities of prostitutes. German officials even specified where the sex workers could sit in church, and some French town governments had prostitutes fined and whipped for conducting business outside the jurisdiction of official brothels.

Prostitution was held to be useful not only as a source of government revenue but also as a so-called treatment for male homosexuality. In the early fifteenth century, the city leaders of Florence sponsored a brothel for foreign prostitutes who would be allowed to dress as they liked within the city. It was thought that they would entice young Florentine men and wean them from youthful homosexuality, a practice that was so widespread in Florence at the time that the birthrate had precipitously dropped. Perhaps not surprisingly, many of the Florentine prostitutes were transvestites, dressing as boys and wearing their hair short in order to attract those clients who preferred male sexual partners to female ones. These women often appear in court records, as transvestism, or cross-dressing, was against the law.[10] In other towns that did not provide so lavishly for such women, successful prostitutes might nonetheless buy their way out of the special dress requirements for a fee. The poorest women were in constant danger from all the diseases of poverty: starvation and illness of all sorts, including sexually transmitted diseases, for which there were no effective treatments. Syphilis was a European-wide epidemic by the beginning of the sixteenth century. In response to the uncontrolled spread of the disease, some authorities attempted to outlaw brothels; in addition, they savagely punished prostitutes with beating, dunking in an iron cage, or mutilation. By the end of the sixteenth century, however, many officials of both church and state decided that prostitution was a necessary evil. Many brothels were reopened. A Spanish church authority explained the public service performed by the brothel: "It is like the stable or latrine for the house. Because just as the city keeps itself clean by providing a separate place where filth and dung are gathered, etc., so … acts the brothel: where the filth and ugliness of the flesh are gathered like the garbage and dung of the city."[11] Regarded as the "sewers" of society, prostitutes were constantly vulnerable to public humiliation and violence. Some men, for either "moral" reasons or as a kind of violent and cruel sport, slashed prostitutes' faces, threw acid at them, and even cut off their noses (the punishment deemed appropriate for such women).

Other prostitutes lived in relative comfort and were able to secure economic stability by saving and investing money and perhaps running a house of prostitution where they employed younger women and took a cut of their profits. More highly educated courtesans might offer their clients a variety of cultural services like musical and dramatic performance in addition to sex. Mistresses of elite men might be regally treated for a few years with gifts of jewels and perhaps private apartments, though they could easily be cast off either when they became too old or when they became pregnant. Aemilia Bassano (Lanyer) (1569–1645), the daughter of court musicians to Queen Elizabeth I, was the mistress of the queen's Lord Chamberlain, Henry Carey, Lord Hunsdon (45 years her senior). During their affair, he gave her an allowance of £45 a year and presents of fine jewelry. When she became pregnant at 23, she was married off to a court musician, Alphonso Lanyer, and Carey no doubt moved on to another, younger mistress. Other mistresses of kings and noblemen were often given a title and an income for life (as were the many mistresses of Charles II of England). They might even hob nob with nobility and royalty, as did Ninon de Lenclos (1620–1705), who socialized with the future queen of France and was the mistress and friend of French luminaries like the politician François de la Rochefoucauld (1613–1680) and the playwright Molière (1622–1673).

The delivery of babies was almost exclusively the purview of female midwives in Europe until the middle of the seventeenth century. Women supervised the entire birthing process from labor through postpartum care. The midwife as well as the new mother's friends would assist her for weeks after the delivery, fix-

Woman on a birthing chair with astrologers casting the baby's horo-
scope, Eucharius Rösslin, *The Byrthe of Mankynde,* trans. Thomas Ray-
nalde (London, 1565). *Source:* © Bodleian Library, University of Oxford, 4°
R 1 Med.Seld., folio 3r.

ing meals, caring for any older children and other family members, and keeping house so that the mother had ample time to
recover and to care for the new baby. Those in charge were either
professional midwives or, in rural areas where there were no
trained specialists, women experienced in having babies or assisting with deliveries. Glückel of Hameln, who was pregnant and
ready to deliver her child, wrote of her mother attending the birth,
even though her mother herself was pregnant and about to
deliver a child of her own.

About the time we came to Hamburg I became pregnant, and my mother, long may she live, was in the same condition. Though I was still a child to whom such unaccustomed things came hard, I was happy when the All Highest presented me with a beautiful, healthy baby. My mother expected her child about the same time, but was pleased that I had had mine first and that she could attend me and the child the first few days. Eight days later she also gave birth to a daughter, so there was no envy or reproach between us. We lay in one room, beside each other, and had no peace from the people who came running to see the wonder of mother and daughter lying in childbed together.[12]

Their proximity later resulted in an amusing mix-up:

It was winter time and my mother and I lay together in a small room…. I left childbed eight days before my mother, and to make the rooms less crowded returned to my own chamber. As I was still so young, my mother would not let me take my baby to my room at night. So, the baby was left in her room, where she and also her maid slept. My mother told me not to worry; if the baby cried she would send the maid with it for me to suckle it and later return the babe to its cradle…. For several nights all went well: usually, as I lay in bed, about midnight, the maid would bring the baby to be fed. One morning, about three o-clock, I awoke with a start and cried to my husband, "What can be the matter? the maid has not yet brought the baby!" … I ran to my mother's room to see what had happened to the babe. I went straight to the cradle: it was empty! … I went over to the maid and began to shake her, hoping to rouse her quietly. But she was in a deep sleep. I had to shout before I could rouse her from her torpor…. My mother—long may she live—woke up. She too cried to the maid, "Where is Glückel's baby?" … Then I said to my mother, "Mumma, perhaps you have my baby in bed with you?" She answered, "No! I have *mine* in bed with me," and held it close to her as though someone was trying to snatch the baby away. I bethought me to go to the other cradle, and there lay her baby, fast asleep! I said, "Mumma, give me *my* baby, *yours* is in the cradle." But she would not believe me, so I had to fetch a light and take her baby to her, so that she could see for herself before she returned my own to me. The whole household had been awakened and alarmed, but soon the consternation turned to laughter, and they said we would really have needed King Solomon soon.[13]

Husbands were not allowed in the birthing room unless the wife was dying. Early in this period, male doctors did not become involved in childbirth cases unless the mother, baby, or both were dead or dying. Gradually, however, women lost control of midwifery, and "male midwives," or physicians, began to dominate the field of child-birth as well as all other areas of medical practice. The shift occurred partly because midwives' earnings increased during the period as they ministered to a wealthier, middle-class, urban population; when the profession became more lucrative, male practitioners became interested in pursuing it. At the same time, women were excluded from the universities and medical centers that trained students in dissection, anatomy, and technological innovations. Among the latter was the forceps, an instrument that pulled the baby through the birth canal and in some cases enabled successful deliveries that might otherwise have ended in death for mother, child, or both. Only male midwives were trained in the use of forceps, so women were perceived as having less scientific and technological expertise. (In fact, records suggest that the forceps caused far more damage than good in most deliveries.) Gradually, women's lack of access to developments in the study of anatomy, combined with time-honored views about the intellectual and moral inferiority of females, contributed to their disenfranchisement in the profession, though midwives remained numerous and important among the rural and urban poor and have survived as an integral part of the European medical system to the present day.

Throughout the Renaissance, female midwives were trained in apprenticeships with experienced practitioners. Often the training period lasted for many years before a woman would oversee a delivery on her own. This was true in unregulated practices as well as in countries that controlled the accreditation of the profession. The typical period of apprenticeship in Germany and Spain was four years, while it was three or four years in France and the Netherlands; in England as much as seven years of tutelage was required. In the fifteenth and sixteenth centuries, licensing of midwives became increasingly common in Europe. Often town councils hired midwives who would be licensed to practice locally; the midwives in such areas could not practice until they were approved by both secular and church officials. In Lille, Paris, Regensburg, and Strasbourg, for example, doctors questioned midwife applicants to determine their competence, and the local bishop administered an oath of office before they would be granted a license. In England, regulating midwives was the provenance of the Church of England from the early sixteenth century.

Parish priests in Italy supervised female practitioners, who were not, however, required to obtain licenses from secular authorities. Physicians regulated midwives in seventeenth-century Spain, while city governments and town councils controlled them in Germany and the Netherlands.

Ecclesiastical licensing of midwives took place for a number of reasons. After the Reformation, both Protestant and Catholic nations were anxious to ensure that baptisms were performed in "the true faith." Midwives were allowed to administer the rite of baptism to newborns and even to babies that died during delivery, but they were required to swear an oath that they would follow the ceremony dictated by the ruling church. In addition, they promised to report truthfully all details of the birth, including parentage, so that officials could track bastardy; they swore never to switch babies, extort fees, perform abortions, or harm infants, and they promised to report the malpractice of other midwives. They also swore to summon male physicians when mother, baby, or both were likely to die. This was because doctors and surgeons had the instruments to cut, hook, and dismember bodies in deliveries that required catastrophic measures.

Although historians disagree about the degree of competence midwives possessed in the period, many concur that the profession was rigorously supervised by the seventeenth century. In addition to their years of apprenticeship with an experienced practitioner, most women had to demonstrate both expertise and integrity. These attributes were attested to by witnesses who provided testimonials about the midwife's character and competence. In a few cases, women were allowed a more formal training. In sixteenth-century Padua, for example, a clinic for teaching midwives was founded, and in 1560 the surgeons of the Hôtel Dieu in Paris established a course in childbirth, culminating in a comprehensive exam that towns throughout France adopted. In the Netherlands, midwives took exams in anatomy, delivery procedures, and childbirth complications before they could be licensed. Formal training was rare, however, and the most common sources of information for midwives were the manuals that female practitioners published during the period and what was learned from other midwives to whom they were formally or informally apprenticed.

One of the most celebrated of these manuals was by the Frenchwoman Louise Bourgeois (1563–1636). A mother of three and a lace maker, she apprenticed herself to a midwife at the age of 24 and began practicing in Paris by 1593. Bourgeois became the most respected authority on midwifery in Europe. She was midwife to the Queen of France, Marie de' Medicis (1573–1642), and she published the definitive reference work on childbirth in 1609. Having supervised nearly two thousand deliveries, she provided detailed illustrations and specific instructions for prenatal care, miscarriages, premature births, hemorrhaging, stillbirths, breach births, induced labor, and postpartum care. Another authoritative guide was Jane Sharp's *The Midwives Book on the Whole Art of Midwifery* (1671), written after Sharp had practiced midwifery for 30 years. The Dutch midwife Catharina Schrader (1656–1746) participated in more than three thousand deliveries during her career. In her eighties, she published a collection of cases that were culled from numerous notebooks she kept during her long and extraordinarily successful practice.

Dutch midwives were unusually privileged in the seventeenth century. They were exempt from taxes on tea, coffee, beer, and some spirits. Town councils throughout the country provided midwives with a salary, free accommodations, and even retirement benefits. Midwives in London during the same century were typically middle-class wives or widows with a remarkably high literacy rate of 86 percent. They needed to be economically solvent to afford the relatively expensive licensing fees. Given the considerable time and cash required to establish oneself in the profession, it was rare for London women to be unskilled—what were known as "dilettante midwives," those with no expertise who assisted in deliveries simply to make quick money. Records suggest that most of the practitioners were committed professionals with years of training and experience.

Women also served as healers beyond their role as midwives, as the care of the sick had traditionally been women's purview. But, like midwives, healers were gradually supplanted in this work by men, who had access to the increasingly professionalized training that was confined to educational institutions from which women were barred. There were notable exceptions to this rule—Isabel Warwike was permitted to practice medicine in York, England, in 1572 because she had "skill in the scyens of Surgery and hath done good therin," and other documents record women's licensing and payment for medical services.[14] But most women practiced medicine without an official license, some working alongside their licensed fathers or husbands and others carrying on the tradition of women's healing that was passed from mother to daughter. Nonetheless, hospitals—places where the impoverished and chronically ill went to be cared for as they died—were staffed almost entirely by women, and women continued to provide home remedies to the great majority of the population who could not afford the fees of a licensed male physician. Indeed, housewives were expected to be able to provide most basic medical care, including herbal remedies, for the members of their households; every woman with even the smallest plot of land at her disposal was expected to grow medicinal herbs. Women's exclusion from the emerging medical schools may have contributed to the prolif- eration during this period of many books by women on nursing techniques as well as recipe books, which usually had as many recipes for potions and cures as for food preparation. In her *Choice Manuall, or Rare and Select Secrets in Physick*, the English- woman Elizabeth Grey, Countess of Kent (1581–1651), provided instruction on a wide range of medical practices and medicines. Here is her cure for anemia:

> *A powder for the green sickness, approved with very good success upon many.* Take of cloves, mace, nutmegs, of each one quarter of an ounce, beat them severally [separately], and then altogether very well, fine sugar very small beaten and one quart of a pound, and then mix and beat them all four together, pearl the sixth part of half an ounce very finely beaten, mingle it with the rest, and beat them altogether again, the filing of steel or iron one ounce and quarter, sift it very fine, and mingle it with the rest....
>
> *The manner of using this powder.* In the morning when you rise take half a spoonful of it, take as much at four o'clock in the after- noon, and as much when you go to bed, walk or stir much after the first takings of it, or more, and then eat some sugar sops or thin broth.
>
> *The patient's diet.* She must forbear oatmeal in broth or any other thing, cheese, eggs, custards, or any stopping meat [food that would make her constipated]. Take care that this be not given to any woman that hath conceived, or is with child.[15]

Even in death, women cared for their family, friends, and neigh- bors; they washed the bodies of the dead and dressed them for burial.

The single largest occupation for women in the Renaissance was domestic service; sixty percent of European urban women were employed as domestic servants in the late fifteenth century. Male servants had been the ideal in the aristocratic country houses and palaces in the late Middle Ages, but women gradually came to supplant men in the great houses. In rural England, however, the bulk of the household staff were male well into the seventeenth century; men outnumbered women in aristocratic country households by as much as 20 to 1, a holdover from the Middle Ages when such great houses were military strongholds. The predominance of men also represents social and economic relationships of clientage and patronage, the ladder of professional success for men of the era. Being "in service" to a powerful nobleman was the only way to get political appointments of all sorts or to rise within the ranks on the estate itself and take on supervisory roles. Because of the mythical association of the household with military service and its ties to professional and political work, women were systematically excluded from even what today might be considered "women's work," such as cooking and cleaning. The only activities that seem nearly always to have been in women's purview were child care and laundry, and even laundresses often lived away from the estate, reducing women's numbers in the house even further.[16] Aristocratic women would have their personal female attendants, but they and the elite women living in the house, including the lady, her daughters, and female relatives of rank, would have been mostly confined to limited areas of the house. One notable exception to this pattern was in the household of Elizabeth Talbot, Countess of Shrewsbury (1527–1608). She was better known as Bess of Hardwick on account of the great house she built, Hardwick Hall. Bess's housekeeper, Mrs. Digby, was the best-paid servant in Bess's household, earning three times as much as her husband (who was also Bess's servant). Digby's high status is no doubt attributable to Bess's own sense of women's capabilities and worth; Bess survived four husbands to inherit and manage one of the wealthiest estates of her era. But the situation in her household was exceptional.

Women servants gradually came to supplant men in the noble households, and they always predominated in lesser households. In seventeenth-century France, more than 60 percent of the servants in noble households were female, and, in professional families, the number rose to 94 percent. In England, women ultimately supplanted men in nearly all domestic work, even in the great households. But the significance of that work shifted absolutely with the change, a phenomenon that is now known as "occupational resegregation": when a job previously held exclusively (or nearly so) by men comes to be seen as "women's work," that work ceases to have the status it previously had and is compensated more poorly than before.[17] Furthermore, women were never able to advance from some kinds of household service into political and public employment; for them, being in service in an aristocratic house was dead-end employment with no opportunity for advancement outside the household, while men could move into political work by serving a powerful aristocrat or courtier.

In most households women were paid significantly less than men, in some areas only one-third what men earned, while they put in even longer hours than their male counterparts. This gender imbalance in terms of numbers shifted over the sixteenth and seventeenth centuries as opportunities for men's advancement moved out of the traditional estate and became increasingly urban and professionalized. And urban households in England always had a preponderance of women servants, though there were certain roles that were always reserved for men—butler, footman, and coach driver, for instance. The tendency to employ women in urban areas of England may have been brought about by repeated epidemics of the Black Death (bubonic plague) that ravaged the population and made all laborers, including servants, less plentiful. Besides making women domestic servants more common and even fashionable, the shortage of laborers in the late Middle Ages also opened previously proscribed urban mercantile activities to women. This phenomenon survives in English family names (and the resulting common words) ending in the feminine suffix "ster," including spinster (spinner), webster (weaver), sempster (seamstress), huckster (originally someone who sold bulk foods, but now a peddler of any sort), and brewster (brewer of beer), to name only a few. Particularly in areas of textile production, women might significantly outnumber men in Renaissance cities. Spinning tended to remain women's work in all eras; even noblewomen were encouraged to spin thread and yarn and to do needlework to keep their hands and minds from idleness. Penelope, the wife of Odysseus in Homer's epic Greek poem, was often cited in the Renaissance as a

Geertruydt Roghman, *A Woman Cleaning* (ca. 1640). *Source:* Reproduced by permission of Davison Art Center, Wesleyan University. Photo by R. J. Phil.

model of womanliness for her faithfulness to her husband, symbolized by her weaving.

Women and men who lived on smaller parcels of land (that they either owned or rented from a large landowner) would work alongside the household servants, supervising that work but also pitching in and getting their hands dirty. In the very poorest of these tenant families, both women and men would work in the fields, sometimes even pulling the plows, as only the most prosperous would own draft animals like horses or oxen. Other farm

Geertruydt Roghman, *A Woman Spinning* (ca. 1640). *Source:* Museum of Fine Arts, Boston. Harvey D. Parker Collection. Photograph © 2004 Museum of Fine Arts, Boston.

laborers, women and men, were mobile, following the harvest from farm to farm and village to village. But, in general, women's work on a small estate would be differentiated from men's. While the husband (a term that refers to the "husbanding" or care of the land and all that lives on it, from plants to birds, to beasts, to people) would be responsible for the oversight of the entire estate, most treatises on husbandry charged wives with the care of the household and nearby crops and animals. So women would oversee the kitchen garden, where they grew plants for medicinal as well as food use (herbs, onions, peas, beans, and other vegetables), while their husbands would oversee the planting of crops like barley and other grains. Similarly, women would tend to the chickens and other domesticated fowl, while men were responsible for cattle, pigs, sheep, and horses. Women usually milked cows and oversaw the dairy with its production of cheese and butter, the "white meats," as they were called, that were essential to early modern diets. These traditional divisions were not absolute; everyone on a small estate, women and men alike, would have been capable of turning a hand to a wide variety of tasks as needed. In harvesttime, for instance, everyone on the estate would have been involved in the crucial task of getting in the grain before it spoiled. And widows were both housewife and husband, responsible for overseeing all farmwork.

A sixteenth-century English book on "good houswifery" by Thomas Tusser (1524–1580) specified the duties of a woman responsible for overseeing a large estate. Tusser's descriptions and admonitions provide many details of the work of all the servants in the household, not only the woman in charge. The housewife was to set her servants to work as soon as the morning cock crowed (at 5:00 A.M. in the winter and 4:00 A.M. in the summer, though some accounts show servants rising as early as 2:00 A.M.) so that a considerable amount of work could be done before breakfast. Only when some work was done and the sun was up was the household to sit down to breakfast: a dish of pottage (stewed vegetables and dried peas) with a little meat. Immediately afterward, the estate's beasts were fed. Housewives were particularly admonished to oversee the brewing and baking themselves. Beer, sometimes called liquid bread as it was made of the same grains as bread, was much lower in alcohol content than beer today and was an important part of early modern diets for children as well as adults. Bread itself was truly the staff of life. The housewife also oversaw the preserving of all foodstuffs and their cooking. To accomplish this work, she needed a good servant not only to help with the animals and in the dairy, but also to gather eggs from the hens as soon as they were laid; such a servant was more useful, said Tusser, than those who dressed in fine clothes. The dairy needed a cat as well as a trap to keep the vermin out of the grain and the dairy products, and the housewife was to take especial care if she put out poison for the rats, lest she poison the entire household.[18]

The Copperplate Map of London (ca. 1553–1559), including Moorfields where laundresses laid out clothes to dry. *Source:* © Museum of London.

The housewife was also to manage the washing, seeing that the clothes were well beaten, trampled, or boiled to remove stains and wrung out well, especially in the winter when there was little sun to dry them. Laundry might be washed in a running stream, in a special room or building, or even in the yard, depending on the weather. Homemade soap, made from a mixture of ashes and grease (mutton or pig fat, for instance), was used for washing some kinds of clothing. In more prosperous households, homemade soap tended to be used more for washing floors and pots than for laundry because it was so caustic and because it required the extra expense of warm or hot water to be effective. (Of course, all of these cleaning products were as caustic to the skin as they were to the linens they washed.) Milder commercially made soaps were available for laundry and personal use, but they were expensive. Linens and some clothing might be cleaned by soaking them in lye (made from ashes), stale urine, or water in which chicken dung had been steeped. They were then rinsed well and given a final rinse in an herbal infusion to take away any offensive smell. Linens might also be stored with dried herbs, especially lavender, to perfume them and to keep out bugs. Ashballs, ashes mixed with water and rolled into balls, were also used for scrubbing and cleaning, and some poor country women and children made a small income producing and selling them. They would set fire to cut wild ferns (which made the best cleaning ash) and other plants, pulverize the ashes, and roll them into balls for sale.[19] But the most popular and widely used cleaning product was elbow grease; everything from laundry to floors to fireplace grates was scrubbed and polished by hand, with or without some kind of soap.

Dinner, the largest meal of the day, was served at noon. The housewife would make sure that grace was said before that and every meal. The standard dinner was three courses. The housewife was urged not to give servants delicacies but to make sure they had enough to eat, because famished servants were less efficient. Most scraps went to the farm animals, but fat was particularly precious and was saved for a variety of uses: to grease farm implements, to make soap, and to make candles. After dinner, the housewife was to oversee household sewing, including mending grain sacks as well as blankets, sheets, and other linens, and, in some households, spinning and cloth making. All households collected feathers from their fowl for stuffing pillows and coverlets. Before supper, the cattle would need to be milked again, and servants would bring in wood for the fire and collect any clothes hanging out or tools left about; the only ones to come indoors empty-handed at the end of the day were the dogs, according to Tusser. Only then would the house be locked up and supper served, a portion of which was to be set aside for poor neighbor children and for the household dogs, who got the scraps. After supper, the housewife was to set aside the leaven, the yeasty starter that raised the bread to be baked the next day, and to set aside coals that would smolder until needed for the next morning's fires. The housewife sent the staff to bed (at 9:00 in the winter and 10:00 in the summer) and then checked to make sure that all the storecupboards were locked up (so that none of the servants could help themselves to food at night) and all fires put out.

Tusser described what he thought was the ideal household system, and it should not be assumed that all households ran like clockwork. Then, as today, some housekeepers were fussier than others. Furthermore, events like war, disease, and famine would interrupt even the best-managed estate, cutting rations, reducing available laborers, and devastating families in countless ways. Mass starvation was rare in England during this period, but it was still a feature of life in France, for instance, and events like the Thirty Years' War (1618–1648) disrupted the production and distribution of food in northern Europe and created poverty and hunger. Furthermore, all of Europe was becoming more urbanized. Consequently, there were fewer people living on farms and producing food, while at the same time, more people lived in cities and were in need of food (though often the cities had good food-distribution networks, and it was the smaller towns and rural areas that suffered most in times of bad harvest). But unlike Italy or Germany or France, England had only one really large city (London) until the nineteenth century and was quite rural in comparison to other countries; in the 1520s only 5.5 percent of the English population lived in towns of more than five thousand. Of those who were located outside towns, many would have lived in areas so remote that they might never in their lifetimes travel more than a few miles from home or visit even a village of more than a few dozen people.

Nonetheless, in England as elsewhere, economies in the small towns were well developed by this period, and local industries such as silk weaving, glass blowing, pottery making, and the production of cheese, soap, and other products were flourishing; many women found opportunities for work in those fields. But by 1670, town dwellers in England had more than doubled to 13.5 percent of the population, and by 1801, the figure had more than doubled again, to 27.5 percent. These figures show a significant shift in the way people lived their lives as well as the kind of work they did. But whether in rural or urban areas, women throughout Europe were limited to the least prestigious jobs, and they earned significantly less than males who performed the same work. An unskilled female laborer in late fourteenth-century Florence, for example, was paid less than half of what her male counterpart earned.

In addition to household work, domestic service, and agricultural labor, women in the period worked at construction sites and performed heavy labor. In Germany and what is now the Czech Republic, women worked alongside men in mines, panning for ore and hauling stones and boulders. In fourteenth-century Italy and France, females were part of the labor force that constructed cathedrals and colleges; they carried sand and bricks, dug ditches, and cleaned out latrines. Another source of heavy labor was in tending to the armies that traversed Europe during the Renaissance. Typically, only one half of the armies were soldiers, while the other half was made up of women and men who dug trenches; constructed campsites; gathered wood for fires; worked as prostitutes; cooked; cleaned; and ministered to the sick, wounded, or dead. As many as one in four of those marching in European armies were women.

Many fewer women than men managed businesses or joined guilds. Men controlled artisan activity, regulated training standards and work conditions, and determined how many artisans could practice a trade in any one town. When women did learn such trades, they tended to do so as wives or daughters of men who belonged to the guilds. There were many exceptions to this rule, of course; there were exclusively female guilds in sixteenth-century Paris, including the Lingères, who made handkerchiefs and linens, and the washerwomen, who rented space along the river Seine to do their washing. In all areas, women as well as men could serve apprenticeships, a period of years when young people would live in an artisan household and learn a trade or a craft. But girls were less likely to be apprenticed with the aim of learning an economic skill that would ultimately make them financially independent and were more likely to serve as household servants, a dead-end job for them. Though in some towns women could join guilds, there was hostility to their being licensed to practice their craft or trade even when they were highly skilled. In 1601, for example, the Genevan watchmakers' guild allowed the wives and daughters of guild members to practice their craft. But by the end of the century, any member who taught his skills to a female was fined and reproved. Particularly in times of low wages and food shortages, women were seen as a threat to men's financial security, as women were traditionally paid less than men and might be given hiring preference in times of economic crisis. Because of these impediments, in some eras it was easier for urban widows to get out of the family business altogether and to make a living as money lenders rather than as manufacturers and merchants. This put them in the same category as Jews, the other large social group that served as early bankers; moneylenders were at best tolerated and at worst despised for the practice of usury, or lending money at interest, which was considered a sinful practice.

The Jewish merchant Glückel of Hameln left a record of her trading activities, including buying trips that took her and her husband all over northern Europe. Glückel came from a family of working women, and she wrote in her diary of other women in her village who were artisans and traders. One such woman, Esther, was "a pious, upright woman who understood business well and supported the household. She went regularly to the fairs, taking not too much stock with her, for at that time people were satisfied with little. She spoke well and God gave her favour in the eyes of all who saw her; the aristocratic ladies of Holstein esteemed her very highly."[20] Glückel's grandmother, too, had been the sole support of her family after her husband had died of the plague:

> My grandmother was left bare and destitute with two unmarried daughters. They fled from the house [after the father died], just as they were, taking nothing with them. Often did she tell me of the terrible hardships she underwent. They had no bed to sleep on but plain boards and stones, and though she had a married daughter, this daughter could not help her.... So my poor grandmother and her daughters underwent severe trials and had to go from house to house until the plague had passed. When she returned to disinfect her house, she found all her best things gone and little left. The very floorboards had been pulled up by the neighbours and the rooms were bare. What could they do? My grandmother still possessed some pledges [debts owed to her] and with these managed to bring up her remaining children.... My grandmother scraped and economized.

Later Glückel's mother worked to support herself and her mother, both of whom "knew how to make pointed gold and silver lace":

> My mother found favour in the eyes of the Hamburg dealers; they gave her gold and silver to work.... When the dealers saw that she was honest and prompt in her work, they trusted her, so that in time she was able to take in girls and teach them the trade. She and her mother lived from this, and clothed themselves neatly and cleanly. But besides this they had little, and at times no more than a crust of bread all day.[21]

Glückel and her husband attended the great fairs in Germany (in Frankfurt, Leipzig, and Brunswick), where they traded money and sold precious metals and jewels. They imported silver from parts of Europe where it was mined and minted into coins. After her husband's death, Glückel took over his business, which thrived under her oversight. She also raised 12 children and negotiated their marriage settlements.

In many parts of Europe, growth in urban mercantile wealth in the late seventeenth and early eighteenth centuries meant that a number of women artisans and merchants had sizable incomes. Even women involved in textile work and needle trades were often able to support themselves dependably in times of prosperity. In such times, the marriage rate declined, as such women did not need to marry to survive; evidently, when given the choice, a significant number of women chose not to marry but rather to maintain their financial and personal independence. Such a choice is enthusiastically urged in the following verses by the sixteenth-century Antwerp schoolteacher Anna Bijns:

> How good to be a woman, how much better to be a man!
> Maidens and wenches, remember the lesson you're about to hear.
> Don't hurtle yourself into marriage far too soon.
> The saying goes: "Where's your spouse? Where's your honor?"
> But one who earns her board and clothes
> Shouldn't scurry to suffer a man's rod.
> So much for my advice, because I suspect—
> Nay, see it sadly proven day by day—
> 'T happens all the time!
> However rich in goods a girl might be,
> Her marriage ring will shackle her for life.
> If however she stays single
> With purity and spotlessness foremost,
> Then she is lord as well as lady. Fantastic, not?
> Though wedlock I do not decry:
> Unyoked is best! Happy the woman without a man.

* * *

> A man oft comes home all drunk and pissed
> Just when his wife had worked her fingers to the bone
> (So many chores to keep a decent house!),
> But if she wants to get in a word or two,
> She gets to taste his fist—no more.

And that besotted keg she is supposed to obey?
Why, yelling and scolding is all she gets,
Such are his ways—and hapless his victim.
And if the nymphs of Venus he chooses to frequent,
What hearty welcome will await him home.
Maidens, young ladies: learn from another's doom,
Ere you, too, end up in fetters and chains.
Please don't argue with me on this,
No matter who contradicts, I stick to it:
Unyoked is best! Happy the woman without a man.

* * *

A single lady has a single income,
But likewise, isn't bothered by another's whims.
And I think: that freedom is worth a lot.
Who'll scoff at her, regardless what she does,
And though every penny she makes herself,
Just think of how much less she spends!
An independent lady is an extraordinary prize—
All right, of a man's boon she is deprived,
But she's lord and lady of her very hearth.
To do one's business and no explaining sure is lots of fun!
Go to bed when she list [likes], rise when she list, all as she will,
And no one to comment! Grab tight your independence then.
Freedom is such a blessed thing.
To all girls: though the right Guy might come along:
Unyoked is best! Happy the woman without a man.

> (Excerpt from Anna Bijns "Unyoked Is Best! Happy the Woman
> without a Man," published in Katharina M. Wilson, ed. *Women
> Writers of the Renaissance and Reformation* [Athens: The Uni-
> versity of Georgia Press, 1991]. © 1991 by Katharina M. Wilson.
> Reprinted with permission.)

A growing and distinct group of workers during this period were black servants. Beginning in the sixteenth century, the wealth of many port cities was significantly based on the import of peoples and goods from colonies in the Americas, Africa, and India. Spaniards trafficked in slavery as early as the Middle Ages, buying and selling Muslims from within Spain and from north Africa and the Ottoman Empire. Early modern exploration and colonization brought increased traffic in slaves from west Africa. Slavery was outlawed in some countries in Europe, such as England, from the mid-sixteenth century, and Poland, where slavery was replaced by serfdom in the fifteenth century. In Spain and Italy, however, slavery was legal. The earliest African servants or slaves were domestic servants and were valued for their rarity and as a sign of mercantile wealth and status; in some areas, every elite family would have had at least one black servant and sometimes even two, one male and one female. Although the Africans were considered slaves, their children were generally freeborn, and the children born of master-slave relationships were sometimes raised as "legitimate" children of the master. As European imperial activity grew, the presence of blacks, particularly in towns with significant ties to merchant activity, became more common, their status declined, and they ceased to be a prized "possession." At the same time, a massive slave trade with a brutal system of plantation slaves was developing. Slaves supported the economy not only in the Caribbean and the Americas, where their existence is perhaps best known, but also in Cyprus and Crete, for instance, where Italian speculators and adventurers used slaves, as they were used in the Caribbean, to farm sugar cane. In the Americas, Spanish conquistadors began bringing African slaves to Spanish colonies in South America in the early sixteenth century. The Portuguese brought so many Africans to Brazil that most areas had at least 50 percent blacks during this period. In fact, the Americas were the destination of half of all Africans captured and enslaved before slavery was outlawed in the nineteenth century. Initially, only west African men were enslaved, while the women and children were kept by the African suppliers to the Atlantic slave trade for their own households. Only later, when masters began to see the advantage of systematically breeding slave women to produce more slaves, were women enslaved in the Americas in numbers that equaled those of men.

Women's work in the Renaissance was varied, evolving in response to new economic possibilities, to changes in women's roles, and to the continuing urbanization of Europe. Although the majority of European women lived on the land and were more affected by the cycle of season and harvest than by political change, they were nevertheless very vulnerable to the dislocation of social and cultural upheaval. War, famine, and disease could bring profound change in their work lives. Rural economic depression might drive agricultural workers off the land and into the city, where they would confront a new set of economic circumstances that might lead to poverty, begging, and vagrancy, or possibly to an independence and income they had never before known. While moralists insisted, perhaps more vehemently than ever, that women's activities should be restricted to home and family, some women, especially middle-class urban women, were, in fact, becoming more mobile and economically independent. New kinds of work were opening up for urban dwellers, particularly in northern Europe, much of which was officially Protestant. But Christian women in Protestant countries no longer had the opportunities of convent life open to them, a life that offered independence from marriage and motherhood and sometimes the possibility of learning and public service unavailable to women outside the convent. Jewish women throughout Europe engaged in trade and banking, though always vulnerable to prejudice and even violence. But whatever the political system, dominant religion, or economic structure, women always saw to the birthing and rearing of children and the bulk of the day to day work that fed and clothed the world. Women always worked, and their work, though often invisible and undervalued, was essential to the survival and success of their families, towns, and countries.

NOTES

1.   Glückel of Hameln, *The Life of Glückel of Hameln 1646–1724 Written by Herself,* trans. and ed. Beth-Zion Abrahams (London: Horovitz, 1962), 40.

2.   Qtd. in Susan C. Karant-Nunn and Merry E. Wiesner-Hanks, eds. and trans., *Luther on Women: A Sourcebook* (New York: Cambridge University Press, 2003), 107–08.

3.   Jacques Guillemeau, *Child-birth or, The happy deliuerie of women Wherein is set downe the gouernment of women.... To which is added, a treatise of the diseases of infants, and young children: with the cure of them. Written in French by Iames Guillimeau [sic] the French Kings chirurgion,* part 2, *The Nursing of Children,* 50.2.5. (London, 1612). This treatise is available online through EEBO, <http://eebo.chadwyck.com>, and in a modern facsimile reprint (New York: Da Capo Press, 1972).

4.   Bonnie S. Anderson and Judith P. Zinsser, *A History of Their Own: Women in Europe from Prehistory to the Present,* vol. 1 (New York: Harper and Row, 1989), 137. See also Norman E. Himes, *Medical History of Contraception* (New York: Schocken Books, 1970), 137–73.

5.   On early modern infanticide, see James R. Farr, *Authority and Sexuality in Early Modern Germany, 1550–1730* (New York: Oxford University Press, 1995); Ulinka Rublack, ed., *The Crimes of Women in Early Modern Germany* (New York: Oxford University Press, 1999); Mark Jackson, ed., *Infanticide: Historical Perspectives on Child Murder and Concealment,*

1550–2000 (Aldershot, UK: Ashgate, 2002); and Deborah A. Symonds, *Weep Not for Me: Women, Ballads, and Infanticide in Early Modern Scotland* (University Park: Pennsylvania State University Press, 1997).

6.   See Alain Bideau, Bertrand Desjardins, and Hector Perez Brignoli, eds., *Infant and Child Mortality in the Past* (New York: Oxford University Press, 1997).

7.   Glückel of Hameln, book 2, *The Life of Glückel of Hameln,* 33.

8.   Paul Slack, ed., *Poverty in Early-Stuart Salisbury Wiltshire Record Society* 31 (Devizes, UK, 1975), *passim.*

9.   On poverty and poorlaws, see Brian Pullen, *Rich and Poor in Renaissance Venice: The Social Institutions of a Catholic State, to 1620* (Cambridge, MA: Harvard University Press, 1971), and Sandra Cavallo, *Charity and Power in Early Modern Italy: Benefactors and their Motives in Turin, 1541–1789* (New York: Cambridge University Press, 1995).

10.   Richard C. Trexler, "Florentine Prostitution in the Fifteenth Century," in *The Women of Renaissance Florence: Power and Dependence in Renaissance Florence,* vol. 2 (Asheville, NC: Pegasus, 1998), 49.

11.   Mary Elizabeth Perry, "Lost Women in Early Modern Seville: The Politics of Prostitution," *Feminist Studies* 4.1 (1978): 206.

12.   Glückel of Hameln, book 2, *The Life of Glückel of Hameln,* 39.

13.   Glückel of Hameln, book 2, *The Life of Glückel of Hameln,* 39–40.

14.   Sara Mendelson and Patricia Crawford, *Women in Early Modern England, 1550–1720* (New York: Oxford University Press, 1998), 318–19.

15.   Charlotte F. Otten, ed., *English Women's Voices, 1540–1700* (Miami: Florida International University Press, 1992), 184.

16.   See Pamela A. Sambrook, *The Country House Servant* (Stroud, UK: Sutton, 1999) for more information on laundry.

17.   The term *occupational resegregation* was coined by Barbara Reskin, "Occupational Resegregation," in *The American Woman,* ed. Sara Rix (New York: Norton, 1988), 258–63.

18.   Thomas Tusser, *Five Hundred Points of Good Husbandry as well for the Champion or Open Countrey, as also for the Woodland or Several, Mixed, in Every Moneth, with Huswifery, over and besides the Book of Huswifery* … (London, 1585). This book is available through EEBO, <http://eebo.chadwyck.com>.

19.   Katharina M. Wilson, ed., *Women Writers of the Renaissance and Reformation* (Athens: University of Georgia Press, 1991), 382–83.

20.   Glückel of Hameln, book 2, *The Life of Glückel of Hameln,* 17.

21.   Glückel of Hameln, book 2, *The Life of Glückel of Hameln,* 17–18.

SUGGESTED READING

Anderson, Bonnie S., and Judith P. Zinsser. *A History of Their Own: Women in Europe from Prehistory to the Present.* Vol. 1. New York: Harper and Row, 1989.

Anderson, Michael. *Approaches to the History of the Western Family, 1500–1914.* Cambridge: Cambridge University Press, 2000.

Benedict, Philip. *Cities and Social Change in Early Modern France.* Boston: Unwin Hyman, 1989.

Cavallo, Sandra. *Charity and Power in Early Modern Italy: Benefactors and Their Motives in Turin, 1541–1789.* New York: Cambridge University Press, 1995.

Cressy, David. *Birth, Marriage, and Death: Ritual, Religion, and the Life-Cycle in Tudor and Stuart England.* New York: Oxford University Press, 1997.

Davis, Barbara Beckerman. "Poverty and Poor Relief in Sixteenth-Century Toulouse." *Historical Reflections/Réflexions Historiques* 17 (1991): 267–96.

Evenden, Doreen. *The Midwives of Seventeenth-Century London.* New York: Cambridge University Press, 2000.

Perry, Mary Elizabeth. "Lost Women in Early Modern Seville: The Politics of Prostitution." *Feminist Studies* 4.1 (February 1978): 195–214.

Pullam, Brian. *Rich and Poor in Renaissance Venice: The Social Institutions of a Catholic State, to 1620.* Cambridge, MA: Harvard University Press, 1971.

Schomberg Center for Research in Black Culture. *The African Presence in the Americas, 1492–1992.* <http://www.si.umich.edu/CHICO/Schomburg/index.html>.

Sharpe, Pamela. *Women's Work: The English Experience, 1650–1914.* New York: Arnold, 1998.

Slack, Paul. *The English Poor Law, 1531–1782.* Cambridge: Cambridge University Press, 1990.

Trexler, Richard C. *The Women of Renaissance Florence: Power and Dependence in Renaissance Florence.* Vol. 2. Asheville, NC: Pegasus, 1998.

Wiesner, Merry E. *Women and Gender in Early Modern Europe.* 2nd ed. New York: Cambridge University Press, 2000.

Wilson, Katharina M., ed. *Women Writers of the Renaissance and Reformation.* Athens: University of Georgia Press, 1991.

Zumthor, Paul. *Daily Life in Rembrandt's Holland.* Stanford, CA: Stanford University Press, 1994.

4

Women and Politics

The role of women in early modern politics, though primarily unofficial, was extensive. While females were instructed to be submissive and in some countries held no legal authority or agency, they nevertheless exerted a significant influence on politics at every level of society. In the early modern networks of power relations—whether international, governmental, or domestic—they were active participants. There were, of course, the female monarchs and regents who were high-profile exceptions to the norm of women's subordination, but there were also more informal means whereby women shaped the course of politics.

> Through the arrangement of marriages, they established ties between influential families; through letters or the spreading of rumors, they shaped networks of opinion; through patronage, they helped or hindered men's political careers; through giving advice and founding institutions, they shaped policy; through participation in riots and disturbances, they demonstrated the weakness of male authority structures.[1]

The influence of women on politics, then, was not restricted to queens and powerful aristocrats. Insofar as politics informs any relationship of power, femininity was a political category of subordination, just as masculinity was one of authority. The relationship of male to female was held to be an image of the relationship between ruler and subject, parent and child. If women challenged such power differentials, whether by armed revolt or simply by altering the fashion of their clothes, they threatened the political distinctions that were at the heart of early modern social structures.

For example, when English women adopted masculine attire at the beginning of the seventeenth century, King James I fulminated that such "hermaphrodites" were disrupting the laws of nature, man, and God. Even the association of women and authority by costuming alone was a violation of proper order. The king convened the clergy of London in 1620 and commanded them to "inveigh vehemently against the insolence of our women, and their wearing of broad brimmed hats, pointed doublets, their hair cut short or shorn, and some of them with stilettos or poniards." The king added that "if pulpit admonitions will not reform them, he would ... fall upon their husbands, parents, or friends that have—or should have—power over them, and make them pay for it; the truth is the world is very much out of order."[2] The degree to which the king and the Church were vested in the political signification of women's appearance and behavior was a measure of the potential for disruptive power that females were held to possess in the early modern period.

Any discussion of women's experience of politics and disruption in the Renaissance must include a consideration of war. Military and civil conflicts shaped every aspect of women's lives. The poverty, starvation, and displacement that attended war threatened members of all social classes. Early in the period, there were local and larger-scale struggles among powerful families who were ambitious for territorial control. As power and governments became more centralized, conflicts were more often between monarchs, although there were also civil wars, religious wars, and other forms of internecine strife. Women were not simply the victims of such disruption; they were also involved as agents. Noblewomen often participated in the politics of war, and some were key figures in the course of regional or international conflicts: "They acted as surrogates administering conquered territories, defending lands and privileges, negotiating the restitution of lands, the release of prisoners, and truces."[3]

A celebrated example of such political force was Margaret of Anjou. Descended from generations of ruling matriarchs, Margaret of Anjou lived from 1429–1482. She married Henry VI of England and fought for his power far more effectively than he did. Acting on behalf of her less competent husband, she raised money

The Man-Woman:

Being a Medicine to cure the Coltish Disease of the Staggers in the *Masculine-Feminines* of our Times.

Exprest in a briefe Decla [...] tion.

Non omnes possumus omnes.

Miftris, will you be trim'd or truss'd?

London printed for I. T. and are to be fold at Chrift Church gate. 1620.

Woman getting a "manly" haircut and man in "womanly" clothing admiring himself in a mirror, from a pamphlet decrying the blurring of gender distinctions through dress and hairstyles. [Anon.], *Hic Mulier, or, The Man-Woman* (London, 1620), title page. *Source:* © Bodleian Library, University of Oxford, Malone 632.

for troops, rallied support and political allies, and fought attacks from the King of France as well as from English opponents. She was finally defeated in 1471. Equally skillful and more successful was Elenore de Roye, who married Louis de Bourbon, Prince de Condé, in 1551. When her husband was imprisoned for plotting to overthrow the French throne, she negotiated with the king for his release. Years later, Louis was again imprisoned for treason, this time for attempting to oust the regent, Queen Catherine de'

Medicis. Elenore raised money in support of his coup and again secured his freedom when he was captured. Upon her death at the age of 28, her husband wrote to their sons, "Ordinarily boys are expected to try to grow up to be like their fathers. I would urge you to try to be like your mother."[4]

Few women who were not also monarchs were as active in politics and in the military as was Anne-Marie-Louise d'Orléans, Duchesse de Montpensier (1627–1693). Her father aspired to overthrow the French monarch, but he was too frightened to follow through on his ambition. The duchess, instead, acted brilliantly:

> She made the alliance with the leader of the opposition against the monarch; she marched into the town of Orléans and won the assembled town notables with a speech. During the 1652 attack on Paris, when she found her father hiding in his room, she went to the fortress of the Bastille and ordered the men to fire on the royal troops. When the queen, Anne of Austria, and her advisor, Cardinal Mazarin, had put down the Fronde, they acknowledged Montpensier's bravery and initiative by sending her, not her father, into exile.[5]

As the leadership and courage of Anne-Marie-Louise d'Orléans demonstrate, some early modern women seized commanding roles in the wars and politics of the period. The participation of most women in military planning, however, was extremely rare.

The displacement caused by war in both the national and international arenas became a way of life for Elizabeth von der Pfalz, later Princess Elizabeth of Bohemia, Princess Palatine (1618–1680). Born in Heidelberg (1 of 13 children), she was the daughter of Elizabeth Stuart of England (daughter of King James VI and I) and Friedrich V, ruler of the Palatine. When Elizabeth was an infant, her parents moved to Prague, where they were crowned King and Queen of Bohemia. In less than 12 months, at the outbreak of the Thirty Years' War (1618–1648), they were deposed and returned to the Palatine. But they were soon driven out of their homeland as the war spread; displaced again, they fled to Holland. Elizabeth, who spent the early war-torn years of her life with relations in Germany, did not join her parents in exile in Holland until she was nine. It was there (much later) that she met the French philosopher René Descartes (1596–1650), with whom she began a correspondence that lasted for seven years until his death. War defined nearly every decade of Elizabeth's life. Her uncle, Charles I of

England, was deposed and beheaded in 1649 in his country's civil war, and three of Elizabeth's brothers fought with him. Eventually, Elizabeth's older brother returned to the Palatine when the Thirty Years' War ended. Elizabeth never married and seemed to prefer her life of scholarly inquiry to both the advantages and burdens of marriage. In 1667 she joined the Protestant Monastery of Herford in Westphalia, where she eventually became abbess, overseeing the order's extensive holdings, including farms and towns and over seven thousand inhabitants. But Elizabeth did not retire from international politics; until her death, she provided political asylum to refugees of wars and other conflicts, including William Penn (1644–1718) and other Quakers as well as the Dutch scholar and champion of women's rights, Anna Maria van Schurman (1607–1678).

What of the common woman's role in politics? Were French and German peasants' wives, who faced starvation because of inflated grain prices, merely invisible victims, or could they force authorities to heed their condition? Were Dutch and English farming women, dispossessed of public lands that were enclosed for livestock, able to join in protest and make themselves heard? Did common women throughout Reformation Europe register their resistance to politically imposed restrictions on their faith and religious practices? The answer to all of these questions is yes: women were central participants in bread riots, tax revolts, land-reform movements, religious protests, and other civic disturbances. Despite their legal status as "*sexus imbecillus*" (the imbecile sex), they challenged oppressive laws in mass marches. And though the 1642 *Law's Resolutions of Women's Rights* by Thomas Edgar insisted that females in England "have no rights in Parliament, they make no laws, they consent to none, they abrogate none," women made up a large number of the rioters against enclosure of common land.[6] In defense of their religious freedom, they threatened ecclesiastical authorities and plundered churches. In Edinburgh in 1637, popular resistance to the Book of Common Prayer, which had been imposed on the Calvinist Scots by King Charles I and the Church of England, was led by "rascally serving women" at Saint Giles' Church, whose voices drowned out the dean. When they were evicted from the sanctuary, they threw stones at the doors and windows of the church. Similarly, working women led by "la Branlaïre" precipitated a 1645

Sébastien Bourdon, Christina, Queen of Sweden. *Source:* Reproduced by permission of The National Portrait Gallery, London.

tax revolt in Montpellier. They called for the death of the tax collectors "for taking the bread from their children's mouths." And in 1629, in a grain riot in Essex, another woman, "Captain" Alice Clark, led a mob of male and female weavers who were all dressed as women, a sign of the disruption to society represented by both the riot and the lack of grain.[7]

Such protests over specific crises were held to be less socially subversive than were more broadly articulated political revolts. For example, Irish women who joined in rebellion against English colonialism were savagely punished for inverting the natural order of female submission. Detractors condemned their political agency in sexual terms, calling them whores and abusers of their "weak" Irish men. Cultures throughout Renaissance Europe sought to preserve gender hierarchies in politics even as some of those cultures battled to redefine power relations between monarch and subject. While some of the radical groups of the English civil war called for absolute equality between women and men, most of them left untouched the gender hierarchy of society while calling for a revolution in the class hierarchy. Though the power of the monarch was seen to be unjust, the power of husbands over wives was understood as divinely ordained and natural. In the words of the radical Henry Parker, "The wife is inferior in nature, and was created for the assistance of man, and servants are hired for their Lord's mere attendance; but it is otherwise in the State between man and man, for that civill difference … is for … the good of all, not that servility and drudgery may be imposed upon all for the pompe of one."[8]

Despite resistance to women's moving out of their proper place in the social order, they continued to assert their political voice. As one scholar has argued, the mid-seventeenth-century "collapse of structures of authority that had traditionally enforced women's subjection allowed them to come close to articulating a program of political and cultural entitlements. Such a program never finally materialized, yet the mass collectivization of women in the protests of the 1640s and 1650s, the mid-century petitions by women that declare their 'equal share' with men in the commonwealth, and the activities of sectarian women in preaching, missionary work, and issuing prophetic warnings to the nation indicate … a window of opportunity for the mass mobilization of women and their re-envisioning of themselves as citizens with specific political rights and obligations."[9] One can read in the language of English women's petitions both conciliatory deference and demanding assertions. They "expressed grievances over the decay of trade (relying on women's recognized status as nurturers and domestic managers), and more controversially pleaded for reconciliation between the two Houses of Parliament, for religious reformation, and for the punishment of [Archbishop] Laud and prosecution of delinquents." The women claimed a public voice because of their common lot with men: "Women are sharers in the common calamities that accompany both Church and Commonwealth, when oppression is exercised over the church of Kingdome wherein they live; and an unlimited power has been given to

Prelates to exercise over the consciences of women as well as men."[10] The women's petitions were widely lampooned in a series of satires that, as was typical, equated women's public speaking with their sexual desire. In spite of this harassment, ten thousand women put their names to a petition of 1649, calling for religious and political reform and asserting "an equal interest with men of this Nation."[11] Five hundred women presented the petition to Parliament, which refused to accept it, arguing that "the matter you petition about is of an higher concernment than you understand.... The House gave an answer to your husbands.... You are desired to goe home, and looke after your owne businesse, and meddle with your huswifery."[12] Whether they were merchants, peasants, artisans, nuns, or aristocrats, women who participated in political struggles during the Renaissance did not achieve equal rights for their gender in any country in Europe.

Given that the prescribed sphere for women was the domestic household, or "huswifery," there was fierce opposition to female rule. The Scottish Presbyterian polemicist John Knox (1505–1572) condemned female heads of state as monstrous and as cause for rebellion. His 1558 *First Blast of the Trumpet Against the Monstrous Regiment of Women* was directed at three Catholic queens named Mary: Mary Tudor, Queen of England; Mary of Guise, wife of James V of Scotland; and their daughter, Mary, Queen of Scots, who succeeded her father as ruler of Scotland. Knox asserted that "A woman promoted to sit in the seat of God, that is, to teach, to judge or to reign above man is a monster in nature, contumely to God, and a thing most repugnant to his will and ordinance." Knox continued with a series of analogies to female rule. A woman leading a man is like a diseased invalid tending the healthy or a lunatic counseling the wise:

> for who can denie but that it be repugneth to nature, that the blind shal be appointed to leade and conduct such as do see? That the weake, the sicke, and impotent persones shal nourishe and kepe the hole and strong, and finalie, that the foolishe, madde and phrenetike, shal gouerne the discrete, and give counsel to such as be sober of mind? And such be all women, compared unto men in bearing of authority.[13]

In more measured tone but with equal conviction, the French political theorist Jean Bodin wrote in 1576 that female rule controverted both scriptural and natural law. Just as the father is the head of the domestic realm, he argued, so should the male monarch be the head of state. Those who defended female rule in the Renaissance did not advocate the innate ability of women; rather, they invoked the notion of the sovereign's "two bodies": her natural body and her political body. The former was weak and fallible, but the latter was invested with the authority, power, and legitimacy of its office. Thomas Smith and John Aylmer made such arguments on behalf of Elizabeth's sovereignty in England. The queen herself promoted the notion of the monarch's two bodies in order to disarm those threatened by female power while still maintaining her absolute control. As she asserted in her 1588 speech to the troops assembled in anticipation of battling the Spanish Armada, "I know I have the body but of a weak and feeble woman; but I have the heart and stomach of a king, and of a king of England too."[14]

Despite prevailing objections to women's rule, there were powerful queens and female regents in Renaissance Europe. Most were the only dynastic heirs, empowered in the absence of male alternatives; others were acting on behalf of minors or incompetent husbands. Isabella of Castile, later Queen of Spain; Catherine de' Medicis and Anne of Austria in France; Christina of Sweden; Anne de Beaujeu (1460–1522), Regent of France for her brother after the king died in 1483; Mary and Elizabeth Tudor of England; Margaret of Austria, Regent of the Netherlands; and Mary Stuart of Scotland each shaped the territories they ruled. All exerted tremendous political influence both within and beyond their domain, but it is important to recognize that the power they wielded was framed in patriarchal terms.

> Nothing of these women's actions, goals, or successes altered the institutions and the attitudes that left women of the nobility, however well-born, vulnerable to loss of privilege and abuse. Nothing of their lives secured a better position for women, a position that would protect and empower them regardless of circumstances. The traditional patterns of life and the traditional views of women had been circumvented, not challenged.[15]

Not only were sovereign women exceptions, but their effect on the material conditions and cultural status of women in general were not transformative.

The most common route to the throne was by way of marriage or dynastic inheritance in the case of no male heir. When there

Elizabeth I, Queen of England, on her throne in the House of Lords, contemporary woodcut. *Source:* © Fotomas Index.

were multiple or conflicting claims to the monarchy, it took extraordinary skill, intelligence, and ambition for a woman to establish sovereignty. All three factors—marriage, inheritance, and iron leadership—worked in favor of Isabella of Castile's sovereignty in Spain. The daughter of John II, King of Castile, Isabella was born in 1451. After her father and two brothers died, she seized the Royal Treasury in 1474 and declared herself queen. The only other contender to the throne was her half niece, but Isabella negotiated the support of the most powerful factions in the civil war–torn country by promising to establish order. Married to Ferdinand of Aragon in 1468, Isabella had united the most formidable families in Spain. Together, they "created a dynasty with enough resources to impose peace and strong enough to pass on the united kingdom—again through the female line—to their daughter's son, the future Charles I of Spain (who also became Charles V of the Holy Roman Empire)."[16]

Isabella's marriage settlement with Ferdinand of Aragon attests to her remarkable control and ambition. Her terms for the alliance were that she would maintain absolute sovereignty over her own kingdom of Castile, including sole authority over the treasury and over royal decrees. While Ferdinand was to have no jurisdiction over her territories, he agreed that she would jointly reign with him over the lands of Aragon. Isabella's independence and statecraft were indomitable. She crushed civil war, launched forces against Portugal, centralized power, and created a royal bureaucracy that kept control of the government away from ambitious nobles. It has been noted that "she delayed a military campaign only once, for the birth of her second daughter, Catherine, a future wife of Henry VIII of England."[17] She was also the primary force behind the destruction of the Jewish community in Spain. In 1492, Jews were given the so-called choice of converting to Christianity or being exiled from Spain, the place that had been their families' homeland for hundreds of years. At the same time, Isabella held sway over the Spanish church. While resolutely Catholic, she refused to allow the pope to limit her authority, and she appointed her own ecclesiastical officials. Not even the most potent patriarch in fifteenth-century Europe, the pope, could dominate Queen Isabella of Spain.

Less ruthless but as politically motivated as the Spanish monarch was her daughter-in-law, Margaret of Austria. Regent of the Netherlands for more than twenty years, skilled negotiator, patroness of the arts, and guardian of her brother's four young children, Margaret lived from 1480–1530. She was the daughter of an Austrian prince, Maximillian, and a Burgundian duchess, Mary. Margaret's father was relentlessly committed to the practice of securing political allies and consolidating wealth by way of arranged marriages. As a result, Margaret was first betrothed when she was two years old, and she had been widowed three times by the age of 24. As commonly occurred, she had been sent as a young girl to the home of another noblewoman, Anne de Beaujeu (daughter of King Louis XI), to be educated for her life in the political arena. Later Maximillian arranged to unite two powerful dynasties—the house of Hapsburg and Spain—by marrying two of his children (Margaret and her brother Philip) to two children of Ferdinand and Isabella, Juan and

Juana. Margaret was married by proxy in 1495 and did not join her husband until nearly two years later. Five months into their lives together, Juan died. After the death of her third husband (Philibert, Duke of Savoy in France), Margaret resolved never to marry again.

European politics had informed Margaret's life from the day of her birth, but in 1506 she assumed an even more active role. In that year, her brother, King Philip of Spain, died. She was promptly appointed Regent of the Netherlands for her seven-year-old nephew, Charles, and guardian of not only Charles but also his three sisters. In the course of their lives, Margaret's wards came to dominate Europe. With the assistance of his shrewd and resourceful aunt, Charles became Holy Roman Emperor, and his sisters "divide[d] among themselves most of the crowns of Europe, Eleanor as queen of Portugal and then of France, Isabel the queen of Denmark, Sweden, and Norway, and Marie, briefly the queen of Hungary and eventually Margaret's successor as governor of the Netherlands for her brother."[18] At her new court in Malines, from which she ruled the region that is now the Netherlands, Belgium, and a northern section of France, Margaret skillfully conducted the business of government and diplomacy. She also established a flourishing oasis for the arts, where musicians, poets, architects, and artists enjoyed her patronage and her participation in their craft. She composed both music and verse, and she engaged in dialogue with humanists from the cultural centers of Europe.

Margaret's success as a leader among rulers was extraordinary. She steered the civil war–torn region toward reconciliation, and she negotiated with France the triumphant Treaty of Cambrai. Vying for the imperial crown, Charles V and Francis I had a long history of antipathy. In 1525 Charles captured both Francis and his two sons but released the father with the Treaty of Madrid a year later. Francis immediately broke the terms of the treaty, despite his sons' continued imprisonment as hostages. Fearing for her grandchildren's lives, the mother of Francis I, Louise of Savoy, met with Margaret to negotiate a resolution to the political crisis. Margaret represented Charles's interests, but at the same time, she made strategic and sage concessions. Her brilliant diplomacy resulted in what was known as "the Ladies' Peace," or the Treaty of Cambrai.

> Margaret was intelligent and adept enough to exploit every personal and practical advantage, showing a knowledge of facts and a power of decision that once more marked her as a woman of extraordinary ability. The treaty signed on August 3, 1529 was almost

entirely favorable to her nephew Charles…. It is recorded in a bulky
document that deals with innumerable territorial questions and the
respective rights of the two monarchs and of their subjects.[19]

By the terms of the treaty, Charles freed his two royal captives and
was recognized as sovereign over a large area of what is now
France and Italy. In addition, Francis agreed to pay Charles's considerable debts to England and to marry Charles's sister Eleanor,
thus allying the empires of Hapsburg, Burgundy, and Spain. Margaret's political acumen was central to many of the most powerful relationships forged among Renaissance sovereigns.

As was the case with Margaret, the opportunity for political capital via marriage was central to the life of Elizabeth I of England
(1533–1603). Unlike Margaret, however, Elizabeth exploited her
potential for marriage without ever actually submitting to a husband. Indeed, she parlayed her eligibility for marriage into a powerful tool to avoid submission—to forge alliances, force concessions
from other nations, and ward off hostilities both at home and
abroad. She gave audience to dozens of suitors during her 45-year
reign, strategically using their courtship to mollify, coerce, or otherwise influence the myriad factions that she needed to navigate
among in order to sustain the peace and prosperity of her nation.
These factions included English Protestants and Catholics, the
French, the Dutch, the Spanish, and the papacy. By putting her marital potential on the market but never conceding it, she was able to
maintain her independence, augment her power, and wield a
potent diplomatic weapon.

But exploiting her marriageability was only one of many successful tactics in Elizabeth's enormous repertoire of political skills.
She was a brilliant statesperson, commanding the respect of her
subjects while also nurturing their affection. She cleverly used
both verbal and painted representations of herself to construct a
persona that was both authoritative and seemingly nonthreaten-
ing to a culture that found powerful women to be disturbing and
unnatural. She cultivated multifaceted images of herself as a
faithful wife to her nation (a "marriage" that her coronation ring
signified), a loving and self-sacrificial mother to her people, and a
chaste beloved virgin—and not just any virgin, but an image of the
Virgin Mary. Elizabeth's virgin body came to symbolize the invio-
late and impregnable state of England. The 1633 paean to Elizabeth *A Chaine of Pearle* praises her "impregnable Virginity" and
claims that her subjects' love for her "guard[s] Her surer, then an

Armie Royall."[20] The many portraits of Elizabeth that circulated throughout England and on the Continent during her lifetime show a body so stiffened and bolstered by dazzling clothing that the weakness of her female body ceases to be a debility. Elizabeth's sovereignty destabilized the patriarchal hierarchy, but Elizabeth was careful to defuse resulting hostilities while still maintaining control. Elizabeth's success in achieving such a balance was also due to her consummate rhetorical abilities. Educated in the richest humanist tradition, adept at many languages, and learned in philosophy and the arts, she was a master at manipulating words and audiences. Her public speeches demonstrate a genius for adapting her discourse to her auditor, whether addressing an unruly House of Commons, a loyal army poised for battle with foreign enemies, or an assembly of university dignitaries (to whom she discoursed at great length in eloquent Latin). Her understanding and appreciation of the power of language contributed to the florescence of literature in Renaissance England. Elizabeth was inspiration and patron to some of the most celebrated poets and dramatists in Western history. Her presence in both the culture and the politics of her age was formative.

Mary, Queen of Scots (1542–1587), was Elizabeth's contemporary, the daughter of Mary of Guise and King James V of Scotland and the mother of James VI, the future James I of England, who followed Elizabeth on the throne. Mary's father died within a week of her birth, and she was crowned queen of Scotland, with her mother serving as regent. Though it was once proposed that she would marry Henry VIII's son, the future Edward VI, Henry's actions against Scotland—his so-called rough wooing of a bride for his son—and his break with Rome discouraged Mary's Scottish Catholic family and political advisers from pursuing this course. Instead, they sent her to live at the French court when she was five. There she was treated according to her royal title, essentially adopted into the French royal family, and betrothed to the dauphin, the future King François II. At the French court, she was educated in modern languages as well as Latin and Greek, in the Catholic religion, in dancing and music, and in statecraft. In 1558, she and the dauphin were married. When his father died the next year, the two were crowned, with Mary holding the title Queen of Scotland and France. It was expected by many that she would also inherit the English throne from Mary Tudor on her death, but Elizabeth I succeeded her sister. Thus, though they never met face to face, the two queens were set up as rivals from the beginning. Meanwhile, in Scotland, Mary's bastard half brother, the Protestant James Stewart, the Duke of Moray, deposed Mary's mother, Mary of Guise, in 1559 and declared himself regent for the young Mary. Mary's mother died in 1560; her husband died six months later, and she returned to Scotland to assume the throne under Moray's direction, a Catholic queen in a Protestant country.

The young queen—tall, beautiful, and accomplished—was beloved by her people. But a woman's rule always held a great potential for noble rivalry, especially if the queen was unmarried. Elizabeth staved off such disruption by endlessly playing the mar-

Mary, Queen of Scots, *Liber Grisiensis* (1565–1692), fol. 11. *Source:* Photograph courtesy of the Scottish Catholic Archives.

riage game with a number of European monarchs and noblemen while retaining her independence. The danger for Elizabeth was that she would leave no clear heir to the throne, something Mary did not dare chance. (Indeed, in a kind of grim historical joke, Mary would ultimately provide Elizabeth with the heir she never bore.) While Elizabeth maintained her royal power until the end of her reign, Mary's life was repeatedly endangered as she was subject to the rule of a series of lovers, suitors, and husbands—all ruthless, ambitious men. In 1565, Mary married Henry Stewart, Lord Darnley, a handsome but shallow and volatile man, but she did not have him crowned king in his own right; rather, he was her prince consort. He clearly wanted more than that, and in 1566 his cronies brutally murdered Mary's Catholic French secretary, David Rizzio (or Riccio), whom Darnley suspected was having an affair with Mary. The killers dragged Rizzio from the table where he was dining with Mary and her counselors (including James Hepburn, the Earl of Bothwell, who was also a target but who escaped out a window); they stabbed Rizzie more than fifty times.

In the utter disruption and perfidy of court politics, Mary was believed to have participated in the murder plot, and the Scottish nobles imprisoned her at Holyrood House palace in Edinburgh. Mary was six months pregnant at the time, and Darnley may even have hoped that witnessing the brutal murder of Rizzio might cause her to miscarry and die, leaving him with a good shot at the throne. Mary, however, was strong and healthy and carried to term the future king James VI of Scotland and James I of England. The birth of a son and heir strengthened Mary's position; she and Darnley reconciled, and he helped her escape. Some of the nobles who had previously assisted Darnley felt understandably betrayed, and they murdered him in 1567. It is possible that Mary herself was involved in the plot to murder Darnley; she was certainly tired of him and his dangerous ambitions at that point. She was, at any rate, charged with his murder, along with Bothwell, by other nobles led by the Duke of Moray. Bothwell abducted Mary and took her to his castle, where he raped her and then "proposed" marriage. The traumatized Mary feared for her own life and that of her infant son, so she agreed to marry him (following his hastily arranged divorce), to give up her Catholicism, and to grant him greater powers than Darnley had held.

At this, Moray and other nobles, some of whom had previously pressed Mary to marry Bothwell, revolted and threatened her life and her son's; she agreed to give herself up to them if Bothwell were given safe passage out of the country. Bothwell unsuccessfully tried to raise an army in support of Mary, but her cause—the Catholic cause—was moribund. He escaped to the Continent but was captured and imprisoned in Denmark, where he died, insane, 10 years later. The Scottish nobles gave Mary and her son safe passage to Edinburgh, where they forced her to abdicate, crowned her son king, took him from Mary, and put him and Scotland under the authority of the Presbyterians and the Duke of Moray, who was named regent for the young king. Mary was imprisoned on the Isle of Lochleven, where she miscarried Bothwell's twins. Mary later escaped to England, where she put herself under the protection of Elizabeth I, who, unbeknownst to Mary, had been sending aid to the Protestant faction in Scotland throughout Mary's short and tumultuous reign.

Mary was never again free. Rather, she was held captive in England under Elizabeth's authority and housed in a series of noble houses (including Bess of Hardwick's Hardwick Hall). During her imprisonment, Mary was the focus for a series of plots supported by those who wished to return England to Catholicism and put Mary on the throne. Elizabeth finally agreed to Mary's execution in 1587, having been persuaded that her own rule would never be safe from such intrigue so long as Mary lived. At the last minute, however, Elizabeth dispatched a document rescinding her earlier order for execution, but only when it was too late to prevent Mary's death. The tragic life of Mary, Queen of Scots, demonstrates how difficult it was for a woman to negotiate the tricky politics of marriage and statecraft and makes it clear why Elizabeth I would avoid marriage and its troubling political consequences, both for a queen personally and for her nation.

Another woman who met a tragic end through her involvement in politics was Lady Jane Grey (1537–1554), queen of England for nine days. Like Elizabeth, Jane received a superb humanist education. Her parents were not much interested in learning, but, as a distant heir to the Tudor throne, she was fostered in the household of the dowager queen Katharine Parr (1512–1546), widow of Henry VIII, a learned woman herself and an ardent Protestant. (That was also where the future queen Elizabeth I was raised.) There Jane was able to pursue her studies in Latin, Greek, and modern languages, and she became a devotee of Reformation theology. Later, when she returned to her parents' household, they hired John Aylmer to

tutor her. Aylmer was a close friend and follower of the pedagogue and author Roger Ascham (1515–1568), who had tutored
Princess Elizabeth and whose book *The Scholemaster* (1570) advocated teaching young students through encouragement and gentleness rather than anger and beatings. In that book, Ascham
recalled his meeting with Grey and her love for learning:

> I found her, in her Chamber, reading Plato's Phœdon in Greek, and
> that with as much delight, as some gentleman would read a merry
> tale in Boccaccio [fourteenth-century Italian novelist]. After saluta-
> tion, and duty done, with some other talk, I asked her, why she
> would lose such pastime in the park? Smiling she answered me: I
> think, all their sport in the park is but a shadow to that pleasure,
> that I find in Plato.[21]

Soon after this meeting, Jane was told by her parents that she was
to be betrothed to Guildford Dudley, son of John Dudley, Duke of
Northumberland. The Northumberland family had been strong
supporters of Protestantism and of the Protestant King Edward VI.
But Edward, who had been sick for much of his life, was dying by
1553, and many Protestant political leaders feared for their lives
under the rule of Edward's successor, the Catholic Mary Tudor.
They had persuaded Edward to sign a document naming Jane, who
had a distant claim to the throne, to succeed him instead. They
proceeded to ally themselves through marriage to Jane as well as
to other women from powerful families. Jane was hastily married
to Dudley and then told of his family's plans for her. On Edward's
death, Jane was crowned Queen of England, while Dudley was
named her prince consort, as Jane refused to make him king in his
own right. But she reigned only nine days before Mary Tudor
claimed the throne with wide support from the English people,
and Jane was imprisoned in the Tower of London. Seven months
later, Mary signed Jane's death warrant, and she was executed,
having just watched from her prison window as first her husband
was taken to his execution on Tower Hill and then as his body and
severed head were brought back.

As befit a woman destined for rule, Princess Leonora Christina of
Denmark (1621–1698) was educated in the same humanist tradition
as Mary Tudor, Elizabeth I, and Mary, Queen of Scots, as well as the
ill-fated Lady Jane Grey. Leonora was fluent in French, Danish, and
High and Low German; in addition, she knew Italian, Spanish,
Swedish, and Latin. A precocious child, she read extensively in his-

tory and literature, played a number of musical instruments, was famous for her needlework, and became a talented artisan of works in amber and ivory. But Leonora's skills were not confined to bookish or traditionally feminine pursuits. Indeed, she insisted on women's rights and her own independence: "In all things she asserted her equality with men, just as she enjoyed the manly sports of riding, hunting, shooting, and ball playing more than most ladies of her time; she wore men's clothes not only for convenience or disguise but also out of preference."[22] Such self-possession and strength of character would serve her well during her adulthood of political crises and personal misfortunes.

Leonora Christina was married at the age of 15 to Corfitz Ulfeldt, her father's high steward of the realm and, after the king, the most powerful person in Denmark. Throughout her twenties, Leonora effectively was a presiding queen of Denmark, since her mother had died. However, on the death of Christian IV in 1648 and the accession of her half brother, Frederik III, Leonora's fortunes changed drastically. Early in his reign, Frederik launched an investigation into the financial affairs of the ambitious and mentally unstable Ulfeldt. In 1651, Leonora and her husband fled to Holland and then to Sweden; they lived in exile for the next 12 years until Leonora was imprisoned in 1663 and Ulfeldt died in 1664. The couple was dispossessed of their lands and titles, but they managed to smuggle a tremendous amount of money out of the kingdom. Ulfeldt used the money to finance Queen Christina of Sweden's war against his enemies in Denmark. Sweden seized large areas of Danish land, and Ulfeldt repossessed his lost territories. A year later, however, Leonora's intermittently insane husband decided to support the Danes against the Swedes. The King of Sweden charged him with treason, and Leonora pleaded his defense. An unshakable sense of conjugal duty led her to support him, despite her unhappiness with his behavior. Her petition to King Charles demonstrated "heroic effort—dauntless courage, unfailing presence of mind, and skill in argumentation, as well as a readiness to depart from the truth."[23] Although the king sentenced Ulfeldt to death, the couple escaped Sweden, and three years later Ulfeldt was charged with conspiring again against the Danish government. Leonora was taken prisoner and shut in the Blue Tower at the castle of Copenhagen for nearly twenty-two years.

While in captivity, Leonora wrote her autobiography (in French), a partly fictional memoir entitled *Memory of Sorrow*, a play,

poetry, hymns in German and Danish, and "Ornament of Heroines," a protofeminist account of heroic women. *Memory of Sorrow* was addressed to her seven children who lived to adulthood.
It records her suffering, religious struggle, and unflagging fortitude. In addition, it attests to her keen powers of observation and
her fascination with the world around her, even during her imprisonment.

> The Renaissance spirit persists in Leonora's fascinated interest in
> everything around her, animate or inanimate, animal or human.
> She studies the reproductive habits of fleas and the vagaries of
> caterpillars, reports like a professor of medicine on a "peculiar mal-
> ady" caused by a large stone in her intestine, and gives a rational
> explanation of witchcraft.[24]

Even though she was prevented from exercising the leadership for
which she had been educated, she continued to dominate her circumscribed world.

Another keen observer of human nature who documented her
firsthand experience of the vicissitudes of Renaissance politics was
Helene Kottanner, the first woman known to have written a memoir
in German. The extraordinarily resourceful chambermaid of Queen
Elizabeth of Hungary, Kottanner recorded events of her life at court
with an acuity that is reminiscent of the most engaging (and accurate) history chronicles. In addition, her personal reflections, vivid
development of characters, and storytelling skill anticipate by
many centuries the psychological complexity and narrative movement of the novel. One of her primary aims in writing the memoir
was to remind the Hungarian king of his debt to her heroic service
so that he would reward her appropriately. In doing so, she
"divulged" her own criminal activities while representing "the truth"
about herself as a paragon of loyalty and rectitude.

Very little is known about Helene Kottanner's life, other than
what was recorded in her memoir, *Die Denkwürdigkeiten der
Helene Kottannerin* [The Memoirs of Helen Kottanner]. She was
born ca. 1400 in Ödenburg, Austria, the daughter of Peter Wolfram,
a member of the local gentry. She was married twice, first to the
mayor of Ödenburg—Peter Székeles (1402–1431)—with whom she
had several children. About a year after the mayor's death, she
married Johann Kottanner, who was in the service of the provost to
the Viennese cathedral. By 1436, she and her family were attached
to the Viennese court, and in 1439 they accompanied Queen Eliza-

beth and her husband, King Albrecht II, to Hungary. In the same year, the king died, leaving his pregnant wife under tremendous pressure from powerful Hungarian nobles to marry the King of Poland. Elizabeth was resolved not only to retain power as monarch but also to secure her family's grip on the throne by crowning her son king as soon as he was born. She could have done neither without the valor and intelligent collusion of her chambermaid, Helene Kottanner.

Without an official coronation and possession of the royal crown, Elizabeth's infant son would not have the legitimacy to rule. On the eve of his birth, however, the crown was locked in a heavily secured vault at the stronghold of Plintenburg, and the queen was in confinement in her castle in Komorn. It was imperative that she get possession of the symbolically potent crown and vestments in order to conduct the coronation of her heir. And she had to do so without alerting her Polish enemies and the Hungarian nobles with whom they conspired to seize the throne. According to Kottanner's memoir, the future of the dynasty depended on someone's stealing the crown from under the nose of murderously ambitious contenders. The queen and her advisers agreed that Helene was the kingdom's best hope:

> Then my gracious lady came to me, and she said that I should do it, because no one she could trust was as familiar with the circumstances there as I was. This troubled me deeply, for it would be a hazardous undertaking involving great danger for me and my little children. I weighed the matter and wondered what to do, and there was no one to whom I could turn for advice, except God alone. Then I realized that if I did not do it, and something evil happened, it would be my fault, a sin against God and the world. Hence I agreed to undertake the perilous journey and risk my life, but I did ask for a helper.... They informed him of the secret plan and told him what was desired of him. He became so afraid, however, that he turned pale as if he were half dead, and he did not accept but went out to his horses in the stable.... [S]hortly thereafter the news reached the castle that he had fallen off his horse and was seriously wounded. When his injuries were better, he left the castle and made off to Croatia.[25]

With great difficulty, the queen was finally able to enlist someone courageous enough to assist her chambermaid. The two set off under the pretense of conveying a retinue of ladies-in-waiting from Plintenburg to Komorn. On the night of February 20, 1440,

Kottanner and her accomplice armed themselves with files, hammers, and flint, dressed in black velvet and dark shoes, and broke into the royal vault at Plintenburg. With graphic suspense, the memoir narrates their burglary. Kottanner used Elizabeth's signet ring to set new seals on the locks for which she had keys, so that the theft would not soon be discovered. Other locks they had to destroy. The suspense builds with the alarming noise of the files and hammers when they smash the metal and the smell of the acrid smoke when they melt the unyielding latches. Will the smoke and the clamor waken the enemy?

> [T]he locks on the crown's casing were so tight that it had been impossible for them to file off and they had burnt them open. There was so much smoke that I worried that some people might notice the smell and wonder where it came from, but God prevented that and protected us. Since the Holy Crown was now free, we again closed the doors everywhere, replaced the locks that they had broken off, pressed my lady's seals on them once more, locked the outer door, and left the piece of cloth with the seal as we had found it and as the castellan had put there. I threw the files in the ladies' privy where you can find them, if you break it open, as evidence that I am speaking the truth…. Then my helper took a red velvet bolster, opened it up, removed part of the feathers, put the Holy Crown onto the pillow, and sewed it back up. It was now almost morning, and the ladies and all the men were getting up and preparing themselves for the journey.[26]

Tension mounts in Kottanner's account as she emphasizes the need for quiet stealth while describing the din of the burglary; she reminds her reader of the inexorable passage of time as she describes their delays, setbacks, and the urgency of finishing by dawn. Even when she has safely absconded with her plunder, the author does not relax her narrative. The travelers stop at an inn to eat—will the pillow remain safe? She has it carried from her sled to the table, where she can constantly guard it. More suspense builds at nightfall as they attempt to cross the frozen Danube. In the middle of the river, the ice breaks, and Kottanner fears that she and her kingdom's future will perish in the frozen dark:

> Then we reached the Danube. It was still frozen, but in some places the ice was very thin. When we were in the middle of the river, the carriage with the ladies proved too heavy; it broke the ice and fell over. The women all screamed, and there was much chaos and con-

fusion. I was frightened and feared that we and the Holy Crown would perish in the Danube. But God came to our rescue; none of our people went through the ice, and of the things that were on the carriage only a few fell into the water and disappeared into the deep. Then I took the duchess of Silesia and the highest-ranking ladies with me on the sled, and with the help of God we all made it safely across the ice.[27]

Kottanner's memoir ends after the infant Ladislaus has been crowned and given safe passage by the author herself, who describes the grief with which she leaves her own children so as to serve the heir apparent. The narrative makes clear King Ladislaus's debt to her, not only for his position on the throne, but for his very life as she protected him from the conspiracies of his childhood enemies. Because Elizabeth died before she could inform her son of his obligation to Kottanner, the memoir serves as a revelation of events and an implicit reminder of his responsibility as a patron. The author's eyewitness account of history is an extraordinary blend of personal sensibility and formative political developments. It predates the heyday of the memoir genre by many centuries. Free of the gossip and scandal that distinguish later "confessions," it configures the relationship between Queen Elizabeth and her chambermaid as one of mutual respect between allies. While limning her individual perspective on international politics, social injustice, intimate relationships, and domestic service, Kottanner's memoir also creates a richly detailed image of her culture.

Like that of Helene Kottanner, the life of the Italian Camilla Faà Gonzaga was shaped by national and international politics. And like her Austrian predecessor, Gonzaga composed her memoir to set the record straight regarding her character. The autobiographical account, or *Storia,* was written in 1622 at the request of the mother superior who presided at the convent where Gonzaga spent the last 40 years of her life. Held to be the first memoir written by an Italian woman, the *Storia* was not published until 1895. It is an elegant reflection on the web of power relations that constrained women in the period, and it is the indomitable assertion of a self that maintains integrity despite the betrayal and malice of friends, family, and political associates.

Camilla Faà Gonzaga was born in 1599. Her father, Ardizzino II, was a nobleman who served as an army captain for the ruling Gonzaga family. He was later appointed ambassador to Turin and

Milan. Her mother died when Camilla was very young, so she was sent to live with her aunt in a convent; it was common practice during the period for motherless girls to be put under the supervision of female relatives in order to keep the young women safe from scandal. At 13, Camilla began service as a lady-in-waiting to Duchess Margherita of Savoy. In 1615, the new Duke Ferdinando Gonzaga of Mantua first met Camilla at court. He wooed her persistently, but she refused to have sex with him out of wedlock; early in 1616, they were secretly married. Ardizzino sanctioned the union when he learned that his daughter was to receive the marquisate of Mombasuzzo, which provided a regular income. Camilla's insistence on the decorum of wedlock was one of the few times in her life that she was able to exercise power over her destiny.

The marriages of rulers were crucial bargaining chips in international politics during the Renaissance. Fernando's choice of a wife whom he loved rather than one who was politically expedient was considered outrageous and irresponsible. The duke yielded to public criticism and to the counsel of his courtiers; he sought from the pope an annulment of his vows to Camilla so that he could forge an alliance with the powerful and wealthy Medici family by marrying Catherine de' Medicis. He urgently needed both the money and the political backing to support his recently declared war with the Savoy. In case the pope refused his petition, Fernando also agreed to legal proceedings that would declare the wedding technically invalid on the grounds that a court bishop rather than a parish priest had officiated. The pope did release Fernando from his union with Camilla, however, and two months after she gave birth to their son, Giacinto, the duke married Catherine. The *Storia* describes the new duchess's apprehension about Camilla's influence on the malleable duke and Giacinto's claim to the inheritance. Catherine insisted that her husband force Camilla either to marry someone else or to join a convent. Slandered, exiled, bereft of her child who had been taken away from her to be educated at court, and abandoned by her family who could no longer benefit from her political connections, Camilla resisted for five years yet another campaign to dispossess her. At the age of 23, with no recourse, she capitulated. Upon taking her religious vows in 1622, she acknowledged her complicity in the cultural doctrine that a woman's greatest contribution is self-sacrifice:

Signor Antonio, you may tell His Highness that I have sacrificed my freedom over the altar of obedience in order to serve him, since everyone believes that on this resolution of mine depends the peace and happiness of his house. God grant it to be so for our common benefit. I have only my life left now and this too I offer to serve His Highness, if necessary. More I cannot give, and I do not long for anything.[28]

Camilla's memoir illustrates the extent to which women in Renaissance Italy were legally powerless over their own lives. Subject first to the ownership of her father, virtually sold to her husband, and then in thrall to various institutions—marital, legal, and ecclesiastical—the author examines the nature of authority and the conflicts of obedience and integrity. Despite isolation and deprivation, she would not be silenced. The narrative asserts self-respect and enacts an authorial control over the events that threatened to write her out of her own history. Although Camilla's manuscript remained unpublished for more than two hundred seventy years, the very act of writing her life established her self as a subject that would not be erased. Her memoir provides a window on ways in which the personal and the political were inextricably interwoven in the experiences of Renaissance women.

In sum, though all early modern political theory argued for women's relative or total exclusion from the realm of politics and government, women nonetheless participated in the public sphere, either as rulers, who were seen as extraordinary—indeed, seen as hardly women at all—or as commoners who added their voices to the many popular protests against economic, religious, and social changes and conditions of the day. All women's lives were shaped by politics, particularly the political changes that defined the early modern period. Women, like men, developed a sense of national identity during the period as nation-states emerged from the more regional and local political units of the Middle Ages. And women, particularly middle-class women, came closer to the centers and exercise of power as the middle class came to dominate the political life of many nations during this period.

NOTES

1.   Merry E. Wiesner, *Women and Gender in Early Modern Europe,* 2nd ed. (New York: Cambridge University Press, 2000), 289.

2.   Qtd. in Edward Phillips Statham, *A Jacobean Letter-Writer: The Life and Times of John Chamberlain* (New York: E. P. Dutton, 1920), 182–83.

3.   Bonnie S. Anderson and Judith P. Zinsser, *A History of Their Own: Women in Europe from Prehistory to the Present,* vol. 1 (New York: Harper and Row, 1989), 279.

4.   Anderson and Zinsser, *A History of Their Own,* 278.

5.   Anderson and Zinsser, *A History of Their Own,* 278.

6.   Thomas Edgar, section iii, "The Punishment of Adam's Sin," *The Law's Resolutions of Women's Rights: Or, the Law's Provision for Women* (London, 1556); Pearl Hogrefe, "Legal Rights of Tudor Women and Their Circumvention," *Sixteenth-Century Journal* 3 (1972): 98. Edgar's pamphlet is also excerpted in M. H. Abrams et al., eds., *The Norton Anthology of English Literature,* vol. 1, *Early Seventeenth Century Topic: Gender, Family, Household* (New York: Norton, 1993), <http://www.wwnorton.com/nael/ 17century/topic_1/laws.htm>.

7.   Natalie Zemon Davis, "Women on Top," in *Feminism and Renaissance Studies,* ed. Lorna Hutson (New York: Oxford University Press, 1999), 173–75.

8.   Qtd. in Wiesner, *Women and Gender in Early Modern Europe,* 301–02.

9.   Katherine Romack, "Monstrous Births and the Body Politic: Women's Political Writings and the Strange and Wonderful Travails of Mistris Parliament and Mris. Rump," in *Debating Gender in Early Modern England, 1500–1700,* ed. Cristina Malcolmson and Mihoko Suzuki (New York: Palgrave Macmillan, 2002), 210–11.

10.   Joad Raymond, *Pamphlets and Pamphleteering in Early Modern Britain* (New York: Cambridge University Press, 2003), 302.

11.   [Anon.], *To the supream authority of England…The humble petition of diverse wel-affected woeman of the cities of London…and places adjacent…*(London, 1649).

12.   Qtd. in Raymond, *Pamphlets,* 305.

13.   John Knox, *The First Blast of the Trumpet Against the Monstrous Regiment of Women* (Geneva, 1558), sig. 9v. Knox's pamphlet is available through EEBO, <http://eebo.chadwyck.com>. Though directed at the three royal Marys, Knox's pamphlet was published on the heels of the coronation of Elizabeth I of England.

14.   Qtd. in Abrams et al., eds., 999. Elizabeth's speech is also available online through Luminarium at <http://www.luminarium.org/renlit/tilbury. htm>.

15.   Anderson and Zinsser, *A History of Their Own,* 331.

16.   Anderson and Zinsser, *A History of Their Own,* 323.

17.   Anderson and Zinsser, *A History of Their Own,* 323.

18.   Anderson and Zinsser, *A History of Their Own*, 325.

19.   Charity Cannon Willard, "Margaret of Austria: Regent of the Netherlands," in *Women Writers of the Renaissance and Reformation*, ed. Katharina M. Wilson (Athens: University of Georgia Press, 1987), 356–57.

20.   Diana Primrose, *A Chaine of Pearle or A Memoriall of the peerles Graces, and Heroick Vertues of Queene Elizabeth, of Glorious Memory* (London, 1630), 4, 7. This paean is available through Renaissance Women Online, <http://www.wwp.brown.edu/texts/rwoentry.html>.

21.   Roger Ascham, *The Scholemaster* (London, 1570), 201. This book is available online through Richard Bear's Renascence Editions <http://darkwing.uoregon.edu/~rbear/ascham1.htm>. Ascham included this anecdote about Lady Jane Grey as an illustration of the superiority of his pedagogical methods. He quoted her as saying,

> One of the greatest benefits, that ever God gave me is that he sent me so sharp and severe parents, and so gentle a schoolmaster. For when I am in presence either of father or mother, whether I speak, keep silence, sit, stand, or go, eat, drink, be merry, or sad, be sewing, playing, dancing, or doing anything else, I must do it, as it were, in such weight, measure, and number, even so perfectly, as God made the world, or else I am so sharply taunted, so cruelly threatened, yea presently some times, with pinches, nips, and bobs, and other ways, which I will not name, for the honor I bear them, so without measure misordered, that I think my self in hell, till time cum, that I must go to M. Elmer, who teacheth me so gently, so pleasantly, with such faire allurements to learning, that I think all the time nothing, whiles I am with him. And when I am called from him, I fall on weeping, because, what soever I do else, but learning, is full of grief, trouble, fear, and whole misliking unto me: And thus my book, hath bene so much my pleasure, & bringeth daily to me more pleasure & more, that in respect of it, all other pleasures, in very deed, be but trifles and troubles unto me. (201–2)

22.   Sverre Lyngstad, "Leonora Christina: The Danish Princess," in *Women Writers of the Seventeenth Century*, ed. Katharina M. Wilson and Frank J. Warnke (Athens: University of Georgia Press, 1989), 378.

23.   Lyngstad, "Leonora Christina," 379.

24.   Lyngstad, "Leonora Christina," 385.

25.   Maya C. Bijvoet, "Helene Kottanner: The Austrian Chambermaid," in *Women Writers of the Renaissance and Reformation*, ed. Katharina M. Wilson (Athens: University of Georgia Press, 1987), 337.

26.   Bijvoet, "Helene Kottanner," 340.

27.   Bijvoet, "Helene Kottanner," 341–42.

28.   Valeria Finucci, "Camilla Faà Gonzaga: Italian Memorialist," in *Women Writers of the Seventeenth Century*, ed. Katharina M. Wilson and Frank J. Warnke (Athens: University of Georgia Press, 1989), 136.

SUGGESTED READING

Anderson, Bonnie S., and Judith P. Zinsser. *A History of Their Own: Women in Europe from Prehistory to the Present.* Vol. 1. New York: Harper and Row, 1989.

Hufton, Olwen. *The Prospect before Her: A History of Women in Western Europe, 1500–1800.* New York: Alfred A. Knopf, 1996.

Hutson, Lorna, ed. *Feminism and Renaissance Studies.* New York: Oxford University Press, 1999.

Kelso, Ruth. *Doctrine for the Lady of the Renaissance.* 1956. Urbana: University of Illinois Press, 1978.

Lerner, Gerda. *The Creation of Feminist Consciousness, from the Middle Ages to 1870.* New York: Oxford University Press, 1994.

Malcolmson, Cristina, and Mihoko Suzuki, eds. *Debating Gender in Early Modern England, 1500–1700.* New York: Palgrave Macmillan, 2002.

Raymond, Joad. *Pamphlets and Pamphleteering in Early Modern Britain.* New York: Cambridge University Press, 2003.

Trexler, Richard C. *The Women of Renaissance Florence: Power and Dependence in Renaissance Florence.* Vol. 2. Asheville, NC: Pegasus, 1998.

Wiesner, Merry E. *Women and Gender in Early Modern Europe.* 2nd ed. New York: Cambridge University Press, 2000.

5

⸺∞⸺

Women and Religion

Religion influenced everyday life in the Renaissance in ways so deep and wide-reaching that it is hard to even imagine now. Religion was central to people's experience, whatever their faith or their individual belief or lack of belief. For most early modern Europeans, the Reformation was the most important religious "event" of the period. The Protestant Reformation brought profound change to those who lived in countries like Great Britain, Switzerland, the Netherlands, parts of France, and the many German states that embraced Reformed theologies, religious practice, and church structure; it also affected people living in those countries and states that remained Catholic, as Protestantism had its adherents even in Catholic countries. And Catholics living in Protestant countries often found themselves having to choose between their faith and their homelands, even their very lives. Furthermore, Catholic theology and practices underwent a Reformation as well, what is known as the Counter-Reformation or Catholic Reformation, driven by reforming forces within and shaped by the Catholic response to emerging Protestantism. Jews living throughout Europe were also affected by shifting attitudes of Christians who might call for forced conversion of the Jews at one historical moment and then consult them as biblical scholars at the next, who might require them to lend money to support political ventures and then drive them from their houses and confiscate their goods as religious attitudes shifted. At the same time, other appeals to the supernatural, such as ancient folk religions and astrology, existed alongside these historic religions with their hierarchies of clergy and structures of belief. Early modern peoples might see no contradiction in worshipping in a church or a synagogue, using a charm or a spell to prevent illness, and having their futures predicted through horoscopes.

It is difficult to separate religion from other social and cultural aspects of the Renaissance, because political life, the economy, family structure, and even the disposition of space were influenced by the religious practices of every town and country of the time. For some groups, religion remained nearly inseparable and indistinguishable from other aspects of their collective identity. For devout Jews, there was no real separation between their ethnic, cultural, social, and historic identity and their religious identity, no way to carve out religion, even theoretically, from everything else one knew and experienced from day to day. Religion was also central to the culture of Christians, and many aspects of everyday life, from education to family relationships to politics, were infused with religious ideas and practices. However, it was during this period that Christian thinkers began to be able to think of culture, politics, and social relations as separate from religion, even though it was almost universally agreed that all such systems should be guided by religious principles. When monarchs could change the religion of a whole country by royal mandate and proclaim themselves head of the church, it was almost inevitable that politics and religion would come to be seen as distinct.

All of Europe was marked by the architecture of the dominant religion, Christianity. The most notable buildings were the massive gothic cathedrals and monasteries that had been built in the Middle Ages (from the late twelfth through the fifteenth centuries). The building of churches in northern Protestant Europe mostly ceased in the Renaissance, but some of the most magnificent ecclesiastical structures of Rome were built in the sixteenth century. These included St. Peter's Basilica in the Vatican, the largest church in the world and the mother church of Catholicism, and the Gesù, the home church of the Jesuit religious order that was at the forefront of the Catholic Reformation. Cathedrals as well as parish churches dominated the cityscapes from Italy to northern England; often the spire of a cathedral or a church would be visible from many miles off, since churches tended to be built on the highest point in town, and their spires could reach as much as four hundred feet. Other buildings, whether civic or domestic, rarely grew higher than a few stories. Churches and cathedrals also served as the civic space of the day; on rainy days, their naves would be filled with women and men coming and going to strike deals, sign contracts, barter, and share news. Even towns relatively small by modern standards could have twenty or thirty parish churches and other ecclesiastical buildings, so that there might be some kind of church or chapel on nearly every corner. In addition to churches, towns and cities might have dozens of monasteries and convents; chantries (small chapels where a cleric prayed for the soul of the deceased nobleman or noblewoman who built the structure and supported the prayers); perhaps a school or university, each with its own private chapel (sometimes as grand as a cathedral); and small private chapels in the homes of the wealthier citizens. In Britain and other parts of Europe that embraced the Protestant Reformation and suppressed monasticism, some of these establishments, especially their larger buildings, continued to be used for worship even after the communities of monks and nuns were disbanded; the presence of religion would have remained ubiquitous. Throughout Catholic countries, monastic orders and their buildings endured. In Spain, Christianity became the only accepted religion in the late fifteenth century following a long period when people of Jewish, Muslim, and Christian faiths lived and worshipped side by side in relative mutual toleration and peace. The great mosques of the Moors (Spanish Muslims of Arab descent) were often reconsecrated for Christian use, but their particular architecture and Arabic inscriptions remained a witness to the history of Islam in Spain. And in towns throughout Europe where Jewish communitites were established, schuls (schools) and synagogues would be visible signs of Jewish religious life.

Walking through any town in early modern Europe, one would have been aware of the centrality of religion by hearing alone: the sound of church bells announcing the start of a service or, in Catholic communities, other bells signaling the elevation of the host—when the priest lifts up the bread, representing Christ's body, for the faithful to adore (the moment in the Mass considered most holy). In addition to bells, one might have passed a preacher calling sinners to repentance or speaking of God's love for the world. Franciscans and Dominicans (the latter known as "the order of preachers") were founded in the thirteenth century with a mission to preach to the laity, and the friars of those orders continued to do so in Catholic countries through the Renaissance. Protestant cities, though no longer friendly to such religious orders, often had open-air pulpits where rival preachers would dispute the finer points of doctrine and theology. In those parts of Europe where Jews were able to practice their religion openly, one might have passed men studying and discussing the Torah, heard a cantor singing the liturgy, or heard a Sephardic woman singing songs in Ladino (a mixed Spanish and Hebrew dialect that had first developed among Jews in the Iberian Peninsula). Shabbat candles would have shown in the window of every Jewish household on Friday evenings at sunset.

Christian architecture would have been highly visible on the rural landscape as well as in the cities. In places like England (where

Lighting the Sabbath candles (Luces Sabbathinae), Johannes Leusden, *Philologus Hebraeo-Mixtus* (Utrecht, 1699). *Source:* Reproduced by permission of the Syndics of Cambridge University Library, 2.24.9.

Washing the household vessels before Passover (*Purgatio Vasorum ante Pascha*), Johannes Leusden, *Philologus Hebraeo-Mixtus* (Utrecht, 1699). *Source:* Reproduced by permission of the Syndics of Cambridge University Library, 2.24.9.

there were few large cities, and most of the people lived in the country), the wild and undeveloped forests and fields were dotted by monasteries. Some of them were great and wealthy, with churches that rivaled the massive cathedrals in magnificence. Until the English Reformation, when the monasteries were dissolved (disbanded) the monastic churches would be surrounded by a complex of buildings—kitchens, refectories, dormitories, libraries, infirmaries, and guest houses—that made them like little towns unto themselves. The nuns or monks, along with lay sisters and brothers and other residents, oversaw the clearing of forest land, the draining of swamps, and the raising of crops and beasts. The monasteries provided a highly visible religious presence in the countryside and a safe place for travelers, as hospitality to strangers was one of the prime monastic duties. The sound of monastic church bells and the voices of the monks and nuns chanting "the office" (the prayer services that were sung throughout the day and night) would have been heard in the country along with the sounds of birds and cattle. Following the Reformation, when the monasteries of England were dissolved and their stone walls, lead roofs, and rich furnishings put to other uses (often for building grand private houses), the very massiveness of the monastic structures made it nearly impossible to disassemble them fully. The ruined buildings, with their roofs open to the sky, their blank windows denuded of stained glass, and their crumbling walls covered with vines, remained a significant feature of the landscape and a reminder of the continuity of the old religion in the midst of the new. In Catholic countries, the monasteries and friaries in town and countryside continued to chant the holy offices and to serve the poor.

Renaissance women's roles in religion, as in other spheres of life, were often circumscribed when compared with men's opportunities for religious leadership and expression. Not surprisingly, the Reformation affected women quite differently from men. When the monastic orders were disbanded in Protestant countries, the monks, many of whom were already ordained priests, could continue their vocations as clerics by serving cathedrals and parish churches; in England, many of the monastic churches already served as cathedrals, so the monks did not even need to move to another location to take up their new duties. But the women's houses in England were impoverished compared with most of the men's, and they lacked the great churches and other magnificent buildings that could become parish churches or cathedrals. Furthermore, there were no religious vocations or roles for nuns to fill in the Reformed churches, so the women who were turned out of the convents had no religious vocational options and, indeed, few employment options at all. Some of them married (the German theologian and reformer Martin Luther, who had been a monk, married Katharina von Bora, a nun who had proposed to him), but others would have had to beg housing and support from relatives or from local authorities. Some English Catholic women became exiles, joining or founding religious orders in Catholic areas of northern Europe. Laywomen could assume an activist religious role by tending to the poor, caring for the sick, and providing relief for orphans and the elderly, but their contributions were typically limited to the acts of nurturing and sacrifice considered appropriate to female virtue. However, during unstable times of social change or crisis, such as the early years of the Reformation, the Thirty Years' War (1618–1648), or the English civil wars (1642–1651), women took advantage of opportunities for more public expressions of their religious ideas. Some were able to assert their beliefs in print and in preaching, and others assumed roles as organizers and leaders of the faithful. But as males consolidated their authority and reestablished hierarchies of order and privilege, women's public participation in religious leadership was severely limited and almost always condemned.

It is perhaps not surprising that gender roles in religion would be affected by cataclysmic events like religious reformation and war. It is also important to keep in mind the way that everyday, ongoing social factors, in terms of class, nationality, and even geogra-

Martin Luther and Katharina von Bora, Centenary Medal. *Source:* Reproduced by kind permission of the Ashmolean Museum, Oxford, Hope Collection 66772.

phy, determined just how people of the Renaissance experienced both religious change and continuity. For instance, elite women and men living in urban political centers would have been affected immediately and profoundly by a sovereign's decision to adopt a Reformed religion, as royal mandate might quickly bring new clergy, new ceremonies, and new prayers into royal chapels and churches under the monarch's eye. Those people living in remote rural areas, on the other hand, might not feel the effects so abruptly or deeply. And, of course, the sovereign might be a woman herself, but the consequences for her people could be quite different from those experienced by the people of a male monarch's nation. When Henry VIII rejected the authority of the pope and declared himself head of the English church, the whole country experienced a reformation of religious polity and praxis. But when, for instance, Queen Christina of Sweden (1626–1689) changed her religious allegiance and embraced Catholicism, she had to move to Rome, leaving the religious settlement of her country intact. Considered among the great leaders of Protestant Europe, Christina became Queen of Sweden in 1644 at the age of 18. Ten years after assuming the throne, she announced her conversion to Catholicism, named her cousin as her successor, and then abdicated. One of the most dramatic spectacles of the Counter-Reformation was her triumphant entry into Rome. There, Pope Alexander VII gave her a magnificent welcome and proclaimed a victory of the Catholic Church over Protestant rule. But her victory was in some sense only theoretical, as Christina, unlike her fellow male monarchs, did not have the power to force her country to follow in her footsteps toward Catholicism.

Christina was converted by the French and Spanish ambassadors to her court as well as by two Jesuit priests who were sent to assure her that Catholic doctrine would not interfere with her strong commitment to scholarship and learning. But the queen was by no means just a pawn in diplomatic and religious struggles. She originated and vigorously carried out her plans to abdicate (no small feat for a woman ruler), and she dictated her own terms of conversion. In giving up her throne, she did not give up her ambition or her place on the international political stage. She was a forceful participant in Vatican politics, and she tried (unsuccessfully) to become both Queen of Naples and Queen of Poland. In addition, Christina founded several prominent academies of learning, and she was an important patron of artists, musicians, playwrights, and actors. Her father had groomed her to be queen by insisting that she receive the kind of extensive education usually available only to males, and she was renowned throughout Europe for her intelligence and learning. Fluent in five languages, she wrote treatises on political philosophy and several collections of maxims or wise teachings. Unlike most women of the time, she was able to assert her authority in public and to prevent religious and social restrictions from stifling her education and her options.

But even those women and men with little education—even the masses who were illiterate—knew about religious changes and discussed them, for everyone could hear sermons and public disputations. An Italian visitor to England in the late sixteenth century noted that even women and shopkeepers engaged in religious discussions.[1] It is evident that women attended public religious events, for their contemporaries criticized weekday religious lectures precisely because they attracted women. Women might also draw criticism for expressing their theological preference by going outside their own parish to hear a preacher whose views they preferred to their local minister's. Perhaps as a result of the public involvement of women, shopkeepers, and other socially marginalized groups in religious discussion, a 1543 act of Parliament prohibited all but men and upper-class women from reading the Bible, while those upper-class women were forbidden to read the Bible aloud to others.

Elsewhere in Europe, everyday life was subject to thoroughgoing religious scrutiny under Calvinist Protestants. By the middle of the sixteenth century, Switzerland, the Netherlands, present-day Belgium, and parts of France were dominated by the religious ideas of the Swiss reformer John Calvin (1509–1564), whose *Institutes of the Christian Religion* called for an utter obliteration of the Catholic Church in favor of Reformed religion. Calvinist religious authorities proscribed dancing, fancy dress, tobacco, coffee, village fairs, and even laughter and levity. Instead, people were to go about in severe sobriety and reserve with strict limitations on any kind of exuberance or spontaneity. On Sundays in Calvinist communities, money markets were closed, and no trade or business was allowed; any payments or economic transactions made on Sundays were legally invalid. In Amsterdam, the town gates were closed during the hours of worship, and in Calvinist areas throughout northern Europe, streets and village lanes were deserted except for the brief minutes before and after the morning and afternoon church services. Children were often tested after each service to make sure that they had paid close attention to the sermons that might run many hours long.

Most women and men who lived in rural areas throughout Europe, though they would have had little formal education, nonetheless had opinions about religious change, a fact evidenced by the many large and small popular revolts in protest against or in support of new theologies or practices. For a number of reasons, women would sometimes be in the forefront of such revolts, especially when the demonstrations were sparked by food shortages, which particularly affected women, as they were responsible for feeding their families. In other cases, women and men dressed as women would lead demonstrations either because women were thought (incorrectly) to be immune from prosecution or because the vision of women taking leadership roles in a public place was the ideal symbol of a world turned upside down.[2] And, of course, women cared every bit as much as men about religious as well as economic issues. In 1536, for instance, a group of English women armed with farm implements attacked workmen who were dismantling a monastery under orders from the king, and other records from the period depict groups of German women attacking clergy they found unacceptable. In another instance, English worshippers of the late sixteenth century, who objected to the overly Puritanical tendencies of their local priest, each brought a Book of Common Prayer to church one Sunday morning to force the priest to conform to the practices of the Church of England as specified in the Prayer Book.[3]

Most religious protests were small and local, but other demonstrations were large, protracted, and violent, and religious change often sparked rioting about a wide range of grievances. In Germany, the Peasants' Revolt of 1524–1525 drew on Martin Luther's ideas such as Christian liberty and the primacy of divine law over secular law to protest social and economic wrongs. Though Luther initially supported the peasants, he became increasingly horrified by the spreading violence and disregard for hierarchical order. He ultimately called for the peasants to cease their revolt, supporting a violent crackdown on the demonstrators. In England, King Henry VIII's Dissolution of the Monasteries in 1535–1536—his action to seize the wealth, buildings, and land of the English monasteries and to secularize the monks and nuns as part of England's Reformation—sparked massive public demonstrations. One such revolt was the Pilgrimage of Grace, which favored a retreat from the Protestant Reformation and the restoration of Catholicism. Tens of thousands turned out and marched to protest religious change, not only the Dissolution but also England's rejection of papal authority and its espousal of Luther's ideas. In England as in Germany, the protests were violently quashed, and many demonstrators were executed. Though these and other protestors always had a wide range of social and economic grievances, the protestors tended to express those grievances in religious terms. The Reformation thus often provided an occasion for political protest and a language of dissent.

Likewise, the motives of political and religious leaders who initiated the reforms were always political as well as religious. For instance, while there were serious reformers in England in the early sixteenth century, Henry VIII broke with the Catholic Church so as to secure a divorce, to establish his sole political authority over church matters, and to seize the great wealth held by the monasteries in order to enrich the coffers of the monarchy; he actually seems to have had very little interest in making substantive religious change. Similarly, when Henri IV of France opted to remain faithful to Catholicism, his motives, too, were political. Henri famously declared in 1594 that "Paris vaut bien une messe" (Paris is well worth a Mass). Though he had Protestant sympathies, he was willing to retain Catholicism, represented by the Mass, as France's official religion in exchange for control of Paris, the political center of the country. While the pope remained the nominal head of the church in France, the French monarch had, in actuality, great power and leeway in religious matters, making Reformation there less necessary to the monarch's political authority than it was in England. In northern Europe, the official religion of any of the German states, whether Catholic or Protestant, depended entirely on the decision of the local prince or duke, and those political leaders made their decisions for chiefly pragmatic and political reasons related to their ability to maintain power and exercise authority within their domain. Throughout Europe at the time, a country's break with Rome or its adherence to Catholicism depended on the political support of the sovereign and a host of social and economic factors.

The profound ways in which religion and politics informed each other and the defining effect they had on the course of women's lives is illustrated in the experiences of Kata Szidónia Petrēzi

(1662–1708). Born in what is now the Czech Republic, she was the daughter of Lutheran parents who resisted Catholic Hapsburg rule. Her mother died when Kata Szidónia was an infant, probably from difficulties in childbirth. Forced to flee her place of birth and stripped of her assets because of her family's religious and political resistance, Kata Szidónia was restored to wealth upon her husband's conversion from Lutheranism to Catholicism. But they were dispossessed of their fortune when he changed his political alliances and renounced Catholicism. After his second "conversion," she was imprisoned for nearly a year and suffered a stroke in jail. Despite her husband's vacillations, Kata Szidónia remained resolute in her resistance to Catholicism and the Holy Roman Empire. From the time of her release from prison until her death, she lived in exile as a political and religious refugee. Throughout her struggle with the government, with the distress caused by her opportunistic husband, and with the difficulties of bearing 11 children (five girls and six boys, of which only the girls survived), Kata Szidónia expressed her personal and religious convictions in writing. She never published her numerous poems of political defiance, betrayed love, and religious faith, but she did pay to have printed her translation of a German treatise entitled *The Agony of the Acquaintances of Those Lutheran Souls Who Have Converted to Catholicism*. She also translated and published several collections of Johann Arndt's (1555–1621) spiritual poetry. Both the life and writing of Kata Szidónia eloquently demonstrate the ways in which religion and politics were fused in the Renaissance, and both illustrate the material and emotional consequences of that conjunction.

Just as individuals vacillated between religious camps, states and countries often wavered before settling on a particular Christian practice and structure. England moved back and forth between Catholicism and Protestantism under succeeding monarchs before finally settling under Elizabeth I into a *via media*; this Protestant "middle way" was between the two religious poles in terms of theology, ecclesiastical structure, and praxis. In the interim, many clerical leaders and laypeople, including women, were executed by both Catholic and Reformed monarchs. Anne Askew (1521–1546), a member of the Reformed church, was imprisoned, tortured, tried, and executed during Henry VIII's reign for holding opinions considered to be too Protestant. Askew left a record of her "examinations" (her questioning and torture) in which she recorded her statement that she believed salvation lies in personal study of the Bible and prayer, not in church sacraments. She wrote, "I would rather read five lines in the Bible, than hear five masses in the temple." She was accused of heresy for "uttering the scriptures" in defiance of the supposed Pauline command that women were not "to speak or talk of the word of God," but she noted:

> I knew Paul's meaning so well as [the religious authorities examining her], which is, 1 Corinthians 14, that a woman ought not to speak in the congregation by the way of teaching. And then I asked him, "How many women he had seen go into the pulpit and preach?" He said, "He never saw none." Then I said, "He ought to find no fault in poor women, except [unless] they offended the law."[4]

Askew was condemned as a heretic to be burned at the stake; though she was given an opportunity to recant her beliefs just before her execution, she refused, and was burned to death. She became a celebrated martyr, both to those who sympathized with her and even to some who condemned her. However, the Jesuit priest Robert Parsons (1546–1610) claimed that "she did in secret seek to corrupt divers people, but especially women," and he saw her sins as particularly related to her gender. She was, he said, "a coy dame, and of very evil fame for wantonness in that she left the company of her husband Master Kyme to gad up and downe the country a-gospelling and gossiping where she might and ought not."[5] But Parsons's was a minority opinion, and Askew's fame spread through the publication of her writings and those of other authors who memorialized her, as well as through "The Ballad of Anne Askew," purported to have been written by her. It reads in part:

> My spirit within me is vexed sore,
> My flesh striveth against the same:
> My sorrows do increase daily more and more,
> My conscience suffereth most bitter paine:
> I with my selfe being thus at strife,
> Would faine have bin at peace and rest:
> Musing and studying in my mortall life,
> What thing I might doe to please God best.[6]

Askew had been supported by Henry VIII's sixth and last wife, Katherine Parr, who offered Askew financial assistance through her ladies-in-waiting and who was probably instrumental in getting Askew pardoned the first time she was arrested. Askew's examinations were in part an attempt to get her to name her supporters, particularly those at court. Parr was an ardent Protestant and far more radical in her religious inclinations than her royal husband; she was known to have lectured Henry on religious doctrine (which incurred his wrath). Though Parr had been given a good education as a young girl, it was not sufficient to her passion for religious study, and she learned Latin and Greek as an adult in order to be able to read the New Testament in the original as well as the many religious commentaries and studies that were written in Latin. In 1545, two years after she became queen, Parr published *Prayers or Medytacions … Collected out of Certayne Holy Workes,* and she published *The Lamentacion of a Synner* in 1547, after Henry's death. While the first work was primarily a compilation of prayers from other sources, *The Lamentacion* is a record of Parr's spiritual journey in overtly Protestant terms, with an emphasis on justification by faith.

> This dignitie of fayth is no derogation [abrogation] to good workes, for out of this fayth springeth al good workes. Yet we may not impute to the worthynes of fayth or workes, our iustificacion before God: but ascribe & geue the worthines of it, wholly to the merites of Christes passion, and referre and attribute the knowledge & perceiuyng therof, onely to fayth.[7]

Parr promoted the careers of the biblical translator Miles Coverdale, Bishop of Exeter (1488–1569), and Thomas Cranmer (1489–1556), Archbishop of Canterbury and author of the first Book of Common Prayer. Though she was loved by Henry, his children, and those at court, she also had her detractors, and her books were seized by religious authorities just before Askew's execution. Indeed, the Catholic priest Parsons claimed that Askew had implicated Parr, asserting that "by her confession [Henry] learned so much of Q. Catherine Parr, he had purposed to have burned her also, if he had lived."[8] But Parr saved her own life by disavowing some of her more evangelical books and bowing to Henry's mastery in matters religious.

There were many individuals, both Catholic and Protestant, who were martyred for their particular faith in England and on the Continent. But far more devastating were the protracted struggles called the Thirty Years' War (1618–1648), a horrific series of battles in central Europe among Catholics, Lutherans, and Calvinists that involved the leaders and peoples of the Holy Roman Empire (centered in Austria and allied to Spain), against France, Germany, Denmark, and Sweden. As always, the participants' religious differences were inextricably connected to dynastic struggles and economic problems. The Thirty Years' War was fought on battlefields across Europe and made death and suffering an everyday part of the lives of all peoples living there; some countries lost as much as 30 percent of their population to the widespread destruction. As is often the case, people sought scapegoats to blame for their troubles, and witch hunts intensified in many parts of Europe during this time. Most of those accused, tried, and executed for being witches were women. (See also chapter 2: "Women and the Law.")

All religions of the period agreed generally that religion was important to women's lives and that women had particular religious roles to play. The duties associated with those roles varied depending on whether a woman was Jewish or Christian, Protestant or Catholic. But, for the most part, women's religious duties tended to be marked by their relationship to a private sphere, whether in a family home or in a convent. Many women found strong voices within these circumscribed arenas, but others protested against the limitations placed on their religious expression and sought to expand their sphere of activity and influence. Then as now, there were some who found religion burdensome and meaningless. Though religious conformity among Christians—that is, the acceptance of a particular religious confession and attendance at services a minimum number of times per year—was legally required in many countries and socially compelled in all, many women and men met the minimum obligations of church attendance and lived relatively secular lives in the midst of a culture whose language, art, and politics were permeated with religious imagery and meaning.

Most religious leaders thought that women's particular religious roles should be confined within the private household. Women were responsible for the religious education of the youngest children, and, as most girls did not receive formal education either at home with a tutor or in a school, their entire education would usually be the responsibility of their mothers. (See also chapter 1: "Women and Education.") In larger households, where the family included servants, the mother of the house would have some responsibility for ordering the religious life of those who worked in the household and for participating in daily prayers at meals and other times. In England, Lady Margaret Hoby (1571–1633) kept a diary from 1599–1605 in which she detailed her daily activities, including her prayer life. Hoby's religious life—family and private prayer, reading the Bible as well as contemporary religious works like sermons, and copying such material into her commonplace book—gave meaning to everyday activities like cleaning, sewing, and food preparation as well as neighborly activities like attending the birth of a child. On Wednesday, August 15, 1599, she wrote:

> In the morning at 6 o'clock I prayed privately: that done, I went to a wife in travail of child, about whom I was busy till 1 o'clock, about which time she being delivered and I having praised God, returned home and betook myself to private prayer two several [separate] times upon the occasion: then I writ the most part of an examination or trial of a Christian, framed by Mr. Rhodes, in the doing where[of] I again fell to prayer, and after continued writing after 3 o'clock: the Lord made me thankful, who hath heard my prayers and hath not turned his face from me: then I talked with Mrs. Brutnell till supper time, and after walked a little into the fields, and so to prayers, and then to bed.[9]

Though Hoby was not a nun—indeed, she was a thoroughgoing Protestant—her daily life was as ordered and suffused by prayer and other religious activities as if she had lived in a convent.

In Jewish homes, women had particular Sabbath responsibilities for lighting candles and saying prayers. Because Judaism was restricted or outlawed in some areas, Jewish women, particularly in Sephardic communities, might bear a crucial responsibility for preserving religious customs and practices for many generations in times when there were no synagogues or schools and the Jewish religion was practiced primarily in the home. The Sephardim were descendants of Iberian Jews who had lived in Spain for many centuries before their expulsion in 1492 under the joint monarchs Ferdinand and Isabella, or later, in 1497, from Portugal. Jews in these countries were given the choice of forced conversion to Christianity or exile. Many Jews at this time became Conversos, or Christian converts, but some few faithfully practiced their religion secretly, what is called "crypto-Judaism." Both those Conversos who stayed in Spain and those who migrated to other European countries were often subject to social and economic discrimination, as there was often a distinction made between "Old Christians" and "New Christians," that is, between those who had been born Christian and those who had converted from Judaism (Conversos). Those who retained their Jewish religious identity and practices experienced varying degrees of tolerance or persecution.

In some parts of Europe—such as Poland (at least for a time) and in the Ottoman Empire (the Turkish Islamic Empire of eastern Europe and North Africa), where many Jews migrated and where they were more fully accepted—they practiced their religion openly and legally. Synagogues were built within the Jewish quarters of many European towns in the late Middle Ages and early in the Renaissance, and Jewish communities might bloom and thrive for decades before some community catastrophe—the plague or another epidemic—would make the Jews victims of scapegoating. Then they would be driven from town and their buildings would be razed. A few Jewish religious structures have survived, like the Alteneuschule in Prague (now in the Czech Republic), the oldest synagogue in continuous use, which was built in the late thirteenth century and resembles Christian churches of the same era. A tiny building for women's public worship was added to the Alteneuschule several hundred years after it was first built, since women were not allowed to worship alongside men in public, but Jewish women's primary religious activity would have been in the home. Notwithstanding the romantic story told in the novel and, later, the 1983 movie *Yentl*, women were discouraged from learning Hebrew and studying the Torah, just as Christian women of the time were discouraged or prevented from learning Greek and Latin, the languages of Christian theology and scholarship. Nonetheless, there were some women in Renaissance Italy who had learned Hebrew and who "prayed daily and on the Sabbath, some wearing *tefillin*," or phylacteries, small boxes containing scriptural texts written in Hebrew worn typically by Jewish men during their recitation of morning prayers. Some women even led prayers in the women's section of the synagogue. Other Italian Jewish women, denied "direct access to the Torah" during services because men and women were seated in separate sections of the synagogue, created lavishly embroidered *mappot,* the binder that wrapped the Torah scrolls. They identified themselves as the makers of the *mappot* (though always in relationship to a man, whether husband, father, or grandfather), thus making them-

selves present to the central rituals of Judaism through their handiwork if not their bodies.[10]

Though they were barred from the rabbinate, Jewish women
nonetheless experienced and contributed to their rich religious
heritage and took leadership roles among other women worshippers. Though the historical sources on Jewish women are scanty,
special women's prayers called *tkhines,* supplications recited in
Yiddish by central and eastern European Ashkenazic Jewish
women (first collected and published in the sixteenth century),
provide a window into these women's religious lives. The collected
tkhines include directions for when and how the prayers were to
be said, for example, "Every woman should say this every day,
morning and evening"; or "When a woman becomes pregnant, she
should say this every day or when she is giving birth"; or "On the
eve of the Day of Atonement at nightfall before *Kol nidrei* one
should say this *tkhine* with devotion."[11] As these rubrics suggest,
the prayers were sometimes connected to Jewish holidays and
liturgies or salient to occasions in a woman's life. Other prayers
accompanied the actions and events of everyday life, as this
prayer for baking:

> Lord of all the world, in your hand is all blessing. I come now to
> revere your holiness, and I pray you to bestow your blessing on the
> baked goods. Send an angel to guard the baking … as you blessed
> the dough of Sarah and Rebecca our mothers.[12]

This *tkhine* shows women who consecrated their days and works
and who understood themselves to be connected to the matriarchs of their history and culture.

In addition, just as Christian women often wielded political
power or found a religious voice during times of social disruption,
so also did some Jewish women in periods when rabbinical and
patriarchal authority were unstable, in spite of the greater danger
to which their transgressive actions exposed them, both as Jews
and as women. Beatrice Benveniste de Luna (1510–1569) was born in
Portugal soon after the forced conversion of the Jews there in 1497.
She and her family escaped to Venice when the Inquisition, newly
established in Portugal, ordered a crackdown against "judaizers,"
those converts who were suspected of secretly practicing Judaism.
Indeed, Beatrice's family were crypto-Jews who lived for a time in
Venice as wealthy Christians while helping to resettle other Iberian Jews in safety. But Beatrice's dispute with her sister over the

terms of their father's will brought the family to the attention of the authorities once again, and the two split apart, with Beatrice moving to Ferrara (in Italy). There she was ultimately joined by her sister, with whom she had reconciled, and both women took Jewish names (Beatrice became Doña Gracia Nasi) and lived openly as Jews. She ultimately immigrated to the Ottoman Empire, where she was free to practice her religion and lived as a prominent and wealthy citizen. Indeed, religious toleration under the Muslim Turks was such that her nephew, openly Jewish and once under sentence of death in Venice, was appointed by the sultan as Duke of Naxos, an island the Turks had recently captured from the Venetians.[13]

It was not only Jews who were subjected to forced conversion. During this same era, Christian explorers and "planters" (colonists), both Catholic and Protestant, compelled thousands of indigenous peoples in the Americas to convert to Christianity. Indeed, explorers and colonizers often justified their brutal actions by claiming they conquered in the name of God and for the "true faith." Some women converts became famous as symbols of Native American submission to the supposed superiority of European male political, marital, and religious rule. Malintzín, known popularly today as La Malinche, was an Aztec woman who served as a translator for the army of Hernán Cortés (1485–1547) in his conquest of Mexico. She was mistress to Cortés and had a son by him before she was married off to one of his followers. Malintzín was used by the Spanish chroniclers as a vehicle for propaganda about Christian preeminence and womanly submission. Cortés's biographer, Bernal Díaz del Castillo, wrote that "Doña Marina," as the Spanish called her, refused all local honor because

> God had been very gracious to her in freeing her from the worship of idols and making her a Christian, and giving her a son by her lord and master Cortés, also in marrying her to such a gentleman as her husband Juan Jaramillo. Even if they were to make her mistress of all the provinces of New Spain, she said, she would refuse the honour, for she would rather serve her husband and Cortés than anything else in the world.[14]

The story of Pocahontas is remarkably similar. The daughter of a Powhatan chief in present-day Virginia, she was taken captive by the English in 1612 and instructed in Christianity. It might be wondered how free she was, as a prisoner of the English, either to refuse to convert to Christianity or to refuse to marry John Rolfe; in any case, she did both, was renamed Rebecca Rolfe, and traveled to England in 1616 with her husband and baby son. She died just after beginning the return voyage to North America. Like Malintzín, she stands for the subordination of "inferior races" to European religion and culture and for what was seen as the proper submission of women to men in marriage.

In Europe, Christian women's opportunities for religious expression and activity as well as their ability to choose celibacy differed

Cannoness of Cologne in a choir habit (Chanoinesse de Cologne en habit de choeur), L'Abbaie de Nôtre Dame du Capitole à Cologne, Pierre Hélyot and Maximilien Bullot, *Histoire des ordres monastiques* (Paris, 1714–1719). *Source:* Reproduced by permission of the Syndics of Cambridge University Library, 5.29.72.

widely depending on their religious denomination. In Catholic countries and cities, a small number of elite women could become nuns, a vocation that provided them with educational opportunities and access to learning and books unavailable to most women. The women in these religious houses contributed to their communities by providing education for some privileged girls in convent schools, copying and illustrating books, providing medical care for the poor, giving spiritual counsel to other women, and praying for the world around them. Jacqueline Pascal (1625–1661), sister of the French philosopher Blaise Pascal (1623–1662) and daughter of a minor noble and politician caught up in the French wars of religion, was a learned nun of the Port-Royal Abbey and headmistress of its boarding school for girls. She was a published author by the age of 12, and her later verse won her both acclaim at court and a national prize. She had wanted to join the order at Port-Royal since visiting there at age 21, but her father intended her for marriage. However, his poor health forced him to depend on Jacqueline, and she negotiated an agreement with him that would allow her to live a religious life at home so long as she continued to oversee his care and act as his secretary. Within three months of his death, she entered the convent of Port-Royal, eventually taking the name Soeur Jacqueline de Sainte Euphemie. Though her brother Blaise initially opposed her choice, he ultimately came to agree with her and to ally himself with the monks of Port-Royal. Ultimately the Abbey was engulfed in the religious struggles between warring factions, and its confessors, postulants, and students were turned out. The remaining nuns, including Jacqueline, were forced to pledge allegiance to a particular religious formula. After both Jacqueline and Blaise had died, their older sister, Gilberte, wrote their biographies, *On the Life of Soeur Jacqueline de Sainte Euphemie Pascal's Sister* and *Monsieur Pascall's Thoughts, Meditations, and Prayers*. The Abbey itself was destroyed in the early eighteenth century as the religious wars raged on.

Although Jacqueline's achievements as a writer were well known, most female religious were unknown beyond their communities and remain unnamed or obscure to us today. But a few nuns made a larger impact, and their names have become important to religious history for their significant contributions to theology and spiritual practice. For instance, the works of the Spanish nun Teresa of Avila (1515–1582) are widely read today, and her spiritual practices still guide many nuns as well as laypeople. When she was 20 years old, Teresa entered a Carmelite convent against her father's consent, though he ultimately relented and supported her decision. Her health was very poor, and she was in spiritual agony because of the great faults she supposed herself to have. But she ultimately developed a strong spiritual practice and came to accept her repeated experiences of the supernatural, both in visions and sounds. In her later years, she wrote an autobiography (*Life Written By Herself*) where she described, in very personal terms, her spiritual journey. She also authored a kind of handbook for the faithful called *The Interior Castle,* a metaphor for the soul's journey, room by room, toward union with God. Teresa ultimately founded a number of Carmelite convents in Spain that followed a spiritual practice based on her writings, and her method influenced houses of friars (male religious) as well. While her religious life was traditional in many ways, and she did not advocate for wide social change, Teresa nonetheless defended women's goodness and their place in Christianity. One of her prayers begins, "Lord, thou didst not despise women, but didst always help them and show them great compassion. Thou didst find more faith and no less love in them than in men."[15]

Like Teresa of Avila, Marie Guyart (1599–1672) was a pioneering nun and author of a spiritual autobiography. Born in Tours and married at age 17, she had a son at 18 and was widowed and bankrupt six months later. She refused to remarry, and in 1634 she became an Ursuline nun, adopting the name Marie de l'Incarnation. It was extraordinarily rare for nuns, who were usually cloistered, to work as missionaries in the Renaissance, but Marie volunteered to assist the Jesuits in establishing the first religious house of women in New France. In 1639, she sailed to Quebec, Canada, to found an Ursuline school for Native Americans. She learned Algonquin, Iriquois, Montagnais, and Ouendat and wrote several dictionaries and other texts in those languages. In addition, she wrote over thirteen thousand letters as well as her spiritual autobiography, *A Relation,* one of the classics of the spiritual life.

Sixteenth-century Italy saw a florescence of women with religious vocations. Among them were those who followed the example of the noted saint Catherine of Siena (1347–1380) by becoming "tertiaries" to established orders like the Dominicans or Franciscans. Tertiaries, or members of monastic "third orders," are women and men who for some reason cannot or do not wish to take religious vows but who ally themselves with an order and live by its rules, sometimes within convent walls and sometimes in family homes. Many of these women were illiterate; during their lifetimes, their fame and influence came through their teaching and counseling, and, after their deaths, through the *vitae,* or life stories, about their beliefs, practices, and visions. Colomba of Rieti (1467–1501) founded a convent of Dominican tertiaries that included young women and widows, while Osanna Andreasi of Mantua (1449–1505) lived as a Dominican tertiary in her own home, where she dedicated her life to charitable works. Chiara Bugni (1471–1514) joined a group of Franciscan tertiaries when she was 18 and lived in the Ospedale del Santo Sepolcro, a hospice or inn for pilgrims traveling to the Holy Land (Jerusalem). The hospice ultimately became a cloistered convent, and Bugni was named prioress, or head, of the women living there. Caterina Mattei of Racconigi (1486–1547) was a silk weaver and Dominican tertiary who lived in a private home with two other tertiaries until she was exiled from the city by a new local governor. She was revered during her lifetime and dictated a record of her life to her confessors (priests to whom she would make a regular confession of her sins). Perhaps the most famous holy woman of Italy at this time was a Dominican nun, Caterina de' Ricci (1522–1590). She was known for her mystical experience and for bearing stigmata, wounds on her hands, feet, side, and forehead that resembled the marks of Christ's crucifixion. (Francis of Assisi [ca. 1181–1226] was the first person recorded to have manifested the stigmata, and Catherine of Siena had stigmata as well.) Caterina's stigmata appeared regularly in periods of extended "ecstasy" or visions of the Passion (the events of Christ's arrest, trial, and crucifixion). She would emerge from the visions with the marks of Christ's torment. These Italian holy women are not, for the most part, remembered for their writings or teachings so much as for their lives of devotion, their ecstatic visions, and the miracles they performed during and after their deaths.[16]

Elsewhere in Catholic Europe, confraternities (religious guilds) provided urban laywomen with opportunities for acts of devotion and charity. Many confraternities admitted both men and women, and some elite groups preserved an equal but limited number of spots for women, each of whom would be paired with an ordained or professed cleric who would direct her life of prayer and holy acts. Confraternities sometimes overlapped with guilds and the interests of artisans and professionals, and the confraternities were often brought under the scrutiny of authorities, who saw the piety of their members as a guise for political agitation and economic unrest. Confraternities also courted official reprimand when they encroached on practices reserved for clergy, such as serving "holy bread" at their communal gatherings; the confraternities then were seen as competing with ecclesiastic structure and undermining the authority of the ordained ministry. But confraternities remained popular, and the numbers of women who joined grew through the sixteenth century, in part because they offered women a devotional practice less confining and regimented than that available to nuns or even tertiaries, who were increasingly restricted during this time. The charitable work of women members of confraternities might be directed toward other women in particular, and they often provided dowries for impoverished girls, trained midwives, and cared for women in hospitals. In sixteenth-century Krakow, Poland, all the confraternities were open to both women and men. People could join as part of a group (whole parishes, families, masters and their apprentices) or as individuals. The great majority who joined were women, and they were not among the wealthy or the influential; rather, the bulk of members were poor, including great numbers of widows and the working poor. Confraternities thrived throughout this period in the Catholic countries of Europe as well as the Catholic settlements in the Americas.

Catholic women in Europe who defied conventional ideas about women's place and limitations could also find themselves in trouble with church authorities. In England under Elizabeth I, where Catholicism was outlawed, Catholic women and men who refused to swear allegiance to the English Protestant Church and to Elizabeth as its head (called "recusants" because they recused or refused the authority of the English church) put their lives in danger for practicing their faith and for harboring priests. Women were particularly active in hiding priests from the law, sometimes in defiance of their Protestant husbands. Dorothy Lawson (1580–1632) had a secret chapel built in her home during her husband's repeated absences on business and, after his death, harbored many Catholic priests. Margaret Clitherow (ca. 1556–1586), whose husband supported her activities on behalf of Catholics though he himself remained Protestant, was repeatedly impris-

Pope-ass Monster, anti-Catholic satire, STC 17797. *Source:* Reproduced by permission of the Folger Shakespeare Library.

oned for harboring priests and for having the Mass celebrated at her house. When last arrested, she refused to plead guilty or not guilty so as to save her children and servants from having to testify against her; as a result, by the requirements of the law, she was condemned to suffer *peine forte et dure,* crushed to death by heavy stones. She walked to the site of her execution barefoot, having sent her socks and shoes to her daughter with the hope that she might follow in her mother's footsteps.

Mary Ward (1585–1645) was another Englishwoman who remained true to the Catholic faith in defiance of the law, but her ideas and practices got her in trouble with Catholic authorities as well. Ward came from a Catholic family, and she was pious and devoted from her youth. She entered a convent in France when she was 21 but found herself unsuited to the cloistered life. Instead, she and the friends she had gathered around her—her Companions—founded an order of uncloistered women who would carry forth their work in the world. Ultimately called the Institute of the Blessed Virgin Mary (IBVM), the order was modeled on the Society of Jesus (the Jesuits) and made its mission the education of women. But the idea that women would do religious work in public spaces was unacceptable to the Catholic authorities. Indeed, her detractors called Ward and her Companions "the galloping girls" because of their insistence that they be able to move about freely. Pope Pius V (1504–1572) had declared that women in religious orders were to be strictly cloistered, that is, they had to stay inside the bounds of the convent and do the kind of work suited to that life. As a result, Ward's new order was suppressed by Catholic authorities. Ward traveled to Rome more than once to defend her work to succeeding popes, but the order was suppressed, and Ward was, for a time, imprisoned. She was allowed to found a house for women in England under the patronage of Queen Henrietta Maria, wife of Charles I and a Catholic herself, but the religious conflicts in England undermined any sustained attempt by Ward or her followers to educate girls in England. After Ward's death, her followers did found some houses in England (under the protection of another Catholic queen, Catherine of Braganza, wife of Charles II), in Catholic Ireland, and on the Continent in Catholic as well as Protestant countries and states. The order, now called the Congregation of Jesus, continues today, faithful to its founder's goal of educating women.

Other groups of recusant Catholic women, some of them descendants of Sir Thomas More (1478–1535), who was executed by Henry VIII when More refused to support Henry's break with Catholicism, left England for the Continent, where they joined and founded convents in Flanders and northern France. One scholar notes that

> [b]etween 1539 and 1598 when the first post-Reformation English monastery was established, a steady stream of English women had flowed in Continental convents, but membership in "foreign" houses had posed many logistical and cultural problems. Therefore, in collaboration with exiled lay Catholics and clergy, various women determined to begin expatriate English cloisters, which would serve their particular needs. From the late sixteenth century, in France,

Execution of Sir Thomas More, John Fisher, Bishop of Rochester, and Margaret, Countess of Salsbury (mother of Cardinal Reginald Pole) for refusing to acknowledge the supremacy of King Henry VIII in the English Church, Giovanni Battista de Cavalleris, *Ecclesiae Anglicanae Trophaea…* (Rome, [1584]), plate 22. *Source:* Reproduced by permission of the Syndics of Cambridge University Library, P.2.33(2).

the southern Netherlands and Portugal, 22 such institutions were founded, which adhered to the rules of St Benedict, St Augustine, St Clare, St Brigid, St Dominic, and the reformed Carmelite constitutions.

The nuns at these establishments "ran small schools and guesthouses, wrote devotional works, and sometimes engaged in overt political activities in the quest for their long held desire to return eventually to English soil." Like More's daughters, these expatriate English nuns benefited from—and made available to other girls—the best education of the day, far beyond what most women could even dream of, and they left to posterity a number of religious treatises and one of the finest poems of the era, religious or secular.[17] In her short life, Gertrude More (1601–1633) wrote a number of spiritual treatises, including "The Holy Practices of a Divine Lover, or the Saintly Idiot's Devotions" (a title that underscored her humility) and a few poems, including "Magnes Amoris Amor" [The Magnet of Love is Love]. In the poem, Gertrude speaks of the suppression of Catholics in England and her ardent love for Christ:

> Renowned *More* whose blessed Fate
> England neer yet could expiate,
> Such was thy constant *Faith,* so much
> Thy *Hope,* thy *Charity* was such,
> As made thee twice a Martyr prove,
> Of *Faith* in Death, in Life of *Love!*
> View heer thy Grandchilds broken *Hart,*
> Wounded with a *Seraphick Dart.*
> Who while she liv'd mortals among
> Thus to her *Spouse Divine* she sung
> *Mirrour of beauty in whose face*
> *The essence lives of every grace!*
> *True lustre dwels in they Sole Spheare.*
> *Those glimmerings that sometimes appeare*
> *In this dark vale, this gloomy night,*
> *Are shadows tipped with glow-worm light.*
> *Show me thy radiant parts above,*
> *Where angels unconsumèd move,*
> *Where amorous fire maintaines their lives,*
> *As man, by breathing air, survives.*
> *But if perchance the mortal eye,*
> *That views thy dazzling looks must dye,*
> *With blindfaith here I'll kiss them and desire*
> *To feele the heat, before I see the fire.*[18]

Though women were discouraged both from writing and from expressing their amorous desire, the license of religion allowed Gertrude to do both.

Queen Elizabeth I (1533–1603), under whose reign Catholicism had been outlawed, had herself been endangered for her religion under the reign of her sister, Mary, who was a Catholic. Elizabeth was the daughter of Anne Boleyn, for whom Henry VIII, Elizabeth's father, broke with the Church in Rome and established the Church of England with himself as head. Henry wanted a divorce from the Catholic Catherine of Aragon—who in their more than twenty years of marriage had given birth to only one child who survived into adulthood, a daughter—in order to marry Anne, who had Protestant leanings. For a variety of political reasons, the pope would not grant Henry's petition for a divorce, though papal consent for royal divorce was not uncommon at the time. Henry's solution was to take over the church, an action that put him in good company with other European rulers and with the politics of Reformation and Counter-Reformation. Henry had hoped that Anne would provide him with a son and heir to the throne, but she gave birth solely to Elizabeth.

Thus, in a way, Elizabeth was the embodiment of the Reformation in England. When she became queen, she was a magnet for animosity on the part of both Catholics, who wanted her to return England to the old religion, and radical Protestants, who did not think she had reformed the English Church enough. But the moderate form of religion that she instituted suited her own inclinations, a combination of Protestant theology and Catholic liturgies and church structure. For a while after her consecration as queen, the pope thought that, in spite of her Protestant origins, Elizabeth might turn the English church back to Catholicism. Elizabeth fostered that line of thinking by her extended courtship with a number of Catholic princes, including Philip II of Spain and the French Duke of Anjou. At the same time, she sent military and financial aid to Protestants in Scotland and in France (to the Huguenots). When it became clear to all involved that she had no intention of either marrying or changing the English religious settlement, Pope Pius V excommunicated her as a heretic and forbade her Catholic subjects to obey her. The most radical Catholics took this papal edict as a mandate to work for Elizabeth's overthrow and even assassination, and Elizabeth cracked down on Catholic recusants.

Catholic queens were also attacked by Protestant religious authorities for their leadership of nation and church. John Knox (1505–1572), who had been ordained as a Catholic priest as a young man but was converted to the Protestantism of Scotland (what would ultimately be the Presbyterian church) in his early thirties, wrote a diatribe against three Catholic queens named Mary: Mary Tudor, Elizabeth's elder sister and her predecessor on the English throne; Mary of Guise, wife of James V of Scotland; and their daughter, Mary, Queen of Scots, who succeeded her father as ruler of Scotland. Unfortunately for Knox, the publication of his book *The First Blast of the Trumpet Against the Monstrous Regiment of Women* coincided with Elizabeth I's accession to the throne in 1558, something that did little to endear Knox to Elizabeth. Furthermore, the kind of argument he made about the blasphemous nature of female rule was very similar to the reasoning of Elizabeth's Catholic critics. In the tract, Knox links the acceptance of a Catholic woman ruler (whom he calls Jezebel) to what he saw as the incomplete reformation of the Church and its continuing ties to its Catholic past:

> Wonder it is, that amongst so many pregnant wits as the isle of Great Britain has produced, so many godly and zealous preachers as England did sometime nourish, and amongst so many learned, and men of grave judgment, as this day by Jezebel are exiled, none is found so stout of courage, so faithful to God, nor loving to their native country, that they dare admonish the inhabitants of that isle, how abominable before God is the empire or rule of a wicked woman (yea, of a traitress and bastard); and what may a people or nation, left destitute of a lawful head, do by the authority of God's word in electing and appointing common rulers and magistrates.

Knox then proceeded to "prove" by quoting the Bible and a series of church authorities through the ages that it is against God's law for women to rule, that "[t]o promote a woman to bear rule, superiority, dominion or empire above any realm, nation, or city, is repugnant to nature, contumely to God, a thing most contrarious to his revealed will and approved ordinance, and finally it is the subversion of good order, of all equity and justice." Women are inferior in every way, he asserted, and unfit for leadership: "weak, frail, impatient, feeble and foolish," they are also "unconstant, variable, cruel and lacking the spirit of counsel and regiment." Rather, Knox argued, "woman in her greatest perfection was made to serve man." He challenged the English to become more manly and to reject the rule of a woman. Though Knox did not call outright for deposing these queens—to "suppress [their rule] is in the hand of God alone," he said—many would have seen Knox's argument as an incitement to rebellion.[19] Whether Protestant or Catholic, then, women rulers were subject to open and potentially violent attack. (See also chapter 4: "Women and Politics.")

However, not all women who found a public religious voice, either through writing or speaking openly, were persecuted or endangered for their ideas. Women—and men—were less likely to be threatened with silencing, persecution, or death when their thinking was orthodox (that is, in accordance with the dominant perspective) and their particular religious practices matched those of the political regime under which they lived. So it was safest to be a Christian, since all states and countries were Christian, and, within Christianity, it was safest to be Catholic under a Catholic monarch or Protestant within a Protestant state. Nonetheless, at a time when women's writing and theological thinking were suspect and often open to condemnation, even the orthodox religious writings of women were, to a certain extent, transgressive and groundbreaking. Soeur Anne de Marquets (1533–1588), a Dominican nun born of a noble family in Normandy, wrote a book in support of the French Catholic Church against the Huguenots, the French Calvinist Protestants. Her work was published at a time when political leaders like Catherine de' Medicis were trying to mend divisions between the two religious groups. Consequently, Marquets's work provoked a strong negative response both from Huguenots and from those Catholic leaders who had hoped to avoid further conflict. She also published a collection of religious poems, *Spiritual Sonnets* (1605), which included translations of other poets' works along with her own compositions. Her own poems show her creativity and insight in reading biblical passages in ways that foregrounded women's religious experience and memorialized a lineage and tradition of faithful women. Her "Sonnet 381" connects two "Maries" from the Bible. The first is "Marie" (Miriam) of the Hebrew Bible, the sister of Aaron and Moses who sang when the Jews triumphed over the Egyptians; the second is the Virgin "Marie," whom Christ took as mother, who also sang a holy song (the "Magnificat"). That Marie is in turn associated with the many nuns of Marquets's own day who, following the first Marie, sin and praise God for his gracious blessings and who, following the second Marie, dedicate their virgin bodies to God and sing praises night and day.

Similarly, Glückel of Hameln (1646–1724), a Jewish merchant woman of the seventeenth century, saw her own life story in the larger terms of the survival of the Jews, God's chosen people. In her memoirs, written sporadically over a period of almost thirty years (1690–1719), she details her family life, its tragedies and successes, and her business activities, placing everything in the context of her faith. Glückel's marriage at age 14 to a successful merchant who traded money, precious metals, and jewels was arranged by her parents, as was typical of the time. She gave birth to 14 children, 12 of whom survived to adulthood, and worked alongside her husband as his trusted companion and adviser. His death prompted her to begin writing her memoirs as a consolation. Widowhood compelled her to become more active as a merchant herself, since her husband left her all his property (something that was by no means typical of the time) as well as his debts. She saved the business and expanded it, becoming a trader, shopkeeper, and banker.

The survival of Glückel and her family never seemed like a certain thing, given the danger and uncertainty of life for Jews in any part of Europe. Glückel noted in her diary:

> I was born in Hamburg and as my parents and others told me, I was not yet three when Jews were driven thence and went to Altona which then belonged to the King of Denmark, where they enjoyed many privileges…. Some twenty-five Jewish families lived there at that time and had a synagogue and cemetery. They lived there for a time and through the efforts of prominent men of the Community obtained permits to trade in the town…. Still, it was a very hard life especially for the poor and needy…. In the mornings, as soon as the men came from the synagogue, they went to town, returning to Altona towards evening when the gates were closed. When they passed through the gates their lives were in continual peril from attacks by sailors, soldiers and all sorts of hooligans. Each woman thanked God when her husband returned safely home.[20]

Glückel's memoirs are filled with prayers and religious tales, and she sometimes uses metaphors of motherhood to express her understanding of Jewish life, often with a humorous twist. So, in describing the Jewish people's response to a messianic figure of the time who, in the end, proved false, she wrote:

> O Lord of the Universe, at that time we hoped that you, O merciful God, would have mercy on your people Israel and redeem us from our exile. We were like a woman in travail, a woman on the labour-stool who, after great labour and sore pains, expects to rejoice in the birth of a child, but finds it is nothing but wind. This, my great God and King, happened to us. All your servants and children did

> much penance, recited many prayers, gave away much in charity,
> throughout the world. For two or three years your people Israel sat
> on the labour-stool—but nothing came save wind.[21]

Glückel was unusual in her success as a merchant and in the fact
that she left a record of her life in her diary, but she always understood her mercantile activities as part of her motherly care for her
children. Her words did nothing to disturb the traditional distinctions made between women's and men's religious or social roles in
her culture, however much her actions may have pushed the
boundaries of womanhood. (See also chapter 3: "Women and
Work.")

But other women of the era were articulate in their rejection of
women's traditional religious roles. The Anabaptists ("re-baptis-
ers," so called because they rejected infant baptism), a radical
sect founded in the 1520s in Saxony and Thuringia (modern Germany), believed in the absolute equality of men and women and
the communal sharing of all property. The movement spread to
other parts of Germany, Switzerland, and England, where women
outnumbered men in Anabaptist congregations. Other English
radical Protestant sects included the Levellers (who wanted to
"level" social class distinctions), Diggers (who advocated for land
reform), Ranters (so called for their style of preaching), and the
Society of Friends, or Quakers (who "quaked" or shook with fervor
when they prayed or preached). These sects called for a reformation of women's social status and roles in addition to other more
narrowly religious or economic demands. The Digger Gerard Winstanley (1609–1676) wrote of an ideal world where

> every man and woman shall have the free liberty to marry whom
> they love, if they can obtain the love and liking of that party whom
> they would marry; and neither birth nor portion [dowry] shall hinder
> the match, for we are all of one blood, mankind; and for portion,
> the common storehouses are every man's and maid's portion, as
> free to one as to another.[22]

Some Ranters went even further, advocating complete sexual
freedom and the abolishment of the strictures of marriage. The
Quakers believed that divine inspiration came to women equally
with men, and many women were preachers and traveling minis-
ters from the earliest days of the movement. (Not surprisingly,
perhaps, many of the most prominent members of the late nine-

teenth- and early twentieth-century suffragist movement in the United States, such as Lucretia Mott and Susan B. Anthony, were Quakers.)

Margaret Fell (1614–1702), a relative of Anne Askew, was an outspoken Quaker who wrote *Woman's Speaking Justified* to elaborate her particular ideas about women's place in religion. She had come from a prosperous Protestant family (she inherited £6000 on her father's death) and married a member of the landed gentry, the barrister (lawyer) and later judge Thomas Fell of Swarthmoor. During one of her husband's absences from home, she and her household were converted to a new understanding of religion by the traveling preacher George Fox, the founder of the Society of Friends. Fox held radical ideas, including a belief in the ministry of all believers rather than an ordained clergy. He also argued for equality of men and women in the church. God speaks equally to all believers, he said, each of whom possesses the "inner light" of divinity and discernment. When Judge Fell returned, he listened to Fox's ideas and found them appealing. Both he and Margaret, who was more enthusiastic for Fox's ideas than was her husband, protected Fox and other Quakers who were regularly beaten by mobs and imprisoned.

When her husband died in 1658, Margaret Fell became even more active in support of the Friends, sheltering them on her estate and pleading repeatedly for their release from prison. She herself ultimately took to the road with two of her daughters as an itinerant Quaker preacher, a vocation nearly unheard of for women at that time. Fox and other Quakers continued to be imprisoned and harassed; ultimately, Fell herself was imprisoned and lost all her property for refusing to take an oath of religious obedience to the king. (Swarthmoor went to her son, who was no longer a practicing Quaker.) During her four and a half years in prison, she wrote the pamphlet *Women's Speaking Justified*. In an extended discourse, she argues for women's equality to men in every way. She ends with the exhortation,

> And so let this [treatise] serve to stop that opposing Spirit that would limit the Power and Spirit of the Lord Jesus, whose Spirit is poured upon all Flesh, both Sons and Daughters, now in his Resurrection; and since that the Lord God in the Creation, when he made Man in his own Image, he made them Male and Female.... And thus the Lord Jesus hath manifested himself and his Power, without Respect of Persons; and so let all Mouths be stopt that would limit him, whose Power and Spirit is infinite, who is pouring it upon all Flesh.[23]

In 1668, Fell was released from prison, and she and George Fox married the next year. Both continued to be active in their travels and preaching, and both were again imprisoned. In 1686, the Act of Toleration restored civil rights to Catholics as well as to various dissenting groups like the Quakers, and many of them were freed from prison. A Friends meeting house was built near Swarthmoor, where Margaret Fell Fox spent her remaining years following the death of George Fox in 1691.

Margaret Fell Fox is an extreme example of the way in which religion might justify women's speaking in a culture that required them to be silent, especially in matters of religion. Many other less radical women also expressed themselves through religion, either speaking publicly or daring to publish their religious insights by claiming divine authorization. In addition to writing original religious works, many women translated biblical passages and other ancient religious works into their own language or, in the case of the Psalms, into verse forms, either for singing or simply for reading and meditation. For instance, Mary Sidney, Countess of Pembroke (1561–1621), completed the translation of the Psalms that her brother, the author Sir Philip Sidney (1554–1586), had begun before his death. Two-thirds of the metrical translations, which circulated widely in manuscript among the literati of England, were Mary's own. (See also chapter 6: "Women and Literature.") Women translators like Mary Sidney were, for the most part, members of a tiny educated elite with the wealth and leisure to support such literate activities. But the lives of women without such advantages were also marked by daily religious activities, in prayer, hymn singing, teaching, and worshipping. Despite restrictions on females' speech, writing, public access, and education, the Reformation gave voice to many powerful expressions of women's faith and conviction.

Catharina von Greiffenberg (1633–1694), for example, was an extraordinarily intelligent and talented Protestant author in the largely Catholic country of Austria. Her religious and literary mission was to convert the Holy Roman Emperor to Protestantism, and she composed a number of widely acclaimed works to that end. Religion was central to Catharina's ambitions and to her accomplishments. She was 28 years old when she published a collection of religious poems that were celebrated by some of the most respected literary circles in the country. Although most women were condemned both for writing and for publishing,

Catharina's work was so well received that she was allowed to become the sole female member of one of Austria's leading literary societies. Primarily self-educated, she learned and wrote in isolation most of her life. Without standardized training, she expressed herself in unconventional ways that were considered innovative and original. As in the case of other learned women writers, she was able to turn the disadvantage of exclusion from mainstream education to the advantage of original perspectives and forms of expression. Her religious convictions informed all that she wrote. In addition to lyric verse, she composed an epic poem about the history of contact between Christianity and Islam, where she portrayed Islam as a source of evil. Written during the Turkish invasion of Austria in 1663, the work is framed as both moral instruction and patriotic tribute. Her most popular publications were several devotionals (*Andachtsbücher*) in which she interpreted biblical passages and wrote poems on Protestant doctrine.

Lady Mary Wortley Montagu (1689–1762) also wrote about Islam, but her goal was to persuade her English audience that Islam was a religion equal in ethics and theology to Protestant Christianity and that those who practiced that religion were as civilized as any European. Montagu was born to an elite English family and was fortunate to have been raised in a household where there was an extensive library. She taught herself Latin so that she could read the classics of ancient Rome; when her father discovered her ability, he was so pleased that he hired a tutor to teach her not only Latin but also Italian. Her future husband, Edward Wortley Montagu, who believed that women should receive the same education as men, was attracted by her ability to quote the Latin poet Horace in the original. They carried on a seven-year correspondence before their marriage as he established his political career, during which time Mary's father arranged her engagement to another lord. So Mary and Edward eloped. As Edward's career advanced, she began to establish herself as a writer and member of England's most elite literary circle.

Mary Wortley Montagu came into close contact with Islam when her husband was appointed ambassador to Turkey in 1716. While she was there, she learned Turkish, studied the Koran (the holy scriptures of Islam), socialized with elite Turkish women, and began wearing a modified Turkish costume instead of traditional English dress. Montagu was also interested in the Turkish practice of inoculation against smallpox, something virtually unknown in Europe, where smallpox was a continuing peril. She had her own son and daughter inoculated and introduced the practice to England on her return. While she was in Turkey, she wrote a series of letters to family members and important people in England in which she related her voyages and discoveries. She clearly intended the letters for a larger reading public, as she kept a manuscript in which the best of her letters were revised; they were ultimately published as the *Turkish Embassy Letters* (1763). The work particularly criticizes English men who have written (inaccurately, she claimed) about Turkish women. As she pointed out, Turkish society was very much gender segregated, and only a woman would be able to enter the harems and converse with Islamic women. She praised Islam, or Mohametism as she called it, saying that it is "so far from the nonsense we charge it with." Rather, "it is the purest morality delivered in the very best language." She further noted that "Mohametism is divided into as many sects as Christianity.... I cannot here forbear reflecting on the natural inclination of mankind to make mysteries and novelties. The Zeidi, Kadari, Jabari, etc. put me in mind of the Catholic, Lutheran, Calvinist, etc., and are equally zealous against one another." However, the toleration Montagu brought to Islam did not extend to Catholicism. She wrote of her visit with a Muslim holy man, "I explained to him the difference between the religion of England and Rome, and he was pleased to hear there were Christians that did not worship images or adore the Virgin Mary. The ridicule of transubstantiation [the Catholic doctrine that the bread and wine of the Eucharist become the actual body and blood of Christ] appeared very strong to him."[24]

Montagu's criticism of Catholicism was common among Protestants who saw Catholic ritual as superstition and magic rather than so-called true religion. That criticism was also leveled at other women who maintained rituals unconnected with established religions, rituals that were part of folk practices and folk magic that had a long history in Europe and that often survived alongside Christianity in its many forms. For several reasons, women were particularly responsible for keeping these traditions. Many of them involved protecting the household, food, and children, all of which fell in women's purview. Furthermore, these practices were not controlled by an elite male clergy. In a sense, women could "own" this avenue to the realm of the supernatural in ways that they could never have access to the rituals of established religions. When day-to-day housekeeping activities went awry or when children became ill, the cause was often thought to be some kind of bewitchment. A woman might, therefore, perform a magical cure to solve the problem. Such cures often involved heating objects in the fire to purify them and saying some special blessing. During childbirth, a very dangerous time for both mother and baby, women were given special drinks—almost like potions—to bring them safely through their travail. Recipes for such drinks appear in Gervase Markham's (ca. 1568–1637) *The English hous-wife:*

> For ease in childbearing. If a woman have a strong and hard labour, take four spoonfulls of another womans milk, and give it the woman to drink in her labour, and she shall be delivered presently.
>
> A generall purge for a woman in child bed. Take two or three eggs, and they must be neither rost [roasted, cooked] nor raw, but between both, and then take butter that salt never came in, and put into the eggs, and sup them off, and eat a piece of brown bread to them, and drink a draught of small Ale.
>
> For a woman that is new brought in bed, and swooneth much. Take Mugwort, Motherwort, and Mints, the quantity of a handfull in all, seeth them together in a pint of Malmsey [wine], and give her to drink thereof two or three spoonfuls at a time, and it will appease her swooning.[25]

Midwives would oversee the careful shutting up of the birthing room where the expectant mother's "gossips," her woman friends and relatives, had gathered to support her and help her. Men were excluded from the room, and it might further be protected from contamination, both natural and supernatural, by heavy curtains and the plugging of keyholes and other openings. After the birth, women would join the mother in sharing the special drink. The room was only gradually opened to the world following this feast. Women would not have seen such an activity as conflicting with the church; in fact, the new mother would probably end her confinement by attending the local parish for "churching," a Christian purification rite with magical overtones of its own.

Renaissance peoples mixed religion and astrology as well. Queen Elizabeth, like many of her contemporaries, consulted astrologer John Dee (1527–1608), who was also a mathematician, astronomer, and navigator, all interrelated fields of inquiry at that time. Astrol-

Mother and her friends sharing a posset or special drink after the birth of a child, Albrecht Dürer, *Birth of the Virgin. Source:* Reproduced by permission of the Art Gallery of Greater Victoria.

ogy was understood to be a kind of science through which one could determine the will of God, and Dee helped Elizabeth decide the timing of important personal and public events, such as her coronation. Another Englishwoman, Aemilia Lanyer (1569–1645), known for her religious poem on the Passion of Christ, *Salve Deus Rex Judaeorum* [Hail, God, King of the Jews], and her defense of women within that work consulted the popular astrologer Simon Foreman. Lanyer wanted to know whether her husband, a minor courtier, would be promoted and whether she would be able to have more children, as she had had a number of miscarriages.

Women's religious roles in the Renaissance were as varied as their economic or social roles, depending on where and when they lived during the period; whether they were Christian or Jewish, Protestant or Catholic; whether they lived in the city or the country; whether they were high born and privileged or members of the peasantry or artisan class; whether they were educated or unlettered; whether they married or remained single; and whether they were inclined to religious experience or dismissed the influence of the supernatural. But wherever women found themselves in this network of cultural possibilities, religion was part of the fabric of life and one that determined everyday experiences for all people.

NOTES

1.   Qtd. in Christopher Hill, *A Turbulent, Seditious and Factious People: John Bunyan and his Church* (New York: Oxford University Press, 1996), 34.

2.   On women in popular revolts, see Natalie Zemon Davis, *Society and Culture in Early Modern France: Eight Essays* (Stanford, CA: Stanford University Press, 1975).

3.   Judith Maltby, *Prayer Book and People in Elizabethan and Early Stuart England* (New York: Cambridge University Press, 1998), 13.

4.   Elaine V. Beilin, ed., *The Examinations of Anne Askew* (New York: Oxford University Press, 1996), 1.276–84. The printer John Bale (1495–1563) published his edited version of Anne Askew's own records of her examinations as *The First Examinacyon of Anne Askewe Lately Martyred in Smythfelde, by the Romysh Popes Vpholders, with the Elucydacyon of Iohan Bale* (London, 1546) and *The Lattre Examinacyon of Anne Askewe Latelye Martyred in Smythfelde, by the Wycked Synagoge of Antichrist, with the Elucydacyon of Iohan Bale* (Marburg, Germany, 1547). Both books are available through EEBO, <http://eebo.chadwyck.com>. In 1563, John Foxe published *The Two Examinations of Anne Askew* in his Protestant catalog of martyrs, *Actes and Monuments*. It and Bale's *First Examinacion* are available through Renaissance Women Online, <http://www.wwp.brown.edu/texts/rwoentry.html>.

5.   Qtd. in Andrew Hiscock, "'A Supernal Liuely fayth': Katharine Parr and the Authoring of Devotion," *Women's Writing* 9 (2002): 181.

6.   "A Ballad of Anne Askew, Intitled: I am a Woman poore and Blind," appendix 2, in Beilin, *The Examinations of Anne Askew,* 195. The "Ballad" is also available through EEBO, <http://eebo.chadwyck.com>.

7.   Qtd. in Hiscock, "'A Supernal Liuely fayth,'" 189. Parr's *Lamentacions* is available in a modern edition as *Katharine Parr,* ed. Elaine V. Beilin (Aldershot, UK: Scolar Press, 1996). Both Parr's works are also avail-

able through Renaissance Women Online, <http://www.wwp.brown.edu/texts/rwoentry.html>.

8.   Qtd. in Hiscock, "'A Supernal Liuely fayth,'" 181.

9.   Qtd. in Betty Travitsky, ed., *The Paradise of Women: Writings by English Women of the Renaissance* (New York: Columbia University Press, 1989), 85–86. Spelling modernized and punctuation normalized here.

10.   Howard Adelman, "Italian Jewish Women," in *Jewish Women in Historical Perspective,* 2nd ed. (Detroit: Wayne State University Press, 1998), 150.

11.   Qtd. in Chava Weissler, "Prayers in Yiddish and the Religious World of Ashkenazic Women," in *Jewish Women in Historical Perspective,* 2nd ed. (Detroit: Wayne State University Press, 1998), 172.

12.   Qtd. in Weissler, "Prayers in Yiddish," 169.

13.   Howard Tzvi Adelman, "Jewish Women and Family Life, Inside and Outside the Ghetto," in *The Jews of Early Modern Venice,* ed. Robert C. Davis and Benjamin Ravid (Baltimore: Johns Hopkins University Press, 2001), 143–65.

14.   Bernal Díaz del Castillo, *The Conquest of New Spain,* trans. J. M. Cohen (Harmondsworth, UK: Penguin, 1963), 86.

15.   Teresa of Avila, The Way of Perfection (Toledo, 1583), chapter 5, par 7. The book is widely available in print and online, including Christian Classics Ethereal Library, <http://www.ccel.org/ccel/teresa/way.html>.

16.   See Daniel Bornstein and Roberto Rusconi, eds., *Women and Religion in Medieval and Renaissance Italy,* trans. Margery J. Schneider (Chicago: University of Chicago Press, 1996) and Letizia Panizza, ed., *Women in Italian Renaissance Culture and Society* (Oxford: European Humanities Research Centre, 2000).

17.   Claire Walker, *Gender and Politics in Early Modern Europe: English Convents in France and the Low Countries* (New York: Palgrave Macmillan, 2003), 2.

18.   Dorothy L. Latz, *"Glow-Worm Light": Writings of 17th Century English Recusant Women from Original Manuscripts* (Salzburg: Institut für Anglistik und Amerikanistik Universität Salzburg, 1989), 41. Reprinted with permission.

19.   John Knox, *The First Blast of the Trumpet Against the Monstrous Regiment of Women* (Geneva, 1558). This tract is available through Project Gutenberg, <http://www.archive.org/texts/gutenberg.php>.

20.   Glückel of Hameln, *The Life of Glückel of Hameln 1646–1724 Written by Herself,* trans. Beth-Zion Abrahams (London: Horovitz, 1962), 13–14.

21.   Glückel of Hameln, *The Life of Glückel of Hameln,* 45.

22.   Gerard Winstanley, *The Law of Freedom in a Platform* (London, 1652), 88. This work is available through EEBO, <http://eebo.chadwyck.com>, and in print as *The Law of Freedom, and Other Writings,* ed. Christopher Hill (New York: Cambridge University Press, 1983).

23.   Margaret Askew Fell Fox, *Women's Speaking Justified* (London, 1667), EEBO, <http://eebo.chadwyck.com>. The work is also available through the Quaker Heritage Press <http://www.qhpress.org/texts/fell.html>, as well as in print, ed. David J. Latt (Los Angeles: Clark Memorial Library, 1979). On Fell, see Bonnelyn Young Kunze, *Margaret Fell and the Rise of Quakerism* (Stanford, CA: Stanford University Press, 1994).

24. Lady Mary Wortley Montagu, letter to the Abbot Conti, 1 April 1717, Kari Boyd McBride, ed., *Selected Turkish Embassy Letters: Lady Mary Wortley Montagu,* <http://www.jamaica.u.arizona.edu/ic/mcbride/ws200/montltrs.htm>, transcribed from Lord Wharncliffe and W. Moy Thomas, *The Letters and Works of Lady Mary Wortley Montagu,* vol. 1 (London: Henry G. Bohn, 1861).

25. Gervase Markham, *The English hous-wife, containing the inward and outward Vertues which ought to be in a compleat woman…. A work generally approved, and now the eighth time much augmented, purged, and made most profitable and necessary for all men, and the general good of this nation* (London, 1664), 31, 32.

SUGGESTED READING

Baskin, Judith R., ed. *Jewish Women in Historical Perspective.* 2nd ed. Detroit: Wayne State University Press, 1998.

Davis, Robert C., and Benjamin Ravid. *The Jews of Early Modern Venice.* Baltimore: Johns Hopkins University Press, 2001.

Diefendorf, Barbara B. *Beneath the Cross: Catholics and Huguenots in Sixteenth-Century Paris.* New York: Oxford University Press, 1991.

Hiscock, Andrew. "'A Supernal Liuely fayth': Katharine Parr and the Authoring of Devotion." *Women's Writing* 9 (2002): 177–97.

Kunze, Bonnelyn Young. *Margaret Fell and the Rise of Quakerism.* Stanford, CA: Stanford University Press, 1994.

Latz, Dorothy L. *Neglected Writings of Recusant Women: Recusant Writings of the Sixteenth–Seventeenth Centuries.* Salzburg: Institut für Anglistik und Amerikanistik Universität Salzburg, 1997.

McBride, Kari Boyd. "Native Mothers, Native Others: La Malinche, Pocahontas, and Sacajawea." *Maternal Measures: Figuring Caregiving in the Early Modern Period.* Ed. Naomi J. Miller and Naomi Yavneh. Aldershot, UK: Ashgate, 2000. 306–16.

Purkiss, Diane. *The Witch in History: Early Modern and Twentieth-Century Representations.* New York: Routledge, 1996.

6

---∞∞∞---

Women and Literature

Against tremendous odds, women in the Renaissance wrote and published remarkable works of poetry, prose, and drama. Their literary production, however, was seriously constrained by a number of factors. First, the prevailing attitude throughout Europe held that teaching females to write prose or poetry was inappropriate and even dangerous. A woman's proper place was in the domestic sphere, and writing would only distract her from her duties or tempt her into foolish ambition, impertinence, or sedition. For moral and economic reasons, then, women were in large part excluded from a humanist education and discouraged from writing. Silence was held to be one of the greatest virtues a female could practice, and writing was taught as a masculine enterprise. The pervasive contempt for women's speaking and writing is conveyed in one of John Ray's proverbs from his popular 1678 collection, "Many women, many words; many geese, many turds." Female authorship presumed a false entitlement to authority, and a woman who made her thoughts—whether spoken or on paper—available to the public was associated with women who made their bodies available to the public. As another of Ray's proverbs teaches, "Free of her lips, free of her hips." Loose tongues were conflated with loose morals or even the grotesque. Lady Mary Wroth (1587–1651), for example, was branded a hermaphrodite and a lascivious monster for publishing her prose romance, *Urania*. Similarly, Marie Dentière (1495–1561) was labeled a pervert for the printed works in which she insisted on women's right to preach in church and other assemblies. The prevailing view was that such transgressive females were likely to corrupt others or disturb social relations. Nonetheless, throughout Europe there was a small minority of females who could and did write; just how small is difficult to determine because of insufficient records, but scholars have estimated that in England alone, only 0.5 percent of the total number of publications in the early seventeenth century were by women. Earlier in the Renaissance, there would have been even fewer. Restrictions on female writers varied among different cultures and at different times during the Renaissance, "but at no time or place was women's access to cultural institutions the same as men's and at no time was the gender of the creator not a factor in how a work was judged."[1]

There were exceptions to proscriptions against educating women, especially among the wealthy. (See also chapter 1: "Women and Education.") Some aristocratic and even merchant families allowed their daughters to learn to write along with the male children. The French poet Louise Labé (ca. 1520–1566) urged all females to take advantage of any opportunity they were permitted to pursue an education and exercise the privilege of writing: "those of us who can, should use this long-craved freedom to study and to let men see how greatly they wronged us when depriving us of its honor and advantages. And if any woman becomes so proficient as to be able to write down her thoughts, let her do so and not despise the honor, but rather flaunt it instead of fine clothes, necklaces and rings."[2] Mary Ward (1585–1645), the founder of the Institute of the Blessed Virgin Mary, held that women must be educated in order that they might lead a public life not confined to the convent or the domestic sphere. The English almanac writer Sarah Jinner (fl. 1658) similarly rallied women to carve out a place for themselves in the sciences by studying, writing, and publishing their thoughts: "why should we suffer our parts to rust? Let us scour the rust off by ingenious endeavouring the attaining of higher accomplishments."[3] Even the assertive Jinner, however, felt the need to mollify those who might be threatened by her position: "this I say not to animate our sex to assume or usurp the breeches [men]; no, but perhaps if we should shine in the splendour of virtue, it would animate our husbands to excel us: so by this means we should have an excellent world."[4] Jinner and Labé's exhortations to study and write were uncommon instances of encouragement for female authors. Of the minority who shared their view that writing was acceptable for women, many insisted that they should limit themselves to pious or domestic subjects, such as mother's advice books (books addressed to one's children and generally containing pious advice for living a virtuous life) and religious topics; and even then, it was argued, their writing should be for private improvement rather than for publication. To avoid censure, many female authors had their work published under pseudonyms or anonymously (a practice that continued through the nineteenth century). Whether pseudonymously or under their own names, many Renaissance women did make their works public. They either had them printed or circulated them in manuscript, a method that was preferred by aristocratic women and men alike, as it limited the readership to the elite.

In keeping with such restrictions on women's expression, translations (particularly translations of Psalms or other religious texts) were deemed less objectionable than original work; if the piece were published, the male author subsumed the female translator, who professed only to be providing a service by making more widely available the words of men rather than asserting her own creative individuality. Such professions of modesty, however, were often a smokescreen for innovation and literary agency. By altering the diction, elaborating metaphors, or making omissions, women translators were able to vary the emphasis and shift the tone of the original source; they shaped the text as mediators from one language to another, and in the process, they made important contributions to the development of the literary vernacular. One scholar has noted that "Elizabeth of Nassau Saarbrücken (1379–1456) and Elenore of Austria (1433–1480)... reform[ed] German courtly language by their translations of chivalric romances; ... and Lea Ráskai's many translations of hagiographic and other sources not only aided lay piety but helped to establish Hungarian as a literary language."[5] Despite these and many other literary accomplishments, cultures throughout Europe taught that by far the most preferable role for a literate woman was as a patron or muse of a man's creative efforts rather than as an active author herself.

Nonetheless, women in every country did write, and they created local and extended networks that connected and supported learned women like themselves. A popular venue for female patronage of the arts and the development of women's writing in

France was the salon. Socially prominent women hosted gatherings of both female and male authors, wits, philosophers, and other literati in their homes. Many of the groups met for years or even decades, and their members significantly shaped the development of French thought and literature. Among the most celebrated and influential Parisian salons were those of Madeleine de Scudery (1607–1701), Catherine de Vivonne, Marquise de Rambouillet (1588–1665), and Madeleine de Souvre, the Marquise de Sablé (1599–1678), author of a collection of maxims on human nature. Similar to the more well known maxims of François, Duc de la Rochefoucauld (1613–1680), Madame de Sablé's collections include sayings such as

> Mediocre and ill-born spirits, especially those only half educated, are the most likely to be opinionated. It is only the strong souls know how to correct themselves and abandon a bad position.
>
> The shame we feel when we see ourselves praised without merit often leads us to achieve things we otherwise could not have accomplished.
>
> Social relationships—and even friendship among the majority of people—are nothing more than a business arrangement that lasts only as long as there is a need.[6]

In addition to la Rochefoucauld, Sablé's salons included such luminaries as Marie de Rabutin-Chantal, Marquise de Sévigné (1626–1696), the philosopher Blaise Pascal, and Marie-Madeleine Pioche de la Vergne, Madame de Lafayette (1634–1693). Lafayette was the author of *La Princesse de Clèves* (first published anonymously in 1678), a novel about court politics in sixteenth-century France. The novel is unusual for its combination of historical accuracy concerning the events and people of the period and its complex psychological portraits of historical and quasi-historical figures. Madame de Lafayette (separated from her husband, who was 18 years her senior) hosted her own literary salon, which brought together this same group of luminaries to discuss art and literature. (See also chapter 1: "Women and Education.")

As is the case today, different genres carried different political significance and aesthetic value in the Renaissance. History, poetry, philosophy, and the epic were considered more weighty, public, and important than were letters, journals, and advice books. Much of the literature produced by women was in the latter three genres, although there were also notable female poets, philosophers, playwrights, and fiction writers. Generally excluded from schools and literary circles, women were also taught that the self-advancement involved in seeking patronage was offensive in a woman. Their access to training, audiences, certain genres, and the financial means to support their creative drive, then, was severely limited. In the rare cases that a woman was judged to have written something of merit, she "was said to have 'overcome the limitations of her sex' and set herself apart from all other women, or she was judged a hermaphrodite, or the work was attributed to her male teacher or a male member of her family."[7] And even then, such judgments were usually reserved for the wealthy and powerful, such as Vittoria Colonna, Marchesa di Pescara (1492–1547), or Mary Sidney, Countess of Pembroke (1561–1621). Writings by women who lacked social status, such as Aemilia Lanyer's *Salve Deus Rex Judaeorum* (Hail, God, King of the Jews), were often ignored by contemporaries and fell into oblivion upon their publication.

Female authors who did publish were often apologetic or defensive. Many protested that they were obliged to make their work public because of friends' insistence or the need to curtail unauthorized versions of their manuscripts. Margaret Tyler, whose romance translation *The Mirror of Princely Deeds and Knighthood* was first published in 1578, assured her audience that it was neither her idea to write the piece nor her desire to finish it, "Gentle reader, the truth is, that as the motion to this kind of labour came not from myself, so was this piece of work put upon me by others, and they which first counselled me to fall to work, took upon them also to be my taskmasters and overseers."[8] Writers of advice books justified their publication out of a sense of responsibility as a practitioner: sick or dying mothers owed a legacy of instruction to their children; conduct manual writers had a duty to their society, and so forth. Women who published religious works claimed to have been inspired to do so in dreams, by God's direct calling, or as a solemn act of piety. So Aemilia Lanyer (1569–1645) wrote at the end of *Salve Deus Rex Judaeorum,*

> Gentle Reader, if thou desire to be resolved, why I give this Title, Salve Deus Rex Judaeorum, know for certain, that it was delivered unto me in sleep many years before I had any intent to write in this manner, and was quite out of my memory until I had written the Passion of Christ, when immediately it came into my remembrance, what I had dreamed long before; and thinking it a significant token, that I was

appointed to perform that Work, I gave the very same words I received in sleep as the fittest Title I could devise for this Book.[9]

The "deliverance" of the title in a dream signified to Lanyer a divine command to write, one that her readers can hardly gainsay and one that thoroughly justified her decision to publish. Women writers of polemical tracts maintained that the injured cause of justice warranted their defense; otherwise, they assured their audience, they would never presume to enter the public arena. Such protestations register the significant extent to which women's publication was considered objectionable or illegitimate.

One of the forms of expression that was culturally sanctioned for females was letter writing. This genre was not as private in the Renaissance as it is today; before the advent of newspapers, letters were an important source of political information as well as personal messages, of public as well as domestic details. Letters were often passed along to a circle of friends and family, and their writers paid close attention to style, narrative voice, and the construction of authorial personae. Some collections, like the letters of Dorothy Osborne (1627–1695), are distinguished by their intimate self-examination. Others were used as political tools for self-assertion. Such was the case with a number of Lady Arbella (or Arabella) Stuart's (1575–1615) letters. Stuart's lineage made her a claimant to the English throne; she was descended from Henry VIII's sister, Margaret, and was also the granddaughter of Bess of Hardwick. Because Stuart stood in line for the throne, the court imposed severe restrictions on her activities, lest she become the focus of an attempted coup. Indeed, for periods of time, she was virtually under house arrest, a prisoner to her political marriage potential. In an effort to attract Queen Elizabeth I's attention to her plight of disenfranchisement and isolation, she addressed letters to a fictional lover, knowing that all her correspondence was intercepted and monitored. The letters constructed an affair that, as expected, forced the queen's counsellors to contend with the resourceful and unhappy Stuart. After Elizabeth's death, Stuart was initially a favorite at the court of King James VI and I, where she strengthened her status by revealing to him any attempt to co-opt her for the opposition. However, as she had been under Elizabeth, she was still prevented from marrying. But Stuart secretly wed William Seymour, who also had a distant claim to the English throne and who had been specifically prohibited as a marriage partner by the king. When the king heard of their marriage, he had Stuart and Seymour arrested and imprisoned. The two made multiple attempts to escape and rejoin each other, but they were repeatedly thwarted. Seymour finally escaped to France, but Stuart spent the rest of her life as a prisoner in the Tower of London. She wrote to the king frequently, attempting to restore herself to his good favor. Indeed, by comparing drafts and finished versions of those letters, one scholar has shown how Stuart crafted a humble persona in her bid to sway the king.[10] But her efforts were unsuccessful, and she died in the tower at the age of 40. Letters by early modern women, then, served political as well as personal ends.

Marie de Rabutin-Chantal, the Marquise de Sévigné (1626–1696), was considered one of the most talented letter writers in Europe. Thanks to the esteem in which her correspondence was held, more than fifteen hundred of her letters are extant. With insight and wit, they record the civil wars, court spectacles, criminal abuses, and intimate domestic news that informed the period of her life in France from 1648 to her death in 1696. Marie de Rabutin-Chantal was born into the nobility in Paris in 1626. Orphaned at the age of seven, she became a wealthy heiress and lived in luxury with grandparents, uncles, aunts, and cousins until her marriage at 18 to Henri de Sévigné. She was allowed an extraordinary education for a woman. An inexhaustible reader, she mastered a number of languages and studied history, philosophy, literature, and theology. Like most upper-class young girls, she was also trained in singing, dancing, and riding. She developed a penchant for traveling, which was uncommon for a woman of the period, partly because women were not encouraged to cultivate the independence or curiosity to provoke such an interest and partly because travel conditions were both dangerous and uncomfortable. Seven years and two children into their marriage, her husband—whose extramarital affairs scandalized even the French aristocracy— died in a duel over another married woman. Although the wealthy young widow was vigorously courted for many subsequent years, she chose never to remarry. Preferring freedom, she wrote at the age of 63, "The state of matrimony is a dangerous disease: far better to take a drink in my opinion."[11]

Madame de Sévigné enjoyed her celebrity among the fashionable and intellectual elite of Paris, and her letters render in vivid detail the culture in which she lived. She had a wide range of correspondents, but many of her letters were addressed to her son and daughter, both of whom were her self-professed passion. (Indeed, her priest once refused to absolve her when she confessed that she loved her daughter more than God.) Poignant letters record her distress when her granddaughter was discarded by the child's other grandparents. The in-laws of Madame de Sévigné's daughter were so disappointed when their son's first child was a girl that they exiled her at the age of five to a convent, where she remained for the rest of her life. A graphic cultural picture emerges in the letters, not only of gender inequities but of the rigidity of class structures and assumptions. For example, in a message to her daughter—dated April 26, 1671, and sent from Paris—Madame de Sévigné recounts the suicide of a French noble's steward Vatel who was driven to despair by the strain of a visit from the king. The dialogue, characterization, and evocative narration strikingly anticipate the novel, a genre that acquired increasing popularity soon into the next century and that was on occasion structured as a sequence of letters (the epistolary novel). Madame de Sévigné's account is laced with irony, and her understated conclusion conveys a chilling sense of social values and callousness.

> The King arrived on Thursday evening. Hunting, lanterns, moonlight, a gentle walk, supper served in a place carpeted with daffodils—everything was perfect. They had supper. There was no roast at one or two tables because of several unexpected guests which upset Vatel, and he said more than once, "I am dishonored; this is a humiliation I cannot bear." He said to Gourville, "I am bewildered; I haven't slept for twelve nights. Assist me giving orders." Gourville comforted him as best he could, but this roast missing, not from the King's table, but from the twenty-fifth down, was constantly on his mind. Gourville told all this to Monsieur le prince who went to Vatel's room and said to him, "Vatel, everything is all right; nothing was so perfect as the king's supper." "Monseigneur, your kindness is overwhelming," he replied, "but I know that there was no roast at two tables." "Not at all," said Monsieur le prince, "don't upset yourself; all is going splendidly." Night falls. The fireworks are a failure owing to fog, and they cost 16,000 francs. By four in the morning Vatel was rushing around everywhere, finding everyone wrapped in slumber. He met a small purveyor who had only two loads of fish. "Is that all?" he asked. "Yes, Sir." He did not know that Vatel had sent men around to all the seaports. Vatel waited a short time, and other purveyors did not arrive; he lost his head and

thought there would be no more fish. He found Gourville and said, "Sir, I shall never survive this disgrace; my honor and my reputation are at stake." Gourville laughed at him. Vatel went to his room, put his sword up against the door and ran it through his heart ... only on the third attempt, for the first two were not mortal. Then he fell dead. At that moment fish was coming in from all quarters. They looked for Vatel to distribute it, went to his room, broke in the door, and found him lying in his own blood. They rushed to Monsieur le prince, who was terribly upset.... However, Gourville tried to make up for the loss of Vatel, which he did in great measure. There was an elegant dinner, light refreshments, and then supper, a walk, cards, hunting, everything scented with daffodils, everything enchanting. Yesterday, Saturday, the same thing, and in the evening the King went on to Liancourt where he ordered *medianoche* [midnight mass]; he is to stay there today.[12]

Comparing the novelistic rendition of Vatel's suicide to the report of a marriage rumor, dated a year earlier, illustrates the remarkable range of tone and style in Madame de Sévigné's literary repertoire. The 1670 letter is addressed to a favorite cousin, Monsieur de Coulanges. It transforms a piece of gossip into an exuberant romp of breathless questions and teasing answers. The tone is playful and tongue-in-cheek, and the speaker's witty, hyperbolic persona is constructed with impressive rhetorical agility.

I am going to tell you the most astonishing thing, the most surprising, the most marvelous, the most bewildering, most triumphant, most astounding, most outrageous, most singular, most extraordinary, most unbelievable, most unforeseen, the greatest, the smallest, most rare, the most common, the most talked about, the most secret until today, the most brilliant, the most enviable, in short, a thing of which one finds only one example in past centuries, and yet that example is not accurate; a thing nobody can believe in Paris (how can one believe it in Lyon?); a thing that makes everyone cry for mercy; a thing that fills Mme de Rohan and Mme de Hauterine with joy; finally a thing that will happen on Sunday and those who see it will fancy they are seeing visions—a thing which will happen on Sunday and which perhaps will not happen on Monday. I cannot make up my mind to say it. Guess what it is; I give you three guesses. Do you give up? Very well, it is necessary to tell you: M de Lauzun is marrying on Sunday at the Louvre—guess who? I give you four guesses, I give you ten, I give you a hundred. Mme de Coulanges will be saying: That is not very difficult to guess; it is Mlle de La Vallière—Not at all, Madame. Mlle de Retz then? Not at all. You are very provincial. How silly we are, you say. It is Mlle Colbert. Still less close. It is surely Mlle de Créquy? You are not there yet. I shall have to tell you in the end: he marries, on Sunday, in the Louvre, with the King's permission, Mademoiselle, Mademoiselle de … Mademoiselle … guess the name. He marries Mademoiselle, my word! by my word! my sworn word! Mademoiselle, la Grande Mademoiselle; Mademoiselle, daughter of the late Monsieur; Mademoiselle, granddaughter of Henri IV; Mademoiselle d'Eu, Mademoiselle de Dombes, Mademoiselle de Montpensier, Mademoiselle d'Orleans; Mademoiselle, first cousin of the King; Mademoiselle, destined for a throne; Mademoiselle, the only match in France worthy of Monsieur. There is a fine subject for discourse. If you shout out loud, if you are beside yourself, if you say that we have lied, that it is false, that we are making fun of you, that this is a good tale, that it is too insignificant to be imagined; if, in short, you insult us, we shall say that you are right. We did the same as you.

Adieu, the letters carried by this post will show you if we are telling the truth or not.[13]

(Excerpts from Madame de Sévigné's letters, published in Katharina M. Wilson and Frank J. Warnke, eds. *Women Writers of the Seventeenth Century* [Athens: The University of Georgia Press, 1989]. © 1989 by the University of Georgia Press. Reprinted with permission.)

The narrative vitality and immediacy of Madame de Sévigné's letters differ markedly from the more formal and didactic letters by women earlier in the Renaissance. Between 1447 and 1470, the Italian Alessandra Macinghi Strozzi (ca. 1407–1471) wrote to her banished sons a collection of 72 letters. Each is structured according to exact epistolary conventions. Following the model developed by the Roman rhetorician Cicero (ca. 106–43 B.C.E.) and that predominated in the Renaissance, each begins with a formal greeting and progresses to an opening, narrative, appeal, and conclusion (*salutatio, exordium, narratio, petitio, and conclusio*). The primary concern is with moral instruction and advice about how to conduct a godly household. Domestic responsibilities to children, spouse, servants, and guests are set forth in terms of passages from scripture, and even the longing of an absent mother is expressed in a religious context. This didactic disposition informs the letters of Italian women well into the seventeenth century. One of the most celebrated epistolary collections was the 1544 *Litere* [Letters] of Vittoria Colonna. Studiously addressing the subject of spiritual development, her published correspondence was the first to specify the female author's first and last names. Colonna's popular collection paved the way for Lucrezia Gonzaga da Gazuolo's 1552 publication *Lettere a Gloria del sesso femminile* [Letters in Praise of Women], Celia Romana's 1563 *Lettere amorose* [Love Letters], Veronica Franco's 1580 *Lettere familiari* [Letters to friends], and Chiara Matraini's 1595 *Lettere* [Letters]. All of the women wrote and published letters in order to edify their readers, whether male or female, and in the process asserted their intellectual and moral entitlement to be heard and respected.

Women were also active as pamphleteers in sixteenth- and seventeenth-century England. Pamphlets, or tracts, small books that reported the news of the day and engaged its most compelling issues—from religion to politics to the nature of women— sold for a penny or two and were the *vox populi* until the invention of newspapers in the late seventeenth century. The earliest female pamphleteers wrote in response to misogynist tracts like Joseph Swetnam's *The Arraignment of Lewd, idle, froward, and unconstant women or the vanity of them, choose you whether, With a Commendation of wise, virtuous, and honest Women, Pleasant for married Men, profitable for young Men, and hurtful to none.* Swetnam's tirade, first published in 1615, was so popular that it was reprinted again in 1615 and in 1616, 1617, 1619, 1622, 1628, 1634, 1637, 1645, 1660, 1667, 1682, 1690, and several times in the eighteenth century. Many pamphlets were written in response to Swetnam, defending women's virtue and goodness, many of them using pseudonyms like Esther Sowernam (*Esther hath hanged Haman; or, An Answer to a lewd Pamphlet entitled The Arraignment of Women, With the arraignment of lewd, idle, froward, and unconstant men and Husbands,* 1617) and Constantia Munda (Pure Constancy) (*The Worming of a mad Dog; or, A Sop for Cerberus, the Jailor of Hell. No Confutation but a sharp Redargution [reproof] of the baiter of Women,* 1617). There is no way to know whether the authors of these tracts were men or women, but there were some protofeminist pamphlets written by women who published under their own names, such as Rachel Speght (1597–aft. 1621), who answered Swetnam with *A Mouzell for Melastomus* [A Muzzle for Badmouth] (1617).

Speght also wrote a religious tract, a poetic reflection on death entitled *Mortalities Memorandum* (1621), which, like *A Mouzell,* relies on a protofeminist reading of biblical passages. Many other women wrote pamphlets to engage the religious debates of the day. Lady Eleanor Davies (1590–1652) used pamphlets to report her prophetic dreams and to prophesy to the English people of the wrath of God that would attend their reversion to Catholicism. She published more than sixty tracts during her lifetime. *A Warning to the Dragon and all His Angels* (1625) advances an allegorical interpretation of the book of Daniel to criticize the "catholicizing" court of King Charles I. (Charles's wife, Henrietta Maria, was openly Catholic, and Charles was tolerant of English Catholics.) Not surprisingly, Davies attracted the attention of the civil and religious authorities with her many pamphlets, and she was imprisoned twice for a number of years each time.

Women also wrote advice books or conduct manuals in which they constructed themselves and their domestic work as both honorable and influential. Although most conduct manuals were written by men, women could engage the genre by drawing on their authority as mothers. Especially popular in England, mother's advice books simultaneously embraced patriarchal values and claimed for motherhood a powerful role in shaping culture and challenging antifeminist slurs. Dorothy Leigh's *The Mother's Blessing* (1616) professes to be a private address to the author's sons, written solely to fulfill her deceased husband's will:

> At his death being charged in his will by the love and duty which I bare him, to see you well instructed and brought up in knowledge, I could not choose but seek (according as I was duty bound) to fulfill his will in all things…. I know not how to perform his duty so well as to leave you these few lines, which will show you as well the great desire your father had both of your spiritual and temporal good, as the care I had to fulfill his will in this.[14]

Despite Leigh's insistence, however, that the book is meant for her sons, that it is informed by her husband's will rather than her own, and that it is motivated by her commitment to subjection and obedience, *The Mother's Blessing* frequently addresses all women and parents in general, and it confidently reminds its readers of the public impact of maternal counsel and practices. Leigh assumed a position of authority that was born of her personal experience as a woman. Her knowledge—and therefore herself, as instructor—is the subject of the book. Nourishing her readers with "the spiritual food of the soul," she described her work as performing an important social and spiritual function.[15] *The Mother's Blessing* was extremely well received; more than twenty editions and reprints were published during the seventeenth century. Similarly, Elizabeth Grymeston's (ca. 1563–1603) *Miscelanea, Meditations, Memoratives* appeared in four editions within 15 years, and Elizabeth Joscelin's (1595–1622) posthumous *Mother's Legacie to her Unborne Childe* was similarly successful. Although all three authors reinscribe dominant notions of women's subordination—apologizing for the effrontery of writing and insisting that they do so only in anticipation of their death—they also affirm a powerful nexus between motherhood and knowledge, femininity and authority.

Creating an instructive persona is also central to the work performed in women's memoirs of the Renaissance. Until late in the period, most autobiographies, whether male- or female-authored, were narratives of spiritual development, describing conversion experiences and teaching by example the means to forge a vital relationship with God. Increasingly, however, memoirs began to focus on a wider range of personal experience. Reflection about emotions and about the self in relation to the world became a defining concern of female autobiographies. The "Memorandum of Martha Moulsworth/Widdowe" (written in 1632 but not published until 1993) is a good example. One of the first autobiographical poems in the English language, the "Memorandum" expresses a spectrum of emotions and reflections about the author's life of 55 years and her three marriages. Moulsworth noted that she was brought up

> in Godly piety,
> In modest chearefulnes, and sad sobriety.
> Nor only so, beyond my sex and kind,
> [My father] did wth learninge Latin decke [my] mind.

The poem includes one of the first exhortations and defenses by an Englishwoman for the founding of a university for females:

> Two Universities we haue of men;
> O that we had but one of women; then
> O then that would in wit and tongues surpass
> All art of men that is or euer was.[16]

As the following passage from Margaret Cavendish, Duchess of Newcastle (1623–1673), illustrates, women were self-conscious about asserting a public persona. But they nevertheless constructed themselves as subjects worthy of their own and others' attention.

> But I hope my readers will not think me vain for writing my life, since there have been many that have done the like, as Caesar, Ovid, and many more, both men and women, and I know of no reason I may not do it as well as they. But I verily believe some censuring readers will scornfully say, why hath this lady writ her own life? Since none care to know whose daughter she was, or whose wife she is, or how she was bred, or what fortunes she had, or how she lived, or what humour or disposition she was of? I answer that it is true, that 'tis no purpose to the readers, but it is to the authoress, because I write it for my own sake, not theirs. Neither did I intend this piece for to delight, but to divulge; not to please the fancy, but to tell the truth. Lest after-ages should mistake, in not knowing I was daughter to one Master Lucas of St. John's near Colchester in Essex, second wife to the Lord Marquis of Newcastle; for, my lord having had two wives, I might easily have been mistaken, especially if I should die and my lord marry again.[17]

Cavendish's announced motives for writing her autobiography—"to divulge" and "to tell the truth"—are similar to those of Helene Kottanner, the first woman known to have written a memoir in German. (See also chapter 4: "Women and Politics.") Kottanner's eyewitness account of history is an extraordinary blend of personal sensibility and formative political developments. It predates the heyday of the memoir genre by many centuries. Free of the gossip and scandal that distinguish later "confessions," it configures the relationship between Queen Elizabeth of Hungary and her chambermaid as one of mutual respect between allies. In the process of limning her individual perspective on international politics, social injustice, intimate relationships, and domestic service, Kottanner's memoir also creates a richly detailed image of her culture.

While memoirs, letters, and conduct books were common genres in which women constructed themselves as subjects, recorded their experiences, and expressed their creativity, female authors also wrote poems, plays, scientific treatises, polemics, prose fiction, and translations. For their literary efforts, most were criticized and many were ignored, but some achieved varying degrees of success and acclaim—particularly the wealthy or powerful few whose social status could command attention and respect. It is fascinating to study the ways in which women adapted historically male forms of expression to articulate their own perspectives. The Petrarchan lyric, that is, the verse form and subject matter popularized by Francesco Petrarch (1304–1374), was extremely popular throughout the European Renaissance; conventionally, it expressed the emotional vicissitudes of a suffering male subject whose consuming love was either unrequited or painfully difficult to articulate. The speaker alternated between abjection and ecstasy; eventually, his love might follow a trajectory that led him "beyond" the lady to a prospect of union with God. Whether used as a stepping stone to spiritual fulfillment or treated as a frame of reference for the speaker's emotional development, the beloved female object was just that: an object that was the premise for the speaker's emergence into language. Often, she was described in dissociated images of body parts: ruby lips, alabaster breasts, golden hair, pearly teeth—parts that rarely cohere into a three-dimensional character. Their significance is the effect they have on the male speaker. Women authors who engaged the Petrarchan paradigm altered the gender roles of speaker and beloved, claiming for themselves an emotive agency that was untraditional for females. Some readers argue that women love poets simply reversed the subject/object positions in their verse, so that the male beloved underwent the same flattening as his traditional counterpart. Other scholars make the claim that female speakers were less vested in objectifying their constructed lovers. But whether the poet was revisionist or imitative, the very fact of her asserting authority *as* an author of love lyrics can be considered remarkable.

One of the early writers of Petrarchan verse in France was Louise Labé, an important poet and member of the most illustrious literary circle in Renaissance France. The friend of authors Pierre de Ronsard (1524–1585), Clément Marot (1496–1544), Joachim du Bellay (1522–1560), and Jean-Antoine de Baïf (1532–1589), she published a popular collection of her own works in 1555. The collection includes 3 elegies, 24 sonnets, a prose work entitled "Debate Between Folly and Love," and a dedicatory epistle to a Lyonnaise noblewoman, Clémence de Bourges. The epistle has been celebrated as a feminist manifesto, although in it she affirms men's right to command and govern women. The letter does, however, "beg excellent Ladies to raise their minds a little above their distaffs and spindles" and to provoke "men to devote more study and labor to the humanities lest they might be ashamed to see us surpass them when they have always pretended to be superior in nearly every-

An image satirizing the dismemberment of the beloved in love poetry: her breasts are globes, her teeth are pearls, her cheeks are roses, her hair is gold wire, her eyes are suns shooting arrows of desire, and Cupid sits on her forehead. *Source:* Charles Sorel, *The Extravagant Shepherd* (London, 1652), © Bodleian Library, University of Oxford, Douce P42, Title Page.

thing."[18] The veiled threat that women might surpass men in learned accomplishments is at the same time a call to women to "devote more study and labor to the humanities." The poems published in Labé's collection include one of the earliest sonnet cycles written in France and several acclaimed elegies in imitation of the Roman poets Propertius (ca. 50–16 B.C.E.) and Ovid (43 B.C.E.–ca. 17

C.E.). Like the lyrics of Petrarch and his imitators, nearly all of Labé's poems are concerned with passionate and often anguished and unrequited love.

Little is known of Labé's life. She was born around 1520 near Lyon, the daughter of Etiennette Deschamps (who died when Louise was a young child) and Pierre Charly, a comfortably well off rope man-ufacturer. Her parents provided her with an extraordinary edu-cation that included Latin, Italian, Spanish, Greek, and her native French as well as music, needlework, and martial arts. Her military skills were legendary, even after her marriage in 1543 to Ennemond Perrin, a prosperous rope maker. Further biographical details are scarce. She spent virtually all of her life in or near Lyon, one of the centers of humanism in Renaissance Europe; her collected works were reprinted in three editions just one year after their first publi-cation (a fact that alone provides evidence of their considerable success); and she died in 1566, about four years after her husband's death. Labé's love poetry is intensely emotional and rhetorically skillful. It elevates love to a cosmic force and draws on a host of Petrarchan conventions, such as nature's participation in the lover's passion ("The pitying gaze of the heavenly stars"), oxy-morons ("I live, I die: I'm drowned and burned. / Enduring freezing cold, I feel excessive heat. / For me, life is too hard, too soft; / My melancholy mixes with my joy"), martial imagery ("Let love take aim at me again, / Fling new fires and new darts at me / … For I am so torn in every part / That he can no longer find a place / To make me worse by wounding me once more"), and a personified Love who inflicts acute physical suffering:

> Since cruel Love first poisoned
> My heart with his fire,
> Always burning with his divine madness,
> He has not left my breast for a single day.
>
> Whatever pain he has given me,
> Whatever threat of impending ruin,
> Whatever thought of death that ends it all,
> Nothing can shake my passionate heart.
>
> The more Love comes to assault us hard,
> The more he makes us gather our forces,
> Forever fresh in his battles.

Like Petrarch, Labé found in her suffering the inspiration to write:

And when I am completely broken,
Arranged exhausted on my bed,
I must cry out my agony all night long.[19]

(Excerpts "From the Works of Louise Labé of Lyon," published in Katharina M. Wilson, ed. *Women Writers of the Renaissance and Reformation* [Athens: The University of Georgia Press, 1991]. © 1991 by the University of Georgia Press. Reprinted with permission.)

The Italian Gaspara Stampa (1524–1554), a contemporary of Labé's, was also a Petrarchan poet. Although only three of her sonnets were published during her lifetime, many critics maintain that Stampa was the most talented female poet of the Italian Renaissance. Like Labé's, most of Stampa's lyrics treat the pain of unfulfilled love. Also like Labé, she does not simply construct herself as the unrequited victim of a cruelly indifferent beloved. Rather, she represents her passion as ennobling and enabling, as the inspiration of her writing, and as the source of her moral authority to teach others. Blending the physical with the spiritual, the sexual with the sacred, is a hallmark of Stampa's verse. Even in the penitential poems that conclude her collected works, the intensity of divine love is sometimes rendered in sensuous terms. According to her poems the experiences of body and soul are not mutually exclusive.

Interest in the uncertain but titillating details of Gaspara's life has eclipsed attention to the literary merit of her work. An eighteenth-century biographer popularized the romantic legend that she was poisoned, and critics throughout the twentieth century debated whether she was a "kept woman." But, in the Italian Renaissance, the status of *cortigiana onesta* (respectable courtesan) was sometimes conferred on cultured, attractive women who engaged in unmarried sexual relationships in exchange for protection and economic security. One scholar has argued that the position actually enabled women to create, influence, and participate in the culture in ways that the prescriptions and proscriptions of marriage made impossible.

The institution of *cortigiana onesta* was perhaps a response to a social situation in which marriage choices were normally determined by commercial or familial considerations rather than by mutual attraction or shared intellectual interest. The relation between *cortigiana* and protector was in some limited respects one of equality: the patron sought in the *cortigiana* intellectual and artistic qualities he would not demand in a wife. It is perhaps for this reason that, during the centuries of the Renaissance and the Baroque, so many distinguished women poets came from the class of the *cortigiana onesta:* it was an identity which, like that of the *grande dame* or the nun, at least made poetic creativity possible.[20]

Whether or not the bourgeois Stampa forged such a relationship with a wealthy nobleman remains unclear, but it is known that she was born in Padua ca. 1524. As a young girl, she moved to Venice when her father, a jeweler, died; there, she mingled with celebrated artists, writers, and aristocrats of Venetian society. Her poetry circulated in manuscript, except for three sonnets that were published in a 1553 anthology. Soon after her death, her collected *Rime* [Rhymes or Verse] was published. The poems are Petrarchan in theme, tone, and imagery, but they are suffused with her own vivid rendition of the desiring female subject rather than the woman as passive object of male desire.

While the connection between Stampa's poetry and her possible livelihood as a courtesan has been debated, there is no doubt about either Veronica Franco's profession or its bearing on a good deal of her erotic lyrics. Like her mother, Franco (1546–1591) was an expensive Venetian prostitute who openly practiced her vocation. She was well received in both aristocratic and literary circles, and an edition of her poetry was published in 1575 or 1576. Her verse is frankly sensual, and her personae are often aggressively erotic, employing martial imagery and extended metaphors of domination and sexual power. As is the case in Stampa's work, Franco's lyrics construct the female speaker's active desire and not the passivity, remoteness, or victimization of women that is conventional in Petrarchan verse. The following lines are from Franco's "Terze rime":

> No more words! To deeds, to the battlefield, to arms!
> for, resolved to die, I wish to free myself
> from such merciless mistreatment....
> Perhaps I would even follow you to bed,
> and, stretched out there in skirmishes with you
> I would yield to you in no way at all:
> To take revenge for your unfair attack,
> I'd fall upon you, and in daring combat,

as you too caught fire defending yourself,
I would die with you, felled by the same blow.[21]

(Translation of Veronica Franco's "Terze Rime," quoted in Ann Rosalind Jones and Margaret F. Rosenthal, eds., *Poems and Selected Letters*, pp. 133–37. © 1998 by The University of Chicago. All rights reserved. Reprinted with permission.)

Another accomplished poet of the Italian Renaissance was Vittoria Colonna (1492–1547). Widely respected for her creative power, erudition, and social prominence, she was also one of the artist Michelangelo de Buonarotti's closest friends. The two exchanged letters, poems, and visits throughout the latter part of her life, and Michelangelo attended her on her deathbed. He described her as his muse, spiritual beacon, and friend. Many of their contemporaries shared his admiration of Colonna, especially for her poetry; some of the most famous writers and humanists of the period in Italy celebrated her verse: Ludovico Ariosto (1474–1533), Spinello Aretino (ca. 1346–1410), Marguerite of Navarre (1492–1549), Giovanni Guidiccioni (1500–1541), and her artistic and spiritual mentor, Cardinal Pietro Bembo (1470–1547). Veronica Gambara (1485–1550), a fellow Petrarchanist, sent several of her own sonnets in homage to Colonna. Modern readers have been similarly impressed; she has been declared "the most famous woman of Italy," and the "literary queen."[22]

In its broad outline, Colonna's life mirrored that of many aristocratic women in Renaissance Italy. Her parents were wealthy and politically influential. When Colonna was three years old, they arranged her marriage to a five-year-old aristocrat in order to solidify regional and state alliances. The parents of the betrothed children signed their wedding contract when Vittoria was 13 and her fiancé, Ferrante Francesco d'Avalos, was 15. The marriage took place two years later. She and her husband saw little of each other, which neither seemed to regret. Ferrante spent only one year with his new wife, after which he was almost continually engaged in military campaigns until his death in 1525 at the age of 35. Colonna, who had no children but raised her husband's orphaned cousin, remained a widow for the last 22 years of her life. Deeply religious, she lived in a number of convents during her widowhood but chose never to become a nun. Unlike most girls of the period, she had received a rigorous humanist education, and she traveled extensively throughout Italy. Both privileges, along

Vittoria Colonna, Marchesa de Pescara, undated letter to Michelangelo Buonarotti. *Source:* Reproduced by permission of The British Library, Add. 23139.

with her wealth and political connections, enabled her to establish herself at the center of a network of powerful and gifted acquaintances.

While Colonna's early and politically motivated wedding, her loveless marriage, and her education were characteristic of European noblewomen, her intellectual and literary abilities were distinguished. Pietro Bembo (1470–1547), poet, scholar, publisher, and cardinal of the church, published her first poem in a 1535 collection of his own verse. Three years later, she published an entire volume of her poetry, and in the next 60 years at least twenty more edi-

tions of her verse appeared. Nearly all of her early poetry is amatory. The metrical form and content are strongly influenced by
Petrarch, and the style of her later spiritual poems is informed by a
Christianized Platonism. As did Petrarch, Colonna traces the development of her earthly love into a transcendent desire for union
with God. Religious rapture replaces the suffering of the early
speakers as she ascends a Neoplatonic ladder toward the divine:

> The great Father draws the soul to heaven,
> bound with string of love, and the knot is tied
> by His dear Son's hand; and so lovely a manner,
> no less than the act itself, contents the heart.
>
> Such is it that I feel a subtle, living ardor
> so penetrate within that, burning, I rejoice,
> and I listen and hear a clear, high sound
> that recalls me to true honor and glory.
>
> Oh steps of faith and charity and hope,
> and of the humility that exalts mankind,
> make us a ladder leading up to highest heaven,
>
> where the blessed souls, together united,
> one after the other, from last to first, all
> gaze at themselves in the great eternal mirror.
>
> (Vittoria Colonna, "Di lacrime e di foco nutir l'alma," trans. Helen
> Moody. Reprinted with permission.)

The opening quatrain of another sonnet describes the speaker's
progress from mortal cares to the respite of God's love:

> From joy to joy, from one to another train
> of sweet and lovely thoughts, Divine Love
> guides me out of the cold, barren winter
> and leads me to His green, warm springtime.

Inspired by divinity rather than earthly desire, the speaker claims
to lose herself in her own creative celebration. She suggests that
praising God in verse, like loving God, is effortless pleasure:

> I move my pen, impelled by inner love;
> and without being fully aware myself of
> what I am saying, I write His praises.[23]

Praising God was a respectable pastime for women, especially if
the praises were translations of men's words rather than original

works. Some female translators of religious texts, however, produced works that were so innovative they became distinctly the translator's own. Such was the case with Mary Sidney's (1561–1621) literary production. One of the most intellectually influential women in Renaissance England, Mary Sidney later became Mary Herbert, Countess of Pembroke. Her illustrious family connections and the extraordinary literary circle to which she was patron have so dazzled students of the period that her own intellectual accomplishments are often overlooked. But those accomplishments are considerable and warrant attention in their own light. She composed the most varied and metrically sophisticated translations of the Psalms ever written in the language. The lyrics have been applauded as "a school of English versification," and they "influenced, directly or indirectly, a good number of English poets of the seventeenth century, chief among them the Countess's kinsman by marriage, George Herbert."[24] In addition, she extensively revised and expanded her brother's prose romance, the *Arcadia,* and she translated Philippe de Mornay's *Discourse of Life and Death,* Robert Garnier's drama *Marc Antoine,* and Petrarch's *Trionfo della morte* [Triumph of death]. Her modifications and revisions of the original works were so substantial that the translated texts were more her own creative productions than the original authors'.

Few families in Elizabethan England were as close to the center of power and prestige as the one to which Mary Sidney was born. Her mother was a close friend of the queen, as was Mary from her young adulthood on. Elizabeth I's relationship with Mary's uncle—Robert, Earl of Leicester—was famously passionate; the two were alternately intimate and adversarial. Mary spent much of her childhood at Penshurst, which was one of the most famous manor houses in the nation and which the Crown had awarded Mary's father for his lifetime of service. She benefited from a lavish education, learning at least six languages as well as needlework, music, and other traditionally feminine arts. When she was 14, she moved into Queen Elizabeth's household, where she lived until her marriage two years later to Henry Herbert, Earl of Pembroke. The couple had two sons and two daughters. Her husband died in 1601, and she remained a widow until her death in 1621. Throughout her years at the Herberts' ancestral seat, Wilton House, she entertained not only Tudor and Stuart royal families and their court, but also many of the best writers in England's golden age. John

Aubrey (1626–1697), the English antiquarian and biographer, described her as perhaps the most intelligent patron in the history of the country. "In her time, Wilton House was like a College, there were so many learned and ingenious persons. She was the greatest patroness of wit and learning of any lady in her time."[25] Authors, scientists, and philosophers praised her intellect and hospitality:

> Francis Meres, Edmund Spenser, Abraham Fraunce, Nicholas Breton, Thomas Moffet, Fulke Greville, Thomas Nashe, Gabriel Harvey, Samuel Daniel, Michael Drayton, John Davies of Hereford, Ben Jonson, John Donne—it would be hard to find a major writer of the period who, though he may not have had some acquaintance with the Countess, at least had friends who did. Her son William was of course one of Shakespeare's most important patrons, and it has often been conjectured that the "W.H." to whom the *Sonnets* are dedicated was the third earl of Pembroke, Mary's son.[26]

Sister to the consummate courtier and author Sir Philip Sidney, the countess completed his translation of the Psalms after his death. Of the 150 poems, Mary composed 107. Her interests were not limited to the humanities; she was an avid student of the sciences, and she had a laboratory built at Wilton, where she was the benefactor of a research chemist.

Among women who contributed to the sciences, it is not surprising that most were aristocrats. There were notable exceptions, such as herbalists and midwives (an overwhelmingly female group until late in the period) and a few women of the middling class scattered throughout Europe whose anomalous training enabled them to pursue their interest in science. An example of the latter was Maria Sibylla Merian, a botanist and entomologist who published her *Wonderful Metamorphosis and Special Nourishment of Caterpillars* in 1679. As was true in the arts, daughters and wives of scientists were more likely to develop their own interests in the discipline, although very few were accorded any authority. Maria Cunitz (ca. 1610–1664) was the wife and daughter of prominent scholars; she became an expert in astronomy and dedicated her published scientific teatise, *Urania propitia* [She who is closest to the muse of astronomy], to the Emperor Frederick III. Generally, female participants in Renaissance science were aristocrats who had access to, and often were patrons of, learned scientific communities. The French geologist Baroness Martine de Beausoleil (ca.

1602–1640) and the natural philosopher Anne Finch, Viscountess Conway (1631–1679), attracted a coterie of scientists to their noble households. Perhaps the most progressive (and certainly the most prolific) of female scientists was Margaret Cavendish, Duchess of Newcastle (1623–1673). Her *Philosophical and Physical Opinions* (1665), among other treatises, embraced the "new science" of the Royal Academy in Britain. (The Royal Academy, however, did not embrace her; indeed, the first woman was admitted to that reigning body of scientists in 1945.)

Cavendish was born Margaret Lucas, the eighth child of a family who believed that a girl's education should be limited to learning the lute, needlework, singing, and dancing. In addition to her traditional education, however, Margaret was taught how to read and write, and she developed a passion for doing both. As a child, she wrote 16 books, each between 50 and 70 pages long. Her ambition to excel as an author grew as she became older. In 1651 she published her first work, a collection of poems that earned her both praise for its originality and criticism for being the work of a weak and ignorant woman. Like her family, Margaret supported the king during the Civil War. When she was 17, she was forced to flee from the home where she was raised in Colchester, England, to Oxford, where the king and his court were in exile. She became a maid of honor to Queen Henrietta Maria and escaped with her to France as the rebels gained more power. While in exile, Margaret married William Cavendish, the first duke of Newcastle, in 1645. Her husband encouraged her to learn and even taught her science and philosophy. Both subjects were important to her later works, including *The Blazing World,* the first book of science fiction published by a woman. In addition,

> she wrote seven works of philosophy and science, giving her opinions on current topics of interest including matter and motion, the vacuum, atoms, sense perception, truth, perfection, and the mind. She based her first works solely on her own perceptions, arguing, like [the English philosopher Thomas] Hobbes, that one's own rational capacity was more valuable than outside authority, but by her later works she was also incorporating ideas from [the philosophers John] Locke, [René] Descartes, and [Jan Baptista] van Helmont.[27]

When Cavendish returned to England, she continued to write fiction, plays, and poetry. Although politically traditional, she was a trailblazer in many ways. Her play *The Convent of Pleasure* sympathetically depicts a lesbian relationship and proposes an ideal community of women separated from patriarchal degradation. She published 22 works and repeatedly had to defend herself against accusations that women who published were arrogant and indecent. She respected her own husband but complained that most men forced women to "live like bats or owls, labor like beasts, and die like worms."[28] In her *Philosophical and Physical Opinions,* she addresses a prefatory letter to "The Two Most Famous Universities of England" in which she exhorts her audience not to condemn her for writing, and she admonishes men for not allowing women intellectual dignity. Offering her treatise to the scholars of Oxford and Cambridge, she urged:

> Receive it without Scorn, for the good Encouragement of our Sex, lest in time we should grow Irrational as Idiots, by the Dejectedness of our Spirits, through the Careless Neglects and Despisements of the Masculine Sex to the Femal, thinking it Impossible we should have either Learning or Understanding, Wit or Judgement, as if we had not Rational Souls as well as Men, and we out of a Custom of Dejectedness think so too, which makes us Quit all Industry towards Profitable Knowledge, being imployed only in Low and Petty imployments, which take away not only our Abilities towards Arts, but higher Capacities in Speculations, so as we are become like Worms, that only Live in the Dull Earth of Ignorance, Winding our Selves sometimes out by the Help of some Refreshing Rain of good Education, which seldome is given us, for we are Kept like Birds in Cages, to Hop up and down in our Houses, not Suffer'd to Fly abroad.

One of the first women in England to write primarily for publication, Cavendish lived her life in observance of her own assertion that "I would rather die in the adventure of noble achievements than live in obscure and sluggish security."[29]

Cavendish's contemporary, Anna Bijns (1493–1575), was a formidable participant in Counter-Reformation polemics of the Netherlands. She was an anomaly among published female authors for several reasons. Although she was born into the middle class—the oldest daughter of master tailor Jan Bijns—after the death of her father when she was a teenager, she spent most of her long life on the verge of poverty. Rarely were writers able to publish under such financially difficult conditions, and it was even rarer still for a woman to admit to the content of poetry like Bijns's. With avenging zeal, she published anti-Protestant lyrics under her own name, lyrics that were renowned for their scatological language and scurrilous epithets. She branded reformers the "children of darkness and stupidity," "poisoned seed," "pus and corruption." Luther was her favorite target, the worst of "the spiders / That from Scripture suck their poison / And revealed to dark malice its reeking bed of dull senselessness." Or as Bijns more plainly put it: "Lutherans stink like goats" and require "a full dozen of faggots under the arse."[30] Her defense of Catholicism, she believed, was divinely inspired. The Holy Spirit was her poetic muse and called her to battle the advances of reformers in the Netherlands.

Bijns was born in Antwerp. She was educated by the Franciscan Minorites and probably spent her young adulthood helping her brother Martaan run a small primary school; together they were barely able to support their family. In 1536 Martaan married, and Anna opened her own one-room school. She refused ever to marry; as a result, she remained impecunious throughout her life and was given a pauper's burial. Bijns's biographers have speculated that she participated in poetry contests sponsored by the Antwerp Chambers of Rhetoric, a popular organization whose members competed in verse of different categories: foolish, amorous, and serious. Some of her readers have attributed to her a number of novels published in Antwerp between 1510 and 1520. Neither speculation has been verified, but Bijns did publish three volumes of pious and militant verse. The first, printed in 1528, contains 23 Counter-Reformation polemics. Within one year of its appearance, it was translated into Latin (so as to circulate among the literati of Europe). The second collection of verse was much longer, and its publication in 1548 was subsidized by the Franciscans. Three editions of the popular *Second Book Containing Many Beautifully Artistic Refrains* appeared by 1565 along with a reprinting of Bijns's first collection. When the author was 74, she agreed to publish her longest collection of poetry (over two hundred fifty pages) as a fund-raiser for a Franciscan prior whose monastery had been destroyed by Protestant arsonists. Her militant lyrics were so popular that one scholar has described her as "the most important and most widely read woman writer of the age in her language."[31]

Not all of Bijns's verses were Counter-Reformation polemics. Her collected secular, amatory, and satirical works were more than twice the length of her religious polemics. The range of tone and

subject matter is vast—from ribald celebrations of women's independence to stinging parodies, satires of marriage, and poignant
love lyrics—all presented variously from the perspective of both
male and female speakers. "Better to fart than to be harmed"
recounts an inventive contest in a convent; "Make Merry and Leap
the Scythe" is a jocular story of nuns who convince their priggish
sister to join in the game of jumping over a scythe, despite her concern that its "edge would kiss my bum!" The eclectic combination
of formal and conversational tone, crusading ire, and reverent
praise distinguish both her religious and secular verse. As one
scholar observed about Bijns's amatory lyrics: "Remarkable mix-
tures of classical topoi (for example, Jason or Aeneas as archetypes
of unfaithful lovers), conventional patterns of fifteenth-century
courtly love poetry, and popular satire, they introduce a new note
in Netherlandic love poetry."[32] Many of her poems are critical of
men, and others caution against the misery of marriage. "Unyoked
is Best! Happy the Woman without a Man," the companion to
another poem that extols the life of a bachelor, warns that financial independence, however meager one's income, and the freedom to govern oneself are far more valuable than any ephemeral
advantages a husband might seem to offer. Enslavement, physical
abuse, betrayal, and grief are the prospects of marriage:

> However rich in goods a girl might be,
> Her marriage ring will shackle her for life.
> If however she stays single
> With purity and spotlessness foremost,
> Then she is lord as well as lady….

> Fine girls turning into loathly hags—
> 'Tis true! Poor sluts! Poor tramps! Cruel marriage!
> Makes me deaf to wedding bells.
> Huh! First they marry the guy, luckless dears,
> Thinking their love just too hot to cool.
> Well, they're sorry and sad within a single year.
> Wedlock's burden is far too heavy.
> They know best whom it harnessed.
> So often is a wife distressed, afraid.
> When after troubles hither and thither he goes
> In search of dice and liquor, night and day,
> She'll curse herself for that initial "yes"….

> A man oft comes home all drunk and pissed
> Just when his wife had worked her fingers to the bone
> (So many chores to keep a decent house!),

But if she wants to get in a word or two,
She gets to taste his fist—no more.
And that besotted keg she is supposed to obey?
Why, yelling and scolding is all she gets,
Such are his ways—and hapless his victim....

A single lady has a single income,
But likewise, isn't bothered by another's whims.
And I think: that freedom is worth a lot.
Who'll scoff at her regardless what she does,
And though every penny she makes herself,
Just think of how much less she spends!
An independent lady is an extraordinary prize—
All right, of a man's boon she is deprived,
But she's lord and lady of her very own hearth.
To do one's business and no explaining sure is lots of fun!
Go to bed when she list, rise when she list, all as she will,
And no one to comment! Grab tight your independence then.
Freedom is such a blessed thing....

Regardless of the fortune a woman might bring,
Many men consider her a slave, that's all....
To women marriage comes to mean betrayal
And the condemnation to a very awful fate.
All her own is spent, her lord impossible to bear.
It's *peine forte et dure* [being pressed to death] instead of fun
    and games....
Unyoked is best! Happy the woman without a man.

(Excerpt from Anna Bijns "Unyoked Is Best! Happy the Woman without a Man," published in Katharina M. Wilson, ed. *Women Writers of the Renaissance and Reformation* [Athens: The University of Georgia Press, 1991]. © 1991 by Katharina M. Wilson. Reprinted with permission.)

A number of female authors shared Bijns's jaundiced view of marriage. The English poet Isabella Whitney (ca. 1548–aft. 1573) remarked in one of her two published collections of popular verse that she couldn't have indulged in reading and writing if she were not single. One of Margaret Cavendish's female characters in *Love's Adventures* scorns the idea of a party in honor of her wedding: "Do you call that a triumphant day, that enslaves a woman all her life after? No, I will make no triumph on that day."[33] Mary Astell (1666–1731) was even more bitter about women's subjection in wedlock. With scathing irony, she presents a third-person defense of herself in *Some Reflections Upon Marriage* (1700). "Far be it from her to stir up Sedition of any sort," she begins.

Nor can she imagine how she any way undermines the Masculine Empire, or blows the Trumpet of Rebellion to the Moiety of Mankind. Is it by exhorting Women, not to expect to have their own Will in any thing, but to be entirely Submissive, when once they have made Choice of a Lord and Master, though he happen not to be so wise, so kind, or even so just a Governor as was expected? She did not, indeed, advise them to think his Folly Wisdom, nor his Brutality, that Love and Worship he promised in his Matrimonial Oath; for this required a Flight of Wit and Sense much above her poor Ability, and proper only to Masculine Understandings.[34]

The "brutality" that Astell mentions is a common theme of marriage in the novellas of María de Zayas y Sotomayor (ca. 1590–ca. 1661). The Spanish author's stories are populated by wife beaters and other abusive husbands. The convent is a haven for many of her female characters. Entering a nunnery is "not a tragic end, but the happiest that could be, since coveted and desired by many, she subjected herself to none."[35] María de Zayas y Sotomayor was born to a noble family from Madrid. Little is known of her life except that she circulated among the most sophisticated and accomplished literary figures of her country, many of whom esteemed her work and wit. She was one of the most renowned writers of novellas (short narratives in prose) in her day. Her work deeply influenced that of the dramatist Ana Caro Mallén de Soto (ca. 1600–ca. 1650) and of fellow novella writer Mariana de Carvajal (ca. 1600–ca. 1663). Zayas's most celebrated collections of stories were *Novelas amorosas y ejemplares* [Romantic Stories and Exemplary Tales] (1637) and *Desengaños amorosos* [Disillusioned Love] (1647). Like Marguerite de Navarre's *Heptameron* and Boccaccio's *Decameron,* the stories are connected by an organizing premise. In the earlier of Zayas's collections, the "framing" circumstances are the convalescence of a noblewoman, Lysis, whose social acquaintances gather each night to tell stories and entertain both Lysis and each other. In the second collection, Lysis allows only women to narrate the tales, and she appoints the order of the speakers. Most of the stories dwell on misplaced love, honor and betrayal, or the abuse of disempowered females whose fortitude and integrity elicit the reader's sympathy. Zayas's novellas move quickly from one dramatic action to the next, and her plots scrutinize with intensity the culture's pervasive victimization of women.

A similar scrutiny took place in the first English play (outside of translations) that is known to be written by a woman. *The*

Tragedie of Mariam, the Faire Queene of Jewry (1613) by Elizabeth Cary (1585–1639) dramatizes the story of Mariam and her murderous husband, Herod. The play both celebrates Mariam for her feminine virtue of chastity and criticizes her outspokenness. It is a conflicted amalgam of conservative and subversive responses to cultural and marital repression of women. Cary seems to embrace both patriarchal values and heroic resistance to the injustice of those values. On the one hand, valorizing a woman's chastity and reproving her speech were central to the platform of Renaissance misogynists; on the other hand, Mariam undergoes a kind of apotheosis at the end of the play and is celebrated even by the husband who had had her decapitated. Other female roles in Cary's closet drama represent similarly conflicted alternatives to Mariam's character. The sexually incontinent, predatory Salome schemes to kill husband after husband, and yet she, not the honest Mariam, is allowed to live. Graphina is in many ways the ideal woman: chaste, silent, obedient, servile, humble, and adoring of her man; yet Cary depicts her as an impotent foil to the more vivid Salome and the more heroic Mariam.

Cary's own life is a history of ambivalence. She was committed to authoritarianism, hierarchy, and political, filial, and wifely obedience, and yet she willfully violated fundamental laws of the kingdom, disobeyed her parents, and disgraced and defied her husband. She converted to Catholicism when doing so was a crime against the state; her conversion nearly cost her husband his position at court. It fueled her father's decision to disinherit her, and it led to her being incarcerated on her estate and nearly starved to death by her own family members. Her children were taken away from her for the protection of their Protestant souls; but, controverting orders of the highest court in the nation, she arranged for two of her sons to be kidnapped, smuggled out of the country, and educated in Catholic schools on the continent. Born Elizabeth Tanfield, she was the only child of wealthy and sternly Protestant parents. Her father was an Oxford lawyer who was later appointed the Lord Chief Baron of the Exchequer. Rigorously self-disciplined, the young Elizabeth is said to have taught herself at least seven languages; she was also a fervent student of theology, but neither of her parents approved of her "masculine learning." When she was 15, they arranged for her marriage to Henry Cary, a knight's son who rose to the rank of viscount. The two were miserably unsuited. According to *The Lady Falkland: Her Life* (written primarily by her daughter Lucy but emended and expanded by two of her other children, Mary and Patrick, and an anonymous Benedictine monk, over the period of 1645–1649), Elizabeth Cary tried to subordinate her desires to those of her repressive husband: "He was very absolute, and though she had a strong will, she had learnt to make it obey his." She is reported to have advised her daughter to "prefer the will of another before her own" whenever possible, and presumably she herself attempted to follow this precept.[36] And yet, just as she insisted on kneeling whenever in her own mother's presence but refused to conform to many of her mother's expectations, Cary repeatedly transgressed against her husband's wishes. During her profoundly unhappy marriage, she gave birth to 11 living children, fulfilling what was held to be her most important role as a woman. But she also wrote *The Tragedie of Mariam* at the age of 17; translated Catholic polemics (at least one of which was publicly burned); and composed religious verse, lives of the saints, and a life of King Edward II. When dispossessed and destitute, she dared to sue her husband before the Privy Council and succeeded in obtaining a subsidy for her maintenance. Six of her eight children who survived into adulthood sought a vocation in the Catholic Church, and all four of her daughters became nuns. No contemporary notice of *Mariam* survives; Cary's most impressive literary production seems to have been ignored or unknown.

The same is true of Aemilia Lanyer's (1569–1645) major work, *Salve Deus Rex Judaeorum.* Much of the information available about Lanyer's life comes from the casebooks of the astrologer Simon Forman, whom Lanyer consulted about her husband's prospects for promotion. Forman tried, evidently unsuccessfully, to seduce Lanyer, and many of his comments are deformed by jealousy and pique and must, therefore, be used with care. Public records show that she was christened in London, the daughter of Baptista Bassano and Margaret Johnson. Nothing certain is known of Aemilia's mother but that she was buried in Bishopsgate on July 7, 1587. Her father's family, the Bassanos, were court musicians who had come to England from Venice at the end of Henry VIII's reign. Internal evidence of Lanyer's poems suggests that she was fostered in the household of Susan Bertie Wingfield, Countess Dowager of Kent (1554–aft. 1596), information also confirmed by Forman, and that she was later attached to the household of Margaret, Countess of Cumberland, and her daughter, Anne Clifford.

Lanyer memorializes her time with these women at the estate of Cookham Dean in "The Description of Cooke-ham." She must have been educated along with the noble girls whom she attended, for her work shows familiarity with poetic genres and verse forms as well as the Geneva Bible and the Book of Common Prayer.

As a young woman, Aemilia frequented the court of Elizabeth I and was mistress to Henry Carey, Lord Hunsdon, 45 years her senior, who "maintained [her] in great pomp," said Forman, and provided her with an income of £40 a year.[37] (There is no conclusive evidence that she was William Shakespeare's mistress, an argument advanced by A. L. Rowse, nor, indeed, that she was the "dark-eyed lady" of John Milton's sonnets, a theory advanced early in this century by John Smart.) She became pregnant at the age of 23, was paid off by Hunsdon, and was married to her cousin by marriage, Alphonso Lanyer, a queen's musician. Alphonso was a member of the recorder consort originally started by the five Bassano brothers that included Aemilia's father, Baptista. Alphonso was one of 59 musicians who played at Elizabeth's funeral, and he moved at her death into the service of James VI and I. He had been preferred by Elizabeth's closest adviser, William Cecil, Lord Burghley, and granted a monopoly for the weighing of hay and straw in London (that is, he had the right to collect a fee for all the hay and straw that came into the city). When he died in 1613, Aemilia Lanyer made over the grant to her brother-in-law, Innocent, evidently with an understanding that she would continue to receive a portion of it, though her right to that income was a source of later dispute.

Lanyer told Forman that she had suffered many miscarriages, but she had at least two children: the first (presumably the son of Hunsdon) was named Henry, born early in 1593, and a daughter, Odillya, born in December 1598, died at 10 months of age. Henry became one of the king's flutists on September 29, 1629. He had two children by his wife, Joyce Mansfield, whom he married in 1623; after his death 10 years later, Lanyer helped support her two grandchildren. When widowed, she opened a school, as she put it, for "children of divers persons of worth and understanding." She experienced financial hardship for much of her later life, although when she died in 1645 at age 76, she was listed as a "pensioner," that is, as someone possessed of a regular income. Lanyer first consulted Forman in 1597; he provided the only physical description available—that she had a wart or a mole in the pit of her throat. He reported that she was unhappy with her husband, and he supposed that her emotional and financial neediness would make her "a good fellow," that is, a willing sex partner. But though she seems to have had continued contact with Forman over the next few years, she ultimately refused to consummate a relationship with him, prompting him in his arrogance to wonder "whether or not she is an incuba" (a demon who was said to descend on women in their sleep to have intercourse with them), which is perhaps why he mentioned the mark on her throat. He also called her a whore.[38]

Lanyer published her volume of poetry, *Salve Deus Rex Judaeorum* (Hail, God, King of the Jews), in 1611 when she was 42 years old. Lanyer's book is radical in its theology and politics and could aptly be called protofeminist. Both the prefatory poems and the title poem argue for women's religious and social equality, and the longer version of the poem addressed to Anne Clifford (to whom the book is actually dedicated) includes a levelling tirade against class privilege. In addition to the prefatory poems, Lanyer's book consists of the long (1,840-line) title poem, "Salve Deus Rex Judaeorum," "The Description of Cooke-ham," and a final prose address "To the doubtfull Reader." "Salve Deus Rex Judaeorum" is a meditation on the Passion that argues that men (not women) were responsible for the crucifixion of Christ. Lanyer further argues in an extended section entitled "Eves Apologie in Defense of Women" that Eve was less culpable than Adam. Lanyer then compares women's sinfulness in the Edenic context to men's sinfulness in the context of the crucifixion to argue for women's social and religious equality with men:

> Then let us have our liberty again,
> And challenge to your selves no Sovereignty;
> You came not in the world without our pain,
> Make that a bar against your cruelty;
> Your fault being greater, why should you disdain
> Our being your equals, free from tyranny?
> If one weak woman simply did offend,
> This sin of yours, hath no excuse, nor end.[39]

"The Description of Cooke-ham" is a country-house poem, predating the more famous exemplar of that genre, "To Penshurst" (1616), by Ben Jonson (1572–1637). Drawing on classical generic features, Lanyer figures the virtue of the "Lady" of the poem, Margaret, Countess of Cumberland, in the homage accorded her by the estate's flora and fauna.

Lanyer's celebration of women united in shared experience and purpose is echoed and personalized in the poetry of Katherine Philips (1631–1664). Philips was renowned for establishing a literary Society of Friendship in which primarily women and some men engaged in correspondence and philosophical discussions. She was the daughter of James Fowler, a flourishing London cloth merchant, and Katherine Oxenbridge Fowler, whose father was a member of the Royal College of Physicians. At the age of eight, Katherine was sent to a Presbyterian girls' boarding school, where she developed lifelong relationships with friends to whom she paid tribute in some of her most famous poems. It was at school that she assumed her pen name, Orinda, and assigned names from classical literature to her friends. When she was 14, her widowed mother married Sir Richard Philips, and two years later Katherine wed her stepfather's son by a previous marriage. She was 16, and her husband, James Philips, was 54. Despite their differences in age and politics (she was a Royalist, and he was an active Parliamentarian), the couple seem to have had a genial relationship. James did not object to his learned wife's writing poetry or devoting time to her female friendships. She gave birth to two children, a son who died after 40 days and a daughter who lived to adulthood. Her literary production was remarkable. Often cited as one of the most important female writers in Renaissance England, she composed more than 100 poems, 5 verse translations, and 2 translations of plays by Pierre Corneille. Her dramatic rendition of *Pompey* was the first play by a woman to be produced in London (1663). It was also performed in Dublin and was acclaimed in both cities.

The theme of pastoral retreat suffuses many of Philips's poems. She contrasts the security and serenity of her friendships with the contentious ambition and violence of national politics. Her poem entitled "A Retir'd Friendship. To Ardelia," for example, sets her relationship apart "from noise of Wars."

> Here is no quarrelling for Crowns,
> Nor fear of changes in our Fate;
> No trembling at the great ones frowns,
> Nor any slavery of State.
>
> But we (of one anothers mind
> Assur'd) the bois'trous World distain;

With quiet Souls and unconfin'd
Enjoy what Princes wish in vain.[40]

Half of her poems are dedicated to Anne Owen, whom she addresses as Lucasia and with whom she maintained an intimate friendship and perhaps a sexual relationship even after Owen had married. In the verse to her female circle, she adapts the language of Renaissance love lyrics, applying it to a nearly unprecedented subject: friendship with a woman. Her poetry invokes the conventional tropes of subjection to love and then defuses the violence by equalizing its effects in mutual friendship:

We court our own Captivity
Than Thrones more great and innocent:
'Twere banishment to be set free,
Since we wear fetters whose intent
Not bondage is, but Ornament.

Our Hearts are mutual Victims laid,
While they (such power in Friendship lies)
Are Altars, Priests, and Off'rings made:
And each Heart which thus kindly dies,
Grows deathless by the Sacrifice.[41]

Platonic love between men was a conventional topic, but it was widely held that women's moral, intellectual, and spiritual inferiority prevented them from being able to form meaningful friendships. As one scholar put it, "When women appeared in literary works about friendship, they were, as a rule, the seductresses who wooed men like John Lyly's Euphues away from his true [male] friend Philautus. It remained for Katherine Philips to assert a philosophy of friendship that took for granted the notion that women could be friends with each other and with men."[42] Not only did she celebrate Platonic love between women, but she broke with tradition in focusing on the woman's perspective in most of her lyrics; for example, her epithalamia, or wedding poems, are more attentive to the bride's experience than to the groom's, and her epitaph on the death of a friend's husband is more about the widow than the dead man. Philips's lyrics circulated in manuscript among her circle, but no authorized collection of the verse was published until three years after her death from smallpox in 1667.

Unlike Katherine Philips, Marie Catherine Desjardins, Madame de Villedieu (ca. 1640–1683), wrote for publication. A member of the minor French nobility, she was a witty participant in the salon of Marie de Rohan-Montbazon, Duchess of Chevreuse (1600–1679), who arranged to have her young protegé's erotic verse printed and who introduced her to the society publisher Claude Barbin. Desjardins's 1659 sonnet "Jouissance" (which means both joy and orgasm) says, in part:

> Today I rested in your arms, overcome by desire;
> Today, dear Tirsis, your passionate love
> Triumphed with impunity over all my shame,
> And I gave in to those transports that seduce the soul.
>
> * * *
>
> A sweet langour deprives me of consciousness;
> I die between the arms of my faithful lover,
> And it is in this death that I find life.[43]

Desjardins and Barbin maintained a working relationship throughout her career. She became a celebrated author whose publications include collections of poetry and letters, 3 plays, and 13 fictional narratives and long novels. Although her work never made her wealthy, she was distinguished as one of the first women in Europe who achieved financial independence through publication.

Aphra Behn (ca. 1640–1689) wrote expressly for publication. Indeed, she was the first woman in Britain (and possibly the first in Europe) to support herself by writing professionally. Her oeuvre of nearly sixty works constituted about one-tenth of the total works published by women in the second half of the seventeenth century. *Oroonoko: or the Royal Slave* is considered the first novel in English. At least eighteen of her plays were performed on stage, many of them frequently and to great acclaim. The most prolific female author in England, she also published translations and volumes of poetry. One scholar has noted that, "as the first woman of letters in English to earn her living by writing, the first female dramatist to forge a niche in the theater, and one of the first to violate traditional expectations about women's secondary status and sexual inactivity or reticence, she has earned a permanent place in the feminist pantheon."[44] For the same accomplishments, however, Behn was also vilified as lewd and unnatural. To write for the public was to be a "public woman," with all the connotations of immorality the term suggested. Indeed, her writing was often equated with the traffic of prostitutes: both entertained male strangers for profit. Behn repeatedly exchanged salvos with critics who condemned the bawdiness of her works. In Behn's comments "To the Reader," which preface her play *Sir Patient Fancy* (1678), she denounces the hypocrisy and bigotry of her detractors. They object, she remarks, because

> The play had no other misfortune but that of [having been written by] a woman: had it been owned by a man, though the most dull unthinking rascally scribbler in town, it had been an admirable play. [Critics protested] *that it was bawdy,* the least and most excusable fault in the men writers, *but from a woman it was unnatural.*[45]

But Behn's most scathing counterattacks were not against those who impugned her morality; rather, they were against those who argued that because she was a woman, the quality of her work was necessarily inferior. Behn's "Epistle to the Reader," which prefaces her play *The Dutch Lover* (1673), constructs an acerbic stereotype of critics who made such arguments, and it asserts that women are capable of producing works that are equal to the very best that men write:

> Indeed that day [the play] 'twas acted first, there comes me into the pit a long, lithe, phlegmatic, white, ill-favored, wretched fop, an offi-cer in masquerade newly transported with a scarf and feather out of France, a sorry animal that has nought else to shield it from the uttermost contempt of all mankind, but that respect which we afford to rats and toads, which though we do not well allow to live, yet when considered as a part of God's creation, we make honorable mention of them. A thing, reader—but no more of such a smelt: this thing, I tell you, opening that which serves it for a mouth, out issued such a noise as this to those that sat about it, that they were to expect a woeful play, God damn him, for it was a woman's.... But affectation has always had a greater share both in the action and discourse of men than truth and judgment have; and for our modern ones, except for our most inimitable laureate, I dare to say I know of none that write at such a formidable rate, but that a woman may well hope to reach their greatest heights.[46]

As has often been the case with controversial female authors, critical attention to Behn has in the past focused more on the details of her life than on the merits of her work. But very few facts about her early life are available. Though neither her family's

Aphra Behn, *Poems upon Several Occasions* (London, 1697), frontispiece.
Source: Reproduced by permission of the British Library, 11626.bb.5.

name nor the year or place of her birth are known for certain, it is conjectured that her father, surname Johnson, was related to Lord Willoughby, who procured his appointment as lieutenant general of Surinam. Born sometime between 1640 and 1649 in the county of Kent, Behn accompanied her father to Surinam; en route, he died at sea, and she returned to England after a brief stay in South America. Most biographers wrote that she subsequently married a Dutch merchant named Behn in England, but there are no records of the marriage, and nowhere in Behn's writing does she mention having a husband; it is possible that she styled herself "Mrs. Behn" as a kind of shield and protection from public scandal. By 1666, she was serving as a spy in Antwerp for Charles II. The English government was persistently negligent in paying her, and two years later she was back in London with debilitating debts. Her first play, *The Forced Marriage,* was a tragicomedy produced in 1670. Most of the drama that followed was comedy, the most popular genre of the period. It is significant that she did not dedicate her plays to a patron for many years; not until she was established as a successful dramatist did she receive aristocratic backing. The absence of support from wealthy benefactors early in her career may well have been because she was the only professional female author at the time. Both her access to the aristocracy and her credibility were limited. Nonetheless, Behn's plays garnered increasing acclaim, and her poems and songs were also well received. Her poetry, like her drama, is characteristically concerned with love, marriage, power relations, and passion. In both genres, she demonstrates a genius for satire. Included among the verse are poems in honor of the royal family. A dedicated Tory, she stalwartly defended the monarchy and celebrated its unpopular members, but her loyalty netted her little profit. At her death in 1689, she was impoverished, socially isolated, and disenfranchised. Throughout her career, Behn was condemned for her unorthodoxy; despite the criticism, however, she refused to quit writing and publishing. As she maintained in her preface to *The Lucky Chance* (1686), "I am not content to write for a Third day only [that is, the day when playwrights would be paid for their work]. I value Fame as much as if I had been born a *Hero.*"[47]

One could argue that all of the women who wrote and published during the Renaissance were to some degree heroic. They braved condemnation, adapted ingeniously, made shrewd tactical concessions when necessary, and in some cases fought attackers with rhetorical ferocity and skill. Taken as a whole, the majority of women's publications were devotional—whether biblical or other pious translations, religious poetry, spiritual autobiographies and meditations, or confessionals—but as the period developed, so did the variety of genres in which they wrote. Far more populist secular works appeared, such as erotic and occasional verse; prose fiction; drama; and manuals about conduct, herbs, cooking, practical medicine, and midwifery. Collections of letters were published, as were memoirs, and the novel began to emerge as a related genre. Early in the period, the Italian Giulia Bigolina (ca. 1516–1569) did not risk the scandal that would have ensued had she published her popular novellas and other prose fiction that treated the subject of love, but increasing numbers of later Renaissance women published in genres that had previously been taboo. One scholar has shown how "the English Civil War saw a dramatic upsurge in women's political writings—from six in the entire period 1600–1640 to seventy-seven in the decade 1641–1650 alone—ranging from political prophesy to women's petitions to Parliament to pamphlets arguing every political position from staunch royalist to radical Leveller." However, "there was no similar expansion anywhere on the Continent, although the horrors of the Thirty Years' War did lead a few women, such as Martha Salome von Belta, to publish their own views of the war's causes and probable consequences."[48] While the Continent did not experience the sudden florescence of women's political writing that took place in England, it did see a significant increase in the genres females employed and in the sheer quantity of their literary production from 1400 to 1700. Women were never as culturally entitled to write as were men, but they nevertheless forged a place for the articulation of their own perspectives during the Renaissance.

Most female writers belonged either to the aristocracy or to wealthy families who allowed their daughters to be educated beyond the traditional confines of a "feminine curriculum" (needlework, music, dancing, and drawing). Even girls privileged with an extensive humanist education, however, had no hope of applying "the new learning" to the career goals of professional service for which it prepared males. Denied most public vocational opportunities, commoners such as Anna Bijns, Aphra Behn, Gaspara Stampa, Aemilia Lanyer, and Louise Labé struggled not only with ostracism but with debt and poverty. The works of wealthy women authors generally met with a better reception—or at least with less overt hostility. Both affluent and lower-class women wrote defenses of their sex and of their right to an education and even an audience. Fourteen-year-old Sarah Fyge (ca. 1670–1723) argued in *The Female Advocate* (1686) that men's attacks on women were born of insecurity, envy, inadequacy, and a lust for power. The Italian Laura Cereta (1469–1499) eloquently argued for equal educational opportunities, and her compatriots, Isotta Nogarola (1418–ca. 1466) and Cassandra Fedele (1465–1558), were renowned for their erudition. There were learned female scholars scattered throughout Europe, in spite of the widely held presumption that girls should be excluded from academic training. In Spain, Beatriz Galindo (Queen Isabella's Latin tutor; 1474–1534) was acclaimed for her intellectual achievements, as were the Portuguese Luisa Sigea (1522–1560); the French Dames des Roches, Madeleine (1520–1587) and Catherine (1542–1587) Neveu, and Pernette Du Guillet (ca. 1520–1545); the English Margaret More Roper (1505–1544) and Bathsua Makin (ca. 1612–ca. 1673); the German Caritas Pirckheimer (1467–1532) and the Dutch Anna Maria van Schurman (1607–1678) and Maria Tesselschade (1594–1649). All of these women defended the right and capacity of their sex to articulate their perspective and to understand and shape their experience. By writing, they were important participants in defining and ordering Renaissance culture.

NOTES

1.   Qtd. in Katharina M. Wilson, ed., *Women Writers of the Renaissance and Reformation* (Athens: University of Georgia Press, 1987), xxiii.

2.   Qtd. in Kate Aughterson, ed., *Renaissance Woman: A Sourcebook: Constructions of Feminity in England* (New York: Routledge, 1995), 256.

3.   Qtd. in Aughterson, *Renaissance Women,* 256. Jinner's almanac includes detailed information about pregnancy and childbirth based on the classical sources used by university-trained male doctors (i.e., Galen and Hippocrates). Her book also includes recipes for abortifacients. See A. S. Weber, "Women's Early Modern Medical Almanacs in Historical Context," *English Literary Renaissance* 33 (2003): 358–402.

4.   Wilson, *Women Writers of the Renaissance,* xxx–xxxi.

5.   Merry E. Wiesner, *Women and Gender in Early Modern Europe,* 2nd ed. (New York: Cambridge University Press, 2000), 177.

6.   Qtd. in Jean Lafond, ed., *Réflexions ou Sentences et Maximes morales suivi de réflexions divers* [Observations or Aphorisms and Moral

Maxims followed by Diverse Observations] (Paris: Editions Gallimard, 1978); our translation.

7.   Wiesner, *Women and Gender*, 177.

8.   Qtd. in Aughterson, *Renaissance Woman*, 235.

9.   Aemilia Lanyer, "To the Doubtful Reader," in *Salve Deus Rex Judaeorum*, ed. Susanne Woods (New York: Oxford University Press, 1993), 139.

10.   See Sara Jayne Steen, introduction to *The Letters of Lady Arbella Stuart*, ed. Sara Jayne Steen (New York: Oxford University Press, 1994).

11.   Qtd. in Katharina M. Wilson and Frank J. Warnke, eds., *Women Writers of the Seventeenth Century* (Athens: University of Georgia Press, 1989), 35.

12.   Madame de Sévigné, letter of 26 April 1671, trans. Jeanne A. Ojala and William T. Ojala, in Wilson and Warnke, *Women Writers of the Seventeenth Century*, 49.

13.   Madame de Sévigné, letter of 1670, trans. Jeanne A. Ojala and William T. Ojala, in Wilson and Warnke, *Women Writers of the Seventeenth Century*, 47–48.

14.   Qtd. in Aughterson, *Renaissance Woman*, 98.

15.   Qtd. in Aughterson, *Renaissance Woman*, 99.

16.   Martha Moulsworth, "Memorandum of Martha Moulsworth/Widdowe," lines 27–30, 33–36. Moulsworth's poem has been edited by Robert C. Evans and Barbara Wiedemann and is available in print in *"My name was Martha": A Renaissance Woman's Autobiographical Poem* (West Cornwall, CT: Locust Hill Press, 1993) as well as online at <http://www.geocities.com/ResearchTriangle/Station/1559/myname1.html>.

17.   Margaret Cavendish, Duchess of Newcastle, "A True Relation of my Birth, Breeding, and Life," in *Natures Picture Drawn by Fancies Pencil* (London, 1656), 391. Cavendish's works are available through EEBO, <http://eebo.chadwyck.com>.

18.   Louise Labé, letter, trans. Jeanne Prine, in Wilson, *Women Writers of the Renaissance*, 149.

19.   Louise Labé, "[Since cruel Love first poisoned]," trans. Jeanne Prine, in Wilson, *Women Writers of the Renaissance*, 151–53.

20.   Frank J. Warnke, "Gaspara Stampa: Aphrodite's Priestess, Love's Martyr," in Wilson, *Women Writers of the Renaissance*, 3–4.

21.   Veronica Franco, "Terze Rime," qtd. in Ann Rosalind Jones and Margaret F. Rosenthal, eds., *Poems and Selected Letters* (Chicago: University of Chicago Press, 1998), 133–37. Used with permission.

22.   Qtd. in Joseph Gibaldi, "Vittoria Colonna: Child, Woman, and Poet," in Wilson, *Women Writers of the Renaissance*, 25.

23.   Gibaldi, "Vittoria Colonna," 41, 40.

24.   Coburn Freer, "Mary Sidney: Countess of Pembroke," in Wilson, *Women Writers of the Renaissance*, 483.

25.   Aubrey qtd. in Wilson, *Women Writers of Renaissance,* 482.

26.   Wilson, *Women Writers of the Renaissance,* 482.

27.   Wiesner, *Women and Gender,* 199.

28.   Qtd. in Wilson and Warnke, *Women Writers of the Seventeenth Century,* 314.

29.   Qtd. in Moira Ferguson, ed., *First Feminists: British Women Writers, 1578–1799* (Bloomington: Indiana University Press, 1985), 85.

30.   Kristiaan P. G. Aercke, "Anna Bijns: Germanic Sappho," in Wilson, *Women Writers of the Renaissance,* 365, 368.

31.   Aercke, "Anna Bijns," 367–68.

32.   Aercke, "Anna Bijns," 374. Jason is a figure of Greek mythology who commanded the ship *Argo* with its crew of Argonauts and captured the golden fleece; Aeneas is the hero of *The Aeneid,* an epic poem about the Trojan War by the Roman poet Virgil (70–19 B.C.E.).

33.   Margaret Cavendish, Duchess of Newcastle, "Love's Adventures," in *Playes Written by the Thrice Noble, Illustrious and Excellent Princess, the Lady Marchioness of Newcastle* (London, 1662), line 66. This work is available through EEBO, <http://eebo.chadwyck.com>.

34.   Qtd. in Ferguson, *First Feminists,* 191.

35.   "Desengaños amorosos," trans. Sandra M. Fox, from "María de Zayas y Sotomayor: Sibyl of Madrid (1590?–1661?)," in *Female Scholars: A Tradition of Learned Women before 1800,* ed. Jean R. Brink (Montreal: Edens Press, 1980), 59.

36.   Heather Wolfe, ed., *Elizabeth Cary, Lady Falkland: Life and Letters* (Tempe, AZ: Medieval and Renaissance Text Studies, 2001), 115.

37.   Aemilia Lanyer, *The Poems of Shakespeare's Dark Lady: Salve Deus Rex Judaeorum by Emilia Lanier,* ed. A. L. Rowse (New York: Clarkson N. Potter, 1978), 11. See also Susanne Woods, ed., *Salve Deus Rex Judaeorum: The Poems of Aemilia Lanyer* (New York: Oxford University Press, 1983), and Kari Boyd McBride's biography of Aemilia Lanyer at <http://jamaica.u.arizona.edu/ic/mcbride/lanyer/lanbio.htm>.

38.   Rowse, *The Poems of Shakespeare's Dark Lady,* 33–35, 11–13.

39.   Aemilia Lanyer, "Salve Deus Rex Judaeorum," in *Salve Deus Rex Judaeorum,* ed. Susanne Woods, lines 825–32. Lanyer's poems are also available online at McBride's Lanyer Web site, <http://jamaica.u.arizona.edu/ic/mcbride/lanyer/lansdrj.htm>, and at Richard Bear's Renascence Editions site at <http://darkwing.uoregon.edu/%7Erbear/ lanyer1.html>.

40.   Qtd. in Ferguson, *First Feminists,* 104. Philips's poems are available as *The Collected Works of Katherine Philips: The Matchless Orinda,* ed. Patrick Thomas (Stump Cross, UK: Stump Cross Books, 1990), and at Luminarium, <http://www.luminarium.org/sevenlit/philips/>.

41.   Qtd. in Ferguson, *First Feminists,* 103–04.

42.   Elizabeth Hageman, "Katherine Philips: The Matchless Orinda," in Wilson, *Women Writers of the Renaissance,* 573.

43.   Our translation. Desjardins's poems are available in French in *Œuvres complètes* (Geneva: Slatkine Reprints, 1971).

44.   Ferguson, *First Feminists,* 143–44.

45.   Aphra Behn, *Sir Patient Fancy* (London, 1678), sig. A_v. The play is available in print as *The Complete Works of Aphra Behn,* ed. Janet Todd (Columbus: Ohio State University Press, 1996) and online through EEBO, <http://eebo.chadwyck.com>.

46.   Aphra Behn, *The Dutch Lover* (London, 1673), sig. $A4_v$–A5. This work is available in print in Todd, *The Complete Works,* and online through EEBO, <http://eebo.chadwyck.com>.

47.   Aphra Behn, *The Lucky Chance* (London, 1673), folios $A5_R$. This work is available through EEBO, <http://eebo.chadwyck.com>, and in print in Todd, *The Complete Works.*

48.   Wiesner, *Women and Gender,* 197.

SUGGESTED READING

Aughterson, Kate, ed. *Renaissance Woman: A Sourcebook: Constructions of Feminity in England.* New York: Routledge, 1995.

Hannay, Margaret P., ed. *Silent but for the Word: Tudor Women as Patrons, Translators, and Writers of Religious Works.* Kent, OH: Kent State University Press, 1985.

Henderson, Katherine Usher, and Barbara F. McManus. *Half Humankind: Contexts and Texts of the Controversy about Women in England, 1540–1640.* Urbana: University of Illinois Press, 1985.

King, Margaret L., and Albert Rabil, Jr., trans. and eds. *Her Immaculate Hand: Selected Works by and about the Women Humanists of Quattrocento Italy.* Asheville, NC: Pegasus Press, 2000.

Summit, Jennifer. *Lost Property: The Woman Writer and English Literary History, 1380–1589.* Chicago: University of Chicago Press, 2000.

Wiesner, Merry E. *Women and Gender in Early Modern Europe.* 2nd ed. New York: Cambridge University Press, 2000.

Wilson, Katharina M., ed. *Women Writers of the Renaissance and Reformation.* Athens: University of Georgia Press, 1987.

Wilson, Katharina M., and Frank J. Warnke, eds. *Women Writers of the Seventeenth Century.* Athens: University of Georgia Press, 1989.

7

———⊶⊷⊶———

Women and the Arts

Interest in Renaissance and baroque women artists has exploded in the past decades, in significant part because of the effort of feminist scholars engaged in a recuperative project to recover the lost and misattributed works of women and to study their reconstituted oeuvres. Early in that recuperative process, much research centered on the question articulated in Linda Nochlin's influential 1971 article, "Why Have There Been No Great Women Artists?" There Nochlin points out that the world is "stultifying, oppressive, and discouraging to all those—women included—who did not have the good fortune to be born white, preferably middle class, and, above all, male":

> The fault lies not in our stars, our hormones, our menstrual cycles, or our empty internal spaces, but in our institutions and our education—education understood to include everything that happens to us from the moment we enter head first, into this world of meaningful symbols, signs, and signals. The miracle is, in fact, that given the overwhelming odds against women, or blacks, so many of both have managed to achieve so much excellence—if not towering grandeur—in those bailiwicks of white masculine prerogative like science, politics, or the arts.[1]

Nochlin further observed that almost all "great" artists have come from the middle class, so one might just as well ask, "Why have there been no great aristocratic artists?"

> While the aristocracy has always supplied the lion's share of patronage and the audience for art, it has rarely contributed any-

thing but a few amateurish efforts to the actual creation of art, despite the fact that aristocrats, like many women, have had far more than their share of educational advantages, and plenty of leisure.[2]

To answer questions about women's, or blacks', or aristocrats' absence from the history of great artists, one must first look to the process of canonization—the social, economic, and cultural forces that decide what kind of art will be designated "great" and will therefore be preserved and studied. Feminist art historians have pointed out that the works that come to be considered *art* and thus to be eligible for canonization are produced mostly by men, while the works that are considered *crafts* or handiwork are produced overwhelmingly by women. So while women were, for the most part, discouraged from working in painting, sculpture, or architecture—modes that have traditionally defined artistic greatness—women's extraordinary accomplishment in, for instance, needlework has been seen as craft rather than art. Women's embroidery, needlepoint, cross-stitch, knitting, crocheting, lace making, and weaving have been seen as a part of the drudgery of housework rather than the exalted realm of genius.

In spite of the cultural hostility to women represented by their exclusion from training, by the disparagement of their art, and by the impediments to their work as professionals, female artists of the early modern period produced extraordinary and influential creative works. As Nochlin and others have shown, the training, audience, genres of expression, opportunities for patronage and commissions, and even the permissible subject matter were significantly limited for female artists. In addition to being banned from life-drawing studios, women were rarely admitted to the academies where painters were taught linear perspective, spatial relationships and proportions, anatomy, and mathematical systems of representation. Rather they were typically trained in the studios of their fathers, husbands, or other male relatives. Their professional lives were made possible by family ties and not by any widespread public encouragement or even social acceptance. Those few who competed with men for commissions were often vilified as morally corrupt, and most were systematically excluded from producing in the most lucrative genres such as oil painting and monumental sculpture. Most, too, were excluded from court and aristocratic commissions.

Moreover, the logistical and cultural constraints of marriage and motherhood prevented many women from developing their abilities or their artistic output. Indeed, the production of gifted and successful young female artists frequently ceased altogether upon their marriage. Either their husbands forbade them to fill such untraditional roles, or the daily demands of the household (which might include carding, spinning, and weaving wool into cloth; sewing clothes; cultivating vegetables; scrubbing; laundering; cooking; child rearing; raising livestock in the yard; butchering animals; preserving meat and fruit; helping with harvesting and planting; milking cows and goats; and making butter, cheese, bread, and beer—or overseeing such work) filled all available time. As Caterina Ginnasio (an Italian church decorator who lived from 1590–1660) remarked, the needle and distaff were the most formidable obstacles to the paintbrush and artist's pencil. Despite fierce odds against women's professional production, however, the Renaissance benefited from increasing numbers of talented, original, vital, and even internationally celebrated women artists. Discrimination and deficient working conditions notwithstanding, they produced in a wide range of media, subjects, and projects. Their achievements were remarkable not only because of the adverse circumstances in which they were created, but because in their own right they were distinguished contributions to one of the most magnificent periods of artistic production in Western history.

Just as literary genres have always been politicized and ranked according to their culturally determined value, there was a hierarchy of genres in which Renaissance painters worked. Large-scale historical or mythological paintings and religious subjects or altarpieces were the most prestigious and remunerative, and therefore they tended to be the male-dominated genres. Such works were considered more important and demanding than were portraits, still lifes, and book illustrations, genres to which women contributed and which were held to be "worth less" both financially and aesthetically. Embroidery, needlework, and miniatures were similarly devalued as women's work; they required the meticulous industry and constrictive manual labor that came to signify a domesticated femininity. The vast majority of porcelain painters and lace makers were women whose production was properly limited to household materials and to the private rather than the public sphere. Domestic subjects and interior settings were the appropriate focus of female painters. They often created small-scale works, the size of which many held to be emblematic of their diminished significance. Ironically, however, several of the "inferior" genres to which women were relegated became so popular during the Renaissance that women still-life painters and miniature portraitists were some of the highest-paid and most-celebrated artists among the courts and monied classes of Europe.

Other creative media were devalued as their status fell from skilled labor to feminine craft. Embroidery, for example, had been a respected guild trade in the Middle Ages, practiced by both males and females and compensated with pay similar to that accorded to painters. During the Renaissance, however, embroidery was designated woman's work and therefore suffered a demotion in both economic and aesthetic value. As one historian explained,

> Middle- and upper-class girls were taught to embroider because embroidered clothing and household objects became signs of class status, and because embroidery was seen as the best way to inculcate the traits most admired in a woman—passivity, chastity, attention to detail, domesticity. As more embroidery was produced in the home for domestic consumption, it was increasingly considered an "accomplishment" rather than an art, and those who embroidered for pay received lower wages, except for the male designers of embroidery patterns and the few men employed as court embroiderers by Europe's monarchs.[3]

Needlework was meant to teach not only patience and restraint but also ideological precepts. Biblical verses and homilies about obedience and other feminine virtues were stitched onto pillows, screens, and other domestic objects. Because embroidery was not considered an art, few women applied their names to the work; consequently, far less is known about the individual creators of needlework pieces than about artists in male-dominated media.

Women in the Renaissance were effectively forbidden from engaging in certain subject matters and media. Most importantly, as Nochlin has shown, females were not allowed to study techniques for representing nude figures or details of male anatomy. As a result, women artists were at a disadvantage in painting the historical scenes with numerous figures that were so popular and lucrative in the period. Even the most accomplished women artists would customarily drape the male bodies in their paintings with

robes or dark shadows so that their lack of training in representing the male nude would be less apparent. Proscriptions against
some media were as rigorously enforced as were conventions
against women studying or depicting naked male anatomy.
Fresco—the application of paint to wet plaster walls—was a
medium from which females were almost always excluded. (The
Italians Onorata Rodiani and Anna Maria Vaiani are among the
few known exceptions.) Fresco required that the artist work out-
doors or in public places, which was considered disgraceful for
women. Landscape painting was another genre in which women's
limited freedom and limited mobility led to their limited participation.

> With very few exceptions, women did not even try landscape paint-
> ing until the nineteenth century. It was evidently not possible for
> women to go on sketching trips and long scenic journeys alone to
> collect the raw material this new genre required. Thus men not only
> controlled the most remunerative and most esteemed public com-
> missions as well as landscape, one of the three popular genres, but
> also had an almost total monopoly over sculpture, architecture,
> and even printmaking before 1800.[4]

Though rare, female architects, sculptors, and printmakers did
distinguish themselves and compete successfully for recognition
during the Renaissance.

One of the few known architects was Plautilla Bricci (1616–1690),
who was born in Rome to a family of artists. Her design of Elpidio
Benedetti's villa near Porta San Pancrazio was commissioned in
1663, and construction was completed in 1665. Benedetti claimed
that Plautilla only assisted her brother, Basilio, with the design,
but surviving documents—including the building contracts and
preliminary drawings—prove that Plautilla was the sole architect.
Although apparently reluctant to publicize his employment of a
female, Benedetti was so pleased with her ability that he commissioned her to design another work, the chapel in San Luigi dei
Francesi in Rome.

Elizabeth of Shrewsbury (1527–1608) was one of the few women
of her era who controlled enough wealth to oversee independently the refurbishment of an existing country house (that is,
English aristocratic estate) or the design of a newly built country
house, and she is known to history as Bess of Hardwick in honor of
her masterpiece, Hardwick Hall. One scholar has described her as

"capable, managing, acquisitive, a businesswoman, a money maker, a land-amasser, a builder of great houses, an indefatigable collector of the trappings of wealth and power, and inordinately ambitious, both for herself and her children."[5] Climbing the only ladder of success available to women of the era, she "married up" four times, surviving all four husbands and accruing, in the process, a magnificent fortune. By the time of her fourth marriage to George Talbot, 6th Earl of Shrewsbury, Bess had purchased the land and houses of her childhood home, Hardwick, from her brother (who had inherited it but proved incompetent to run it). Bess began work on Hardwick right away, replacing the medieval manor house with what came to be known as Hardwick Old Hall because, not long after she began that remodeling project, she launched the massive building project of the new Hardwick Hall. When her husband died in 1590, Bess gained control of all the family properties and received a substantial widow's jointure as well. She spent the next 13 years of her life building, remodeling, buying and commissioning furnishings, and acquiring more property. Even before Hardwick Old Hall had been completed, she had begun work on the great house whose castellations spell out her own initials (ES)—Hardwick Hall, which contemporaries claimed was "more glass than wall."

Hardwick is unusual among Tudor houses in a number of ways. Its situation atop a hill makes it one of the most striking country houses to dominate the landscape. While its plan was probably drawn up by the surveyor Robert Smythson, Bess's influence can be seen particularly in those features that distinguish the houses she modified or built from those of her contemporaries. The most impressive high-ceilinged state rooms are not on the second floor, as was usual, but on the third. Bess presided over ceremonial dinners in the High Great Chamber, "the ceremonial pivot of the house." She conducted business from her withdrawing room, where, "as the inventory shows, she kept her writing table and her books, and stored her papers and her money in a great iron chest and a miscellaneous series of coffers and boxes."[6] Indeed, Bess's apartments were all "conveniently on the warm, south side [of the house], well away from the smells of the kitchens and the noise of the hall, and the chapel was on the same floor: if she wished, Bess had no need to leave that … floor for weeks on end, for everything was conveniently where she could reach it without going upstairs or down."[7] Bess and her ladies-in-waiting occupied the premier places of Hardwick Hall, dominating the social and economic life of the house from her personal and public suite of rooms. Though she remained appropriately domesticated and cloistered in the deepest interior of the house, Bess made that domestic space the power center of Hardwick Hall.

The most impressive of the furnishings at Hardwick were its fabulous embroideries. One scholar has shown the many ways in which Elizabeth of Shrewsbury "made conscientious use of classical and Christian topoi, and of allegorical figures ... to describe female authority in the household," including images of "the virtuous wife," especially Penelope, Ulysses' faithful spouse, and many mythic and historical warrior queens. Bess employed male professional embroiderers throughout her life and put members of her household to work on such projects as well—everyone from her ladies-in-waiting to her grooms. She herself rarely spent time doing needlework (a fact that separates her from Penelope and traditional notions of the ideal woman).[8] Bess's monogram—a stylized ES with the "Hardwick stag and eglantine [wild rose]"—appeared on many of the embroideries, marking her authority over the decoration of the household and its management.[9]

Few women (or men) had Bess's great wealth and the ability to put their stamp on entire houses and estates, but many women contradicted the prevailing wisdom about females' limitations in their choice of artistic medium. Two acclaimed female sculptors in Renaissance Europe were Properzia de' Rossi (1490–1530) and Luisa Ignacia Roldán (ca. 1656–1704). De' Rossi was the only early modern Italian woman known to have worked in marble. Born in Bologna, she trained first as an engraver and became famous at an early age for her astonishingly detailed carvings on peach stones and cherry pits. Her first public commission was to decorate the canopy over the altar of Santa Maria del Baraccano. Subsequently, she won a competition to create a number of sculptures for the church of San Petronio. One of her most famous marble bas-reliefs for the cathedral of Bologna depicts the biblical story of Joseph and Potiphar's wife. Giorgio Vasari (1511–1574), the Tuscan courtier whose published biographies of artists were very popular and influential, applauded the energy and dramatic tension of the scene; he also mentioned that de' Rossi received meager payment for her work because of libelous allegations that an envious painter spread against her. Indeed, both her success and her ambition scandalized contemporaries who believed that women should never compete with men and never join a public profession. Vasari attempted to temper her inappropriate strength of character by assuring his audience that she was beautiful and accomplished at domestic chores. Marveling at her "miraculous" artistic ability, he portrayed her as an exception among women. The implication of all such left-handed compliments, of course, is that a woman is not naturally able to excel in a man's world. This strategy of accounting for the success of an individual at the expense of women in general was a common way of making their achievements less threatening and therefore more tolerable. Use of the strategy was not limited to men; Queen Elizabeth of England, for example, repeatedly described herself as an exception to the rule of otherwise weak women.

Another so-called exceptional sculptor was Luisa Ignacia Roldán. The first known female sculptor in Spain, she was trained in her father's workshop in Seville, along with her older sisters and two brothers. She distinguished herself at an early age and became widely known for her wooden and terra-cotta sculptures. At 15, she married another sculptor, Luis Antonio de los Arcos, whose only recorded works are collaborative pieces that he assisted his wife in producing. Roldán's fame spread throughout the country. King Charles II appointed her sculptor of the chamber, and she moved with her two children and husband to the court in Madrid. Her prolific output included larger-than-life-size wooden statues, relief sculptures, and her acclaimed terra-cotta figures. The small clay sculptures painted in vivid gold and bright colors depicted religious scenes. Roldán's use of polychromy, along with her intimate details from nature, was unprecedented in terra-cotta religious forms. Her clay groups were so treasured that they were kept on permanent display with relics and other sacred icons in many churches throughout Spain.

Roldán's career illustrates one role Renaissance women artists might assume, if rarely—that of court professional. Other women artists served as facilitators to their father's or husband's business. Diana Scultori Ghisi, also known as Diana Mantuana, fulfilled the latter role very successfully. Born in Italy in 1547, Diana was the daughter of an artist who trained her to produce engravings that he then bestowed as gifts to potential benefactors. The purpose of her early art was to procure work and favors for her father. After her marriage to Francesco da Volterra, she continued in her role as facilitator by designing engravings meant to solicit architectural commissions for her husband. The couple moved to Rome, where Francesco served as architect to members of the papal court. There Pope Gregory XIII granted Diana an unusual dispensation to produce, distribute, and market her prints in her own name. That privilege made Diana legal owner of her work, conferring on her some of the protections that modern copyright laws ensure. There is no record of her receiving commissions, and of approximately seventy-five engravings that have survived, most were produced on behalf of her father and husband. Once Francesco was securely established as a prominent architect who could attract commissions on his own, Diana's printmaking career seems to have ended. She died in 1612, 24 years after producing her last dated print.

Like Diana Mantuana, Elisabetta Sirani (1638–1665) was a talented and successful Italian engraver as well as a prolific painter. Her father was an artist in Bologna, where she was born. By the age of 17, she was earning her own living as an artist. Precocious and gifted, she attracted many wealthy, private patrons, and her work was commissioned for several royal collections. Sirani supported her entire family—both parents, three siblings, and herself—not only through her internationally celebrated renderings of mythological and religious subjects but also through her instruction of more than a dozen female students who became professional artists themselves. She died suddenly at the age of 27, having produced an enormous corpus. Public spectacle and solemn orations distinguished her funeral. Sirani's body lay in state on a huge scaffolding that was topped by a life-size statue of the artist. Such an elaborate commemoration was remarkable for a female commoner and was testimony to the esteem in which her engravings and paintings were held.

Another noted engraver was Magdalena van de Passe (ca. 1600–1638). She was born to a Dutch family of engravers who settled in Utrecht and who were all trained by the father, Crispin van de Passe. The family's engravings are so similar that it is often impossible to attribute a particular work to any one of the siblings alone, but Magdalena is known to have made or contributed to engravings of many of the English nobility and members of the royal family, including Henry VIII (1491–1547), Lady Jane Grey (1537–1554), and Katherine, Duchess of Buckingham (d. 1649). Magdalena herself was particularly renowned for her biblical scenes and landscapes, and her work has been praised for its "effective use of chiaroscuro," the artistic technique of sharp contrast between light and dark popularized in the Renaissance by Leonardo da Vinci (1452–1519), Michelangelo Merisi da Caravaggio (1573–1610), and Rembrandt van Rijn (1606–1669) and which Artemisia Gentileschi (1593–1652) used so effectively in her own work. Magdalena worked in the family business alongside her father and brothers until she married at the age of 34. She was widowed two years later and returned to the family home but probably had ceased working as an engraver from the time of her marriage.[10]

A compatriot, fellow engraver, and near contemporary of van de Passe's was Geertruyd Roghman (1625–bef. 1657). Born into a family of engravers, Roghman produced an eloquent series of works that depict women's occupations, including sewing, spinning, pleating fabric, cooking, and cleaning. The engravings highlight the painstaking aspects of domestic labor, humanizing rather than romanticizing or moralizing the daily details of women's work. Comparing the "leisure and reverie" of Jan Vermeer's (1632–1675) *Lacemaker* to the "physical labor" of Roghman's working women, one art historian has observed:

> In Vermeer's painting, a stylish young woman bends over her bobbins completely absorbed in her task. In contrast, Roghman's figures are often in strained poses with their heads bent uncomfortably close to their laps as if to stress the difficulty of doing fine work in the dim interiors of Dutch houses of the period. Surrounded by the implements necessary to their activities—spindles, combs, bundles of cloth and thread—they demonstrate the complexity and physical labor of the task.[11]

Roghman's art emphasizes the arduous material circumstances of domestic work while also conveying the dignity and even beauty of such engagement.

No discussion of Renaissance women engravers would be complete without a consideration of the work of Maria Sibylla Merian (1647–1717). In addition to producing exquisitely detailed etchings and beautiful watercolors, she revolutionized the fields of zoology and botany. Born in Germany to a Swiss engraver and his Dutch wife, Merian studied and sketched plants and animals from a very early age. Her father died when she was three, and her stepfather—the Flemish flower painter Jacob Marrell—trained her to illustrate the meticulous observations of natural life for which she

Geertruydt Roghman, *Two Women Sewing* (ca. 1640). *Source:* Museum of Fine Arts, Boston. Harvey D. Parker Collection, P8117. Photograph © 2004 Museum of Fine Arts, Boston.

became famous. In 1665, she married the painter Johann Graff, with whom she had two daughters. One scholar has noted:

When she was only twenty-three, Merian published a three-volume set of her flower engravings, the first of which appeared in 1670. Her major contribution to entomology and botany came nine years later, with the publication of her second three-volume work, *The Wonderful Transformation of Caterpillars and Their Singular Plant Nourishment*. In an abrupt departure from the traditional method of drawing from preserved insect specimens, she carefully studied living examples of 186 kinds of European moths and butterflies, recording their appearance and activities at various stages in their life cycles. Merian's scrupulously accurate, painstakingly detailed illustrations provided a wealth of new information for the scientific community.[12]

The careful observations recorded in Merian's illustrated books were foundational for the scientific classification of species that the Swedish botanist Carolus Linnaeus (1707–1778) undertook a generation later. Her influence in both scientific and artistic spheres was tremendous.

By the 1690s, Merian had divorced her husband and moved to Holland. Fascinated by the collections of South American flora and fauna that were increasingly popular among Europeans, she resolved to take her two grown daughters with her on a cataloging expedition to the Dutch colony of Surinam. Such an undertaking was extraordinary. The perils of transatlantic travel and the risks of disease in a tropical colony were serious, but considered even more grave—indeed, shocking—was her venturing forth without a male chaperone. Nevertheless, the city of Amsterdam funded her two-year project of studying and drawing indigenous insects, plants, and animals of South America. Merian became one of the first Europeans to observe and record the local peoples and their traditions. Suffering from malaria, she was forced to return to Holland, where she published a lavishly illustrated collection of commentaries that included 60 engravings made from her watercolor paintings. The book was entitled *Metamorphosis of the Insects of Surinam,* and it earned her international acclaim.

International acclaim was a remarkable achievement for any Renaissance artist, whether male or female. The first woman painter whose reputation extended beyond her own country was Sofonisba Anguissola (ca. 1535–1625). The oldest of six daughters, all of whom were painters, she was born in Cremona, Italy, to a minor noble family. Her father supported the artistic training of his children and even consulted with Michelangelo Buonarroti about Sofonisba's skill. She became a respected portraitist at an early age and taught her younger sisters techniques that she had studied with master artists. Her specialties were both formal and informal portraiture; the latter was an innovative variation that she was instrumental in developing. It was characterized by a domestic setting and sometimes a "conversation arrangement" of figures. One of the most famous examples of such a construction is *The Chess Game*, which depicts three of her sisters poised in the midst of their game. Each of the younger sisters looks at her older sibling, and the eldest gazes directly at the viewer.

Anguissola was a prolific painter who produced an extraordinary variety of portraits. She created more self-portraits than any artist between Albrecht Dürer (1471–1528) and Rembrandt van Rijn (1606–1669).[13] Word of her ability spread to Spain, where she was invited to join the court of Philip II. In 1559 she moved to Madrid and served for 10 years as both court painter and lady-in-waiting to the queen. She amassed great wealth in her royal position, setting an example and providing an incentive for subsequent female artists. Even the pope commissioned one of Anguissola's paintings. In 1561 she responded to Pius IV's request for a portrait of Queen Isabella de Valois. A further measure of the high esteem in which she was held is that the Spanish king arranged her marriage to a Sicilian lord in 1570; the monarch also provided her with a sumptuous wedding and a substantial dowry. The couple moved to Sicily, where her husband died four years later. Sofonisba continued to paint during her two marriages (she wedded a Genoese ship captain in 1584) and until her death in 1625.

Anguissola exerted an important influence on her compatriot Lavinia Fontana (1552–1614). Born in Bologna, Fontana was the most prolific female artist in Europe before 1700. Her corpus is exceptional because of its broad range of subjects and format. In addition to portraits, she produced large-scale biblical and mythological works, many of which depicted male and female nudes. Her expertise in representing male nudes was extremely uncommon among women artists. Indeed, she was refused acceptance to the Carracci Academy because instruction there included studying and drawing male models, and it is likely that she learned in her father's studio to paint the nude form. Fontana was also unusual in that she continued to have a successful career after marrying and giving birth to 11 children. Furthermore, her husband, a wealthy painter who had been one of her father's students, gave up his own profession to further hers. He ceased producing his own works so that he could help construct the frames and backgrounds of her paintings and assist with child rearing. His wife supported the family throughout her adult life. She created many works for patrons and private clients, and she began to win public commissions in 1584. Summoned to Rome by the pope, she received a papal commission for a large altarpiece in the basilica of San Paolo Fuori le Mura. The piece depicted the stoning of Saint Stephen the Martyr and was more than twenty feet high. It was a controversial work, but her subsequent paintings won her election to the Roman Academy; this extraordinary distinction for a woman enabled her to charge exceptionally high prices for her work. Ambassadors, princes, Pope Paul V, cardinals, and numerous other dignitaries commissioned her to paint their portraits. King Philip II of Spain paid her one thousand ducats for her painting *The Holy Family with John the Baptist*. Fontana's reputation was so prominent that a medal was struck in her honor three years before she died. Her distinguished oeuvre, illustrious clientele, supportive husband, recognition by academies, and her earning power set invaluable precedents for subsequent female artists.

Fontana's study of male nudes and their inclusion in her work were very unusual for a woman of her time, since women were prohibited from the academic studios where young men perfected their skills drawing the human body.[14] For male artists, on the other hand, the nude—especially the female nude—was a significant sign of their technical skill. Analysis of the role of the nude in early modern art has been important to the scholarship on women artists of the period. The predominance of the naked female form in Western art has become a topic of critical interest over the past thirty years as art historians have moved from simply tracing the development of artistic styles and forms to studying the cultural, social, and economic catalysts for the production of art. John Berger's *Ways of Seeing,* a hugely influential study, shows how oil painting in general, and the nude in particular, are connected to the emergence of capitalism in the early modern period. Berger observes that "the technique of mixing pigments with oil had existed since the ancient world" but that "oil painting did not fully establish its own norms, its own way of seeing, until the sixteenth century" when it started to represent "objects which can be bought and owned." Oil painting "served the interests of the successive ruling classes, all of whom depended in different ways on the new power of capital." Even more importantly, "a way of seeing the world, which was ultimately determined by new attitudes to property and exchange, found its visual expression in the oil painting, and could not have found it in any other art form." Oil painting, more than any other medium, was able to represent things and people with verisimilitude, a kind of realism that made objects on the canvas look in some ways more real than the objects themselves. As a result, Berger argues, "Oil painting did to appearances what capital did to social relations. It reduced everything to the equality of objects. Everything became exchangeable because everything became a commodity."[15]

Among the themes of oil painting that were "reduced" to the status of commodity was the female nude, "the one category of European oil painting [in which] women were the principal, ever-recurring subject." Among the popular historic figures was the biblical Susannah, often portrayed with a mirror. Berger suggests:

> You painted a naked woman because you enjoyed looking at her, you put a mirror in her hand and you called the painting *Vanity*, thus morally condemning the woman whose nakedness you had depicted for your own pleasure. [But t]he real function of the mirror was otherwise. It was to make the woman connive in treating herself as, first and foremost, a sight.[16]

To exemplify how the nude functioned in society, Berger uses the story of Charles II of England, who "commissioned a secret painting from [the portraitist] Lely" of "one of the King's mistresses, Nell Gwynne." The painting

> shows her passively looking at the spectator staring at her naked. This nakedness is not, however, an expression of her own feelings; it is a sign of her submission to the owner's feelings or demands. (The owner of both woman and painting.) This painting, when the King showed it to others, demonstrated this submission and his guests envied him.[17]

Furthermore, Berger suggests that "in the average European oil painting of the nude the principal protagonist is never painted. He is the spectator in front of the picture and he is presumed to be a man." That is why the nude's body "is arranged in the way it is, to display it to the man looking at the picture. This picture is made to appeal to *his* sexuality. It has nothing to do with her sexuality."[18]

Because women were not trained to represent the male body, even Artemisia Gentileschi (1593–1652), probably the most successful female baroque artist, draped men's naked bodies when they formed part of her paintings, as she did in her many renditions of the biblical story of Judith slaying Holofernes. However, when Gentileschi portrayed the female body, as she did most famously in her *Susanna and the Elders,* painted when she was only 17, she often rejected the kind of awkward and eroticized display that marks so many Renaissance and baroque paintings. Whereas Jacopo Tintoretto's (1518–1594) painting of Susanna makes her complicit with her own seduction by portraying her gazing into a mirror and enjoying her own sexuality in anticipation of the arrival of the two elders who will proposition her, Gentileschi's *Susanna* makes it clear that what the elders intend is rape. Rather than placing Susanna in a romanticized pastoral bower, Gentileschi shows Susanna seated naked on cold stone, her body twisted in agony as the two elders lower over her. Moreover, Gentileschi foreshortens the depth of field, so that the figures in the painting seem pressed too close together; the viewer as well feels uncomfortably close to the figures in the painting and even complicit in Susanna's exploitation. In Gentileschi's work, the beauty of Susanna's naked body is placed in tension with the uneasiness the viewer feels at her situation, both her narrative situation and her situation within the field of the canvas.

Though Gentileschi's skill was confirmed by this early painting, she nevertheless met with censure, financial hardship, and ostracism throughout her life. Until recently, she was not even recognized as the creator of many of her most important works. Though only 34 works of a much larger corpus remain, many of them were previously attributed to her father and other male contemporaries. Only the work of feminist art historians has sorted out her oeuvre and returned her to her proper place in the history of painting. Her artistic primacy is based on the excellence of her work, the originality of her treatment of traditional subjects, and the number of her paintings that have survived. She was both praised and disdained by contemporary critics, recognized as having genius, yet seen as monstrous because she was a woman exercising a creative talent thought to be exclusively male.

Like many other women artists of her era, Gentileschi was the daughter of an artist, the successful painter Orazio Gentileschi (ca. 1563–1639). Her father trained her as an artist and introduced her to the working artists of Rome, including Caravaggio, whose *chiaroscuro* style greatly influenced her work. By the time she was 17, she had produced one of the works for which she is best known, her stunning interpretation of *Susanna and the Elders* (1610). Among those with whom Orazio worked was the Florentine artist

Agostino Tassi, whom Artemisia accused of raping her when she was 19. Her father filed suit against Tassi for injury and damage, and, remarkably, the transcripts of the seven-month-long rape trial have survived. According to Artemisia, Tassi, with the help of family friends, repeatedly attempted to be alone with her and raped her when he finally succeeded in cornering her in her bedroom. He tried to placate her afterward by promising to marry her and gained access to her bedroom (and her person) repeatedly on the strength of that promise, but he always avoided following through with the actual marriage. The trial followed a pattern familiar even today: she was accused of not having been a virgin at the time of the rape and of having many lovers, and she was examined by midwives to determine whether she had been "deflowered" recently or a long time ago. Perhaps most galling for an artist like Gentileschi, Tassi testified that her skills were so pitiful that he had to teach her the rules of perspective and was doing so the day she claimed he raped her. Tassi denied ever having had sexual relations with Gentileschi and brought many witnesses to testify that she was "an insatiable whore."[19] Their testimony was refuted by Orazio (who brought countersuit for perjury), and Artemisia's accusations against Tassi were corroborated by a former friend of his who recounted Tassi's boasting about his sexual exploits at Artemisia's expense. Tassi had been imprisoned earlier for incest with his sister-in-law and had been charged with arranging the murder of his wife. He was ultimately convicted on the charge of raping Gentileschi; he served less than a year in prison and, astonishingly, was later invited again into the Gentileschi household by Orazio.

During and soon after the trial, Gentileschi was working on *Judith Slaying Holofernes* (1612–1613). The painting is remarkable not only for its technical proficiency but for the original way in which Gentileschi portrays Judith, who had long been a popular subject for art. Gentileschi's Judith is strong, muscular, and determined, while other contemporary depictions made Judith little more than a fashion plate, pretty, demure, and seemingly incapable of decapitating a ruthless military leader like Holofernes. One month after the long trial ended, Artemisia was married to a Florentine businessman, Pietro Antonio di Vincenzo Stiattesi, and they moved to Florence. While there, she gave birth to a daughter. In Florence, Gentileschi returned to the subject of Judith, completing *Judith and her Maidservant*. Again, Gentileschi's treatment of the familiar subject matter is unexpected and original with both women portrayed as strong and resolute. Gentileschi and her husband worked at the Academy of Design, and Gentileschi became an official member there in 1616—a remarkable honor for a woman of her day, probably made possible by the support of her Florentine patron, the Grand Duke Cosimo II of the powerful Medici family. During her years in Florence, the duke commissioned quite a few paintings from Gentileschi, and she left Florence to return to Rome upon his death in 1621.

From Rome she probably moved to Genoa that same year, accompanying her father, who was invited there by a Genoese nobleman. While there she painted her first *Lucretia* (1621) and her first *Cleopatra* (1621–1622). She also received commissions in nearby Venice during this period and met Anthony Van Dyck (1599–1641), one of the most successful painters of the era. Moreover, it is possible that she became acquainted with Sofonisba Anguissola, a generation older than Gentileschi and one of the handful of women who worked as professional artists. Gentileschi soon returned to Rome and is recorded as living there as head of household with her daughter and two servants. (Evidently she and her husband had separated, and she eventually lost touch with him altogether.) Gentileschi later had another daughter; both her daughters are known to have been painters, though neither their work nor any assessment of it has survived. During this stay in Rome, a French artist, Pierre Dumonstier le Neveu, made a drawing of Gentileschi's hand holding a paintbrush; in the caption, he described the drawing as the hand of "the excellent and wise noble woman of Rome, Artemisia." Her fame is further evident in a commemorative medal bearing her portrait made between 1625 and 1630 that calls her *pictrix celebris* (celebrated woman painter). Also at this time, Jerome David painted her portrait with a caption calling her "the famous Roman painter."

At some time between 1626 and 1630 Gentileschi moved to Naples, where she painted her *Self-Portrait as the Allegory of Painting* (a work unique in its fusing of art, muse, and artist), *The Annunciation* (1630), another *Lucretia,* another *Cleopatra,* and many other works. She collaborated with a number of artists (all male) while in Naples. In 1637, desperate for money to finance her daughter's wedding, Gentileschi began looking for new patrons. In one letter soliciting commissions, she mentions "some small works done by [her] daughter"[20] that she is sending along. The new

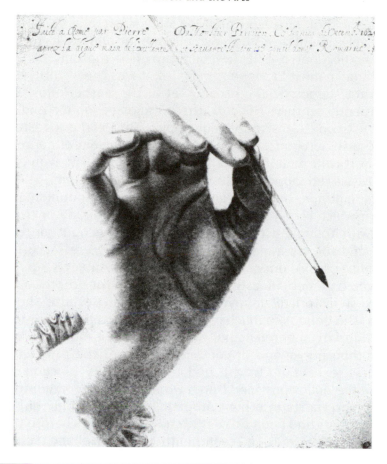

Pierre Dumonstier le Neveu, Artemisia Gentileschi's hand (1625). *Source:* © Copyright The British Museum.

patron to whom she finally attached herself was King Charles I of England. Gentileschi was in residence at the English court from 1638 to 1641, one of many continental artists invited there by the art-collecting king. She may have gone specifically to assist her father, Orazio, in a massive project to decorate the ceilings of Queen Anne's house at Greenwich. After civil war had broken out in England in 1641 (a war that would result in the execution of Charles I), Artemisia returned to Naples, where she lived until her death. She remained very active there, painting at least five variations on Bathsheba and perhaps another Judith. The only record of her death is in two satiric epitaphs—frequently translated and reprinted—that make no mention of her art but figure her in exclusively sexual terms as a nymphomaniac and adulterer.

While the Church and the court provided the bulk of the art patronage in most European countries, it was the wealthy middle class that supported the art market in the Netherlands. By the seventeenth century, Holland was a major economic and naval power with an extensive colonial empire. The aesthetic taste of its prosperous merchants influenced the development of genres that were particularly suited to the limited mobility of women and their restricted opportunities for academic training. Still lifes, flower paintings, and portraits were extremely popular genres, none of which required knowledge of the male nude or travel to study with Italian masters. The Dutch had a penchant for realistic detail and for representations of material culture. Accordingly, paintings of ordinary or even domestic subjects, precisely observed and meticulously rendered, were in far greater demand than vast historical or mythological pieces. Because the merchants who bought so much of the art intended to hang it in their homes, it was generally small-scaled. An open-market economy rather than patronage or commissions drove the production of paintings (except portraits), and the possibility of competition outside the guilds provided Dutch women with opportunities that their counterparts in other European countries rarely enjoyed.[21] Female artists had been successful still-life painters before the florescence of the genre in seventeenth-century Holland. Fede Galizia (1578–1630) in Italy was a leader in the genre, and four women painters of still lifes had been elected to the French Academy in the seventeenth century. However, one scholar has noted that "the most noteworthy women still life painters were Flemish and Dutch, since these schools were the most active and suffered least from the French Academy's low esteem for this genre."[22] Flower paintings, too, were especially marketable in the Netherlands. Growing and selling flowers was a robust sector of the Dutch economy by 1600. Tulips sold for extravagant sums, and middle-class households incorporated flower gardening into their leisure-time activities. In addition, explorers brought exotic floral species back from their voyages to the New World and the East. Intense interest in these nonnative species prompted artists to include them in still lifes and flower works in order to improve the marketability of their canvasses.

One of the early women painters of still lifes in the Netherlands was Clara Peeters (1594–ca. 1657), who had already distinguished herself as an accomplished artist by the age of 14. Little is known about her personal life except that she did not marry until very late, at the age of 45. Born in Antwerp, she was among the originators of a popular category of painting called the "banquet" or "breakfast piece." Such works display a table on which food, a few porcelain or metal dishes, and glass vessels are arranged. Peeters had a superb talent for representing the varied textures and patterns of light reflected in such objects. An early series of four banquet pieces—one a painting of fish, another of game, a third of a dinner composition, and one entitled *Still Life with Flowers, a Goblet, Dried Fruit, and Pretzels*—established her as a leader in her field. Though Peeters was only 17 years old at the time she painted them, they were immediately recognized as "among the masterpieces of early seventeenth-century still life."[23] She was particularly famous for rendering textures and juxtaposing natural objects with manufactured ones. Her 1612 *Still Life with a Vase of Flowers, Goblets, and Shells* is celebrated not only for its vital composition, or arrangement, of objects and their relationships to each other, but also for the exquisite reflections of light. In the metallic surface of one goblet, for example, Peeters's own image is reflected seven times.

Another important innovator from the Netherlands was Judith Leyster (1609–1660), one of the first artists to develop the "intimate genre," a scene of one or only a few figures captured in a narrative moment. The lighting in these scenes often comes from a single source, thus focusing attention on the figures and their ordinary but vitally rendered activity: sewing, singing, drinking, painting, or flute playing. Leyster created an unusual variety of works, including still lifes, genre paintings, and portraits. Born in Haarlem to a brewer and a cloth maker, she supported herself not only as an independent artist but as the head of her own workshop of pupils. In her twenties, she became the only female member of the Haarlem painters' guild. Two years later, she successfully sued fellow artist Frans Hals for violating professional ethics by apprenticing one of her students. Ironically, art critics since her death have enabled another kind of appropriation of Leyster by Hals: they have misattributed a number of her works to her male colleague.

The most prolific period of Leyster's career was between 1629 and the year of her marriage in 1636. After she wed the painter Jan Miense Molenaer (ca. 1610–1688), her artistic production decreased drastically. One of the most intriguing works from her period of greatest artistic output was *The Proposition* (1631). The painting is an excellent example of the intimate genre. It portrays a woman intently sewing as a leering man leans from behind her into the light. The unresponsive woman studiously ignores both the coins that the man offers and his hand on her shoulder as he tries to pull her away from her work. The scene of unwelcome interruption contrasts the looming shadow and dark attire of the male harasser with the illuminated face and startlingly white blouse of the restrained woman. Other Dutch and Flemish renderings of sexual propositions are typically lively and bawdy; their male and female figures are mutually invested in the exchange of money for sex. Leyster's scene, however, presents a different view. As one critic has dryly remarked, the painting suggests that "not every transaction occurs between willing participants."[24]

Born just one year after Judith Leyster, Louise Moillon (1610–1696) was perhaps the best still life painter of seventeenth-century France. Both her father and stepfather were artists in Paris. By the age of 10, she was selling her paintings and contributing to the support of her six siblings and widowed mother. As was true of Judith Leyster, Moillon's artistic production nearly ceased after her marriage in 1640. Before losing her professional independence, however, she achieved a considerable reputation for her work. Especially remarkable was her ability to render texture and reflections. In her still lifes, "she delighted in showing off her technical expertise in passages such as the water droplets on the table and the individual highlights on the shiny berries. Also notable is the dark background, which focuses attention on the fruits themselves, giving the picture a quiet intensity."[25] Despite her talent and success, however, she was not allowed into the Royal Academy of Painting and Sculpture (established in 1648), because its members held that still life was an inferior genre—inferior to the representation of the human form and of historic or mythic scenes. The Royal Academy revised its exclusionary position in 1663 when King Louis XIV decreed that female artists should be allowed membership if they excelled in their medium. Within 20 years, four female still life painters were elected to the academy. Records show that the number of professional women artists in

France grew steadily, from only 3 in the sixteenth century to 28 by the end of the seventeenth century. After the admission of Catherine Perrot to the academy in 1682, however, no woman was elected for another 40 years. In 1706 the policy of banning all females was reinstated, although a small number of exceptions were made over the next century.

Like still life paintings, portraits were a "minor" genre in which women artists throughout Europe excelled. One of the most prolific portraitists was the English Mary Beale (1632–1697), who also taught students in her own workshop. Her contemporaries especially praised—and purchased—her studies of children. Unlike many female painters whose careers waned or ended altogether upon their marriage, Beale began her apprenticeship after she wed her husband, Charles. From his scrupulously detailed notebooks, her extraordinary output is evident; in just one year, for example (1677), he recorded that his wife completed 83 commissions. Mary was the primary wage earner of the family, while Charles managed the household, helped raise their two sons, and assisted his wife with preparing her paints and canvasses. She was distinguished not only for the quality of her art, but also for the variety of materials with which she worked, including oils, watercolors, and pastels.

In the course of the Renaissance, the conditions of artistic production and the social restrictions on women improved gradually. More females engaged in creative vocations, and more enjoyed the patronage and wage-earning power that their male counterparts had long commanded. Art historians have identified 30 women artists of fifteenth-century Italy; that number tripled within the next one hundred years. By the seventeenth century, there were more than two hundred women painters who have left some historical record. Similar increases occurred elsewhere in Europe as both the reputation and the works of female Italian painters, engravers, and graphic artists moved north. As their professional presence grew, so did their income. Court painters often received liberal honoraria, and even their extended family could benefit from royal patronage. The Spanish king paid Sofonisba Anguissola's father an annual salary of eight hundred lire for his daughter's work.[26] The prestige of appointments to European courts significantly enhanced the status of female artists. Caterina van Hemessen (ca. 1527–ca. 1566) served as painter to the court of Maria of Austria, Regent of the Netherlands, accompanying Maria to Spain when she moved her court there in 1556. The Flemish Levina Teerline (ca. 1510–1576) was appointed painter to the court of three English monarchs: Edward VI, Mary I, and Elizabeth I. She was also commissioned to work for King Henry VIII, but she agreed to this only on the condition that her father accompany her to the household of the notorious philanderer. (Henry was also notorious for having his wives beheaded; when Duchess Christina of Milan was approached by Henry's minions as a potential marriage candidate, she is said to have replied that, had she two heads, she might be interested.) Levina's miniatures were so highly esteemed that her annual salary was greater than that of the two most renowned male portraitists of the English court, Nicholas Hilliard (1547–1619) and Hans Holbein the Younger (1497–1543). Maria van Oosterwyck (1630–1693) was a Dutch still life painter whose exquisitely detailed and luminous works were commissioned by royalty throughout northern Europe, including Emperor Leopold, King William and Queen Mary of England, Louis IX of France, and the Elector of Saxony. August II of Poland is said to have paid her 2,400 guilders for two of her flower paintings. Isabella del Pozzo (1660–1700) was court painter to Adelheid, wife of the Elector of Bavaria. Her payment was an annual salary of four hundred guilders as well as a daily allowance of beer, wine, and bread. After she became blind, the elector awarded her an annual pension of two hundred guilders. The English Susan Penelope Rosse (1652–1700) was one of the most popular miniaturists in history. Some of her paintings were only one inch high. She served as commissioned artist to a number of the members of Charles II's court. Late in the period, Rachel Ruysch (1664–1750) was appointed court painter to the Elector Palatine in Dusseldorf. Her productivity included not only a long and successful career of flower painting but also the birth of 10 children.

Court appointments were by no means the only source of revenue for female artists. Although there are few extant records of average earnings, evidence of exceptional wages is more available. Whereas Rembrandt rarely received more than 500 guilders for any of his works, his compatriot Rachel Ruysch charged between 750 and 1,250 guilders per painting. The papal exchequer disbursed 348 scudi to Anna Maria Vaiani (d. 1655) for her decorations of one of the Vatican chapels; for one fresco there, she received the equivalent of half the annual salary of a German town clerk in 1600. Lavinia Fontana's *The Holy Family with John the Baptist,* for which King Philip of Spain paid one thousand ducats, was worth four times the annual salary of a German town clerk. Clearly, many women artists were able to support their families with their earnings, and many did. Elisabetta Sirani was a major source of income for her household. The French artist Elizabeth Chéron (1648–1711) paid her father's debts, supported her mother and siblings, and paid for the education of at least one brother and one sister. Some of the families that women artists were helping to sustain were exceptionally large. As mentioned earlier, Lavinia Fontana had 11 children, and Rachel Ruysch had 10. The Dutch Aleyda Wolfsen (b. 1648) gave birth to eight children. Their financial contributions to such sizable households were essential.

Even if some female artists were not fully supporting their families, their professional lives were closely tied to family life. Most were born into their calling, working in family-operated studios or craft shops and producing art along with their fathers, brothers, husbands, mothers, sisters, and daughters. It was common for several generations of families to collaborate in the production of art, overseeing the business and training of—or serving as—apprentices. Titian employed all of his daughters, and Tintoretto apprenticed four of his eight children. Indeed, the paintings of his daughter Marietta (1560–1590) were often attributed to her father; her talent was so great that even experts have found some of their works indistinguishable. Such misattribution was fairly common. The Italian painter Carlo Dolci taught his daughter Agnese Maria (d. 1686) to copy his works. She became so adept that some art critics believe the picture that the Louvre attributes to her father, *Christ Blessing the Bread,* is probably her own creation. Not only producing art but training others to do so was one of the roles of female painters. Jan Breughel's grandmother, Marie Bessemers (1520–1600), was his first teacher. The French miniaturist Antoinette Hérault (1642–1695) trained her five daughters, all of whom became painters and all of whom married other artists.

Not only did women artists in the Renaissance produce excellent work, but many of them did so at an astonishingly early age. Indeed, women were often far more precocious than their male counterparts. As one scholar has put it:

Fede Galizia's artistic promise was noted publicly when she was twelve. Angelica Kauffman painted her self-portrait at the age of thirteen. Vigée-Lebrun was supporting her family at the age of fifteen. Giovanna Garzoni signed a painting of the Madonna at the age of sixteen. Sirani's own list of her work records five paintings made when she was seventeen, and Artemisia Gentileschi was the same age when she painted her *Susanna and the Elders* in Pommersfelden. Leyster had already attracted public comment on her gifts when she was seventeen, Clara Peeters' first dated work was painted when she was seventeen, and those of Rachel Ruysch and Anne Vallayer-Coster when they were eighteen. Susan Horenbout was eighteen when she sold a miniature to [the German artist Albrecht] Dürer. Louise Moillon's first surviving painting was made when she was nineteen. Caterina van Hemessen and Judith Leyster have both left us works painted when they were twenty. While references to precocious artistic activity by male artists are not unknown, it is by no means usual to be able to discuss works made before they reached their twenties.[27]

It is not certain why women's professional success often came at an earlier time in their lives than did men's; perhaps the latter spent their early years on formal training that was not available to women, thereby delaying men's production for the public. Perhaps accomplished women artists were galvanized at a young age because their career prospects were often diminished significantly upon marriage and childbearing. Whatever the reasons, female artists typically distinguished themselves earlier and overcame far greater cultural barriers to their creativity than did men.

Women's opportunities to create and perform musically were—perhaps even more than their prospects as artists and writers—limited to the private or cloistered sphere. It is certain, however, that women participated in the musical culture of Europe more fully than surviving records document; the records themselves are incomplete or nonspecific, especially in the case of popular music. Songs, lullabies, ballads, and other forms of folk music were often passed from generation to generation vocally rather than in print with the author's name included. Folk songs that were eventually published were often anonymous, but one scholar has wryly commented that "anonymous was a woman." Furthermore, many such folk songs "accompanied traditionally women's work such as child care or weaving," so that singing was connected with women's work.[28] By the seventeenth century, musical training was an integral part of middle- and upper-class girls' education. Singing and playing an instrument were cultivated as accomplishments rather than serious skills, and women's performances typically were private occasions confined to a family audience.

As was the case with artists, most female musicians were the daughters of fathers who composed or performed professionally and who allowed their daughters both training and public opportunities in music. Such were the circumstances of Francesca Caccini (b. 1587–d. aft. 1640), who became the highest-paid performer in the Florentine court of the Medicis. A generation later, another Italian vocalist, Barbara Strozzi (1619–1677), was renowned for her public performances and for her music salon in Venice. Neither woman was permitted to make her career in opera—the most pop-

Bernardo Strozzi, *A Gamba Player* (perhaps Barbara Strozzi; ca. 1635). *Source:* Staatliche Kunstsammlungen Dresden, 381/04.

ular and prestigious musical genre in Italy, where all roles were sung by men at this time—and many of the women's compositions are rather short songs of love. But Strozzi also composed cantatas; indeed, she is sometimes credited with inventing the genre. She was born in Venice and was the "adopted" daughter and heir of the poet and librettist Giulio Strozzi, in whose household her mother, Isabella Garzoni, was a servant. Strozzi was probably Barbara's natural father. He oversaw her extensive education, particularly in music, preparing her for the life of a professional musician and, later, provided her with an opportunity to perform for the elite of Venice. She was a singer, composer, and accomplished performer on many instruments. She published eight volumes of arias and secular cantatas for solo voice and continuo, taking a short break from publication and performance during the years she gave birth to her four children but then resuming her career. Strozzi may have been a courtesan, although the fact that she was labeled so by contemporaries does not by itself provide conclusive evidence of the fact, as many women who excelled in "masculine" occupations were called whores.

Opportunities for females who produced secular music increased gradually in the course of the Renaissance. By 1700, women were creating longer compositions, and there were at least twenty-three published female musicians in Italy. The French Elizabeth-Claude Jacquet de la Guerre (ca. 1664–1727) composed important instrumental works as well as an opera. Also late in the period, the Austrian emperor commissioned Camilla di Rossi to write oratorios and other choral pieces. Indeed the court and the convent were the most common venues for female musicians. Court ladies were expected to have training in voice and choral performance. *The Courtier,* Castiglione's influential work about the values and behavior of the ideal courtier, describes music as not only an ornament but a professional necessity for the women and men whose lives and careers depended on the court. Many female musicians, singers, and composers sought patronage at courts throughout Europe. Anna Magdalena Bach (1701–1760), the second wife of the composer Johann Sebastian Bach (1685–1750), met him when they were both musicians at the court of Prince Leopold at Cöthen in Germany. Perhaps the first woman who ever published madrigals was the Italian lutenist, singer, and composer Maddalena Casulana (ca. 1540–ca. 1590); she attached herself to the Venetian court and in 1568 dedicated her *Primo libro de*

J.W.E., *Musick's Handmaid* (London, 1678), frontispiece. Henry Playford, *The Second Part of Musick's Hand-Maid* (London, 1689). *Source:* Reproduced by permission of The British Library, k.4.b.10. (2.) k.

madrigali a quattro voci [First book of madrigals for four voices] to Isabella de' Medicis Orsina. A second volume of her work appeared two years later. Another prominent singer and published composer at the Medici court was Francesca Caccini. Born in Florence in 1587, she was the daughter of an accomplished musician who taught his entire family to sing and play several instruments. In addition, Francesca was trained in music theory and composition. She made her first professional appearance at the age of 13 when she sang in her father's opera *Euridice.* In 1618, she published her collection entitled *Il Primo Libro,* and she presented her own opera, *La Liberazione di Ruggiero* [The Liberation of Ruggiero], at court in 1625. Extraordinarily talented and celebrated, she became the most highly paid singer at the Medici court. Nobles from other parts of the country similarly sponsored female musicians. The Duke of Ferrara formed an all-female singing group in 1580, and other Italian courts followed his lead. Women who specialized in playing a number of instruments joined the groups, and by the end of the Renaissance, members were writing a significant portion of the music they performed. The professional *concerto delle donne* (concert of women) would typically rehearse from two to six hours each day, and although they are said to have been paid less than their male counterparts, they earned considerable acclaim throughout Italy.

Convents were havens for female composers, singers, and instrumentalists. In Renaissance Europe, more than half of the women who published both secular and religious music were nuns. The musician Gracia Baptista, for example, was a Spanish nun who lived in the first half of the sixteenth century in Avila. Her variations on the chant *Conditor alme siderum* [Creator of the Stars of Night], written for voice and either organ or harpsichord, were published in 1557 in one of the first collections of Spanish keyboard music. In Italy, convents organized choirs for girls who lived in orphanages, training them so well that the city government in Venice, for example, sponsored and even made revenue from their performances.

> The choirs these schools produced became so renowned that girls who were not orphans were taken on as day students, including some daughters of Venice's elite. These Ospedali grandi [orphanages] were not strictly convents, but the girls vowed to sing or play for ten years after they were trained, so could not leave until they were about thirty. They gave frequent public performances, which the city used as a source of income, and it also encouraged the girls and women to develop their talents by sending them to study with distinguished teachers and commissioning special works for them.[29]

In 1563, however, the Council of Trent decreed that convent performances should be strictly curtailed, and the Catholic Church forbade nuns to play any instrument other than the organ. By the time of a 1686 papal injunction against any Catholic woman learning music from any male, opportunities within the church for creating or performing music were significantly diminished. The explanation that Pope Innocent XI gave for prohibiting even daughters to study with their fathers specifically linked music with immorality, "music is completely injurious to the modesty that is proper for the [female] sex."[30] (See also chapter 1, "Women and Education.")

A woman's public display of any art—whether painting, dance, sculpture, or music—invariably invoked questions about her morality. This was particularly true for Renaissance women actors. English law proscribed females from the public stage until the Restoration of the monarchy in 1661. Countries on the Continent were less repressive, but the treatment of even those women who were legally allowed to earn their living in the theater was abusive and discriminatory. Some women sought protection, in addition to supplementary income, as mistresses of wealthy patrons or of men affiliated with the theater. By the late sixteenth century in France and Italy, women were part of itinerant troupes of actors who staged comedy for public audiences. In some instances, they even served as directors as well as players; the French Madeleine Béjart and the German Caroline Neuber were directors of their own troupes, as was Catherina Elisabeth Velten, who published a defense of the morality of actresses in popular comedies.

Madeleine Béjart (1618–1672) came from a family of 11 children, five of whom were professional actors closely affiliated with the great French playwright Molière (1622–1673). Madeleine led the traveling troupe in which her siblings performed until they all joined Molière's company, L'Illustre Théâtre, in 1643. She earned an impressive reputation playing the roles that Molière created for her, as did her sister, Armande Grésinde Claire Elizabeth Béjart (1645–1700). Armande married Molière when she was 17 and he was 40. They had a tempestuous relationship, separating after the birth of their daughter and then reuniting six years later. Even during their estrangement, however, the playwright continued to create starring roles for his talented wife, who was celebrated at the French and English courts for her performances. During the last 20 years of her career, she was the leading comic actress at the Comédie Française.

The Béjart sisters were anomalous in that their father was not associated with the theater. (He was a minor government official on the verge of poverty.) As was the case with female artists and musicians, many women actors on the Renaissance stage had fathers who were professionally involved in the arts. Additionally, many women married men who were similarly affiliated; otherwise, women's careers were far less likely to develop. One of the most successful actors in seventeenth-century France, Marie Champmeslé (1642–1698), was married to the actor and playwright Charles Chevillet (1642–1701). Marie and her husband were sought after by some of the most popular playhouses in Paris, and the dramatist Jean Racine (1639–1699) wrote his greatest tragedies for her to star in. For the last 30 years of her life, she specialized in playing the tragic heroine; her popularity contributed to the tremendous success of the newly established Comédie Française.

Women made a later debut on the public stage in England than did their sisters on the Continent. Although English women performed in plays at court and in private theaters or manor houses, they were forbidden by law until 1660 to appear on public stages. Throughout the golden age of Elizabethan and Jacobean drama, boys had played the roles of girls and women. A notable exception to this practice was the participation of aristocratic women in the elaborate spectacles called masques. This highly stylized genre, which included music, dancing, allegorical poetry, complicated sets, and expensive machinery, involved women of the nobility in the production. For example, both Queen Anne (wife of James VI and I) and Queen Henrietta Maria (wife of Charles I) acted in court masques and achieved notoriety among antitheatrical puritans for doing so. In 1642, the Parliament closed the theaters in London, citing them as dens of immorality. There were a few private performances during the following 18 years while the Civil War raged, but the public playhouses were inoperative until the monarchy was restored with the coronation of Charles II in 1660. At that time, the king ordained that women should play women's roles on the stage. No doubt Charles was motivated to issue the decree because of his experience attending plays while in exile on the Continent, where actresses had been routinely performing since the mid-1500s. (Charles also preferred French musical styles and forms to those that had developed in England during his exile.) But many in England conflated women who performed in public with "public women," or prostitutes, and many considered both professions equally disgraceful.

Although few "respectable" women pursued a career in the theater, it was for some an attractive alternative to being a servant or to poverty. But actors needed to be literate, an attribute that few lower-class females possessed. Many professionals, then, were from straitened circumstances in the middle or lower middle class. They "included women whose good families had come down in the world, like the popular singer and comedienne Charlotte Butler; daughters of tradesmen, like tragedienne Sarah Cooke; and gentlemen's bastards, like Moll Davis. While the expected career for the genteel, dowerless female was domestic service, the less respectable job of actress offered better pay and better prospects."[31] Despite the better pay, the life of an actor was arduous and demanding. She worked every day but Sunday, rehearsing all morning and performing every afternoon. In addition, she might have private performances at court in the evenings. If she missed just one rehearsal, she could be fined a week's wages. The production schedule was grueling:

Each theater seems to have produced between forty and sixty different plays each season. Clearly, in their spare time successful players needed to study their lines: even the best new plays or revivals rarely ran for longer than six days. A leading actor or actress might have to play as many as thirty different parts in the course of a season. During the years from 1673 to 1709 the brilliant Elizabeth Barry is known to have played 142 named parts, with presumably more in cast lists which have not survived. Once a player possessed a particular part, he or she was expected to be prepared to play it at every subsequent revival, no matter how much time had passed since the last performance. Sometimes when a play proved unsuccessful one day, another had to be hastily substituted on the next.[32]

As was the case for Renaissance women who participated in any of the arts, women gradually claimed more authority and earned more entitlement on the stage. In England, for example, Elizabeth Barry became one of the highest-paid performers, male or female, in the 1690s. She was extremely popular with both court and public audiences and was a shrewd businesswoman whose earning power gave her considerable influence over her theatrical company. Such enfranchisement came at a cost, however. Many who resented Barry's self-assertion and financial independence reviled her as unnatural, insatiable, and predatory; her detractors made their allegations in sexual terms, accusing her of prostitution and sexual extortion. Despite the fierce resentment, though, her success made it possible for other women to forge their own place in the theater. Records name more than eighty professional women on the English stage by the end of the century, and many more were earning their livelihood in theaters throughout Spain, France, and other European countries.

Clearly, women in the Renaissance were distinguished actors, artists, sculptors, architects, engravers, scientific illustrators, and musicians. In addition, they were important patrons. Noblewomen provided support and commissions for all kinds of producers of art. In turn, their beneficiaries celebrated their largesse and paid tribute to their discerning taste. Patronage was a means of displaying one's wealth and establishing one's cultural position. Late in the period, for instance, Sophie Charlotte, Queen of Prussia (1668–1705), engaged Gottfried Leibniz (1646–1716) to be the head of the Berlin Academy of Sciences, which she founded and supported. Moreover, noblewomen hired architects and sculptors to transform castles designed for defense into châteaux and palaces where they could live comfortably, and to construct elaborate tombs for themselves and their husbands. They arranged for the building and decoration of convents, churches, hospitals, and orphanages, choosing the architect and often approving the plans down to the smallest detail.[33]

Patronage was the most significant source of maintenance for the majority of Renaissance artists and writers, whether male or female; the latter frequently turned to noblewomen or female monarchs for sympathetic support of their careers and even for protection. Queen Anne of Denmark (wife of James VI and I) not only commissioned and acted in court masques but brought the artist and architect Inigo Jones (1573–1652) to England, initiating a revolution in state architecture. (Jones also designed the fabulous sets for the masques written by Ben Jonson.) Anne had Jones design a private retreat for her at Greenwich, known as Queen Anne's House, and later Jones designed the Banqueting House at Whitehall Palace in London. Of course, women rulers sometimes supported women artists as well: Maria of Austria, Regent of the Netherlands (1505–1558), was the major patron of Caterina van Hemessen, and Sofonisba Anguissola was court painter to Isabella of Valois, Queen of Spain (1546–1568), to name only two. Despite the many shrill public voices of contemporary moralists that excoriated women artists and claimed that they lacked the creative capacity (which, according to this view, was the province of men alone), women were active participants in all fields and artistic media, making a unique contribution to the history of the Renaissance. Though they were inspired by the same developments in technique that influenced male artists, women, by virtue of the particular social and cultural limitations and expectations of their times, brought a different perspective to the subject matter of all the arts, from architecture to painting to music to drama.

NOTES

1.   Linda Nochlin, "Why Have There Been No Great Women Artists?" in *Art and Sexual Politics: Why Have There Been No Great Women Artists?*, ed. Thomas B. Hess and Elizabeth C. Baker (New York: Collier Books, 1971), 5–6.

2.   Nochlin, "Why Have There Been No Great Women Artists?" 9.

3.   Merry E. Wiesner, *Women and Gender in Early Modern Europe,* 2nd ed. (New York: Cambridge University Press, 2000), 178.

4.   Ann Sutherland Harris and Linda Nochlin, *Women Artists: 1550–1950* (New York: Alfred A. Knopf, 1984), 29.

5.   Mark Girouard, *Hardwick Hall* (London: The National Trust, 1989), 6.

6.   Girouard, *Hardwick Hall,* 30, 33, 32.

7.   David N. Durant, *Bess of Hardwick: Portrait of an Elizabethan Dynast* (London: Weidenfeld and Nicolson, 1977), 162.

8.   Don E. Wayne, "'A More Safe Survey': Social-Property Relations, Hegemony, and the Rhetoric of Country Life," in *Soundings of Things Done: Essays in Honor of S. K. Heninger, Jr.,* ed. Peter E. Medine and Joseph Wittreich (Newark: University of Delaware Press, 1997), 278.

9.   Girouard, *Hardwick Hall,* 24, 28.

10.   *Grove Dictionary of Art,* s.v. "Magdalena van de Passe." The *Grove Dictionary* is available online at <http://www.artnet.com/library/index.asp?N=1>.

11.   Whitney Chadwick, *Women, Art, and Society* (London: Thames & Hudson 1990), 115.

12.   Nancy G. Heller, *Women Artists: An Illustrated History* (New York: Abbeville Press, 1987), 37.

13.   Chadwick, *Women, Art, and Society,* 70.

14.   Nochlin, "Why Have There Been No Great Women Artists?" 24.

15.   John Berger, *Ways of Seeing* (New York: Penguin, 1977), 84, 85, 87.

16.   Berger, *Ways of Seeing,* 47, 51.

17.   Berger, *Ways of Seeing,* 52.

18.   Berger, *Ways of Seeing,* 55.

19.   Mary D. Garrard, *Artemisia Gentileschi: The Image of the Female Hero in Italian Baroque Art* (Princeton, NJ: Princeton University Press, 1989), 22. The entire transcript of the rape trial is reprinted in an appendix to Garrard's book. See also Kari Boyd McBride's Web site on Gentileschi at <http://jamaica.u.arizona.edu/ic/mcbride/ws200/gentil.htm>.

20.   Artemisia Gentileschi, letter to Don Antonio Ruffo, 13 March 1649, qtd. in Mary D. Garrard, *Artemisia Gentileschi,* 391.

21.   Wendy Slatkin, *Women Artists in History from Antiquity to the 20th Century* (Englewood Cliffs, NJ: Prentice Hall, 1990), 55–56.

22.   Slatkin, *Women Artists,* 56.

23.   Slatkin, *Women Artists,* 59.

24.   Slatkin, *Women Artists,* 63.

25.   Heller, *Women Artists,* 58.

26.   Edith Krull, *Women in Art* (London: Studio Vista, 1989), 12.

27.   Harris and Nochlin, *Women Artists,* 41–42.

28.   Wiesner, *Women and Gender,* 186.

29.   Wiesner, *Women and Gender,* 187.

30.   Qtd. in Jane Bowers, "The Emergence of Women Composers in Italy, 1566–1700," in *Women Making Music: The Western Art Tradition, 1150–1950,* ed. and trans. Jane Bowers and Judith Tick (Urbana: University of Illinois Press, 1986), 139.

31.   Elizabeth Howe, *The First English Actresses: Women and Drama, 1660–1700* (New York: Cambridge University Press, 1996), 8.

32.   Howe, *First English Actresses,* 9–10.

33.   Wiesner, *Women and Gender,* 168.

SUGGESTED READING

Baldauf-Berdes, Jane J. *Women Musicians of Venice: Musical Foundations, 1525–1855.* Rev. ed. New York: Oxford University Press, 1996.

Berger, John. *Ways of Seeing.* New York: Penguin, 1977.

Bowers, Jane, and Judith Tick, eds. and trans. *Women Making Music: The Western Art Tradition, 1150–1950.* Urbana: University of Illinois Press, 1986.

Chadwick, Whitney. *Women, Art, and Society.* London: Thames & Hudson, 1990.

Garrard, Mary D. *Artemisia Gentileschi: The Image of the Female Hero in Italian Baroque Art.* Princeton, NJ: Princeton University Press, 1989.

Harris, Ann Sutherland, and Linda Nochlin. *Women Artists: 1550–1950.* New York: Alfred A. Knopf, 1984.

Heller, Nancy G. *Women Artists: An Illustrated History.* New York: Abbeville Press, 1987.

Howe, Elizabeth. *The First English Actresses: Women and Drama, 1660–1700.* New York: Cambridge University Press, 1996.

King, Catherine E. *Renaissance Women Patrons: Wives and Widows in Italy c. 1300–1550.* New York: Palgrave Macmillan, 1998.

Krull, Edith. *Women in Art.* London: Studio Vista, 1989.

Nochlin, Linda. "Why Have There Been No Great Women Artists?" *Art and Sexual Politics: Why Have There Been No Great Women Artists?* Ed. Thomas B. Hess and Elizabeth C. Baker. New York: Collier Books, 1971, 1–39.

Slatkin, Wendy. *Women Artists in History from Antiquity to the 20th Century.* Englewood Cliffs, NJ: Prentice Hall, 1990.

Wiesner, Merry E. *Women and Gender in Early Modern Europe.* 2nd ed. New York: Cambridge University Press, 2000.

8

⚬⚬⚬

Women and Pleasures

The many restrictions on early modern women's activities and the widely held contemporary sense of their particular sinfulness might make it seem that women of the Renaissance could find little pleasure in life, but, of course, that is not the case at all. Early modern women took pleasure in many activities, in spite of some moralists' condemnation of frivolity. The very humanist shift that characterized the Renaissance, one that acknowledged the value of earthly, human activities in addition to the life of the hereafter, authorized the enjoyment of life's pleasures. The other chapters of this book discuss at length some of those activities, including women's delight in writing, art, music, needlework, household administration, healing, child-rearing, and even housework—all kinds of work that could be done well and to the satisfaction and happiness of the doer. Women's delight in education, learning, and reading is perhaps most forcefully and persuasively documented, as such women were more likely than others to leave a record of their pleasure in the life of the mind, but illiterate women with no book education also found gratification and fun in many activities of work and play.

Then as now, women took pleasure in their relationships with others. Though marriages were often arranged primarily for economic reasons, many couples grew to love each other and took joy in companionship. The German theologian Martin Luther's marriage to the former nun Katharina von Bora was in part a political act on his part, a symbol of his rejection of the Catholic emphasis on celibacy as well as a witness to his theology regarding the sacred nature of marriage, but it was actually she who proposed to him. None of her letters have survived, but his letters to her are filled with praise and affection, and his will named her executor (contrary to Saxon law, wherein men were typically executors), and he left her everything. (In spite of Luther's instructions to the contrary, Katharina was assigned two male guardians.)[1]

Countless gravestones and monuments attest to the fact that a surviving spouse was often devastated by the loss of his or her life companion. Elizabeth (Cooke) Hoby (1540–1609) composed in Latin an elegy to her husband, the English ambassador to the French court, Sir Thomas Hoby, who died while they were living in France and when she was pregnant. (See chapter 6: "Women and Literature.") Her poem "Elizabeth Hobaea conjux, ad Thomam Hobaeum, Equitem Maritum" [From Elizabeth Hoby, wife, to her Husband, the Knight Thomas Hoby] reads in part:

> While we lived as one, we were equally blessed;
> Though our body was twofold, we shared a single soul.
> But nothing endures in this world;
> You are for me a weeping testament of this truth.
> While you served your country, distracted with public affairs,
> You died, a sorrowful corpse in an alien land.
> Our children, feverish with the flames of grief—
> What could I do for them, alas, immersed in such misery?
> Unhappy wife, unhappy mother, I wander about aimlessly.
> I weep for the man snatched away—I weep for my own limbs.
> So, with a pregnant belly, I return by sea and by land
> To my home, lost in grief, desiring death.
> My dearest husband, my most excellent *Thomas,*
> In whom everything that was, was right and noble,
> Elizabeth, to you once the happiest wife,
> Brings back these words which she recalls with holy tears.
> I cannot prevent death, but these dead limbs,
> Insofar as I am able, I will always honor.
> O God! Either let me have another Thomas,
> Or let me return to my own Thomas.[2]

The form of these sentiments is very stylized, and even the feelings expressed are rather clichéd, but the artifice does not necessarily mean that the poem is hypocritical or false any more than the gift of flowers or a ring to one's beloved today suggests hypocrisy, despite the fact that such gifts are very traditional and even un-original. Then as now, people were likely to use the discourses and rituals available to them to communicate their deepest emotions; indeed, profound feelings may be more likely to find expression through artificial and traditional means than more shallow senti-ments and polite exchanges, which everyday language conveys with ease. And to contemporaries, the fact that Elizabeth Hoby was able to show off her superb skill in Latin versification in the process of declaring her love for her late husband served to make the tribute even more valued and valuable.

Women also took pleasure in other family relationships, with parents, children, and siblings, relationships that are also memo-rialized in epitaphs. Elizabeth Hoby wrote an elegy on the death of her two daughters, Elizabeth and Anne, in which she begins by addressing Elizabeth, who died after her sister Anne: "Your death was cruel, / but that death was even crueller that slew your younger sister Anna with you…. As their mother, I wanted to unite them in a single tomb, / as I had carried them both in my joy-ous womb."[3] In a similar manner, Anne King (1621–aft. 1671), sister of the poet Henry King, Bishop of Chichester, memorialized her sister, Dorothy. Anne was an artist and poet in her own right (though none of her drawings have survived, and only three of her poems). She erected a monument 26 years after her sister's death, sug-gesting a strong bond and love that was not diminished by long absence, and had carved on it an "Inscription on monument of Dorothy, Lady Hubert at Langley, Buckinghamshire M[emoria] S[acra]" [sacred to her memory]:

> Reader upon this field of Marble see
> How Death and Love Contend for mastery.
> Vaunting her spoils, Death warns Thee, Here lies
> One of her Choice pieces of destruction,
> For Wit, Form, Sweetness, So sublime, that higher
> Her Dart nor Malice ever did aspire.
> Love from Friend (scarce willing to survive
> But to preserve the Other's Fame alive,
> A Sister so endeared in Blood and Heart,
> She felt the stroke and still weeps for the smart)
> Informs thee (if Thou'lt help) these Virtues Fate
> Cannot consume or time obliterate.
> But by Thine Eyes embalmed, She will lie
> Living and fresh, till Death Herself must die.

> Then lend some Tears, for mine must needs be spent,
> Being both the Dead's and Living's monument.[4]

All of these memorials to loved ones make use of standard expressions of grief in traditional poetic forms, yet each shows us something beyond the trite and hackneyed—the real love each felt for the other and the pleasure each had taken in another's friendship and affection.

King's characterization of herself as a "Friend" to her sister was a significant claim in an era that theorized extensively on friendship between men, but tended to dismiss or trivialize friendship between women. Writers of the Renaissance took their ideas about friendship from classical authors like the Greek philosopher Aristotle (384–322 B.C.E.) and, in particular, from *De Amicitia* [On Friendship] by the Roman politician and philosopher Marcus Tullius Cicero (ca. 106–43 B.C.E.). These authors and many others held that friendship was a male prerogative and that friendship between two men was the zenith of human relationships. Aristotle had argued that true friendship depended upon the goodness and wisdom of both parties and could emerge only between equals; therefore, a man could never be a friend to a woman, as she was his inferior. For the same reason, women could never enjoy friendship to the extent that was possible for men, as they were not capable of the same degree of goodness and wisdom. Early modern thinkers added to these classical theories the example from the biblical story of David, where, in his lament for the death of Jonathan, David said, "I am distressed for thee, my brother Jonathan, very pleasant hast thou been unto me: thy love to me was wonderful, surpassing the love of women."[5]

This kind of thinking did not prevent early modern women from developing profound friendships with each other and writing about those friendships. The English poet Katherine Philips (1631–1664) was at the center of a Society of Friendship, where women read and exchanged poems and gave each other fanciful pastoral names; Philips herself was known as "the matchless Orinda." Philips's poetry suggests that women's friendship too could have an erotic element, and such relationships are quite well documented in the period. (See also chapter 6, "Women and Literature.") Philips's most important friend was Anne Owen, styled Lucasia in the Philips circle, and their friendship, like that of the biblical David and Jonathan, may have been sexual. It was certainly

Two girls in bed. *Source: Roxburghe Ballads,* courtesy AMS Press.

what would now be called homoerotic (though Philips seems to have been more attached to Owen than Owen was to Philips). Philips's poem "Friendship's Mystery, To My Dearest Lucasia" has immortalized their relationship. In the first stanza of the poem, Philips calls their friendship a "miracle," perhaps referring to the notion that only men could be true friends:

> COME, my Lucasia, since we see
> That Miracles Mens faith do move,
> By wonder and by prodigy
> To the dull angry world let's prove
> There's a Religion in our Love.[6]

Another poem by Philips, "Friendship in Emblem, or the Seal, to my dearest Lucasia," expands on their friendship:

1

The hearts thus intermixéd speak
A Love that no bold shock can break.
For Joined and growing, both in one,
Neither can be disturbed alone.

2

That means a mutuall knowledge too,
For what is't either a heart can do,
Which by its panting sentinel
It does not to the other tell?

3

That friendship hearts so much refines,
It nothing but itself designs.
The hearts are free from lower ends,
For each point to the other tends.

9

So friends are only *Two* in this,
T'reclaim each other when they miss.
For whosoe'er will grossly fall,
Can never be a friend at all.

10

And as that useful instrument
For even lines was ever meant,
So friendship governs actions best,
Prescribing Law to all the rest.

11

And as in nature, nothing's set
So just as lines and numbers met,
So compasses for these being made,
Do friendship's harmony persuade.

13

And like to them, so friends may own
Extension, not division.
Their points, like bodies, separate,
But head, like souls, knows no such fate.

14

And as each part so well is knit
That their embraces ever fit,

So friends are such by destiny,
And no third can the place supply.

15
There needs no motto to the Seal
But that we may the Mine reveal.
To the dull eye; it was thought fit
That friendship only should be writ.

16
But as there is degrees of bliss,
So there's no friendship meant by this,
But such as will transmit to fame
Lucasia's and *Orinda's* name.

Philips also dedicated a poem to Anne Fowler about the joys of a single life called "Advice to Virgins." She originally wrote the poem before her marriage, when she was only 15 or 16, but she later reworked it slightly and published it anonymously. The work, which ends by flouting the proverb that spinsters will be condemned to "leading apes in hell," reads in part:

A Maiden Life affords the best Content,
'Tis always happy as 'tis innocent.
Clear as Olympias bright and full of ease,
And calm as Neptune in the Halcyon days.
There are no sleeps broke with domestic cares,
No crying Children to distract our Prayers,
No pangs of Childbirth to extort our Tears,
No blust'ring Husbands create new Fears,
No rude upbraiding, that Defect or this,
No great Concern, whoever keeps a Miss.
No sighing, nor Affrightment at the Glass,
When it presents us with a Ruined Face;
But such an Object makes a Wife to Start,
And almost tempts her to adulterate Art,
Knowing a Husband's Love doth oft decay,
As Youth and Beauty Fades and wears away.
And therefore, Madam, be advised by me,
Turn, turn apostate to Love's Diety.
Suppress wild Nature, if she dares Rebel,
There's no such Thing, as leading Apes in Hell.

Whether in taboo same-sex unions or in love affairs or in marriage, women enjoyed lovemaking, a fact that is attested in both the medical and the poetic literature of the time. Many forms of Renaissance love poetry attest to men's desire for women, of course, but women were less likely than men to feel free to express sexual desire, given their culture's concern with women's chastity and the dangers of lust. Nonetheless, some women did use the Petrarchan sonnet to express desire, perhaps most notably the Italian women poets Gaspara Stampa (1524–1554), Veronica Franco (1546–1591), and Tullia d'Aragona (d. 1556). Franco and d'Aragona were courtesans, and Stampa may have been; that fact no doubt licensed them to be more frank about the desires that many women felt but were not free to express. All three poets wrote sonnet sequences addressed to a remote and unavailable man, detailing their pains and joys in love (the model that had been established by Petrarch in his sonnets to the unattainable Laura). (See also chapter 6, "Women and Literature.")

Other women expressed their erotic desire through devotional poetry, a tradition with a long history in the West. Because the erotic poem the Song of Songs (sometimes called the Song of Solomon) had been part of the Hebrew Bible since it was first canonized well over two millennia ago, there developed a tradition in the West of expressing longing for God in the same vocabulary used to express sexual longing. Gertrude More's poem, reproduced in the chapter on Women and Religion as well as Aemilia Lanyer's *Salve Deus Rex Judueorum* are good examples of the fusion of the erotic and the devotional, but eroticized spirituality was not limited to English writers or to nuns. The celebrated Italian poet Vittoria Colonna (1490–1547) wrote devotional sonnets modeled very much on the Petrarchan sonnets of erotic desire. Her "Debile e inferma a la salute ver ricorro" reads in part:

> Weak and infirm I run towards true salvation,
> And blindly call out to the sun I worship faithfully,
> And naked, I burn for his heavenly gold,
> And approach his flames, my body pure cold wax.

Another poem of hers, "Di lacrime e di foco nutrir l'alma," reads in part:

> Love teaches me to feed on flames and tears;
> To turn withered hope green through desire;
> To re-enslave my heart each time Love frees
> His noble face from that heavy disdain;

Love also teaches me to bear his weight
When I dream he's there alluring, touching
Me, and in the sweet encounter the pain's
Gone and my beloved enjoys my languors;
Sweet are these tears, delicious this passion.
How is this—that I have lost all hope saves
Me—in the back of my mind the sense I
Can renounce the desire coursing through
My body—that people honor torment
When you smile serenely. Thus Love teaches me.[7]

Devotional poetry like More's, Lanyer's, and Colonna's provided an outlet for the expression of desire that was not otherwise available to women and, at the same time, gave passion to the expression of religious devotion.

Sexuality and desire were also part of Renaissance medical and scientific discourse. When the anatomists and physicians of the era rediscovered the ancient texts on medicine, particularly those of Hippocrates (460–377 B.C.E.) and Galen (131–200 C.E.), they also "discovered" the clitoris as the site of women's sexual pleasure. Early modern physicians believed that both women and men ejaculated and that conception was possible only if both of them experienced pleasure. The English midwife Jane Sharp wrote in detail about both male and female bodies and their sexual organs in her book *The Midwives Book, or, The Whole Art of Midwifry Discovered* (1671). There she said:

> The wings [labia] appear when the Lips are parted, and they are made of soft spongy flesh, and the doubling of the skin, placed at the sides of the neck, these compass the Clitoris, and are like a Cocks Comb. These wings besides the great pleasure they give women in Copulation, are to defend the Matrix from outward violence.... The Clitoris is a sinewy hard body, full of spongy and black matter within it, as it is in the side ligaments of a mans Yard [penis], and this Clitoris will stand and fall as the Yard doth, & make women lustfull and take delight in Copulation, and were it not for this they would have no desire nor delight, nor would they ever conceive.[8]

The advantages for women in this kind of thinking are obvious, but there was also a pernicious piece to the argument: it was thought impossible for a woman to be impregnated in a rape unless she had enjoyed the experience.

Renaissance medical texts and marriage manuals argued that sexual pleasure was a good thing and often encouraged husbands to pleasure their wives thoroughly before penetration to ensure that they would conceive. In 1549, the French physician Ambroise Paré wrote:

> When the husband comes into his wife's chamber, he must entertain her with all sorts of dalliance, wanton behavior, and allurements to venery [desire]: but if he perceive her to be slow, and more cold, he must cherish, embrace, and tickle her, and shall not abruptly, the nerves [penis] being suddenly distended [erect], break into the field of nature [the vagina], but rather shall creep in by little and little, intermixing more wanton kisses with wanton words and speeches, handling her secret parts and dugs [breasts], that she may take fire and be inflamed to venery, for so at length the womb will strive and wax fervent with a desire of casting forth its own seed [semen].

Paré further suggested that if the woman is slow to be aroused,

> it shall be necessary first to foment her secret parts with the decoction of hot herbes made with Muscadine [wine], or boiled in any other good wine, and to put a little muske or civet into the neck or mouth of the womb: and when she shall perceive the efflux [flowing] of her seed to approach, by reason of the tickling pleasure, she must advertise [tell] her husband thereof, that at the very instant time or moment, he may also yield forth his seed.[9]

Even the German theologian Martin Luther (1483–1546) wrote about the pleasures of sex and assumed that women found lovemaking pleasurable. Luther fulminated against those who taught that marital sex was sinful, and he wrote passionately about the naturalness and beauty of sexual desire between wife and husband:

> Some people have argued and discussed in detail about whether it is a sin to desire a wife or husband in marriage, but this is foolish and against both Scripture and nature, for why should people marry unless they have desire and love for another. For this reason God has given such desire to the bride and bridegroom, for otherwise everyone would flee from marriage and avoid it. He has also commanded in Scripture that husband and wife are to love one another and shows that He takes great pleasure when things are well between a husband and wife. For this reason such desire and

"No Love, No Life." *Source: Roxburghe Ballads,* courtesy AMS Press.

love must truly not remain outside, and one has luck and grace if
they last a long time.

He also said of married, or "bridal," love that it is above all other
human love; it

burns like fire and seeks nothing more than its spouse, who says, "I
desire nothing that is yours, neither gold nor silver, neither this nor
that; I desire you yourself, and I would have all or nothing." All other
forms of love seek something other than simply the one who is
loved. Only this kind wants the entire beloved for itself.[10]

Many bawdy lyrics (almost all of them anonymous) expounded
on women's sexual pleasure, including one entitled "My Thing Is
My Own," which dwells on men's inability to satisfy women's
desire, a common theme in English lyrics in particular. This very

popular song had many, many verses in its many editions. Here are a few of them:

> I, a tender young maid, have been courted by many
> Of all sorts and trades as ever was any.
> A spruce haberdasher first spake to me fair,
> But I would have nothing to do with small ware.

> A master of music came with intent
> To give me a lesson on my instrument.
> I thanked him for nothing, and bid him be gone,
> For my little fiddle must not be played on.

> A cunning clockmaker did court me as well,
> And promised me riches if I'd ring his bell.
> So I looked at his clockwork, and said with a shock,
> "Your pendulum's far too small for my clock."

The refrain to the song says repeatedly, "My thing is my own, and I'll keep it so still, / Though other young lasses may do as they will," a remarkable claim in an era when a woman's chastity and, thus, her desire, belonged to her father or her husband. Indeed, the final refrain recoups the speaker's desire in marriage: "My thing is my own, and I'll keep it so still, / until I be married, / say men what they will."[11]

Women took great pleasure in beautiful clothes, in spite of moralists' condemnation of women's vanity. Such pleasure was not limited to elite women, though they had the means to indulge this pleasure far beyond anything a poorer woman could dream of. It is known how widespread the pleasure in dress was because of sumptuary laws, which regulated who could wear what based on their social class. The laws in Tudor England specified that no one could wear cloth of gold or silver or purple silk except those with the rank of countess or higher, though viscountesses were allowed to wear those colors in their kirtles (the top petticoat or skirt). Only baronesses and higher could wear silk or cloth mixed with or embroidered with silk, pearls, gold, or silver. Only barons' daughters and maids of honor could wear headdresses trimmed with pearls. One had to be the wife of a knight or higher to wear velvet, and only the wives of landowning gentlemen or higher were allowed to wear satin, damask, taffeta, or grosgrain in their gowns. Sumptuary laws applied to men as well, for this was a time when wealthy, titled men dressed in velvet, silks, lace, and fur.

These regulations, however, represent the failure to confine particular luxuries to the aristocracy at a time when some

The portraiture of Robert Car, Earle of Somerset, Vicount Rochester, Knight of the most noble order of the Garter &c. And of the Ladie Francis his wife

Robert Carr, Earle of Somerset, and Ladie Francis [sic], displaying clothes of the highest fashion, including a flat-top farthingale. Lady Frances (as it is more commonly spelled) divorced her first husband, Robert Devereux, Earl of Essex, to marry Carr. Both Carr and Lady Frances were part of the infamous Overbury scandal; they were convicted of poisoning Sir Thomas Overbury in 1613 to keep him from revealing that they had been living together before her divorce. Both were pardoned by King James VI and I. *Source:* Engraving by Renold Elstrack, in Michael Sparke, *The Narrative History of King James* (London, 1651), facing p. 56. *Source:* © Copyright The Trustees of The British Museum.

members of the middle class (those whose wealth was based on trade) were becoming as wealthy as those with inherited titles, land, and income. High-born women often passed on their dresses to their maids; that was one of the perks of domestic service. And middle-class women were increasingly able to insist on having clothes and other marks of wealth that were as fine or finer than aristocrats'. Elizabeth Spencer (daughter of John Spencer, a very wealthy merchant and sometime Lord Mayor of London) left a particularly extensive record of the demands she made in 1594 from her fiancé, Lord Compton, on the occasion of their marriage. Her requirements included not only clothes but other marks of status. She wanted an allowance of £2,600 per year for clothing plus another £600 for charitable works, regarding which "I would not, neither will be accountable for," plus £2,000 "to put in my purse," £6,000 "to buy me jewels," and £4,000 "to buy me a pearl chain." These are fabulous sums at a time when most workers would make just pennies a day. In addition, she required

> Two gentlewomen, lest one should be sick, or have some other let. Also, believe it, it is an undecent thing for a gentlewoman to stand mumping alone, when God hath blessed their lord and lady with a great estate…. Also, I will have six or eight gentlemen; and I will have my two coaches, one lined with velvet to myself, with four very fair horses; and a coach for my women, lined with cloth and laced with gold, or otherwise with scarlet and laced with silver, with four good horses.

Her terms of marriage also required appropriate delineation of status among her attendants:

> Also, at any time when I travel, I will be allowed not only caroches and spare horses, for me and my women, and I will have such carriages as be fitting for all, orderly, not pestering [mixing up] my things with my women's, nor theirs with either chambermaids, nor theirs with washmaids.

She was especially particular about the furnishing of her house:

> Also, I will have all my houses furnished, and my lodging chambers to be suited with all such furniture as is fit; as beds, stools, chairs, suitable cushions, carpets, silver warming-pans, cupboards of plate, fair hangings, and such like. So for my drawing-chamber in all houses, I will have them delicately furnished, both with hangings, couch, canopy, glass, carpet, chairs, cushions, and all things thereunto belonging.[12]

Though few women would have had such a fabulous retinue or so much "pocket money," Spencer's demands show us what many women desired and would have taken pleasure in.

Women also enjoyed dancing, whether at country dances or court balls. For wealthy women, dancing was an opportunity to show off their dresses; engage in flirtation; and display their elegance, gracefulness, and knowledge of the latest dances. Such dances might be highly structured, with every move and step predetermined. At other times, couples who knew the possible variations for a particular dance—a galliard, or pavanne, or bransle—might improvise the order of the steps and gestures that defined that dance. Men tended to have more active roles to play in courtly dances than women, and, for the most part, there was little touching, except of hands. Sir Thomas Elyot, in his *Book Named the Governor,* praised the way in which dancing symbolized "perfect harmony" by displaying the man's fierce "male" attributes and "women's gentler virtues."[13] However, a risqué dance of the period called La Volta required the man to lift his partner on his thigh and turn around while holding her there—a very sexy dance, indeed. A painting held at Penshurt Place, the country house of the Sidney family, shows Elizabeth I being lifted up on one of her courtier's thighs, so even queens danced La Volta, though it is said that Elizabeth liked the galliard best of all.[14] (It is probable that she did not know about this painting and would have suppressed its representation of her as being in a man's power in such a way.) Country dances, enjoyed by peasants and commoners rather than aristocrats, tended to be more lively than courtly dances, and the gestures and steps made by women and men tended to be more similar to each other than different.[15] Many dances mimicked courtship, with a man approaching a woman and then withdrawing and with her encouraging him, refusing him, and finally accepting him. In the Bavarian *Schuhplattler,* "the man stamped, slapped his thighs, somersaulted, circled the girl, and even jumped over her to get her attention." And the sarabande, which came to Spain in the late sixteenth century from the Arab world, was described by a contemporary as "a sexual pantomime of unparalleled suggestiveness."[16]

Thoinot Arbeau, a clergyman from Langres, France, wrote a manual of dancing called *Orchesography* [Choreography] (1589) in which he recommended dancing as a safe way for young men and women to meet:

> Dancing is practised to reveal whether lovers are in good health
> and sound of limb, after which they are permitted to kiss their mis-
> tresses in order that they may touch and savour one another, thus
> to ascertain if they are shapeley or emit an unpleasant odour as of
> bad meat.[17]

Though Arbeau wrote from the man's point of view, one can
assume that young women were also scoping out the defects of
their partners. Likewise, the Italian writer Fabritio Caroso published two books on dancing, *Il Ballerino* [The Professional Dancer]
and *Nobilita di Dame* [The Dignity of Ladies] in which he lists
dances whose names imply the "art of love": the Mirror of Love and
the Power of Love.

Aristocratic women enjoyed sports like fishing and hunting.
Book illuminations and tapestries of the period often showed both
noblewomen and noblemen riding to the hunt. Queen Elizabeth I
was noted for her love of hunting, and a structure called Queen
Elizabeth's Hunting Lodge survives as a testament to her enjoyment of this pastime. The building sits in Fairmead Deer Park in
what was then the Royal Forest of Essex. Though the 1543 structure
was built by her father, Henry VIII, she kept it up and used it after
his death, adding a large chimney to make it more serviceable. Its

Women and men gaming. *Source: Roxburghe Ballads,* courtesy AMS
Press.

salient feature is its height; it is many stories tall, and the top two floors are open at the sides to allow spectators to see the countryside many miles in each direction so as to view the hunt as it unfolded. Elizabeth engaged in the hunt herself and was said to be a superb archer; other women are portrayed in contemporary paintings hunting rabbits with bow and arrow. For those aristocrats and members of the royal family who were less athletically inclined, some "hunts" were so arranged that the ladies and gentlemen were arrayed on either side of a plain or corridor through which the deer were driven, providing a much easier target for the hunters and not necessitating any riding at all.[18]

Even more often women were portrayed fishing. The late fifteenth-century work entitled *The Treatyse of Fysshynge wyth an Angle* (1496) was probably written by a nun, the Lady Juliana Berners. She begins her book with a disquisition on happiness (in which she uses "man" to mean both men and women):

> [w]hich are the means and cause to reduce a man to a merry spirit? Truly, unto my simple discretion it seemeth me good and honest disports and games in which a man's heart joyeth without any repentance. Then it followeth that good and honest disports be the cause of men's fair age and long life. Therefore now will I choose of 4 good disports and honest games that is to say, of hunting, hawking, fowling, and fishing, namely angling with a rod or a yarde of line and a hook ... That is to say, if a man lack leaches [physicians] and medicines, he shall make 3 things his medicine or leaches and he shall never need any more. The first of them is merry thought. The 2nd is to labor moderately. The 3rd is good diet of clean meats and sensible drinks.

After discussing the advantages and disadvantages of various modes of hunting, she turns to fishing as the best diversion:

> Thus it seems to me that hunting, hawking, and fowling be so laborious and grievous that none of them may perform to induce a man to a merry spirit, the which is the cause of long life, according to the said parable of Salamon.
>
> Doubtless, then it follows that it must needs be the disport and game of fishing with an angle rod, for all other manner of fishing is also right labor and grievous, often causing men to be right weyth and cold, which many times hath been seen as the chief cause of infirmity and sometimes death. But the angler may have no cold nor

any disease nor anger [for any reason] but that which he causes himself, for he may not greatly lose but a line or an hook, of which he may have plenty of his own making or of other men's.[19]

Other activities included under the "sports" rubric were popular at the time, including tennis, or, as it was called when played without a racquet, handball. Such games were thought by some to be a good preparation for military prowess (the usual justification for sports) and were, thus, thought to be most appropriate for boys and men; even so, young women also enjoyed them when they were allowed to play. Because such sport was usually the occasion for betting and gambling, however, many moralists spoke against it. In England, these qualms about the game led to the argument that tennis should be avoided by genteel men, that it was the sport of the lower classes. In France, however, tennis was seen as a particularly aristocratic recreation, and there were great efforts made there to prevent members of the bourgeoisie and peasantry from playing, including a royal decree that all tennis courts in Paris, except those of the nobility, were to be shut down. In fact, a French visitor to England, Etienne Perlin, commented with surprise that in England "you may commonly see artisans, such as hatters or joiners [carpenters], play at tennis for a crown, which is not seen elsewhere, particularly on a working day."[20]

People of the Renaissance loved all kinds of games, from bowling, to chess, to checkers. Checkers is a very old game, indeed, originating probably in Egypt and brought to Europe through Spain by the Moors (Muslims from northwest Africa). As early as the eighth century, it was called Alquerque, and it was played on a board of 5 x 5 squares. The game became very popular in France in the sixteenth century, where it was first played on a chess board as it is today. Two versions of the game were played: when it involved capturing (or huffing) one's opponents' pieces, it was called *le jeu force* (the game of force); the noncapturing or non-huffing version was called *le jeu plaisant de dames* (the pleasant game of ladies) or simply *dames*. In England, the game was called Draughts, and it was later brought to America with the name Checkers. Card games, which were probably an import from China and which were first played in Europe in the fourteenth century, were also popular; they were an occasion for gambling and for moralists' zealous condemnation. Until the advent of printing, all decks were hand-painted and, therefore, a province of the aristocracy. However, beginning in the fifteenth century, German and Swiss printers began widely distributing cheap decks, and cards were soon played by people of all ranks. Some English royal decrees attempted to limit card playing (and gambling) to the 12 days of Christmas, a traditional time of celebration and even riot, but such decrees were generally ineffective in containing people's pleasure in card games—and in gambling.[21] Often card games were part of aristocratic all-night parties that involved many pleasures, including dancing, eating, drinking, gambling, and probably more than a little kissing and cuddling. The less wealthy had their less extravagant celebrations as well, and many rituals of daily life were the occasion for a party involving food, drink, and dancing—from the bris (circumcision ceremony) and bar mitzvah (coming of age ritual) of Jewish communities, to the baptisms of Christian communities, to the weddings and funerals that marked all people's lives. Each of these ceremonies was also a celebration of community life and personal love or loss, and each prompted a kind of informal holiday and break from the humdrum of work and daily routines.

Festivals of the sacred or secular calendar also provided occasions for celebration and feasting. As noted, the 12 days of Christmas (that is, Christmas Day, December 25, through January 5, the day before Epiphany) were a special time of festivity, but many communities had local feasts as well. For instance, shepherds all over Europe had their own special feasts for saints who were associated with shepherding, such as St. Wendelin, St. Wolfgang, or St. Bartholomew, whose feast day, August 24, marked the move from summer to winter quarters. In south Germany, shepherd communities would on that date elect a king and queen of the season and hold dances accompanied by feasting and drinking. Not surprisingly, given the importance of shepherds to the story of Jesus's birth, shepherds in many communities had special celebrations at Christmastime, including nativity plays.[22] Shepherds had their own musical traditions as well, often focused on the music of the bagpipes, a very ancient instrument common to many European cultures.

Carnival time, the period just before the somber Christian season of Lent, was a time of particularly high spirits and celebration, especially as Lent required fasting and abstaining from certain foods such as meat and drink. Carnivals were known as a time of misrule when society was turned topsy-turvy. Many people wore masks, drank heavily, and engaged in behavior that would not have been permitted at other times of the year. As one historian has argued, at Carnival time,

> young men could openly express their desire for ladies of higher social status, and respectable ladies could walk the streets. Wearing masks helped liberate people from their everyday selves, conferring a sense of impunity like a cloak of invisibility in folktales.

Little wonder that a contemporary proverb said "In Carnival, everything is permitted."[23]

People of the Renaissance also enjoyed "sports" that would be considered barbaric and sadistic today. Bearbaiting, dog and cock fights, and public punishment and executions all brought out good-sized crowds to watch, cheer, gamble, and gossip. The dramatic works of Shakespeare and his contemporaries were staged in playhouses built in "Bankside," the south side of the Thames River, which was outside the regulatory reach of the cities of London and Westminster; it was, therefore, the home to "dicey" activities. Bankside was originally known for its bear gardens and animal-baiting pits, large holes in the ground where animals were placed and from which they could not escape and, so, would fight to the death. The "pleasure" of this activity came not only from observing the contest and slaughter but from the inevitable gambling that accompanied all such activities. In addition to animal fights, Bankside, like the streets of many other European cities at the time, would have been home to a great variety of entertainment, including jugglers, acrobats, singers, musicians, and those selling a variety of cheap wares.

Though some Bankside activities were hardly legal, they were nonetheless popular with people from all ranks of society. Both King Henry VIII and Queen Elizabeth visited the bearbaiting pits of Bankside. The queen even brought along the French and Spanish ambassadors to entertain them and to show off what London had to offer. Initially, the playhouses competed with difficulty against the animal baiting for an audience. But as the plays became more popular, the theater companies were banned from performance on Thursdays, the traditional day for animal baiting. When the Puritans closed down the English playhouses during the Interregnum (the period between the execution of Charles I in 1649 and the Restoration of the monarchy with the return of Charles II in 1660), they did not close down the bear pits, which tells something about what was considered the more wholesome activity by contemporary moralists and religious leaders.[24] In Spain, the most popular form of animal baiting developed into bullfighting, the highly ritualized sport still popular today. In some Italian cities, horse racing became the most favored "animal" sport, often staged in the town piazza.

Animal torture was also part of children's games and even part of some recipes. Dutch children would put cats in a bag, hang it from a tree, and take turns beating the bag with a stick. Other Dutch games, no doubt duplicated in all European countries, involved beating, hanging, or stabbing a variety of animals, including dogs, geese, and peacocks, in addition to cats.[25] A sixteenth-century English recipe for roast goose includes the entertainment of watching the goose die as a kind of appetizer to the feast:

> A Goose, or Duck, or some lively Creature, (but the Goose is best) must be pulled all clear off her Feathers, only the head and neck must be spared. Then make a fire round about her; not too close to her, that the smoke do not choke her, and that the fire may not burn her too soon: not too far off, that she may not escape free; within the circle of the fire let there be set small cups and pots full of water, wherein Salt and Honey are mingled, and let there be set also Chargers full of sodden Apples, cut into small pieces in the dish. The Goose must be all Larded and basted over, to make her the more fit to be eaten, and may rost the better, put then fire about her, do not make too much haste, when as you see her begin to Rost; for by walking about, and flying here and there being cooped in by the fire that stops her way out, the unwearied Goose is kept in by drinking of the water; which cools her heat and all her body, and the Apples make her dung, cleanse and empty her. When she grows scalding hot, her inward parts rost also, then wet with a Sponge her head and heart [breast] continually; and when you see her giddy with running, and begin to stumble, her heart wants moisture: [when] she is Rosted, take her up, and set her upon the Table to your Guests, and as you cut her up she will cry continually, that she will be almost all eaten before she be dead.

Not only was this torture meant to make the goose more tasty, but, as the author commented, "it is very pleasant to behold."[26] Public houses and inns were also known for their animal baiting and animal fights, particularly cock fights, for card playing and gambling, for popular music, and for dancing.

Not all adult and children's games were violent and sadistic. A list of games played by seventeenth-century Dutch children included "the big ball, I spy, flick-fingers, hunt-the-slipper, quoits, clappers, knuckle-bones, little windmill, prinsoners' base, slabs, equal-or-not, conkers, marble-pits and hey-cockalorum." Children also played "blind-man's buff, paper windmills, leap-frog, spinning-tops, bow and arrow, and marbles." Excavations of early modern sites have turned up tops, balls, kites, and boats, as well as toy soldiers and other miniature military equipment. While boys tended to play with toy soldiers, girls played with dolls made from "wood, cloth, paper or even silver, in every possible shape and form, some-times with eyes that moved, or in various provincial costumes" and might own "doll's furniture and miniature cooking utensils."[27] Hundreds of such kitchen utensils have turned up in excavations of early modern sites, including plates, bowls, pitchers, cooking pots, and frying pans. Wealthier children had miniature cupboards with a complete set of serving dishes and cutlery. Some children even had elaborate dollhouses. Such toys were not only for girls' amuse-

Shepherdesses making music, "Aprill. Aegloga Quarta," Edmund Spenser, *Shepheards Calendar* (London, 1586), sig. C$_3$^{v}. STC 23089. *Source:* Reproduced by permission of the Folger Shakespeare Library.

ment but also taught them skills that they were expected to master as future housewives. Older girls from wealthy families might be given fashion dolls wearing the latest styles. But it was not only the very wealthy who owned toys; toys were being mass produced as early as the fifteenth century, and most children would have owned some playthings.

Among the amusements that attracted people of all ages were the annual fairs held in towns all over Europe, often scheduled to coincide with Christian religious holidays. A variety of peddlers would offer their wares for sale at such fairs, including farmers; artisans of all sorts; tooth-drawers (early dentists); those selling medicines; sellers of silks, ribbons, and other luxury goods; orange sellers and others offering rare commodities; recruiting sergeants; players and puppeteers; singers and sellers of broadside ballads; and, of course, thieves. In sixteenth-century Sweden, the king used the annual fair to promulgate royal policy. The fairs near Paris, which lasted for many months in the spring and the fall, boasted coffee shops, toy shops, acrobats, exotic animals, and Italian actors. Bartholomew Fair and Sourbridge Fair in England were famed for their plays, puppet shows, clowns, rope dancers, and waxworks.[28]

Early modern women's lives were rich and varied, encompassing play and pleasure as well as arduous work, serious attention to religion, and the cultivation of "womanly virtues." Though they lived in a world that tended to value order and hierarchy over self-expression and individuality, many of them nonetheless left a record of their pleasure in work and leisure: from the documents of those few women who wielded political power; to the writings of poets and polemicists; to the artwork of embroiderers, engravers, sculptors, and painters; to the obscure and anonymous records of the hundreds of thousands of women whose names will never be known but who make up the history of women's roles in the Renaissance.

NOTES

1.   See Susan C. Karant-Nunn and Merry E. Wiesner-Hanks, eds. and trans., *Luther on Women: A Sourcebook* (New York: Cambridge University Press, 2003), 187.

2.   Elizabeth Hoby, "Elizabeth Hobaea conjux, ad Thomam Hobaeum, Equitem Maritum," in *Early Modern Women Poets 1520–1700*,

An Anthology, ed. Jane Stevenson and Peter Davidson (New York: Oxford University Press, 2001), 45–46. Our translation.

3.   Elizabeth Hoby, "Elizabethae Hobeae, Matris, in obitum duarum filiarum Elizabethae, et Annae, Epicedium," in Stevenson and Davidson, *Early Modern Women Poets,* 47. Our translation.

4.   Modernized, from Anne King, *Kissing the Rod: An Anthology of Seventeenth-Century Women's Verse,* ed. Germaine Greer (London: Virago, 1988), 182.

5.   2 Sam. 1:26.

6.   Katherine Philips's poems are available through *Luminarium,* <http://www.luminarium.org/sevenlit/philips/philipsbib.htm>, through EEBO, <http://eebo.chadwyck.com>, and in print as *The Collected Works of Katherine Philips: The Matchless Orinda, Vol. 1: The Poems,* ed. Patrick Thomas (Stump Cross, UK: Stump Cross Books, 1990).

7.   Trans. Helen Moody.

8.   Jane Sharp, *The Midwives Book, or, The Whole Art of Midwifry Discovered* (London, 1671), sig. D6r, D6v-D7r. Sharp's book is available online through the Brown University Women Writers Online, <www.wwp.brown.edu>, and through EEBO, <http://eebo.chadwyck.com>. It is also available in modern editions, including that edited by Elaine Hoby (New York: Oxford University Press, 1999).

9.   Modernized, from Thomas Johnson's 1634 translation of Paré, *The Workes of the Famous Chirurgion Ambrose Parey,* 889, 886. Also qtd. in Valerie Traub, *The Renaissance of Lesbianism in Early Modern England* (New York: Cambridge University Press, 2002), 85, 94.

10.   Qtd. in Karant-Nunn and Wiesner-Hanks, *Luther on Women,* 145, 90.

11.   "My Thing Is My Own," from V. de Sola Pinto and A. E. Rodway, eds., *The Common Muse: Popular British Ballad Poetry from the 15th to the 20th Century* (Hammondsworth, UK: Penguin, 1965), 435–37.

12.   Qtd. in Mark Girouard, *A Country House Companion* (New Haven, CT: Yale University Press, 1987), 31–32.

13.   Alison Sim, *Pleasures & Pastimes in Tudor England* (Stroud, UK: Sutton, 1999), 114–15.

14.   Greg Lindahl maintains a wonderful Web site on Renaissance dances, cataloging a great range of dances along with their histories and providing instructions on how to execute the various steps. *Society for Creative Anachronism Dance Page,* <http://www.pbm.com/~lindahl/dance.html>.

15.   On the differences between courtly and country dances, see Howard Skiles, "Hands, Feet, and Bottoms: Decentering the Cosmic Dance in *A Midsummer Night's Dream,*" *Shakespeare Quarterly* 44 (1993): 325–42.

16.   Qtd. in Peter Burke, *Popular Culture in Early Modern Europe,* rev. rpt. (Aldershot, UK: Ashgate, 1999), 117–18; Burke also describes the other courtship dances mentioned here.

17.   Qtd. in Sim, *Pleasures*, 114.

18.   Sim, *Pleasures*, 177.

19.   Juliana Berners, *Treatise of Fishing*, from Richard Bear's *Renascence Editions*, 2002, <http://darkwing.uoregon.edu/~rbear/berners/berners.html>.

20.   Qtd. in Sim, *Pleasures*, 184. Sim also cites the decree regarding tennis courts.

21.   Sim, *Pleasures*, 191–93.

22.   Burke, *Popular Culture*, 33.

23.   Burke, *Popular Culture*, 202–03.

24.   See Brittania.com for a history of Bankside, especially the site on *Shakespeare's London,* <http://www.britannia.com/hiddenlondon/shakespeare.html>.

25.   Paul Zumthor, *Daily Life in Rembrandt's Holland* (Stanford, CA: Stanford University Press, 1994), 168–69.

26.   From *Eighteen Books of the Secrets of Art and Nature* (London, 1660), qtd. in Patricia Fumerton, "Introduction: A New New Historicism," in *Renaissance Culture and the Everyday,* ed. Patricia Fumerton and Simon Hunt (Philadelphia: University of Pennsylvania Press, 1999), 2.

27.   Zumthor, *Daily Life,* 169.

28.   Burke, *Popular Culture,* 111, 112.

SUGGESTED READING

Arnold, Janet. *Patterns of Fashion: The Cut and Construction of Clothes for Men and Women c. 1560–1620.* New York: Drama Book Pub., 1985.

Ashford, Jane. *A Visual History of Costume: The Sixteenth Century.* New York: Drama Book Pub., 1983.

Burke, Peter. *Popular Culture in Early Modern Europe.* Rev. rpt. Aldershot, UK: Ashgate, 1999.

Cressy, David. *Birth, Marriage, and Death: Ritual, Religion, and the Life-Cycle in Tudor and Stuart England.* New York: Oxford University Press, 1999.

Fraser, Antonia. *A History of Toys.* London: Weidenfeld and Nicolson, 1966.

Fumerton, Patricia, and Simon Hunt, eds. *Renaissance Culture and the Everyday.* Philadelphia: University of Pennsylvania Press, 1999.

Gröber, Karl. *Children's Toys of Bygone Days: A History of Playthings of all Peoples from Prehistoric Times to the Nineteenth Century.* Trans. P. Hereford. London: Batsford, 1928.

King, C. E. *A Collector's History of Dolls.* New York: Bonanza Books, 1977.

Sim, Alison. *Pleasures & Pastimes in Tudor England.* Stroud, UK: Sutton, 1999.

Selected Bibliography

Abraham, Beth-Zion, trans. and ed. *The Life of Glückel of Hameln, 1646–1724, Written by Herself*. London: Horovitz, 1962.

Amussen, Susan D. *An Ordered Society: Gender and Class in Early Modern England*. New York: Oxford University Press, 1988.

Amussen, Susan D., and Adele F. Seeff. *Attending to Early Modern Women*. Newark: University of Delaware Press, 1998.

Anderson, Bonnie S., and Judith P. Zinsser. *A History of Their Own: Women in Europe from Prehistory to the Present*. Vol. 1. New York: Harper and Row, 1989.

Anderson, Michael. *Approaches to the History of the Western Family, 1500–1914*. Cambridge: Cambridge University Press, 2000.

Ariès, Philippe, and André Béjin. *Western Sexuality: Practice and Precept in Past and Present*. Trans. A. Forster. New York: Basil Blackwell, 1985.

Arnold, Janet. *Patterns of Fashion: The Cut and Construction of Clothes for Men and Women c. 1560–1620*. New York: Drama Book Pub., 1985.

Ashford, Jane. *A Visual History of Costume: The Sixteenth Century*. New York: Drama Book Pub., 1983.

Baernstein, P. Renée. *A Convent Tale: A Century of Sisterhood in Spanish Milan*. New York: Routledge, 2002.

Bainton, Roland H. *Women of the Reformation from Spain to Scandinavia*. Minneapolis, MN: Augsburg Publishing House, 1977.

Baldauf-Berdes, Jane J. *Women Musicians of Venice: Musical Foundations, 1525–1855*. Rev. ed. New York: Oxford University Press, 1996.

Barahona, Renato. *Sex, Crimes, Honour, and the Law in Early Modern Spain: Vizcaya, 1528–1735*. Toronto: University of Toronto Press, 2003.

Barry, Jonathan, Marianne Hester, and Gareth Roberts, eds. *Witchcraft in Early Modern Europe: Studies in Culture and Belief*. New York: Cambridge University Press, 1999.

Baskin, Judith R., ed. *Jewish Women in Historical Perspective*. 2nd ed. Detroit, MI: Wayne State University Press, 1998.

Bates, Catherine. *The Rhetoric of Courtship in Elizabethan Language and Literature*. New York: Cambridge University Press, 1992.

Becker, Lucina M. *Death and the Early Modern Englishwoman*. Aldershot, UK: Ashgate, 2003.

Bell, Ilona. *Elizabethan Women and the Poetry of Courtship*. New York: Cambridge University Press, 1998.

Bell, Rudolph M. *Holy Anorexia*. Chicago: Chicago University Press, 1985.

Bellabarba, Marco. *The Politics of Court Scandal in Early Modern England: News Culture and the Overbury Affair, 1603–1660*. Cambridge: Cambridge University Press, 2002.

Ben-Amos, Ilana Krausman. *Adolescence and Youth in Early Modern England*. New Haven, CT: Yale University Press, 1994.

Benedict, Philip. *Christ's Churches Purely Reformed: A Social History of Calvinism*. New Haven, CT: Yale University Press, 2002.

———. *Cities and Social Change in Early Modern France*. Boston: Unwin Hyman, 1989.

Bennett, Judith M. *Ale, Beer, and Brewsters in England: Women's Work in a Changing World 1300–1600*. New York: Oxford University Press, 1996.

Benson, Pamela J. *The Invention of the Renaissance Woman: The Challenge of Female Independence in the Literature and Thought of Italy and England*. University Park: Pennsylvania State University Press, 1992.

Berger, John. *Ways of Seeing*. New York: Penguin, 1977.

Berry, Philippa. *Of Chastity and Power: Elizabethan Literature and the Unmarried Queen*. New York: Routledge, 1989.

Bonfield, Lloyd, Richard M. Smith, and Keith Wrightson. *The World We Have Gained: Histories of Population and Social Structure: Essays Presented to Peter Laslett on His Seventieth Birthday*. New York: Basil Blackwell, 1986.

Bornstein, Daniel E., and Roberto Rusconi, eds. *Women and Religion in Medieval and Renaissance Italy*. Trans. Margery J. Schneider. Chicago: University of Chicago Press, 1996.

Bowers, Jane, and Judith Tick, eds. and trans. *Women Making Music: The Western Art Tradition, 1150–1950*. Urbana: University of Illinois Press, 1986.

Brailsford, Mabel Richmond. *Quaker Women*. London: Duckworth, 1915.

Brant, Clare, and Diane Purkiss, eds. *Women, Texts, and Histories, 1575–1760*. New York: Routledge, 1992.

Brewer, John, and Roy Porter, eds. *Consumption and the World of Goods: Consumption and Society in the Eighteenth Century.* New York: Routledge, 1993.

Bridenthal, Renate, Susan Mosher Stuard, and Merry E. Wiesner. *Becoming Visible: Women in European History.* Boston: Houghton Mifflin, 1998.

Brigden, Susan. *New Worlds, Lost Worlds: The Rule of the Tudors, 1486–1603.* New York: Penguin, 2000.

Brink, Jean R., ed. *Female Scholars: A Tradition of Learned Women before 1800.* Montreal: Eden Press, 1980.

Brink, Jean R., Maryanne C. Horowitz, and Allison P. Coudert, eds. *Playing with Gender: A Renaissance Pursuit.* Urbana: University of Illinois Press, 1991.

Broomhall, Susan M. *Women and the Book Trade in Sixteenth-Century France.* Aldershot, UK: Ashgate, 2002.

Broude, Norma, and Mary Garrard, eds. *Feminism and Art History: Questioning the Litany.* New York: Harper and Row, 1982.

Brown, Judith C. *Immodest Acts: The Life of a Lesbian Nun in Renaissance Italy.* New York: Oxford University Press, 1986.

Brown, Judith C., and Robert C. Davis, eds. *Gender and Society in Renaissance Italy.* London: Longman, 1998.

Bullough, Vern L. *Women and Prostitution: A Social History.* Buffalo, NY: Prometheus Books, 1987.

Cahn, Susan. *Industry of Devotion: The Transformation of Women's Work in England, 1500–1660.* New York: Columbia University Press, 1987.

Cammarata, Joan F., ed. *Women in the Discourse of Early Modern Spain.* Gainesville: University Press of Florida, 2003.

Carlson, Eric Josef. *Marriage and the English Reformation.* Cambridge, MA: Blackwell, 1994.

Carroll, Jane L., and Alison G. Stewart, eds. *Saints, Sinners, and Sisters: Gender and Northern Art in Medieval and Early Modern Europe.* Aldershot, UK: Ashgate, 2003.

Casey, James. *The History of the Family.* New York: Basil Blackwell, 1989.

Cavallo, Sandra. *Charity and Power in Early Modern Italy: Benefactors and Their Motives in Turin, 1541–1789.* New York: Cambridge University Press, 1995.

Cerasano, S. P., and Marion Wynne-Davies, eds. *Gloriana's Face: Women, Public and Private, in the English Renaissance.* Detroit, MI: Wayne State University Press, 1992.

Chadwick, Whitney. *Women, Art, and Society.* London: Thames & Hudson, 1990.

Charles, Lindsey, and Lorna Duffin. *Women and Work in Pre-Industrial England.* Dover, NH: Croom Helm, 1989.

Charlton, Kenneth. *Women, Religion, and Education in Early Modern England.* New York: Routledge, 1999.

Chedgzoy, Kate, Melanie Hansen, and Suzanne Trill, eds. *Voicing Women: Gender and Sexuality in Early Modern Writing.* Keele, UK: Keele University Press, 1996.

Chojnacka, Monica. *Working Women of Early Modern Venice.* Baltimore: Johns Hopkins University Press, 2001.

Clark, Alice. *The Working Life of Women in the Seventeenth Century.* London: Routledge, 1919. Rpt., New York: A.M. Kelley, 1968.

Clarke, Danielle. *The Politics of Early Modern Women's Writing.* New York: Longman, 2001.

Cohen, Sherrill. *The Evolution of Women's Asylums since 1500: From Refuges for Ex-Prostitutes to Shelters for Battered Women.* New York: Oxford University Press, 1992.

Cohn, Samuel Kline. *Women in the Streets: Essays on Sex and Power in Renaissance Italy.* Baltimore: Johns Hopkins University Press, 1996.

Conley, John J. *The Suspicion of Virtue: Women Philosophers in Neoclassical France.* Ithaca, NY: Cornell University Press, 2002.

Connell, William J., ed. *Society and Individual in Renaissance Florence.* Berkeley: University of California Press, 2002.

Cox, Virginia. "The Single Self: Feminist Thought and the Marriage Market in Early Modern Venice." *Renaissance Quarterly* 48 (1995): 513–81.

Crawford, Patricia. *Women and Religion in England, 1500–1720.* New York: Routledge, 1993.

Cressy, David. *Birth, Marriage, and Death: Ritual, Religion, and the Life-Cycle in Tudor and Stuart England.* New York: Oxford University Press, 1999.

Cuming, G. J., and Derek Baker, eds. *Popular Belief and Practice: Studies in Church History 8.* Cambridge: Cambridge University Press, 1972.

Datta, Satya. *Women and Men in Early Modern Venice: Reassessing History.* Aldershot, UK: Ashgate, 2003.

Davis, Barbara Beckerman. "Poverty and Poor Relief in Sixteenth-Century Toulouse." *Historical Reflections/Reflexions Historiques* 17 (1991): 267–96.

Davis, James C. *A Venetian Family and Its Fortune, 1500–1900: The Dona and the Conservation of Their Wealth.* Philadelphia: American Philosophical Society, 1975.

Davis, Natalie Zemon. *The Return of Martin Guerre.* Cambridge, MA: Harvard University Press, 1983.

———. *Society and Culture in Early Modern France: Eight Essays.* Stanford, CA: Stanford University Press, 1975.

———. *Women on the Margins: Three Seventeenth-Century Lives.* Cambridge, MA: Harvard University Press, 1995.

Dean, Trevor, and K.J.P. Lowe. *Marriage in Italy, 1300–1650.* New York: Cambridge University Press, 1998.

Dekker, Rudolf, and Lotte van de Pol. *The Tradition of Female Transvestism in Early Modern Europe.* Basingstoke, UK: Macmillan, 1989.

Diefendorf, Barbara B. *Beneath the Cross: Catholics and Huguenots in Sixteenth-Century Paris.* New York: Oxford University Press, 1991.

Diefendorf, Barbara B., and Carla Alison Hesse, eds. *Culture and Identity in Early Modern Europe (1500–1800): Essays in Honor of Natalie Zemon Davis.* Ann Arbor: University of Michigan Press, 1993.

Dolan, Frances E. *Dangerous Familiars: Representations of Domestic Crime in England: 1550–1700.* Ithaca, NY: Cornell University Press, 1994.

———. *Whores of Babylon: Catholicism, Gender, and Seventeenth-Century Print Culture.* Ithaca, NY: Cornell University Press, 1999.

Donnell, Sidney. *Feminizing the Enemy: Imperial Spain, Transvestite Drama, and the Crisis of Masculinity.* Lewisburg, PA: Bucknell University Press, 2003.

Donnison, Jean. *Midwives and Medical Men: A History of the Struggle for the Control of Childbirth.* 2nd ed. New Barnet, UK: Historical Publications, 1988.

D'Orleans, Anne-Marie-Louise, Duchess de Monpensier. *Against Marriage: The Correspondence of La Grande Mademoiselle by Anne-Marie-Louise D'Orleans, Duchesse de Monpensier.* Ed. and trans. Joan DeJean. Chicago: Chicago University Press, 2002.

Dresen-Coenders, Lène, and Petty Bange, eds. *Saints and She-Devils: Images of Women in the 15th and 16th Centuries.* London: Rubicon, 1987.

Duby, Georges, et al., eds. *A History of Women in the West: Renaissance and Enlightenment Paradoxes.* Vol. 3. Cambridge, MA: Belknap Press of Harvard University Press, 1993.

Duffy, Eamon. *The Voices of Morebath: Reformation and Rebellion in an English Village.* New Haven, CT: Yale University Press, 2001.

Dugaw, Dianne. *Warrior Women and Popular Balladry 1650–1850.* New York: Cambridge University Press, 1989.

Eales, Jacqueline. *Women in Early Modern England, 1500–1700.* Bristol, PA: UCL Press, 1998.

Edwards, Kathryn A., ed. *Werewolves, Witches, and Wandering Spirits: Traditional Belief and Folklore in Early Modern Europe.* Kirksville, MO: Truman State University Press, 2002.

Erickson, Amy Louise. *Women and Property in Early Modern England.* New York: Routledge, 1993.

Evenden, Doreen. *The Midwives of Seventeenth-Century London.* New York: Cambridge University Press, 2000.

Ezell, Margaret. *The Patriarch's Wife: Literary Evidence and the History of the Family.* Chapel Hill: University of North Carolina Press, 1987.

Faderman, Lillian. *Surpassing the Love of Men: Romantic Friendship and Love between Women from the Sixteenth Century to the Present.* New York: Morrow, 1981.

Fairchilds, Cissie C. *Domestic Enemies: Servants and Their Masters in Old Regime France*. Baltimore: Johns Hopkins University Press, 1984.

Farr, James R. *Authority and Sexuality in Early Modern Germany, 1550–1730*. New York: Oxford University Press, 1995.

Farrell, Michèle Longino. *Performing Motherhood: The Sévigné Correspondence*. Hanover, NH: University Press of New England, 1991.

Fenlon, Iain. *Music and Culture in Late Renaissance Italy*. New York: Oxford University Press, 2002.

Ferguson, Margaret W. *Dido's Daughters: Literacy, Gender, and Empire in Early Modern England and France*. Chicago: Chicago University Press, 2003.

Ferguson, Margaret W., Maureen Quilligan, and Nancy J. Vickers, eds. *Rewriting the Renaissance: The Discourses of Sexual Difference in Early Modern Europe*. Chicago: University of Chicago Press, 1987.

Fildes, Valerie. *Wet Nursing: A History from Antiquity to the Present*. New York: Basil Blackwell, 1988.

————, ed. *Women as Mothers in Pre-Industrial England: Essays in Memory of Dorothy McLaren*. New York: Routledge, 1990.

Fine, Elsa Honig. *Women and Art: A History of Women Painters and Sculptors from the Renaissance to the 20th Century*. Montclair, NJ: Allanheld & Schram/Prior, 1978.

Fletcher, Anthony, and John Stevenson, eds. *Order and Disorder in Early Modern England*. New York: Cambridge University Press, 1985.

Fradenberg, Louise, and Carla Freccero, eds. *Premodern Sexualities*. New York: Routledge, 1996.

Fraser, Antonia. *The Weaker Vessel: Woman's Lot in the Seventeenth Century*. London: Weidenfeld and Nicolson, 1984.

Frick, Carole Collier. *Dressing Renaissance Florence: Families, Fortunes, and Fine Clothing*. Baltimore: Johns Hopkins University Press, 2002.

Frojmovic, Eva. *Imaging the Self, Imaging the Other: Visual Representation and Jewish-Christian Dynamics in the Middle Ages and Early Modern Period*. Leiden, The Netherlands: Brill, 2002.

Frye, Susan, and Karen Robertson, eds. *Maids and Mistresses, Cousins and Queens: Women's Alliances in Early Modern England*. New York: Oxford University Press, 1999.

Fumerton, Patricia, and Simon Hunt, eds. *Renaissance Culture and the Everyday*. Philadelphia: University of Pennsylvania Press, 1999.

Garrard, Mary D. *Artemisia Gentileschi: The Image of the Female Hero in Italian Baroque Art*. Princeton, NJ: Princeton University Press, 1989.

————. "Here's Looking at Me: Sofonisba Anguissola and the Problem of the Woman Artist." *Renaissance Quarterly* 47 (1994): 556–622.

Garrioch, David. *Neighbourhood and Community in Paris 1740–1790*. New York: Cambridge University Press, 1986.

Gélis, Jacques. *History of Childbirth: Fertility, Pregnancy, and Birth in Early Modern Europe.* Trans. R. Morris. Cambridge, UK: Polity, 1991.

George, Margaret. *Women in the First Capitalist Society: Experiences in Seventeenth Century England.* Urbana: University of Illinois Press, 1988.

Gibson, Marion, ed. *Witchcraft and Society in England and America, 1550–1750.* Ithaca, NY: Cornell University Press, 2003.

Gibson, Wendy. *Women in Seventeenth Century France.* New York: Macmillan, 1989.

Gillespie, Katharine. *Domesticity and Dissent in the Seventeenth Century: English Women's Writing and the Public Sphere.* New York: Cambridge University Press, 2004.

Glanville, Philippa, and Jennifer Faulds Goldsborough. *Women Silversmiths 1685–1845.* New York: Thame and Hudson, 1990.

Goldberg, Jonathan, ed. *Queering the Renaissance.* Durham, NC: Duke University Press, 1994.

Goody, Jack. *The Development of the Family and Marriage in Europe.* New York: Cambridge University Press, 1983.

Goody, Jack, Joan Thirsk, and E. P. Thompson, eds. *Family and Inheritance: Rural Society in Western Europe, 1200–1800.* New York: Cambridge University Press, 1976.

Gowing, Laura. *Common Bodies: Women, Touch, and Power in Seventeenth-Century England.* New Haven, CT: Yale University Press, 2003.

———. *Domestic Dangers: Women, Words, and Sex in Early Modern London.* New York: Oxford University Press, 1996.

Graham, Elspeth, ed. *Her Own Life: Autobiographical Writings by Seventeenth Century Englishwomen.* New York: Routledge, 1989.

Greaves, Richard L. *Triumph over Silence: Women in Protestant History.* Princeton, NJ: Princeton University Press, 1990.

Gregory, Brad S., ed. *The Forgotten Writings of the Mennonite Martyrs.* Leiden, The Netherlands: Brill, 2002.

Grendler, Paul F. *Schooling in Renaissance Italy: Literacy and Learning, 1300–1600.* Baltimore: Johns Hopkins University Press, 1989.

Grundy, Isobel, and Susan Wiseman, eds. *Women, Writing, History: 1640–1740.* London: Batsford, 1991.

Habermann, Ina. *Staging Slander and Gender in Early Modern England.* Aldershot, UK: Ashgate, 2003.

Hafter, Daryl, ed. *European Women and Preindustrial Craft.* Bloomington: Indiana University Press, 1995.

Hall, Kim F. *Things of Darkness: Economies of Race and Gender in Early Modern England.* Ithaca, NY: Cornell University Press, 1995.

Hammons, Pamela S. *Poetic Resistance: English Women Writers and the Early Modern Lyric.* Aldershot, UK: Ashgate, 2002.

Hanawalt, Barbara, ed. *Women and Work in Preindustrial Europe*. Bloomington: Indiana University Press, 1986.

Hannay, Margaret P., ed. *Silent but for the Word: Tudor Women as Patrons, Translators, and Writers of Religious Works*. Kent, OH: Kent State University Press, 1985.

Harris, Ann Sutherland, and Linda Nochlin. *Women Artists: 1550–1950*. New York: Alfred A. Knopf, 1984.

Harris, Barbara J. *English Aristocratic Women 1450–1550: Marriage and Family, Property and Careers*. New York: Oxford University Press, 2002.

Harvey, Elizabeth. *Ventriloquized Voices: Feminist Theory and English Renaissance Texts*. New York: Routledge, 1992.

Heller, Nancy G. *Women Artists: An Illustrated History*. New York: Abbeville Press, 1987.

Henderson, John, and Richard Wall, eds. *Poor Women and Children in the European Past*. New York: Routledge, 1994.

Henderson, Katherine Usher, and Barbara F. McManus. *Half Humankind: Contexts and Texts of the Controversy about Women in England, 1540–1640*. Urbana: University of Illinois Press, 1985.

Hendricks, Margo, and Patricia Parker, eds. *Women, "Race," and Writing in the Early Modern Period*. New York: Routledge, 1994.

Herlihy, David, and Christiane Klapisch-Zuber. *Tuscans and Their Families: A Study of the Florentine Catasto of 1427*. New Haven, CT: Yale University Press, 1985.

Hill, Bridget. *The First English Feminist: Reflections on Marriage and Other Writings by Mary Astell*. Aldershot, UK: Gower/Maurice Temple Smith, 1986.

Hills, Helen. "Cities and Virgins: Female Aristocratic Convents in Early Modern Naples and Palermo." *Oxford Art Journal* 22 (1999): 31–54.

Hinds, Hilary. *God's Englishwomen: Seventeenth Century Radical Sectarian Writing and Feminist Criticism*. New York: St. Martin's Press, 1996.

Hobby, Elaine. *Virtue of Necessity: English Women's Writings, 1646–1688*. London: Virago Press, 1988.

Howe, Elizabeth. *The First English Actresses: Women and Drama, 1660–1700*. New York: Cambridge University Press, 1996.

Hsia, R. Po-Chia, and H.F.K. van Nierop, eds. *Calvinism and Religious Toleration in the Dutch Golden Age*. New York: Cambridge University Press, 2002.

Hufton, Olwen. *The Prospect before Her: A History of Women in Western Europe, 1500–1800*. New York: Alfred A. Knopf, 1996.

Hull, Suzanne W. *Chaste, Silent, and Obedient: English Books for Women, 1475–1640*. San Marino, CA: Huntington Library, 1982.

———. *Women According to Men: The World of Tudor-Stuart Women*. Walnut Creek, CA: AltaMira Press, 1996.

Hunt, Margaret. *The Middling Sort: Commerce, Gender, and the Family in England, 1680–1780.* Berkeley: University of California Press, 1996.

Hunter, Lynette, and Sarah Hutton, eds. *Women, Science, and Medicine 1500–1700: Mothers and Sisters of the Royal Society.* Stroud, UK: Sutton, 1997.

Hutson, Lorna, ed. *Feminism and Renaissance Studies.* New York: Oxford University Press, 1999.

———. *The Usurer's Daughter: Male Friendship and Fictions of Women in Sixteenth Century England.* New York: Routledge, 1994.

Ingram, Martin. *Church Courts, Sex, and Marriage in England, 1570–1640.* New York: Cambridge University Press, 1987.

Jackson, Mark, ed. *Infanticide: Historical Perspectives on Child Murder and Concealment, 1550–2000.* Aldershot, UK: Ashgate, 2002.

Jacobs, Fredrika H. *Defining the Renaissance Virtuosa: Women Artists and the Language of Art History and Criticism.* New York: Cambridge University Press, 1998.

Jardine, Lisa. *Worldly Goods: A New History of the Renaissance.* New York: Norton, 1998.

Jelinek, Estelle C., ed. *The Traditions of Women's Autobiography from Antiquity to the Present.* Boston: Twayne, 1986.

Johnson, Geraldine A., and Sara F. Matthews Grieco, eds. *Picturing Women in Renaissance and Baroque Italy.* New York: Cambridge University Press, 1997.

Jones, Ann Rosalind. *The Currency of Eros: Women's Love Lyric in Europe 1540–1620.* Bloomington: Indiana University Press, 1990.

Jones, Ann Rosalind, and Peter Stallybrass. *Renaissance Clothing and the Materials of Memory.* New York: Cambridge University Press, 2002.

Jones, Vivien. *Women and Literature in Britain, 1700–1800.* New York: Cambridge University Press, 2000.

Jordan, Constance. *Renaissance Feminism: Literary Texts and Political Models.* Ithaca, NY: Cornell University Press, 1990.

Kamen, Henry. *Early Modern European Society.* New York: Routledge, 2000.

Karant-Nunn, Susan C., and Merry E. Wiesner-Hanks, eds. and trans. *Luther on Women: A Sourcebook.* New York: Cambridge University Press, 2003.

Keeble, N.H. *The Cultural Identity of Seventeenth-Century Woman: A Reader.* New York: Routledge, 1994.

Kelso, Ruth. *Doctrine for the Lady of the Renaissance.* 1956. Urbana: University of Illinois Press, 1978.

Kermode, Jenny, and Garthine Walker, eds. *Women, Crime, and the Courts in Early Modern England.* London: UCl Press, 1994.

Kettering, Sharon. "The Patronage Power of Early Modern French Noblewomen." *Historical Journal* 32 (1989): 817–41.

King, Catherine E. *Renaissance Women Patrons: Wives and Widows in Italy c. 1300–1550*. New York: Palgrave Macmillan, 1998.

King, Margaret L. *Women of the Renaissance*. Chicago: University of Chicago Press, 1991.

King, Margaret L., and Albert Rabil, Jr., trans. and eds. *Her Immaculate Hand: Selected Works by and about the Women Humanists of Quattrocento Italy*. Asheville, NC: Pegasus Press, 2000.

Klapisch-Zuber, Christiane. *Women, Family, and Ritual in Renaissance Italy*. Trans. Lydia G. Cochrane. Chicago: University of Chicago Press, 1987.

Klein, Joan Larsen. *Daughters, Wives, and Widows: Writings by Men about Women and Marriage in England, 1500–1640*. Urbana: University of Illinois Press, 1992.

Korda, Natasha. *Shakespeare's Domestic Economies: Gender and Property in Early Modern England*. Philadelphia: University of Pennsylvania Press, 2002.

Krull, Edith. *Women in Art*. London: Studio Vista, 1989.

Kuehn, Thomas. *Law, Family, and Women: Towards a Legal Anthropology of Renaissance Italy*. Chicago: University of Chicago Press, 1991.

Kunze, Bonnelyn Young. *Margaret Fell and the Rise of Quakerism*. Stanford, CA: Stanford University Press, 1994.

Kussmaul, Ann. *Servants in Husbandry in Early Modern England*. New York: Cambridge University Press, 1990.

Labalme, Patricia H. *Beyond Their Sex: Learned Women of the European Past*. New York: New York University Press, 1980.

Laqueur, Thomas. *Making Sex: Body and Gender from the Greeks to Freud*. Cambridge, MA: Harvard University Press, 1990.

Latz, Dorothy L. *"Glow-Worm Light": Writings of 17th Century English Recusant Women from Original Manuscripts*. Salzburg: Institut für Anglistik und Amerikanistik Universität Salzburg, 1989.

———. *Neglected Writings of Recusant Women: Recusant Writings of the Sixteenth–Seventeenth Centuries*. Salzburg: Institut für Anglistik und Amerikanistik Universität Salzburg, 1997.

———. *Saint Angela Merici and the Spiritual Currents of the Italian Renaissance*. Lille, France: Université de Lille III, 1987.

Lawner, Lynne. *Lives of the Courtesans: Portraits of the Renaissance*. New York: Rizzoli, 1987.

Lerner, Gerda. *The Creation of Feminist Consciousness, from the Middle Ages to 1870*. New York: Oxford University Press, 1994.

Levin, Carole, and Patricia A. Sullivan, eds. *Political Rhetoric, Power, and Renaissance Women*. Albany: State University of New York Press, 1995.

Lewalski, Barbara K. *Writing Women in Jacobean England*. Cambridge, MA: Harvard University Press, 1993.

Lougee, Carolyn C. *Le Paradis des Femmes: Women, Salons, and the Social Stratification in Seventeenth Century France.* Princeton, NJ: Princeton University Press, 1976.

Lowe, Kate. *Nuns' Chronicles and Convent Culture in Renaissance and Counter-Reformation Italy.* New York: Cambridge University Press, 2003.

Lynch, Katherine A. *Individuals, Families, and Communities in Europe, 1200–1800: The Urban Foundations of Western Society.* New York: Cambridge University Press, 2003.

Mack, Phyllis. *Visionary Women: Ecstatic Prophecy in Seventeenth-Century England.* Berkeley: University of California Press, 1992.

Maclean, Ian. *The Renaissance Notion of Woman: A Study in the Fortunes of Scholasticism and Medical Science in European Intellectual Life.* New York: Cambridge University Press, 1980.

———. *Women Triumphant: Feminism in French Literature, 1610–1652.* New York: Oxford University Press, 1977.

MacNeil, Anna. *Music and Women of the Commedia dell'Arte in the Late Sixteenth Century.* New York: Oxford University Press, 2003.

Malcolmson, Christina, and Mihoko Suzuki, eds. *Debating Gender in Early Modern England, 1500–1700.* New York: Palgrave Macmillan, 2002.

Marland, Hilary, ed. *The Art of Midwifery: Early Modern Midwives in Europe.* New York: Routledge, 1993.

Marshall, Rosalind Kay. *Virgins and Viragos: A History of Women in Scotland from 1080–1980.* London: Collins, 1983.

Martin, A. Lynn. *Alcohol, Sex, and Gender in Late Medieval and Early Modern Europe.* New York: Palgrave, 2001.

Martz, Linda. *A Network of Converso Families in Early Modern Toledo: Assimilating a Minority.* Ann Arbor: University of Michigan Press, 2003.

Maza, Sarah C. *Servants and Masters in Eighteenth Century France.* Princeton, NJ: Princeton University Press, 1983.

McBride, Kari Boyd, ed. *Domestic Arrangements in Early Modern England.* Pittsburgh, PA: Duquesne University Press, 2002.

McKendrick, Melveena. *Women in Society in Spanish Drama of the Golden Age: A Study of the Mujer Varonil.* New York: Cambridge University Press, 1974.

McLaren, Angus. *A History of Contraception from Antiquity to the Present Day.* Cambridge, MA: Basil Blackwell, 1990.

McManus, Caroline. *Spenser's* Faerie Queene *and the Reading of Women.* Newark: University of Delaware Press, 2002.

Meek, Christine. *Women in Renaissance and Early Modern Europe.* Dublin: Four Courts, 2000.

Mendelson, Sara, and Patricia Crawford. *Women in Early Modern England, 1550–1720.* New York: Oxford University Press, 1998.

Menon, Madhavi. *Wanton Words: Rhetoric and Sexuality in English Renaissance Drama*. Toronto: University of Toronto Press, 2004.

Migiel, Marilyn, and Juliana Schiesari, eds. *Refiguring Women: Perspectives on the Italian Renaissance*. Ithaca, NY: Cornell University Press, 1991.

Miller, Naomi J., and Naomi Yavneh, eds. *Maternal Measures: Figuring Caregiving in the Early Modern Period*. Aldershot, UK: Ashgate, 2000.

———. *Thicker Than Water: Sisters and Brothers in the Early Modern World*. Aldershot, UK: Ashgate, 2005.

Monson, Craig A., ed. *The Crannied Wall: Women, Religion, and the Arts in Early Modern Europe*. Ann Arbor: University of Michigan Press, 1992.

Moore, Cornelia Niekus. *The Maiden's Mirror: Reading Matter for German Girls in the Sixteenth and Seventeenth Centuries*. Wiesbaden, Germany: O. Harrassowitz, 1987.

Musacchio, Jacqueline Marie. *The Art and Ritual of Childbirth in Renaissance Italy*. New Haven, CT: Yale University Press, 1999.

Nader, Helen, ed. *Power and Gender in Renaissance Spain: Eight Women of the Mendoza Family, 1450–1650*. Urbana: University of Illinois Press, 2004.

Neuls-Bates, Carol. *Women in Music: An Anthology of Source Readings from the Middle Ages to the Present*. Boston: Northeastern University Press, 1996.

Nevitt, H. Rodney. *Art and the Culture of Love in Seventeenth-Century Holland*. New York: Cambridge University Press, 2002.

Newman, Karen. *Fashioning Femininity and English Renaissance Drama*. Chicago: University of Chicago Press, 1991.

Nochlin, Linda. "Why Have There Been No Great Women Artists?" *Art and Sexual Politics: Why Have There Been No Great Women Artists?* Ed. Thomas B. Hess and Elizabeth C. Baker. New York: Collier Books, 1971. 1–39.

O'Day, Rosemary. *Education and Society, 1500–1800: Social Foundations of Education in Early Modern Britain*. New York: Longman, 1982.

O'Dowd, Mary, and Margaret MacCurtain. *Women in Early Modern Ireland*. Edinburgh: Edinburgh University Press, 1991.

Ogilvie, Sheilagh. *A Bitter Living: Women, Markets, and Social Capital in Early Modern Germany*. Edinburgh: Edinburgh University Press, 1991.

Okin, Susan Moller. *Women in Western Political Thought*. Princeton, NJ: Princeton University Press, 1979.

Orgel, Stephen. *Impersonations: The Performance of Gender in Shakespeare's England*. New York: Cambridge University Press, 1996.

Orlin, Lena Cowen. *Elizabethan Households: An Anthology*. Washington, DC: Folger Shakespeare Library, 1995.

―――. *Material London, Circa 1600*. Philadelphia, University of Pennsylvania Press, 2000.

―――. *Private Matters and Public Culture in Post-Reformation England*. Ithaca, NY: Cornell University Press, 1994.

Otten, Charlotte F., ed. *English Women's Voices, 1540–1700*. Miami: Florida International University Press, 1992.

Outhwaite, R. B., ed. *Marriage and Society: Studies in the Social History of Marriage*. London: Europa, 1981.

Ozment, Steven E. *Magdalena and Balthasar: An Intimate Portrait of Life in Sixteenth Century Europe Revealed in the Letters of a Nuremberg Husband and Wife*. New York: Simon & Schuster, 1986.

Panizza, Letizia. *Women in Italian Renaissance Culture and Society*. Oxford: European Humanities Research Centre, 2000.

Panizza, Letizia, and Sharon Wood, eds. *A History of Women's Writing in Italy*. New York: Cambridge University Press, 2000.

Pardai hé-Galabrun, Annik. *The Birth of Intimacy: Private and Domestic Life in Early Modern Paris*. Oxford: Polity, 1991.

Pelling, Margaret. *The Common Lot: Sickness, Medical Occupations, and the Urban Poor in Early Modern England*. New York: Longman, 1998.

Pendle, Karin, ed. *Women and Music: A History*. Bloomington: Indiana University Press, 1991.

Perlingieri, Ilya Sandra. *Sofonisba Anguissola: The First Great Woman Artist of the Renaissance*. New York: Rizzoli, 1992.

Perrot, Michelle, and Alain Paire. *Writing Women's History*. Cambridge, MA: Blackwell, 1992.

Perry, Mary Elizabeth. *Gender and Disorder in Early Modern Seville*. Princeton, NJ: Princeton University Press, 1990.

Phillippy, Patricia. *Women, Death, and Literature in Post-Reformation England*. New York: Cambridge University Press, 2002.

Phillips, Roderick. *Putting Asunder: A History of Divorce in Western Society*. New York: Cambridge University Press, 1989.

Pollock, Linda A. *Forgotten Children: Parent-Child Relations from 1500–1900*. New York: Cambridge University Press, 1983.

Porter, Roy. *Patients and Practitioners: Lay Perceptions of Medicine in Pre-industrial Society*. New York: Cambridge University Press, 1985.

Prior, Mary, ed. *Women in English Society, 1500–1800*. New York: Methuen, 1985.

Pullan, Brian S. *Rich and Poor in Renaissance Venice: The Social Institutions of a Catholic State, to 1620*. Cambridge, MA: Harvard University Press, 1971.

Purkiss, Diane. *The Witch in History: Early Modern and Twentieth-Century Representations*. New York: Routledge, 1996.

Quaife, G. R. *Wanton Wenches and Wayward Wives: Peasants and Illicit Sex in Early Seventeenth Century England*. New Brunswick, NJ: Rutgers University Press, 1979.

Rabb, Theodore K. *Renaissance Lives: Portraits of an Age*. New York: Pantheon, 1993.

Rapley, Elizabeth. *The Dévotes: Women and Church in Seventeenth-Century France*. Kingston, Ontario: McGill-Queen's University Press, 1990.

Raymond, Joad. *Pamphlets and Pamphleteering in Early Modern Britain*. New York: Cambridge University Press, 2003.

Richards, Sandra. *The Rise of the English Actress*. New York: St. Martin's Press, 1993.

Roper, Lyndal. *The Holy Household: Women and Morals, in Reformation Augsburg*. New York: Oxford University Press, 1989.

———. *Oedipus and the Devil: Witchcraft, Sexuality, and Religion in Early Modern Europe*. New York: Routledge, 1994.

Rose, Mary Beth, ed. *Women in the Middle Ages and the Renaissance*. Syracuse, NY: Syracuse University Press, 1986.

Rublack, Ulinka, ed. *The Crimes of Women in Early Modern Germany*. New York: Oxford University Press, 1999.

———. *Gender in Early Modern German History*. New York: Cambridge University Press, 2002.

Ruff, Julius R. *Violence in Early Modern Europe, 1500–1800*. New York: Cambridge University Press, 2001.

Ruggiero, Guido. *The Boundaries of Eros: Sex Crime and Sexuality in Renaissance Venice*. New York: Oxford University Press, 1985.

Sabean, David Warren. *Property, Production, and Family in Neckarhausen, 1700–1870*. New York: Cambridge University Press, 1990.

Sanderson, Margaret H. B. *A Kindly Place? Living in Sixteenth Century Scotland*. East Lothian, Scotland: Tuckwell Press, 2002.

Sarti, Raffaella, and Allan Cameron. *Europe at Home: Family and Material Culture, 1500–1800*. New Haven, CT: Yale University Press, 2002.

Schama, Simon. *The Embarrassment of Riches: An Interpretation of Dutch Culture in the Golden Age*. New York: Random House, 1987.

Schochet, Gordon J. *The Authoritarian Family and Political Attitudes in 17th Century England: Patriarchalism in Political Thought*. New Brunswick, NJ: Transaction Books, 1988.

Schutte, Anne Jacobson. "Irene di Spilimbergo: The Image of a Creative Woman in Late Renaissance Italy." *Renaissance Quarterly* 44 (1991): 42–61.

Scott, Joan W. "Gender: A Useful Category of Historical Analysis." *American Historical Review* 91 (1986): 1053–75.

Sharpe, James A. *Crime in Early Modern England*. 2nd ed. New York: Longman, 1999.

Sharpe, Pamela. *Women's Work: The English Experience, 1650–1914*. New York: Arnold, 1998.

Sheils, William J., and Diana Wood, eds. *Women in the Church: Papers Read at the 1989 Summer Meeting and the 1990 Winter Meeting of* the *Ecclesiastical History Society.* Cambridge, MA: Basil Blackwell, 1990.

Shephard, Amanda. *Gender and Authority in Sixteenth-Century England: The Knox Debate.* Keele, Staffordshire, UK: Ryburn, 1994.

Sim, Alison. *Pleasures & Pastimes in Tudor England.* Stroud, UK: Sutton, 1999.

———. *The Tudor Housewife.* Buffalo, NY: McGill-Queen's University Press, 1996.

Slack, Paul. *The English Poor Law, 1531–1782.* Cambridge: Cambridge University Press, 1990.

Slater, Miriam. *Family Life in the Seventeenth Century: The Verneys of Clayden House.* Boston: Routledge & Kegan Paul, 1984.

Slatkin, Wendy. *Women Artists in History from Antiquity to the 20th Century.* Englewood Cliffs, NJ: Prentice Hall, 1990.

Smith, Hilda L., ed. *Women Writers and the Early Modern British Political Tradition.* New York: Cambridge University Press, 1998.

Sperling, Jutta Gisela. *Convents and the Body Politic in Late Renaissance Venice.* Chicago: University of Chicago Press, 1999.

Spufford, Margaret. *Contrasting Communities: English Villagers in the Sixteenth and Seventeenth Centuries.* 2nd ed. Stroud, UK: Sutton, 2000.

Stevenson, Jane. "Women and Classical Education in the Early Modern Period." *Pedagogy and Power: Rhetorics of Classical Learning.* Ed. Yun Lee Too and Niall Livingstone. New York: Cambridge University Press, 1998. 83–109.

Stock, Phyllis. *Better Than Rubies: A History of Women's Education.* New York: Putnam, 1978.

Stone, Lawrence. *The Family, Sex and Marriage in England 1500–1800.* New York: Harper & Row, 1977.

Stortoni, Laura Anna, ed. *Women Poets of the Italian Renaissance: Courtly Ladies and Courtesans.* Trans. Laura Anna Stortoni and Mary Prentice Lillie. New York: Ithaca Press, 1997.

Strong, Roy. *The Cult of Elizabeth: Elizabethan Portraiture and Pageantry.* London: Pimlico, 1999.

Summers, Claude J., and Ted-Larry Pebworth, eds. *Representing Women in Renaissance England.* Columbia: University of Missouri Press, 1997.

Summit, Jennifer. *Lost Property: The Woman Writer and English Literary History, 1380–1589.* Chicago: University of Chicago Press, 2000.

Sussman, George D. *Selling Mothers' Milk: The Wetnursing Business in France, 1715–1914.* Urbana: University of Illinois Press, 1982.

Todd, Janet M. *The Sign of Angellica: Women, Writing, and Fiction, 1660–1800.* London: Virago, 1989.

Traer, James F. *Marriage and the Family in Eighteenth Century France.* Ithaca, NY: Cornell University Press, 1980.

Traub, Valerie. *The Renaissance of Lesbianism in Early Modern England*. New York: Cambridge University Press, 2002.

Traub, Valerie, M. Lindsay Kaplan, and Dympna Callaghan. *Feminist Readings of Early Modern Culture: Emerging Subjects*. New York: Cambridge University Press, 1996.

Travitsky, Betty. *The Paradise of Women: Writings by Englishwomen of the Renaissance*. New York: Columbia University Press, 1989.

Trexler, Richard C. *The Women of Renaissance Florence: Power and Dependence in Renaissance Florence*. Vol. 2. Asheville, NC: Pegasus, 1998.

Trill, Suzanne, Kate Chedgzoy, and Melanie Osborne, eds. *Lay by Your Needles Ladies, Take the Pen: Writing Women in England, 1500–1700*. New York: Oxford University Press, 1997.

Turner, David M. *Fashioning Adultery: Gender, Sex, and Civility in England, 1660–1740*. New York: Cambridge University Press, 2002.

Turner, James Grantham, ed. *One Flesh: Paradisal Marriage and Sexual Relations in the Age of Milton*. New York: Oxford University Press, 1987.

———. *Schooling Sex: Libertine Literature and Erotic Education in Italy, France, and England, 1534–1685*. New York: Oxford University Press, 2003.

———. *Sexuality and Gender in Early Modern Europe: Institutions, Texts, Images*. New York: Cambridge University Press, 1993.

Turudich, Daniela, and Laurie J. Welch. *Plucked, Shaved, and Braided: Medieval and Renaissance Beauty and Grooming Practices 1000–1600*. Long Beach, CA: Streamline Press, 2004.

Underdown, David. *Revel, Riot, and Rebellion: Popular Politics and Culture in England, 1603–1660*. New York: Oxford University Press, 1985.

Van Duersen, Arie Theodorus. *Plain Lives in a Golden Age: Popular Culture, Religion, and Society in Seventeenth-Century Holland*. New York: Cambridge University Press, 1991.

Vanhaelen, Angela. *Comic Print and Theatre in Early Modern Amsterdam: Gender, Childhood, and the City*. Aldershot, UK: Ashgate, 2003.

Vigarello, Georges. *Concepts of Cleanliness: Changing Attitudes in France since the Middle Ages*. New York: Cambridge University Press, 1988.

Voaden, Rosalynn, and Diane Wolfthal. *Framing the Family: Narrative and Representation in the Medieval and Early Modern Periods*. Tempe, AZ: Medieval Texts and Studies, 2005.

Waddington, Raymond B. *Aretino's Satyr: Sexuality, Satire, and Self-Projection in Sixteenth-Century Literature and Art*. Toronto: University of Toronto Press, 2004.

Waite, Gary K. *Heresy, Magic, and Witchcraft in Early Modern Europe*. New York: Palgrave/St. Martin's Press, 2003.

Walker, Claire. *Gender and Politics in Early Modern Europe: English Convents in France and the Low Countries*. New York: Palgrave Macmillan, 2003.

Wall, Wendy. *Staging Domesticity: Household Work and English Identity in Early Modern Drama*. New York: Cambridge University Press, 2002.

Warnicke, Retha M. *The Marrying of Anne of Cleves: Royal Protocol in Early Modern England*. New York: Cambridge University Press, 2000.

———. *The Rise and Fall of Anne Boleyn: Family Politics at the Court of Henry VIII*. New York: Cambridge University Press, 1989.

———. *Women of the English Renaissance and Reformation*. Westport, CT: Greenwood Press, 1983.

Wear, Andrew. *Knowledge & Practice in English Medicine, 1550–1680*. New York: Cambridge University Press, 2000.

Weber, Alison. *Saint Teresa of Avila and the Rhetoric of Femininity*. Princeton, NJ: Princeton University Press, 1990.

Weinstein, Roni. *Marriage Rituals Italian Style: A Historical Anthropological Perspective on Early Modern Italian Jews*. Trans. Batya Stein. Leiden, The Netherlands: Brill, 2004.

Welu, James A., and P. Biesboer. *Judith Leyster: A Dutch Master and Her World*. New York: Yale University Press, 1993.

Whitehead, Barbara J., ed. *Women's Education in Early Modern Europe: A History, 1500–1800*. New York: Garland, 1999.

Wiesner, Merry E. *Gender, Church, and State in Early Modern Germany*. New York: Longman, 1998.

———. *Women and Gender in Early Modern Europe*. 2nd ed. New York: Cambridge University Press, 2000.

———. *Working Women in Renaissance Germany*. New Brunswick, NJ: Rutgers University Press, 1986.

Wilcox, Helen, ed. *Women and Literature in Britain, 1500–1700*. New York: Cambridge University Press, 1996.

Wilson, Katharina M., ed. *Women Writers of the Renaissance and Reformation*. Athens: University of Georgia Press, 1987.

Wilson, Katharina M., and Frank J. Warnke, eds. *Women Writers of the Seventeenth Century*. Athens: University of Georgia Press, 1989.

Wiltenburg, Joy. *Disorderly Women and Female Power in the Street Literature of Early Modern Germany*. Charlottesville: University Press of Virginia, 1992.

Wolfthal, Diane. "Picturing Same-Sex Love: Images by Petrus Christus and the Housebook Master." *Troubled Vision: Gender, Sexuality, and Sight in Medieval Text and Image*. Ed. Robert Mills and Emma Barker. Hampshire, UK: Palgrave Macmillan, 2004.

———. "The Woman in the Window: Gender, Spatial Topography, and the Culture of Display in Images of Prostitutes Produced in Early

Modern Italy." *Il Rinascimento della pornografia: Sessualità e modernità in Italia nel Cinque e Seicento*. Ed. Francesco Erspamer. Rome: Bulzoni, 2005.

―――. "Writing the History of Women Artists: The Case of Margaret van Eyck." *Essays on Women Artists "The Most Excellent."* Ed. Liana Cheney. Lewiston, NY: Edwin Mellen Press, 2003. 1.19–40.

Woodbridge, Linda. *Women and the English Renaissance: Literature and the Nature of Womankind 1540–1620*. Urbana: University of Illinois Press, 1984.

Woodford, Charlotte. *Nuns as Historians in Early Modern Germany*. New York: Oxford University Press, 2002.

Wrightson, Keith. *English Society 1580–1680*. London: Hutchinson, 1982.

Zumthor, Paul. *Daily Life in Rembrandt's Holland*. Stanford, CA: Stanford University Press, 1994.

Index

Esther Sowernam, 205; *Hic
Mulier, or, The Man-Woman*, 127;
Joseph Swetnam, 205; *A Mouzell
for Melastomus* (Rachel Speght),
205; *De nobilitate et praecellentia foeminei sexus* [On the Nobility and excellency of the female
sex] (Henricus Cornelius Agrippa
von Nettesheim), 20–21; Sara
Fyge, 236
Woman's Speaking Justified (Margaret Fell), 186
women religious, 155, 157–58,
173–75, 178–80, 183, 222, 270;
Caterina de' Ricci, 175; Caterina
Mattei, 175; Catherine of Siena,
174; Chiara Bugni, 175; Gertrude
More, 180, 284–85; Jacqueline
Pascal, 173; Katharina von Bora,
158–59, 277–78; Louise
Bourgeois, 106–7; Marie Guyart,
174; Mary Ward, 45–47, 51 n.31,
177–78, 196; Osanna Andreasi of
Mantua, 175; Soeur Anne de
Marquets, 183; Teresa of Avila,
173–74; tertiaries, 174–75
women rulers: Anne of Austria,
133; Anne de Beaujeu, 133, 135;
Anne Boleyn, 40, 181; Anne of
Denmark, 272, 274; Anne-Marie-
Louise D'Orléans (Duchesse de
Montpensier), 128; Catharine of
Aragon, 40, 71, 135, 181; Catharine de' Medicis, 127–28, 133, 148,
183; Catherine of Braganza, 178;
Christina, Queen of Sweden, 44,
54, 130, 133, 160–61; Elenore of
Austria, 197; Elizabeth of
Bohemia, 128–29; Elizabeth I
(Queen of England), 5–6, 40, 44,
54, 77, 102, 133–34, 137–42, 164,
176, 180–82, 190, 200, 217, 227,
248, 291, 292–93, 296; Elizabeth
of Hungary, 144–47, 208; Elizabeth of Nassau Saarbrücken,
197; Henrietta Maria, 178, 206,
219, 272; Isabella of Castile
(Queen of Spain), 133–35;
Isabella of Valois (Queen of
Spain), 274; Katharine Parr, 141,
165–66; Lady Jane Grey, 141–42,
249; Leonora Christina of Denmark, 142–44; Margaret of
Anjou, 126–27; Margaret of Austria, 133, 135–37; Maria of Austria, 263, 274; Marie de' Medicis,
107; Mary I (Queen of England),
5, 40, 77, 132, 133, 142, 180, 181,
264; Mary of Guise, 132, 138, 139,
182; Mary, Queen of Scots,
132–33, 138–42, 182; Sophie Charlotte, Queen of Prussia, 273
women's orchestras (*concerto
delle donne*), 269
*Wonderful Metamorphosis and
Special Nourishment of Caterpillars* (Maria Sibylla Merian),
218, 251–52
Worming of a mad Dog, The
(Constantia Munda), 205
Wroth, Lady Mary, 15, 195

Zayas y Sotomayor, María de, 15,
224

About the Authors

MEG LOTA BROWN is Professor of English at the University of Arizona, Tucson.

KARI BOYD McBRIDE is Associate Professor and Undergraduate Director in the Women's Studies Department, Faculty Affiliate in the Department of English, and Director of the Group for Early Modern Studies at the University of Arizona, Tucson.